COMPANY TOWN

Potlatch, Idaho, and the Potlatch Lumber Company

To Dad on his birthday
May 8, 1988
Gordon, Lynn, Peter & Philip

COMPANY TOWN
Potlatch, Idaho, and the Potlatch Lumber Company

KEITH C. PETERSEN

Washington State University Press
Pullman, Washington

and

Latah County Historical Society
Moscow, Idaho

1987

Printed and bound in the United States of America
Washington State University Press
Pullman, Washington

Library of Congress Cataloging-in-Publication Data

Petersen, Keith C.
    Company town.

    Bibliography: p. 270
    Includes index.
    1. Potlatch Corporation–History.
2. Lumber trade–Idaho–History. 3. Company
towns–Idaho–History. 4. Potlatch (Idaho)–
Economic conditions. I. Latah County Historical
Society. II. Title.
HD9759.P63P47 1987   307.7'67'0979686   87-14980
ISBN 0-87422-036-X
ISBN 0-87422-037-8 (pbk.)

This book is printed on pH neutral, acid-free paper.

Research grants and contracts for this study were provided by:

The Idaho Humanities Council, a state-based program of the
National Endowment for the Humanities

The National Endowment for the Humanities

The Idaho State Historic Preservation Office

The Latah County Historical Society

*This book is dedicated to
Mom and Dad, who have always been supportive,
and to my wife Mary, fellow historian,
critical reviewer, sharer of ideas, and,
most of all, friend.*

In one respect at least the Potlatch Lumber Company was from its inception quite different from the others. . . . There was an atmosphere of importance and superiority about it, a sort of grandiosity that at times seemed to annoy father. . . . It enjoyed its full share of . . . publicity.

Frederick E. Weyerhaeuser

CONTENTS

ACKNOWLEDGMENTS

At a bend in the Palouse River, two miles off U.S. Highway 95, in the shadow of Gold Hill, in northern Latah County, Idaho, rests a town named Potlatch. It is not a particularly picturesque place. Instead, it projects an image of gritty working-class living.

I do not remember my initial impression of Potlatch. It is a town, like many others, that does not leave lasting impressions upon passersby. I am sure, when I first viewed it, that the thought never occurred to me that I would someday spend the better part of a decade researching its history. But now I have, and this book is the result. It is the story of a place that was unusual – a town completely owned by a large lumber company. But I was more drawn to the study because of what Potlatch has in common with much of the West. For the story of Potlatch is the tale of the exploitation of natural resources; of the impact of big business upon the development of a rural area; of ordinary people making a place their home.

Over the years I have incurred many debts, and I am pleased to recognize those who have helped on this project. First of all, I must thank my colleague in research and the Director of the Latah County Historical Society, Mary Reed. She assisted me on numerous research trips and read every word in this manuscript, helping with major stylistic and substantive revisions. I cannot imagine that this could have been written without her expertise, even if she did not also happen to be my wife. Thomas R. Cox of San Diego State University and Louie Attebery of the College of Idaho also reviewed the entire manuscript, and I am grateful for their numerous helpful comments and ideas for further study. Frederic Johnson of the University of Idaho and Lee Gale of Potlatch reviewed parts of the manuscript, and the final version is much improved because of their assistance.

As a non-affiliated public historian, I was able to undertake this project only because of financial assistance from several organizations. Research was funded by a two-year research grant from the National Endowment for the Humanities and by two contracts from the Idaho State Historic Preservation Office. Writing was funded by a contract from the Latah County Historical Society and a grant from the Idaho Humanities Council, the state-based committee of the National Endowment for the Humanities. It goes without saying that the book's conclusions do not necessarily reflect the opinions of any of these groups, but I am indebted to each for allowing me the freedom to study the topic.

The Latah County Historical Society, located in Moscow, Idaho, is a historian's delight. I can never adequately repay its staff and Board of Trustees for their friendship and assistance, and for the confidence they placed in me by financially supporting my work and partially underwriting publication costs. They are a farsighted group that has done much to preserve the region's history. In order to pay for the Potlatch project the Society launched a major fundraising drive. That campaign was greatly assisted by a hard-working Potlatch local advisory committee consisting of Florence Anderson, James Dewey, Lee Gale, Nettie Gale, Adeline Howard, Dwight Strong, and Paul Tobin. These people, Potlatch history experts all, also answered numerous inquiries from me as I tried to unravel the town's past.

Others who assisted the Society in making contacts to raise money included Harold K. Steen, Executive Director of the Forest History Society; Judy Austin of the Idaho State Historical Society; Frederick P. Billings and Howie Meadowcroft of the Weyerhaeuser Company; and Elaine Meyer of Moscow. Their efforts were tremendously successful, with over 200 businesses, groups, and individuals contributing. Except for those who wished no publicity, these donors' names appear at the end of these acknowledgments. I am indebted to each, but I would particularly like to acknowledge the generous contribution of George Frederick Jewett, Jr. In many ways, over many years, he and his family have supported numerous historical projects, and I am grateful for his assistance on this one.

Behind every researcher there are good librarians and archivists, and I acknowledge the assistance of several who not only helped in a professional manner but also provided friendship and conversation during hours of poring over documents. When I first began research on this book Terry Abraham was the archivist at Washington State University's Manuscripts, Archives and Special Collections. Later he became head of the Department of Special Collections at the University of Idaho, and in both places lent a high degree of expertise and friendly help. Stanley Shepard was the head of Special Collections before Terry, and in addition to assisting me on research, he was very influential in obtaining the large collection of Potlatch Lumber Company papers which were donated by Potlatch Corporation to the University of Idaho during the course of this project. Chris Talbott, librarian at the Latah County Historical Society, provided access to the Society's large regional history collection. The Weyerhaeuser Company archives in Tacoma were indispensable, as were the archivists there, Laura Cadigan, now with Kraft, Inc., and Donnie Crespo. One of the best-kept secrets among forest historians is the excellent and meticulously organized archives of the Laird-Norton Company in Seattle. I cannot tell Elizabeth Adkins, who was responsible for processing this large collection before she, too, moved to Kraft, how indebted I am to her. Not only did she provide me with materials during my several research trips, but she also kept me informed of new, pertinent additions to the collection via a steady stream of letters and long distance telephone calls. I hope she knows how much I appreciate her many hours of work.

Fred Bohm, Editor-in-Chief at the Washington State University Press, provided encouragement throughout the publication process. I am also indebted to Thomas Sanders, Director of the Press, and Fred for their willingness to cooperate with local organizations in publishing regional history. Others at the Press who assisted on this project included editors Jill Whelchel and Jan Clemens, and designer Jo Savage.

Sam Schrager and Lillian Otness were primarily responsible for gathering the Latah County Historical Society's outstanding oral history collection, which I used extensively. Beyond that, however, they were the two who, nearly ten years ago, interested me in Latah County's rich history. Both have paved the way for later historians by their own research and writing on the area. As I now seem to be spending most of my time writing about one topic or another in that county's history, they are the two who deserve most of the credit—or blame—for getting me started.

Shannon O'Dell accompanied me on many research trips to Potlatch as we sat before space heaters in the cold basement of city hall going over the Potlatch Lumber Company records before they were donated to the University of Idaho. Paul Tobin and Jack Gruber of the Potlatch Corporation deserve special credit for seeing that the records were eventually donated, and many future historians will be indebted to them for preserving this valuable collection.

In May and June 1983 I made several trips to the Potlatch millsite with Latah County Historical Society volunteer, Trustee, and photographer extraordinary John Talbott. John was a true Renaissance man who knew more about many things than most of us do about one. Not only did he provide an invaluable photodocumentation of the mill before it was dismantled, but as he and I walked through every building, he patiently explained what each was. I could not have written chapter four without his assistance. Everyone interested in the preservation of Latah County history was saddened when John died in the summer of 1985. I am sorry he was not able to read this book, but he was often on my mind as I wrote it.

As she has on nearly all of my writing projects, Kathleen Probasco lent her considerable editorial and typing skills while preparing various drafts of this manuscript. Simply deciphering my penmanship alone is worth meritorious mention, but Kathy also caught many errors, and the final manuscript is much better because of her attention to detail. Roy Chatters provided me with access to the Palouse Boomerang Museum's complete run of Palouse *Republics*. Malcolm and Elsie Renfrew and Lee Gale allowed me to interview them. These interviews were invaluable in my research, and I have donated the tapes and indexes to the Latah County Historical Society, where I hope they will assist future researchers. Janice Johnson put me in contact with several helpful Potlatch informants. Donald Meinig, now of Syracuse University but at one time a boy growing up near Palouse City, must be considered the "guru" of all regional historians who follow the publication of his impressive *The Great Columbia Plain*. I am indebted to his writing and documentation in that book, which led me to many obscure sources, as well as to him personally for leading me to even more during our conversations and correspondence.

The chief problem with writing acknowledgments is that you are bound to leave someone out who helped along the way. I no doubt have omitted several because I am indebted to so many. I hope, however, they will forgive me, for the omission was unintentional and I want them to know I value their assistance.

Keith Petersen
Pullman, Washington
August 1987

The following people and companies made generous contributions to the Latah County Historical Society for the Potlatch at 80 Project. Their donations supported the writing and publication of this book. I would like to thank all of them for their assistance.

BENEFACTOR
George Frederick Jewett, Jr., in memory of George Frederick Jewett

PATRONS
Maryanne Decker Henske, in memory of Charlotte Laird Decker
Setsuo Matsura, in memory of Mr. and Mrs. Will Hearn and Roderic Hearn
Jeannette Petersen, in memory of Warren S. and Soloma Benner
Stanley Shepard
Mr. and Mrs. Luke Williams

SPONSORS
Bennett Lumber Products
C. J. Johnson, in memory of Mr. and Mrs. J. L. Johnson
Frances Laird Osgood, in memory of Laird Bell
Kathleen Peck Probasco
An additional contribution in this category was received in memory of Edward and Willard Thompson.

SUPPORTERS
Dagny E. Alsterlund, in memory of Alfred E. and Eugenia E. Alsterlund and Alfred I. Alsterlund
Mr. and Mrs. L. J. Ashbaugh
Norris and Nancy Biggerstaff
Patricia Born, in memory of Dr. Nereus M. Cook
Norton Clapp
Raymond H. Compton, in memory of Edward T. Compton
Helen de Freitas, in memory of Frederic Somers Bell
Dr. Frank C. Gibson, Jr., in memory of Dr. Frank Gibson, Sr.
Amber Gleave, in memory of Gordon Gleave and Mr. and Mrs. Russell Gleave
Catherine Gleave and Inez Gleave Rich, in memory of Harry L. M. and Nellie Gleave
William S. and Janet Groff Greever
Roger Guernsey, in memory of Evon and Viola Guernsey
Pearl Vowell Hanson, in memory of Ray Hanson
Cora Knott
Mr. and Mrs. George Kovich, in memory of Otto and Ferris Leuschel
Otto H. Leuschel, Jr., in memory of Otto and Ferris Leuschel
Richard B. Madden
Alice and Walter Mallory
Sophia Marineau, in memory of William T. Marineau

Jean M. Monnett
Judy and Ralph Nielsen
H. Robert and Lillian Otness
Roland W. Portman
Carol and Malcolm Renfrew, in memory of Earl E. Renfrew
Mr. and Mrs. Edgar E. Renfrew, in memory of Robert James (Rob) Morris
Lois Hodge Shute, in memory of Alice and Shelley Hodge
Felix L. and Jerry Stapleton
Allen and Betsy Strong, in memory of Arthur and Alice Strong
Gary E. Strong Family, in honor of Cleora and Dwight Strong
Nellie E. Trotter, in memory of William Trotter, Sr. and Luther Trotter
Washington Water Power Company
Norma J. Watson, in memory of Harold and Nora Beckemeier
Glen E. Wood, in memory of James E. and Pearl Wood

CONTRIBUTORS
Terry Abraham
Patrick and Elsa Agnew, in memory of Erick and Ida Matson, and William and Margaret Deary
Leonard S. Alsager, in memory of Sven and Gerda Alsager
Vera V. Alsterlund, Marilyn K. Westerkamp, and Ronald A. Alsterlund, in memory of Alfred I. (Pedie) Alsterlund
Richard A. Anderson, in memory of William and Hilda Anderson and Andrew and Carrie Lundquist
Robert Anderson, in memory of Art and Florence Anderson
Sherrel and Dorothy Anderson
Kenneth Andrew, in memory of Signa H. and Shelton E. Andrew
John D. Armstrong, in memory of John David Morrissey
Alexia Asplund, in memory of Elof Asplund
Glen E. Atkison
Marvin and Irene Bain
Beulah J. Baker, in memory of G. Orien Baker
Win Baker, in memory of G. C. Baker
William and Dorothy Barnes
Frances Burrows Bellmont
Mr. and Mrs. Frederick P. Billings, in memory of Mr. and Mrs. Charles Lee Billings
Donna Bray
Nathalie Bell Brown, in memory of Laird Bell
Eugene Burden, in memory of Job, Levi, and Emery Burden
Earl E. Button
David and Kendria Cada, in memory of Mr. and Mrs. Bernie Hansen
Joe and Dorothy Cada, in memory of Mr. and Mrs. Joseph G. Cada, Sr.
Raymond R. Cameron

Martin and Kelly Caturia
Mel and Louise Chandler, in memory of Ethel and Wesley Chandler
Louis E. Chappell
Florence L. Cline
Delfred Cone, in memory of John and Mattie Cone
Construction Services, Ltd.
Josephine Thompson Cox, in memory of Dr. Joseph W. Thompson
Wilmer and Cynthia Cox
Opal Salisbury Cumbie, in memory of Nolen M. Salisbury
Dell R. David
James and Helen Dewey
Hazel Kay Diehl
Dewey M. Dixon
Mrs. Harley Drollinger
Dick and Sharon Dudley
Clifford J. French
Ruth E. Frick
Carl and Ingrid Fynboe
Lee and Nettie Gale, in memory of Homer and Rhoda Peterson
    Canfield
Edward Gambetty, in memory of Victoria and George Gambetty
Mrs. Mark Gleason, in memory of Mr. and Mrs. Arthur G. Burch
Fred R. Gleave, in memory of Mr. and Mrs. H. L. M. Gleave
G. Margaret Gleave, in memory of Fred Gleave
Jack M. Gruber
Kathleen Hardcastle
Flora G. Harris, in memory of John Lienhard
Mr. and Mrs. Bill Hash, in memory of Glee Depee
Philip Hearn, in memory of Mr. and Mrs. W. E. Hearn
Louise M. Heighes, in memory of Hubert H. Heighes
Conrad and Inger Hermsted, in memory of Erick and Ida Matson
Hiawatha Apartments
Adeline B. Howard, in memory of William M. and Emma Lienhard
    Boller and Allison Alfred Boller
Alfred R. Howard, in memory of William T. and Emaline Johnson
    Howard
John A. Howard
Julian G. Humiston, in memory of Walter and Mollie Humiston
Laverna L. Huston, in memory of Ernest Gunderson
Idaho First National Bank
Irvin and Janice Johnson
Richard and Joann Jones
Naoma Keiser, in memory of Stanley "Tommie" Keiser and Fred and
    Hester Kreid
Esmé Kindelan, in memory of John Kindelan and Family

Harold and Ruth King

Ronald M. King

Richard N. King, in memory of Wilson and Laura King

E. R. "Ted" Kirsch, in memory of Ted and Maude Kirsch

Wendell G. Krasselt

Karl H. Krause

Calvin and Elizabeth Kreid

Virgil and Elizabeth Krous, in memory of George and Vickie
    Gambetty

Duvella Kusler, in memory of James E. and Pearl Wood

Rick and Kelly Largent

Cliff and Elsie Lathen, in memory of J. J. O'Connell

Marguerite W. Laughlin

Charles W. Leinbach, in memory of Myra and Walter J. Gamble

Carol Lemke, in memory of William R. (Bill) Lemke

Phillis and Duane LeTourneau

Mr. and Mrs. J. M. Lyle

Jack McBride

Thelma McCrory, in memory of Luther L., Orville L., and Louella
    Miller Vassar

William Ernest McGee

Bessie McKinney, in memory of Dewey McKinney

Patty O. McLaughlin, in memory of James J. O'Connell

Edwin B. Mains

Bess Salisbury Mansur

Lucetta Lindsay Marr, in memory of Jack and Agnes Lindsay

Moscow Auto Service

Charles L. Mundy, in memory of Hazel Mae Colvin

Henry Nygaard and Louise Nygaard Rosenholz, in memory of Martin
    and Corinne Paroz Nygaard

Carol Oberbillig, in memory of Albert F. Hamburg

Daniel W. O'Connell, in memory of J. J. O'Connell

Mr. and Mrs. Bernard L. Odelin, in memory of Mary E. Ackerman

Loyal J. Oien, in memory of Mr. and Mrs. Peter O. Oien

Milton and Blanche Oien, in memory of Mart and Wilda Moore

Mr. and Mrs. Earl J. Olsen, in memory of the Harry Gleave Family

Evelyn Pelton, in memory of Homer Pelton

Rollo P. Perkins

Jack K. Petersen

Keith Petersen and Mary Reed, in memory of John C. and Ida Frick
    Gleason

Agnes C. Peterson

The Children of Homer L. Peterson, in memory of Homer L.
    Peterson

Diana Y. Pieper, in memory of Clarence E. Closson

Plummer and Wagner

Barbara Maxey Porath, in memory of Henry W., Grace M., and Clarence H. Maxey

Larry Poston, in memory of Jack Poston

Potlatch Empire Foods

Potlatch Lions Club

Gretchen Potter

Myrtle E. Powlison

Mr. and Mrs. Barry Rauch

Daisy Paroz Richter and Amie Paroz, in memory of Gilbert Ami Paroz

Bessie I. Roe, in memory of Virgil P. Roe

Malcolm E. Rossman

Philip and Leona Sawyer

Marie and D. F. Scharnhorst

Robert R. Schnurr, in memory of Fred and Gladys Schnurr

O. V. Smiset, in memory of Nels Smiset

Dr. Victor C. Smith, in memory of Dottie Murray Smith

Kemet and Mariel Spence

Bill and Marilyn Stephens, in memory of George H. Turner

Douglas K. and Carol Strong

Dwight and Cleora Strong

Howard I. and Mary Newton Strong, in memory of Lewis Newton

Charles G. Talbott, Jr., in memory of the C. G. Talbott Family

Taylor Insurance Agency

Donald W. Thompson, in memory of Dr. Joseph W. Thompson

Eugene and JoAnn C. Thompson

Louise Trail, in memory of Josephine Alexander

Vina B. Turner, in memory of George T. Cochrane

Cloyd L. Tuttle, in memory of Harold "Snake River Red" Rounds

Eddie and Lorretta Vowels

Thomas Rex Walenta, in memory of Carol Florence Walenta

Maxine Walser

Calvin and Kathleen Warnick

White Pine Drug

Herbert L. Wickstrand

Charles F. Woods

Wilbur W. Wright

Hank and Helen Zimet, in memory of W. J. Gamble

Lee and Nora Eccher Zimmer

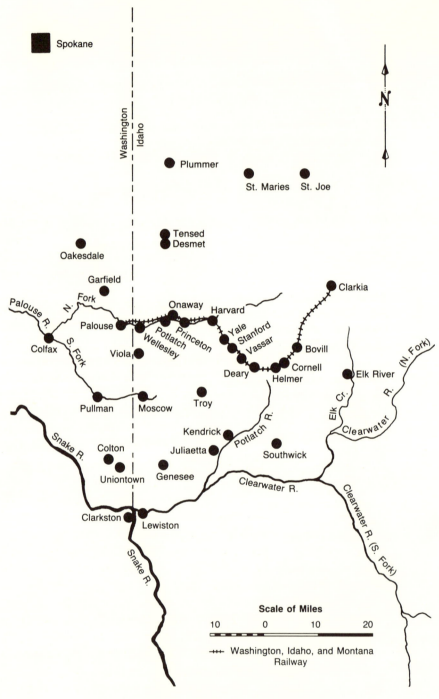

North central Idaho in the early twentieth century.

The Setting

PRAIRIE AND FOREST

The hills are too large, the Palouse landscape too immense to master its shape from eye level. Rolling hill runs into rolling hill, open and undulating, a mesmerizing sameness only occasionally broken by streambed or hollow. Walking the land gives some impression of ocean swells, but to understand its sea-like nature a better view is needed. Seen from a butte's summit, the countryside does indeed resemble an interior sea. Wind ripples through fields bending grasses wave-like, the sea merging into the shores of mountainous forests to the east.

This prairie in southeastern Washington and northern Idaho encompasses some 4,000 square miles, an area slightly smaller than Connecticut. Its southern border is the Snake and Clearwater river canyons, plummeting in spots over 2,000 feet below the prairie above. Forested Idaho mountains define the Palouse on the east, while the north and west are bounded by channeled scablands, a region stripped bare of topsoil 13,000 to 18,000 years ago by some of the greatest floods in geologic history.

These barren scablands starkly contrast with the rich prairie soil they rim. Stacked upon basaltic bedrock, the Palouse hills are actually loess dunes—silt and ash wind-carried here over millions of years, shaped by weather and erosion. In places the loess is 150 feet thick, a foundation for fertile topsoil making the region a leading producer of wheat, peas, and lentils.[1]

Early white travelers named this prairie for the Palouse Indians, who first occupied the land. The name eventually also transferred to a river, a town, a horse—the Appaloosa—and, in a way, to a particular rural lifestyle characterized in earlier times by large horse and mule teams tugging wheat-farming equipment over steep hillsides, and, before railroads, by inventive tramway systems transporting that crop down sheer river canyons to steamboat landings.[2]

The first westward migrations passed over the Palouse because eastern emigrants, accustomed to the thin-soiled hillsides of their native regions, believed the slopes unfarmable. The earliest settlers moved here in the 1860s to fatten cattle on the luxuriant native bunch-grass. A series of ravaging winters gradually reduced the numbers of cattlemen, who were replaced by scattered farmers cultivating the region's few flat bottomlands. Once these farmers discovered that the hills were blanketed with rich, deep topsoil, the area filled quickly. By the mid-1870s permanent population centers were established at Colfax and Palouse City in Whitman County, Washington, and Moscow and Genesee in what would become Latah County, Idaho.[3]

The forests abutting the Palouse's eastern border are distinct from the grasslands they neighbor. The soil is poorer, elevation higher, climate cooler and moister. These forests, though, are linked culturally and economically with the Palouse, for the resources of one aided development of the other.

The Palouse region is defined largely by the drainage of the Palouse River, which flows generally southwesterly from its source in Idaho's Hoodoo Mountains, gradually descending until reaching Palouse Falls, a 170-foot basaltic cliff. A few miles below the Falls the river joins the Snake. The lower third of the stream cleaves through inhospitable scabland while the longer middle section glides gently past Palouse prairie. The upper tenth, lying mostly in Idaho, is mountainous and heavily forested. There is a popular notion that this forest, before whites intruded, consisted solely of pure, stately stands of western white pine,[4] but actually white pine was just one of many intermingled species in the rich Latah County timberlands.

Early settlers did not discover a sea of grass crashing suddenly into a solid, pine-covered shore; the Palouse mixed gently with the forest, woodland undergrowth gradually replacing prairie bunchgrass. The grassland and forest converged in the zone of the ponderosa pine.[5] This tree, which tolerates considerable drought, snaked onto the Palouse wherever streams cut through heavy loess soil – such as along the Palouse River – and also covered slopes on the granite buttes which jutted into the prairie. The ponderosas on the fringes of the Palouse grew far apart, in park-like pine savannas, on ground covered with grasses, kinnikinnick, wild roses, lupine, and numerous other flowers and shrubs.

Moving eastward and upward to a moister land, the forest changed. Douglas fir, lodgepole pine, and western larch joined the ponderosa, the timberland gradually becoming denser, undergrowth thicker.

Ponderosa pine dominated the drier south-facing slopes even at higher altitudes, and transitions between habitats were not distinct, but white pine was reached by about 3,000 feet, especially along wet stream valleys and on mountain slopes with northern exposures. These giants, frequently over 200 feet high and twice as old, dominated the landscape to about 5,000 feet. But they seldom grew in pure stands, sharing their home with a broad assortment of species that also thrived in this damp, luxuriant environment: western larch, western red cedar, Douglas fir, grand fir, lodgepole pine, and Engelmann spruce. The trees stood close, interlacing branches shading the ground below. The forest reeked of dampness as the fine soil and decayed branches and leaves efficiently stored water. Virtually no grass grew here, the ground being covered with mosses and fungi. Tangled masses of larger underbrush thrived in natural openings, including willow, alder, maple, buckbrush, honeysuckle, elder, currants, and thimbleberry.[6]

Early Palouse settlers discovered ten species of coniferous trees in Latah County, as well as numerous deciduous trees of little value. Ponderosa pine, because it grew closest to the prairie, was the most utilized, both for fuel and lumber. Other easily accessible and highly used species were Douglas fir, which was also sawn into lumber; lodgepole pine, cut for corral rails and fuel; western larch, favored for fuel and milled into flooring and ties when railroads came to the region; and western red cedar, used for fencing and shingles. White pine, Engelmann spruce, and grand fir were commercially harvested after rail spurs and logging camps made the entire Palouse River basin accessible to lumbermen.

While these forests lay untouched by ax or saw in the early 1870s, they were not "virgin." The woods constantly changed, even before logging. The average age of the region's merchantable timber when first viewed by whites was probably 150 to 300 years old, and only rarely were trees over 400 years old. Yet, under ideal conditions, the lifespan of most of the area's coniferous species is much longer. Lightning-caused fires created the most significant forest alterations. As early as 1883, General Land Office surveyor Herman Gradou, working inland far away from settlements along the Palouse River, noted that large sections of the forest had "been deadened by fire." Frequently these blazes, in days before loggers left ignitable slash piles, burned themselves out quietly and slowly with little damage to mature trees. Occasionally, though, high winds fanned flames which destroyed even the largest monarchs. If a fire raged through the same area again while downed timber was still flammable, the destruction was even more severe. In some northern Idaho locations, earliest observers found wide expanses of brushy slopes dotted with char-coaled stumps, evidence that several conflagrations had passed through.

While fire did the most damage, other natural forces were also at work. Heavy rains loosened soil around roots, making trees suscep-tible to high winds. Accumulated snows often broke both old and young trees. Various types of fungi and insects attacked many species.

The forests of the Palouse River drainage thus were not stands of pure white pines when first viewed by whites, but they were nonetheless remarkable sights. Their riches eased the settlement of the Palouse, and provided the basis of a gigantic commercial forestry enterprise. The first whites to observe these woodlands were thus understandably impressed with their potential.[7]

A LAND COVERED WITH PINES

Isaac Stevens was pleased as he rode out of the Walla Walla valley on June 16, 1855, accompanied by a packmaster, fifteen teamsters, two Indian guides, and four assistants. Though only thirty-seven, he was perhaps the most important man in the Pacific Northwest: Washington Territorial Governor, transcontinental railroad surveyor, and official United States negotiator with Indian tribes. He had just concluded two weeks of talks at the Walla Walla Council, meeting with chiefs from the Nez Perce, Cayuse, Walla Walla, Yakima, and Palouse tribes. Despite divisions among the Indian leaders, Stevens had wrenched three separate treaties from the gathered nations and felt he had secured agreements amenable to whites and Indians alike. "The effect on the peace of the country hardly admits exaggeration," he immodestly wrote the Commissioner of Indian Affairs. Now he was journeying to other councils to the north and east, concluding two years of hectic negotiating.[8]

As Stevens left Walla Walla, his immediate duties shifted from In-dian negotiator to landscape examiner, for future railroad routes depended upon his detailed observations of the terrain. For five days his party journeyed northward, to the Touchet River, the Tukanen, Pat-tah-haha Creek, and finally the Snake. They followed that river a few miles, noting cornfields and orchards cultivated by Nez Perces, and then ascended into the Palouse country, camping June 20 on the western edge of Paradise Ridge, overlooking the valley of present-day Moscow, Idaho. Here Stevens jotted the first recorded observations of Latah County: "We have been astonished to-day at the luxuriance of the grass and the richness of the soil." Gazing into that valley and beyond, Stevens saw vast beds of wildflowers, abundant fields of blue camas shimmering like clear water reflecting a cloudless sky, and open, rolling grassland. The prairie inspired him, but so did the view to the east: dense forests on ridges "covered with pines." The next day the group traveled farther north to the Palouse River and Stevens, exhilarated by the sight, took time to climb a high hill, observing the stream's source. "So much was I impressed with it," he wrote, "that I directed Mr. [James] Doty to carefully take notes and lay down the river on his map." The country presented an awesome spectacle of heavy forests. Turning downstream Stevens saw trees just as abundant and large as at the headwaters— "trees . . . three and four feet through, with a proportionate height."[9]

Stevens was the first recorder of timberlands that eventually attracted wealthy lumbermen, but other early visitors also noted these forests. Four years after Stevens's trek, Captain John Mullan, surveying sites for the construction of a military road from Walla Walla to Fort Benton in Montana, dispatched Theodore Kolecki to investigate a route along the Palouse River. After trudging across rolling Palouse prairies on a steamy July day, Kolecki reached the base of Steptoe Butte, and, despite the oppressive heat and fatiguing journey, "climbed up this steep and rocky cone that stretches its crown more than one thousand feet above its dingy neighbors." From the top, Kolecki, like thousands who have followed, was treated to a spectacular panorama: grasslands to the west, mountains to the east, and, in close view, the Palouse River basin, "densely wooded" with forests covering the landscape from the river's source to a point within four miles of the Butte.

Thirteen years after Kolecki made his report, a newspaperman from Weiser, Idaho, noted that "we have . . . made inspection of . . . the timber on the Palouse river and its tributaries . . . and we are free to say that much of it is as fine as any we have seen in any country. . . . We saw white pine trees varying in diameter from two to five feet, and from 150 to 360 feet in height, as straight as an arrow, and many of them free from limbs for about 100 and 150 feet from the ground."[10]

From the time of earliest American settlement pioneers logged forests from necessity. Trees needed felling and land clearing before farms could be established, yet timber was also essential for housing, fencing and fuel; and lumbering became one of America's earliest industries, with wood workers some of the new country's most skilled laborers and craftsmen. Forests were exploited both out of necessity and for profit. The rich timberlands observed by the earliest Palouse country explorers were no exception. At first these were logged by homesteaders on the nearby prairie who needed lumber and fuel to survive. Eventually, after the depletion of forests in the upper Great Lakes states, shrewd lumbermen backed by wealthy investors systematically and efficiently harvested these lands.

SAWMILLING BEGINS IN THE PALOUSE

The Palouse country ostensibly had an advantage over many treeless prairies, an advantage recognized by regional boosters who proclaimed that the area's streams afforded "excellent water power and a cheap and easy means for the transportation of lumber from the splendid forests of Idaho, and thus while we live in the best farming country in the world we have all the advantages of a timbered country and escape the disadvantages incident to the same." In reality, though, midwestern farmers living near railroad terminals often had easier access to wood and lumber than did their Palouse counterparts. Palousers suffered through a long period of primitive roads and limited transportation facilities, and, despite the nearness of forests, even some area boosters were at times ambivalent about their surroundings. "The greatest difficulty which the settler will encounter in taking up a farm . . . is the comparative absence of timber," admitted one pro-motional brochure in 1882. Consequently, proximity to timber deter-mined Palouse settlement patterns, the earliest residents being drawn to eastern fringes near the forests or settling along streams large enough for log drives.[11]

While the Palouse River's major branch flows southwesterly out of the Hoodoos, a smaller fork originates at Moscow Mountain, runs to the southwest, then abruptly changes course northward after cross-ing the Washington border. Thirty miles to the north and west it enters a forested valley where the two branches converge. Here James A. Perkins and Thomas Smith, enticed by the trees and the river's current, established Colfax, the first town in the Palouse. Here too they started the area's first and most essential industry, sawmilling.

Anderson Cox, a Waitsburg, Washington, businessman, dispatched Perkins and Smith to the country in 1870, directing them to find a millsite. The Union Flat area south of Colfax was already attracting settlers, and Cox saw economic potential in building a mill to provide them with lumber. The isolated Colfax valley proved too oppressive for Smith, who soon left, but Perkins was joined by Hezekiah Hollingsworth. Using hired labor paid by Cox, Perkins and Hollingsworth constructed a mill and millrace, cutting their first lumber in September 1871. Eventually they added a dam and holding boom.

The mill, a crude affair with a perpendicular blade that locals joked went "up one day and down the next," proved profitable, filling an urgent need for lumber. Anderson Cox died a few months after the mill opened and Perkins sold his share to Hollingsworth, who in turn sold to John Davenport. Davenport apparently operated the mill until 1877 when M. J. Sexton and William Codd bought him out. These two transformed the inefficient plant into a major Palouse business.[12]

Sexton and Codd did not exactly find the field crowded when they began sawmilling, but neither did they have a monopoly. A mill opened northeast of Moscow on the edge of Moscow Mountain's timberlands in 1876, operated a few months, and was replaced in 1877 with a more permanent plant providing most of the lumber for that town's rapid growth in the late 1870s. At about the same time, mills were established on the north fork of the Palouse River at Elberton and in Pullman along the south fork. The most significant activity, however, was the construction, apparently in 1877, of the first sawmill at Palouse City. Surprisingly, given the town's advantageous natural setting, sawmill activity in Palouse City lagged behind other towns until the 1880s. By then people had discovered the potential of the Palouse River for transporting logs to the community, the first sizable town along the north fork and the closest to Latah County's timberlands, and Palouse City became a lumbering boomtown.[13]

Before the heyday of Palouse City's sawmilling, the region's small, scattered mills could not supply the lumber needed for the rapidly populating country. Since Palouse soil was generally unsuitable for sod construction, most of the area's first houses were crude affairs, usually dugouts sunk into hillsides or banks with holes cut to vent smoke. Log houses came next. Roads were almost nonexistent and early settlers laboriously hauled logs from the timber to their homes. As a result, houses were small, fourteen feet square usually sufficing for a family dwelling, with bachelors inhabiting considerably tighter quarters. Floors were dirt, and gaps between logs were chinked with clay mud, the largest holes sometimes first plugged by cedar wedges.[14]

Housing did not automatically improve with the construction of sawmills. One Palouse pioneer lived two and one-half years in a dirt-bottomed log cabin, unable to find enough lumber to buy for a floor. Others draped quilts over door openings and stretched muslin across windowgaps while awaiting finishing materials. Some residents dismantled wagons, using the planks for house siding. It was not unusual to return home with less than a half dozen unplaned, uneven boards after spending a day in line at one of the local sawmills. By 1877 things were so desperate the Colfax newspaper, normally filled with enthusiastic boosterism, warned people against coming to the Palouse:

> The immigration of the Palouse country has been so unusual-ly large this season . . . that no kinds of manufactures have kept pace and the result is we have four consumers to one producer. This is more noticeable in the article of lumber. The three sawmills in the county have not supplied the demand for lumber and never can. . . . There are now more than one hundred families in the county without shelter for the winter because lumber cannot be had to build, and at the present rate of immigration there can be no telling how many will be obliged to burrow in the ground like a coyote, and if the winter should be a severe one, there will probably be some suffering. Every woodshed or shelter of any kind is occupied for a dwelling house, buildings that were ex-pected to be finished before this time are unfinished for want of lumber.[15]

The situation could not last: resources were too plentiful; business-men too keen. Though spot shortages continued until the turn of the century, local lumber demands were gradually met, primarily by the improved Codd and Sexton mill at Colfax, and by mills at Palouse City.

Palouse City—later shortened to Palouse—began like other com-munities in the area. First it was the site of settlers ranging cattle, then of farmers, eventually becoming a neighborhood trading center. Its natural setting, however, guaranteed stronger growth than most other towns.

Palouse lies just across the Washington border along the Palouse River. The stream is narrow but swift here, running through a substantial ponderosa pine grove. The Idaho mountains adjacent to the town contained minerals as well as trees, and mining in Latah County's Gold Hill and Hoodoo districts created Palouse's first boom. These mining districts are some of the oldest in the West, prospecting beginning in 1860, just twelve years after California's golden discovery. Though few people struck mineral riches in Latah County, it was not for lack of trying. Miners traipsed through those hills for well over a century, finding just enough color to maintain enthusiasm. Palouse became the prospectors' staging and trading center. Many town businessmen, if not miners themselves, grubstaked prospectors and by 1895 the town's newspaper reported that "nearly every man in town . . . has a claim staked out somewhere."[16]

The Hoodoo and Gold Hill districts never developed into "the most promising field . . .in the northwest for the prospector, promoter, or investor" despite the assurances of Palouse's boosting editor. But they did give the town its first significant growth. From a sleepy population of 200 in 1882, Palouse mushroomed into Whitman County's second largest town just nine years later, a settlement of 1,200 hoping to become the major metropolis between Spokane and Walla Walla. The trading of thousands of dollars of Latah County gold for supplies fueled Palouse's growth, which was complemented in 1888 by the completion of a Northern Pacific rail line into town. During this same period entrepreneurs discovered the town's potential for sawmilling, and while Palouse's boom commenced with agriculture, mining, and railroads, it was sustained by lumbering.[17]

In 1882 Palouse had one sawmill, in 1884 two, and by 1887 three, with three additional plants nearby. One of these, owned by M. J. Sexton and William Codd, operators of the Colfax mill, was a "mammoth manufacturing establishment" capable of furnishing everything from windowsills to saddle boards. When the railroad built through town, these mills gained access to a wider marketing area. Shipments rolled to Genesee, Colton, Pullman, Garfield, Oakesdale, and other points along the line. By 1889 the Palouse sawmills employed over 100 men ripping out 90,000 feet of lumber a day. Two sash and door factories fabricated finish materials for prairie settlers. The Palouse newspaper gloated over prospects for continued prosperity:

> Almost every day we see some one in Palouse City from one of the many little villages along the S & P[18] contracting for lumber. . . . This condition of affairs must remain as it is on account of the peculiar "lay of the country." The Palouse river being the only water course that can be used for logging purposes, and that stream being crossed at Palouse City by the S & P railroad, it makes this place the natural lumber market for a very large area of the country [and] . . . gives Palouse City a decided advantage in forever controlling the lumber market.[19]

By 1891 the number of employees at Palouse's mills had doubled. In that year the Palouse Mill Company started operation with $87,000 capitalization and soon acquired control of all the town's mills, making it the largest lumbering concern in eastern Washington, cutting twelve to thirteen million board feet a year. The company—manufacturers of lumber, lath, shingles, sashes, storefronts, doors, desks, molding, mantels, and balustrades at "bed rock prices"—operated lumberyards in several nearby towns. When Michigan lumberman Charles O. Brown toured Idaho forests in 1893, he spent a night at Palouse City and was impressed with the company's mills which were "doing a good business. . . . No wonder a sawmill pays here—no culls—no waist [sic]—no stumpage."[20]

Brown visited Palouse just before the wet harvest of 1893, the only disastrous crop failure in the area's history. This, combined with the nationwide Panic of 1893 and the Palouse Mill Company's too-rapid expansion, forced the concern into bankruptcy. In 1895, businessmen incorporated the Palouse River Lumber Company, taking over the plant of the defunct Palouse Mill Company and replacing that firm as the region's largest lumbering business.[21]

The Palouse River Lumber Company also had difficulties. The plant was conveniently located adjacent to the Northern Pacific tracks, a boon to marketing, but in 1898 a passing locomotive ignited sawdust in the yard starting a fire that destroyed the firm's planing mill and sash and door factory. Undaunted stockholders rebuilt in 1899, creating an even larger facility and by 1901 the company managed a string of retail yards throughout the Palouse country, shipping up to seventy-five carloads of lumber monthly to places as distant as Lewiston, Idaho, and Spangle, Washington.[22]

This burst of sawmilling activity in the late 1800s transformed Palouse from an isolated prairie trading center into a boisterous logging town. After a fire destroyed most of the community's frame structures in 1888, Palouse rebuilt with impressive brick buildings belying its small population base. By 1892 a Portland journalist described the place as "decidedly metropolitan." Mile-long plank sidewalks sixteen feet wide ran along Main Street, and major thoroughfares were macadamized, eliminating mud-wading. Electric street lights, telephones, waterworks, and, in the words of the newspaperman, "a system of sewerage that would be a credit to a city of 10,000" contributed to the cosmopolitan aura.

In addition to the sawmills, Palouse had two flour mills, two brickyards, three hardware firms, ten dry goods or grocery stores, a brewery, five saloons, two hotels, two furniture stores, and a surprisingly wide array of other businesses. When the publisher of the Palouse *Republican* hawked his first newspaper in May 1892 he predicted "future prosperity in abundance . . . for the City of Palouse—the dimple in the blushing cheek of nature." His enthusiasm had hardly dimmed six months later when he advised that "people who desire to live in one of the first cities of the land must get in on the tide," for Palouse was experiencing "a state of affairs never dreamed of by the most sanguine prophet of our times."[23]

The town boomed throughout the 1890s, only temporarily slowed by the 1893 depression. Although it appeared metropolitan for such a small place, it also had the feel of a community on the fringe of one of America's last logging frontiers. Woods workers "blowing in" from camps were accommodated by several brothels and taverns, including the "Damfino Saloon," so named by a sign painter who, when inquiring of the owner what name he wished emblazoned upon his storefront was greeted with the reply, "Damn if I know." The town could become rowdy, with too many men toting guns. Charles Farnsworth, co-owner of the community's first sawmill, saw three men killed on Palouse streets in as many gunfights, and local newspapers periodically reported such fracases throughout the decade.[24]

Things were particularly lively each spring during the annual Palouse River log drive, which moved timber from Idaho forests to Colfax, Elberton, and Palouse mills. The river's first drive in 1871 took logs a short distance into Colfax. As timber along the stream banks was cut, drives became longer, originating in Idaho by at least 1880. In that year Sexton and Codd floated two million feet of sawlogs to their Colfax mill. As Palouse grew into the region's sawmilling center, it became the terminus for most of the logs. There were normally so many in the river there by summer that they completely covered the water.

Loggers cut Idaho trees, decked them in a central location, and awaited winter snows when they were sleigh-hauled to the river's banks. Then river pigs, as log drivers were known—"hard-driving, hard-drinking, hard-fighting, blasphemous pioneers picked . . . for their stamina, agility, and strength"—shot them downstream during spring freshets. The Palouse is an unpredictable river with an unpredictable flow. The stream, narrow and winding, stranded logs on banks, and for the length of the drive river pigs, dressed in overalls and calked boots, worked in the water, handspiking logs, rolling and pushing strays back into the stream. A peavy—a pole tipped with a sharp steel point and adjustable steel hook which served as lever, spike, and gripper—was the pig's stock tool, but he occasionally used dynamite to break large log jams. Experienced log drivers working jams developed fine balance, but even the best frequently fell off floating logs, sometimes drowning in whirlpools or under log masses. No log rode easily, but cedar was the toughest, two-thirds of this bouyant tree floating out of the water, turning erratically. Idaho river pigs said all it took to make a cedar log roll was a change in their tobacco chew from one cheek to another. After days of dressing in clothes that never dried, bunking on a barge or in soggy tents along the river edge, eating biscuits, canned fruit, and meat, the river pigs, some of the highest-paid woods workers, eagerly descended upon Palouse City to unwind. "The last night of the drive through Palouse was also pay day," remembered R. H. Bockmier, "and time for celebrating. Some of the men would get just plain and fancy drunk. A number always made the calaboose—to sober up."[25]

By the turn of the century the Palouse River Lumber Company, the Colfax mill, and a few smaller concerns were meeting most regional lumber needs. Idaho timberlands had yielded the fuel, fencing, and building materials needed for settling the prairie. The forests also provided a livelihood for residents in need of cash or bartering material. They could cut cord wood or fence posts for neighbors, or, when mills came in, log during part of the year to supplement meager farm incomes. Yet, despite thirty years of logging, the forests had hardly been touched. Trees bordering the Palouse River were cut, but inland timberlands retained their riches. By the early 1900s Great Lakes lumbermen, searching for places to expand, came upon this treasure in Latah County's forests.[26]

THE WEYERHAEUSER SYNDICATE

A few months before Isaac Stevens set out to explore the Pacific Northwest in the 1850s, Wisconsin Representative Ben Eastman soberly informed his Congressional colleagues that "upon the rivers which are tributary to the Mississippi, and also upon those which empty themselves into Lake Michigan, there are interminable forests of pine, sufficient to supply all the wants of the citizens . . . for all time to come." Even as he spoke, the forests of Eastman's native Maine, once also considered inexhaustible, were rapidly disappearing, forcing lumbermen into Michigan, Wisconsin, and Minnesota. Within thirty years of his speech, upper Great Lakes lumbermen knew that intensive logging would soon leave little but cutover lands even in these tremendous woods, and looked for new opportunities in places like Oregon, Washington, and Idaho. Within fifty years of the optimistic prediction, the Lakes States' pine forests were depleted. Before then, however, these lands supplied lumber to settle the Midwest and provided a training ground for woods and sawmill workers who carried their crafts elsewhere. They also created fortunes for timberland owners, riches so immense these lumber barons looked for other regions in which to invest their money and export their skills.[27]

American settlers began utilizing their forests almost as soon as they stepped off the ships carrying them from the Old World. Initially they cleared land to make way for settlements, farms, and pastures, and the vast eastern forest often seemed more a burden than an asset. But even in the earliest days of American settlement timber was a valuable commodity, for it provided material for heating, cooking, building, and fencing. In fact, the forest touched nearly every aspect of colonial life, providing houses and barns, furniture and utensils, wagons, boats, and carriages, tools and containers. Colonists soon realized that this abundant resource had commercial possibilities. Settlers sent a small shipment of hand-hewn clapboards from Jamestown to England in 1607, and Richmond boasted a water-powered sawmill four years later. Sawmills proliferated along the entire seaboard, especially in New England. By the end of the seventeenth century, Massachusetts Bay Colony had over seventy mills, and at the time of the American Revolution wood products ranked fifth in importance among all colonial exports.[28]

The Northeast, particularly Maine, led the nation in lumber production by the early nineteenth century. As population and lumber demands increased, timber became Maine's most important industry. Here were great forests of white pine, the lumberman's favorite tree. White pine is soft and easily worked, yet resistant to shrinking and splintering. Equally important, it is extremely buoyant, and wood that floated easily was a boon to lumbermen relying upon waterways to transport timber from forest to mill.

The demand for wood products continued to grow while technological advances enabled lumbermen to more successfully attack forests and produce lumber. As a result, the Northeast's timberlands gradually became exhausted and lumbermen looked elsewhere to find adequate supplies. They moved north to Canada's Ottawa valley, south along the Appalachians, west to the middle Mississippi River region, and into the American South. Most significantly, however, lumbering entered the Great Lakes States of Michigan, Minnesota, and Wisconsin, where tremendous white pine forests and excellent natural waterway systems beckoned. In 1839 the Northeast produced two-thirds of the nation's total production of lumber. Just twenty years later its share had shrunk to one-third. The industry had made a great transition, both in geography and technology.[29]

Michigan's commercial logging began in the 1820s, and by 1837 over 400 sawmills were cutting. By 1870 Michigan had replaced Pennsylvania and New York as the nation's leading lumber producer, with output peaking there in 1889. By that time many Michigan lumbermen had moved farther west to Minnesota, one of the nation's leading lumbering regions by the 1890s. The first Wisconsin sawmill opened in 1809, though commercial activity really began in the 1850s, peaking in 1892.[30]

Eastern lumbermen had made fortunes, but these paled when compared to the massive wealth and resource accumulations built up by timbermen in the Lakes States. Continued growth of the nation's population, the settlement of treeless prairie regions, urbanization, industrialization, and railroad construction all spurred increases in lumber demands. Since small local mills could not meet these needs, some entrepreneurs began constructing larger facilities. These large manufacturers came to hold tremendous positions of strength because they produced a basic material necessary for the nation's growth. Frederick Weyerhaeuser was one of the shrewdest of this new style of lumber businessman, and became one of the industry's wealthiest and most influential leaders.

The German-born Weyerhaeuser emigrated to the United States in 1852 at age seventeen. His family settled near Erie, Pennsylvania, where Weyerhaeuser worked on a farm and in a brewery. At twenty-one he moved west to Rock Island, Illinois, a Mississippi River town strategically located between the white pine forests of the Great Lakes and the midwestern prairies then being rapidly settled. Here Weyerhaeuser worked at a variety of jobs, including sawmilling. In 1860 he, along with brother-in-law Frederick C. A. Denkmann, purchased a Rock Island sawmill, an investment that initially pushed both men to the edge of bankruptcy. The gamble paid handsomely, however. By 1869 the partners were free of debt and owned a mill delivering annual profits. They bought large Rock Island homes and prepared to expand into new areas.

Rock Island provided the foundation for their fortune, but these energetic entrepreneurs realized the future clearly lay farther north, in the dense Wisconsin and Minnesota forests. Downriver Mississippi sawmill owners, such as Weyerhaeuser and Denkmann, faced a dilemma in the late 1860s. The meager forests of Illinois and Iowa were inadequate, and lumbermen relied on logs floated to mills from Wisconsin and Minnesota to meet demand. Though these downriver Mississippi lumbermen were competitors with one another, they recognized their common problem and the potential for cooperation. In 1868 they dispatched Weyerhaeuser to Wisconsin to investigate pine lands with an eye toward guaranteeing the supplies of timber needed to maintain their operations.

Weyerhaeuser journeyed to the Chippewa River valley. The Chippewa flows through Wisconsin's richest pine lands before joining the Mississippi south of Minneapolis-St. Paul. The river and its tributaries drain an area encompassing more than a third of Wisconsin's pineries. The region's rich holdings—over 46 billion board feet—were unusually accessible, with the valley's lakes, streams, and rivers forming a natural transportation web. Enthralled by this bonanza, Weyerhaeuser worked diligently to convince downriver timbermen of the need for cooperating to win control of the Chippewa pineries from local lumbermen who also coveted them. Such control would ensure the flow of Chippewa logs to their own Mississippi River sawmills.

Weyerhaeuser's task was difficult, for competition far outdistanced cooperation as an operational mode among lumbermen. Nevertheless, in 1871 he succeeded in forming the Mississippi River Logging Company, a combination of seventeen lumber firms. Many people involved in the company later expanded with Weyerhaeuser into Minnesota and the Pacific Northwest—men like William H. Laird, James L. and Matthew G. Norton, and Peter Musser—and the Mississippi River Logging Company provided the embryonic beginnings of a complex conglomerate that was a major force in shaping the development of American lumbering.

The company was created as a vehicle to purchase Chippewa valley timberlands and float logs from these holdings downstream in sufficient number to maintain operations at lower Mississippi mills. For ten years Chippewa valley mill owners, naturally concerned about this incursion into their timberlands, battled the downstream interests—on the river, in the courts, and in the legislature. The conflict came to a head in 1880. Tremendous flooding that spring carried the entire season's supply of logs well past the traditional holding areas of the Chippewa sawmills. They could be retrieved, but only at great cost. Chippewa sawmillers, on the verge of ruin, had no choice but to come to terms with the downriver mill owners. For its part, Weyerhaeuser's group was eager to increase the area it controlled without vast capital outlay. Weyerhaeuser argued that cooperation was the answer, and the upriver and downriver interests in 1881 permanently united in an arrangement for purchasing, driving, and distributing Chippewa valley logs. But there was no question that, thanks to the effects of the flood, Weyerhaeuser and his downriver allies clearly dominated the enlarged organization.[31]

Frederick Weyerhaeuser emerged from the Chippewa struggle as the most influential and powerful lumberman in the United States. The incursion into the Chippewa valley demonstrated his organizational skills and launched him into a new aspect of the lumber business: timberland ownership. Downstream Mississippi mill owners had traditionally acquired logs from others, but in 1868 Laird-Norton & Company bought its first timberland—in the Chippewa valley— and Weyerhaeuser and Denkmann followed with an 8,000 acre purchase there in 1872. In the future, massive timberland acquisitions by Weyerhaeuser and his associates were to be the basis for enormous fortunes. The Mississippi River Logging Company also connected Weyerhaeuser with lumbermen who remained trusted associates during the dramatic periods of expansion that followed. People like Peter Musser, E. S. and A. B. Youmans, and especially Laird and the Nortons were not only able partners, but faithful friends.[32]

By the 1880s Weyerhaeuser knew enough of lumbering to realize that—in times before reforestation and sustained yields—constant expansion keyed survival. Even the lush merchantable timber of the Chippewa forest would one day be gone. Lumbermen needed to search relentlessly for new timberlands. In 1890 Musser and Company, the Laird-Norton Company, and Weyerhaeuser and Denkmann formed the Pine Tree Lumber Company which acquired thousands of acres of Minnesota timberland. The associates were making the first of many steps westward, but for several years Minnesota was the center of their activities, with Weyerhaeuser eventually moving his home and office to St. Paul.[33]

By the turn of the century, Frederick Weyerhaeuser was America's predominant lumbermen—president of twenty-one companies, holder of staggering timberland acreages, director of several banks. Though he did not invent the concept of interlocking management, he raised it to new levels of efficiency in American lumbering. He and his associates directed the destinies of a dizzying number of timber-related firms, sitting on each others' boards, owning each others' stock. As Weyerhaeuser was usually the bellwether and most visible spokesman for these firms, he and his associates became commonly known as the "Weyerhaeuser syndicate."[34]

Minnesota lumber manufacturing peaked in the late 1890s. Just as resources had played out along the banks of the Mississippi and the Chippewa, they were now declining in Minnesota. Realizing this, Weyerhaeuser investigated the Douglas fir and pine forests of Washington, Oregon, and Idaho, as well as the pineries of the Gulf States. In the Pacific Northwest, sharp-eyed and hopeful boosters could also see the impending depletion of Great Lakes forests. They anticipated the syndicate's need to move—to purchase lands, build mills, and create wealth—and worked to lure these entrepreneurs into their region. The Weyerhaeuser group was not the first to market timber in Wisconsin and Minnesota, and they were far from the first to harvest the rich Pacific Northwest forests. Washington's earliest sawmill started in 1827, Idaho's in 1840, and Oregon's in 1842. But just as in the Lakes States, the Weyerhaeuser group dramatically altered the nature of Pacific Northwest lumbering. Turn-of-the-century boomers eagerly awaited the Weyerhaeusers, the syndicate came, and the region has never been quite the same since.[35]

CHAPTER TWO

Move to Idaho

C. O. BROWN AND THE IDAHO TIMBERLANDS

Charles O. Brown wearily marked his fifty-second birthday. April 20, 1893—it should have been spring, but Michigan weather pays no heed to calendars. "My berth-day [sic] [and] . . . there is two feet of snow here in the Northern Michigan forests," Brown wrote in his diary. "Will I have to pass another berth-day here? I hope not. This is a little too much winter for comfort."[1]

Brown, born in Maine, a Civil War veteran who had withered to eighty-six pounds as a prisoner of war in South Carolina, knew discomfort. And he knew he would forever suffer as a timber cruiser and woodland trader in Michigan's icy climate. Besides, it did not take extraordinary foresight to realize that "the end of the pine on the Menominee waters is very neer [sic]." So, at the precise age of fifty-two years and two months, Brown headed west seeking greater opportunity and better conditions.[2]

Brown traveled by train, first to the Chicago World's Fair, then to Colorado, Utah, and finally Idaho, trekking west across the state's southland, stopping in Boise, then swinging northward. On July 22 he reached Moscow. Over the next few days he observed mill operations at Palouse City and surveyed north central Idaho timberlands, finding tall, clear white pines and "the largest cedar I have ever seen." By the end of August he was back in Michigan. But Brown, the first significant Lakes States timberland trader to view Latah County's forests, planned to return and seek his fortune.[3]

Ecstatic about the state's potential, Brown attempted to convince Great Lakes lumbermen to invest in Idaho timberlands, but found an unreceptive audience. Lumber prices tumbled during the Panic of 1893, and the industry did not recover for another half dozen years. Expansion was out of the question. Disappointed but undeterred after a year of unsuccessful proselytizing, Brown returned to Idaho in 1894 with his son, Nat, and son-in-law Theodore Fohl. All three claimed homesteads near Bovill in eastern Latah County.[4]

Brown reappeared in Michigan in 1895 attending to business affairs, then set out for Idaho again with his remaining family, determined this time to stay and prosper despite other Lakes Staters' reluctance to follow. For the next six years he preached the gospel of Idaho timberlands to prospective investors. He boasted at an Idaho Immigration Association convention that there stood in Latah County "the largest single group of white pine . . . in the United States, upon no tree of which the lumberman's ax has yet fallen." Investors could purchase these lands reasonably from the state or from homesteaders. For years miners had unsuccessfully trudged through this forest, "ever seeking the phantom of wealth in the gray old mountains . . . heeding not the sure fortune that capital and experience will . . . glean from the dark forest." Though speaking in Boise, Brown aimed his remarks at the Great Lakes region where "there are plenty of men who, having accumulated wealth in the manufacture of their own forests, are now looking elsewhere for others. . . . To these people we must appeal."[5]

Brown fired verbal appeals. He published publicity brochures. He journeyed frequently to Minnesota, Michigan, and Wisconsin. He tenaciously sought investors, but few listened, preoccupied as they were with the depression. Still he struggled doggedly on, never doubting Idaho's potential profitability. Finally, in 1899 the economy veered upward, kindled by patriotism and optimism following American military victories over Spain. Woodlands appreciated wildly, timber around the Great Lakes became increasingly scarce, and lumbermen prepared to move on once again. C. O. Brown was on the ground, ready to pilot them into Idaho.

Brown's first converts were George Scofield, a Michigan sawmiller, and his father, Edward, a wealthy lumberman and Wisconsin's governor. The Scofields, apparently representing "a syndicate of wealthy lumbermen," journeyed to Moscow in the summer of 1899 and toured Latah County timberlands with Brown. Duly impressed, Edward outlined plans for sawmills and a logging railroad. But after further thought the Scofields backed out. Much of northern Idaho's forests were state-owned. Investors could purchase trees but not the land, and the state, hoping to discourage timberland speculation, imposed a twenty-year logging limit. After that, all uncut stumpage would revert to the state. The Scofields felt the policy prohibited profitable investment. A company would have to accumulate vast timberlands to justify the expense of building railroads and sawmills, and it could not expect to clear all that land within twenty years. Wisconsin's governor shook "Idaho's dust from off his feet," and returned home. Brown was devastated. After years of sweat he had finally lured potential investors to Idaho only to see them leave, money still in hand.[6]

Brown labored for another nine months until John Glover and James Johnson visited. Brown had no idea that the two represented the Lakes States' largest timber syndicate. Glover owned the Willow River Lumber Company in New Richmond, Wisconsin; Johnson was his ace timber cruiser. They traveled to Moscow at the instigation of John A. Humbird, a wealthy Wisconsin lumberman and acquaintance of Frederick Weyerhaeuser. Brown had persistently written Weyerhaeuser and Humbird, and now the two had secretly dispatched Glover and Johnson to scout the area he extolled. Brown toured the two through forests around his Bovill homestead. Glover and Johnson, overwhelmed, immediately offered Brown a job with their company, though it was still unclear to Brown who they represented. Brown accepted a $150 a month salary as "local agent," hoping for the best but remaining skeptical. "Will this deal stick?" he wondered. "I certainly hope so—I am getting old and cannot always hold my breath waiting—well if we do go on with this enterprise I believe I can make a pile of money for the company—and incedently [sic] a living for myself." A few weeks later Brown learned he was on Humbird and Weyerhaeuser's payroll. His bulldog perseverance had finally paid off.[7]

Despite Latah County's obvious wealth, Weyerhaeuser and Humbird instructed Brown to concentrate purchasing efforts farther south, in the Clearwater River area. For years Brown had roamed these forests, seeing no one but homesteaders. Now his isolated travels were interrupted as the Clearwater teemed with timber cruisers. Agents representing the Scofields, who had changed their minds about Idaho's potential, wealthy Wisconsin lumberman Warren E. McCord, and other groups scouted the same lands as Brown in a feverish race to claim the richest property. This Idaho invasion began suddenly for a number of reasons. First, Brown had advertised well, and the Weyerhaeusers were not alone in recognizing Idaho's potential. Second, the improved economy encouraged expansion. Finally and perhaps most importantly, lumbermen gained access to Northern Pacific Railroad scrip, enabling them to purchase timberlands without relying on Idaho state lands encumbered with their burdensome rule requiring cutting within twenty years. Congress encouraged railroads to construct transcontinental lines by granting them title to every odd numbered land section along their rail beds. If the land was occupied by settlers or was part of an Indian reservation, national park, or national forest reserve, railroads were instead given certificates, called scrip, entitling them to property elsewhere. When Washington's Mt. Rainier National Park was created in 1898, the Northern Pacific acquired tremendous quantities of scrip in exchange for those parts of its land grant lying within the park. The railroad willingly sold to lumber companies, and lumbermen, realizing the impossibility of acquiring large tracts of land by buying out individual homesteaders and unwilling to rely solely upon purchases of state stumpage, eagerly bought the scrip. As a result, timber buyers rushed to Idaho in the summer of 1900, and C. O. Brown was in the middle of the flurry.

In August Brown and his son sighted some of the Clearwater's finest timber stands. Guided by a trapper, the Browns found a high point crowned by a huge rock providing a vista of incredible forests. Clambering to the top, Brown spread his arms wide, telling Nat they should claim all the good timber that could be seen from the rock. Returning to Moscow, Brown wired Glover of his discovery. "Go at once" and claim the timber, Glover telegraphed back on August 24. Charles and Nat Brown, Theodore Fohl, and four other men set out for the woods, only to find that McCord's survey crew had already been working the area for a month. Brown prodded his men, working them every daylight hour, taking no time off, attempting to catch up. McCord's team had been forced to spend most of its head start running township lines in the unsurveyed country. Taking advantage of his rivals' survey markers, Brown devoted his energy to cruising—estimating the amount of standing timber. On September 9 he cabled Glover to speed to Idaho and be prepared to file scrip on enormous timberlands. Five days later Brown met Glover in Lewiston, handing him the requisite survey and cruise information. Glover rushed to the land office, filing on 30,000 acres of Idaho's choicest timberlands. One day later, McCord appeared, discovering to his disgust that he was too late. "We only secured the land by the skin of our teeth," Brown gleefully recorded in his diary, adding that it was "one of the sharpest pieces of work I have ever accomplished."[8]

Bitterly disappointed, McCord ordered his crew to continue on, hoping to claim adjacent timberlands. Brown and his weary men also returned to the forests, cruising an additional 20,000 acres. On September 24, Brown received word that one of McCord's men had already left for Lewiston to file. Exhausted from the previous weeks' whirlwind activity, Brown dispatched Nat to overtake him. McCord's man had a three-hour start, but Nat, with an excellent horse, a sack of oats, a small lunch, and a "palouser"—a lard pail with a candle stuck through a jagged side hole to provide light—rode after him into the night woods. After twenty-five miles Brown came to a lighted cabin. Extinguishing the palouser, he stealthily approached the window and found McCord's man resting inside. Creeping to the barn, Brown discovered two horses. One was wet and covered with mud, exhausted from a hard ride through the forest. The other was fresh. He saddled the fresh one, turned his own and the tired one loose, and hastened on into the woods, reaching Orofino before dawn, where he found a waiting railroad engine. When asked if he had requested the engine for a special run to Lewiston, Nat replied that he was indeed heading for that town. Having stolen a horse and commandeered a train, Brown once again beat McCord to the land office, and on September 25 Glover filed on the additional 20,000 acres. A furious McCord threatened to sue. Glover hustled to a hotel across the river in Clarkston, Washington, while Nat hid at a friend's house, both hoping to escape arrest. McCord eventually cooled and filed no lawsuit. Though the ethics of its agents were questionable, the Weyerhaeuser syndicate had made its first Idaho timberland purchases.[9]

In October, Weyerhaeuser visited Idaho to personally view woodlands there. Accompanied by his son Charles, J. A. Humbird, and Glover, he traveled first to Sandpoint where he and Humbird purchased the Sandpoint Lumber Company, renaming it the Humbird Lumber Company. The group then departed for Moscow where Charles Brown greeted them. A nine-day junket into Latah County and Clearwater forests followed. It was Brown's first meeting with Weyerhaeuser, then sixty-five years old with blue eyes, salt and pepper beard, still supple and strong. Brown described him as "hale and hearty . . .and very spry." Charles Weyerhaeuser struck Brown as "intelligent, courteous and will evedently [sic] make a sharp business man—and one that will not waste the millions he will inherit."

Brown escorted the group by horseback along narrow forest trails. Near Fohl's Bovill homestead they marveled at a 400-year-old, 227-foot-tall monarch that came to be called the "King of White Pines," one of the largest of the species ever found. Pressing on, Brown pointed out the choice timber they already owned, as well as uncruised lands. Despite incessant rain, primitive lodgings, and poor food, the party—with the exception of Glover who was in a continuous "ill temper"—took "every thing cheerfully" and tried "to put the best foot forward." After leaving the woods, Weyerhaeuser expressed delight over the timberlands, congratulated Nat for his night ride, and thanked Charles for an enlightening tour.[10]

Horseback riding through a cold, soggy forest, sleeping in homestead shacks, and eating cold meals was not exactly the type of travel to which Humbird and the Weyerhaeusers were accustomed. But these were shrewd timbermen who realized Brown had not exaggerated Idaho's riches. In December 1900 they formed the Clearwater Timber Company with Humbird as president, Weyerhaeuser vice president, Glover secretary, and Brown local agent. Capitalized at $500,000, the company expanded upon Brown's original purchases, eventually acquiring over 200,000 acres of prime white pine. In January 1901 they organized the Potlatch Timber Company, Ltd., again with Brown as local agent. This company, considered by the stockholders as a prelude to future timberland acquisitions and lumber manufacturing in Latah County, duly segregated activity there from the Clearwater region. Although the Potlatch Timber Company acquired small land parcels, it was never very active in Idaho. Within a few months after its incorporation, the Weyerhaeuser syndicate engaged another Latah County representative – William Deary – who pursued a more aggressive, expansionistic policy than that originally envisioned for the Potlatch Timber Company.[11]

When Charles Brown died in Moscow on August 2, 1902, all the town's businesses closed for the funeral. He had helped build the small community and brought big lumbering concerns to the state. Although he died before the Weyerhaeusers began sawmilling there, Brown had envisioned the huge mills, railroads, and immense logging operations that eventually came. Nat replaced his father as local agent for the Clearwater Timber Company, remaining with the firm until 1912. Then Theodore Fohl, formerly chief cruiser and fire warden for the company, became agent, serving until 1927 when Clearwater opened its large Lewiston sawmill.

WEYERHAEUSER MOVES WEST

Frederick Weyerhaeuser understood that survival depended upon acquiring more timberlands. He was not sure where those timberlands should be purchased. Expansion was destined; investment in the West was not.

By the 1880s, Lakes States lumbermen prepared to move into the only two great timbered regions remaining in America – the South and the West. For a time Weyerhaeuser considered southern expansion. The issue divided his family, with one of Frederick's sons,

Charles, favoring the West while another, Frederick E., preferred
the South. "Brother Fred is the enthusiastic Southern member of
our family," Charles wrote. "I would rather be interested in property even if the profits are smaller, in a place where I would be per-
fectly willing to live. The South may be better than I think it is,
but I have always been prejudiced against it."[12]

The elder Frederick shared Charles's southern biases. He feared
the region's heat and malaria; questioned it as a proper home for family
and friends; held lingering Civil War antagonisms. Still, Weyerhaeuser
open-mindedly investigated all possibilities, potential profitability occasionally overriding prejudices. He, along with the Laird-Norton
group and other investors, even organized the Southern Lumber Company, operating in Arkansas and Louisiana under the leadership of
son Frederick. Had northern railroads been less assertive in luring
Great Lakes lumbermen to the West, the history of the Weyerhaeuser
companies might have more of a southern than a northwestern flavor.
Young Frederick always regretted that they did not move more aggressively into the South at that time. "Almost any investment in
southern pine lumber made in 1900 by competent lumbermen would
have been exceedingly profitable," he noted many years later. As it
was, the Southern Lumber Company remained the group's only
significant southern venture during the early 1900s.[13]

As early as 1885 the Northern Pacific Railroad offered Weyerhaeuser timberlands in the Pacific Northwest along with a Tacoma,
Washington, millsite. Two years later he visited Puget Sound.
Although Weyerhaeuser came away feeling the region held great opportunity for future generations of his family, he was not yet ready
to invest. Then in 1893 he moved to a fashionable St. Paul
neighborhood, close to railroad magnate James J. Hill's home. The
two became fast friends, sharing evening fireside discussions when
Hill discoursed upon the fertility of Pacific Northwest woodlands
and the ability of his railroads to provide access to markets.[14]

Railroads transformed lumbering in the Pacific Northwest. From
the time of the region's first sawmill in 1827, commercial activity
had centered in the area west of the Cascade Range, with lumber
reaching markets by sea. By the 1890s railroads criss-crossed the
region, opening interior forest lands, while transcontinental lines
delivered lumber to lucrative markets farther east. The railroads also
owned land and scrip that they eagerly proffered to lumbermen.[15]

Hill made sure Weyerhaeuser knew all this. Jim Hill was "an old
fellow with long whiskers [who] . . .used to come over to call and

. . . stay awfully late," remembered Frederick K. Weyerhaeuser of his grandfather's late-night neighborly visits. "Everybody would get pretty sleepy." The senior Frederick Weyerhaeuser believed in retiring early and rising at dawn; Hill loved the evening. Weyerhaeuser occasionally dozed as Hill, absorbed in monologues about the railroads' opening of the West, droned on, but he heard enough to realize Hill's financial needs meshed with his own ambition. Hill required cash to pay debts. Weyerhaeuser wanted new timberlands. Hill informed Weyerhaeuser that he planned to retire eight million dollars of Northern Pacific Railroad bonds by selling 900,000 acres of Pacific Northwest timberlands. One night late in 1899, sitting before a fire in Hill's den, the two sealed one of the biggest real estate deals in American history. Weyerhaeuser's syndicate would purchase all the Northern Pacific property for six dollars an acre, with Weyerhaeuser and Denkmann underwriting one-third of the cost and the Laird-Norton group bankrolling nearly another third.[16]

This enormous transaction established the land base for the Weyerhaeuser Timber Company, headquartered in Tacoma, the largest of Weyerhaeuser's Pacific Northwest ventures. It also opened the door to other investments. With the Northern Pacific acquisition, the associates clearly opted to emphasize western over southern expansion. Weyerhaeuser, believing the only time he lost money on timberlands was when he did not buy, now sought additional property on both sides of the Cascade Mountains. His excursion with C. O. Brown confirmed his suspicion that Idaho offered another promising investment opportunity.

Weyerhauser's purchase also inspired western expansion by other Lakes Staters who judiciously followed the syndicate's moves. While most activity centered on the Pacific slope—the location of the greatest forests—many turn-of-the-century investors also rushed into northern Idaho and other pine regions east of the Cascades and in the Rocky Mountains. In 1899 the entire northern Rocky Mountain region produced less than one percent of the nation's lumber supply, but by 1910 production had tripled, the selling price of Idaho lumber nearly doubled, and the Rocky Mountain region was manufacturing over 3 percent of America's lumber. Of all the interior lumber businesses established during this period, the largest was based in Potlatch, Idaho.[17]

WILLIAM DEARY

Matthew Norton, Peter Musser, and Frederick Weyerhaeuser gained friendship and mutual respect during their association with the Mississippi River Logging Company. By 1890 these seasoned, wealthy lumbermen sought new challenges, anticipating the time when it would become necessary to transfer some of their authority to the next generation of their families. Thus the Laird-Norton group, Weyerhaeuser and Denkmann, and the Mussers purchased vast northern Minnesota timberlands from the Northern Pacific Railroad in the early 1890s and incorporated the Pine Tree Lumber Company. They constructed a mill at Little Falls and placed the million-dollar operation under the leadership of Charles A. Weyerhaeuser, Frederick's son, who served as general manager, and R. Drew Musser, Peter's son, as secretary-treasurer. Drew and Charles had apprenticed in other family firms, but this was their first independent venture. Each received paternalistic advice from elders, but Pine Tree was clearly theirs to manage.

The firm could not have started at a worse time. Just when milling began, the 1893 depression hit and Musser and Weyerhaeuser agonized through several lean years. The two bachelors lived frugally in small quarters above their office and were equally Spartan with company funds. They realized, though, as Frederick Weyerhaeuser had before them, that one seldom erred when purchasing timberlands. Even while manufacturing profits were slim, Pine Tree's woodlands gradually appreciated in value, and Charles and Drew sought other sound timber purchases.

In 1894 the two met William Deary. Born in Canada in the 1850s, Deary was a squat, broad-bodied, deep-chested man five feet nine inches tall, weighing over 200 pounds. An experienced logger and woodsman, he was vigorous and visionary. Moving to the Great Lakes region in the 1880s, Deary successfully speculated in timberlands and made an immediate impression on Musser and Weyerhaeuser, who occasionally bought Minnesota timber tracts from him. In 1895 Deary formed a partnership with J. B. Kehl of Chippewa Falls, Wisconsin, a moderately successful flour miller and timberland trader well acquainted with Frederick Weyerhaeuser.

The Pine Tree Lumber Company maintained a working relationship with Kehl and Deary, but large timberland purchases were impossible while Musser and Weyerhaeuser struggled to become financially solvent. By 1898 prospects had brightened and Deary, always an aggressive purchaser, approached Pine Tree about buying 350 million feet of northern Minnesota timber. Deary had ambition but needed money. The Weyerhaeuser associates had money and liked Deary's assertive style. As a result, they incorporated the Northland Pine Company with Kehl and Deary, Weyerhaeuser and Denkmann, Laird-Norton and Company, and the Musser family each owning one-fourth interest. At first the company speculated in Minnesota timberlands, but Deary proved to be overly optimistic about the possibility of purchasing large tracts of these northern lands. Too many investors already operated there, and the small, scattered available acreages had limited value. "It is becoming more difficult to pick up pine and it is only a question of time when all of the cheap timber will have been purchased," Musser commiserated to Frederic S. Bell at the Laird-Norton Company in 1899. The future lay elsewhere. Northland Pine Company, with William Deary as general manager, thus became the Weyerhaeuser associates' vehicle for probing new territories, and Deary spent much of the next two years on the road, searching for timberlands.[18]

In November 1899 Deary traveled to Saskatchewan, Canada, but found trees there scrubby and small, noting that "the spruce timber in that country will never cut any figure with the lumber market." By April 1900 he was scouting in Texas, Louisiana, Alabama, and Florida. Impressed with timberland near Beaumont, Texas, he wrote to Laird-Norton that "there is no other timber that can be bought as well located as that for these prices." Northland's directors disagreed, making no purchases. Suffering from the heat, fearing quarantine because of an outbreak of yellow fever along the Gulf of Mexico, and concerned about his children at home who had contracted whooping cough, Deary cut short his southern trip and returned to Minnesota. In the fall, Northland's directors authorized him to travel again to the South and into Mexico, scouting timber during cooler winter months. He did, but found little property of interest.[19]

Even while looking over Canadian and southern timber, Deary wanted to explore Idaho's woodlands. "Let me know what you think about my going out to the coast this winter and into Idaho to look up, and see if I could get something that would be a good thing for the Northland Pine Co.," he wrote in 1899. A year later, he traveled by train to Seattle, scouted Puget Sound timberlands, then went to Oregon, and eventually spent a couple of days in Lewiston where he probably met up with J. B. Kehl. Kehl at this time was playing all options, working with W. E. McCord against the Weyerhaeuser interests in the Clearwater area, and had been in Lewiston just two days earlier when he got the disappointing news that Nat Brown had beaten the McCord group to the land office and filed on Clearwater timberlands. Deary made a hurried trip through Idaho woodlands, perhaps not even getting into Latah County. He was far from overwhelmed. "From what I saw of Idaho I do not think it is a very good place to invest money," he wrote to Laird-Norton. "I am very much more impressed with the southern timber and the prospects of getting money out of it, than I am in the West." A month later, though, C. O. Brown led Charles Weyerhaeuser and his father on their more extended trip, convincing them that Idaho was the place to invest. Though the Northland Pine Company's directors authorized one more southern excursion for Deary, for all practical purposes the nod had gone to the West instead of the South. Deary, too, eventually became a convert, strongly advocating timberland purchases in Idaho, but Frederick and Charles Weyerhaeuser were the strongest early advocates among the Northland Pine Company's owners.[20]

In the spring of 1901 Northland's directors again sent Deary to Idaho to scout the timberlands more thoroughly. There was still some wavering on the part of the company's directors. On the eve of Deary's second Idaho excursion Drew Musser wrote to the Laird-Norton Company: "Kindly let me know what you think of Idaho investments. It seems to me that the South is the better place." But Deary, after taking a closer look, liked Latah County's potential. The pine, fir, cedar, and tamarack were abundant and merchantable. After logging, this land bordering the rich Palouse country also seemed to offer agricultural potential, which would enable the company to make back some of its investment by selling cleared lands to farmers. By the fall of 1901 Deary had become a true believer, urging the Northland Pine Company's other directors to sell all their Minnesota timberlands, freeing money for Idaho investments. "The more I go through the different locations here," he wrote, "the more favorably I am impressed with the timber."[21]

Recovered from the battering it had taken during the depression of 1893, the Weyerhaeuser group looked forward to expansion. After forming the Northland Pine Company the only question was whether it would move to Idaho or to the South. First Frederick and Charles Weyerhaeuser and J. B. Kehl became convinced that Idaho offered the greatest rewards. Eventually William Deary became a champion of that state's resources. Other company directors, some reluctantly, agreed to forego the South in favor of Idaho. Once the decision had been made, Northland moved into the state dramatically, purchasing huge timberland tracts.

FIRST PURCHASES IN LATAH COUNTY

With the Browns and Fohl busily working the region south of Latah County after the Clearwater Timber Company's formation, Deary needed help estimating stumpage on possible Northland Pine Company purchases. When sent into Latah County in spring 1901, Deary took a number of timber cruisers with him. He placed most of his confidence, though—and the future of the Northland Pine Company—in the estimating capabilities of William Helmer, a fellow Canadian and acquaintance from Minnesota's woods.

Capable timber cruisers, land lookers, estimators—they went by different names—ensured the survival of timber purchasing companies. Cruisers' estimates of merchantable lumber in standing forests determined whether a company bought, and at what price. Inaccurately low timber estimates might cause a firm to forego purchases, possibly losing profitable acquisitions, while high estimates could bring bankruptcy. Cruisers had to note quickly how many merchantable trees stood in a particular tract and ascertain how many of the valued species actually contained good lumber, for on any piece of land there were decayed and defective trees that looked healthy to all but the best-trained observers.

Cruisers, usually working in small groups, established base camps and then ventured off on individual estimating excursions to pre-designated sections. Because the forest was already surveyed in most areas, establishing locations by using a compass and surveyors' field notes to find witness tree section markers proved relatively easy. Once a corner was established, cruisers paced off a section. Pacing was of utmost importance, for if an estimator stutter-stepped his whole cruise was thrown off. The best cruisers paced with astonishing accuracy. Estimators next walked off a 200-square-foot tract within the section, counted the number of merchantable trees in that area, and estimated the board feet in a few of them. The average number of board feet per tree was multiplied by the average number of usable trees per acre, which was multiplied again by 640, the number of acres in a section.[22]

Good estimators accomplished these tasks quickly and accurately, and few were better at them than Bill Helmer, chief cruiser on Weyerhaeuser properties north of the Clearwater for many years. Born in 1863, Helmer grew up hiking the white pine forests of his native Quebec province. Branching out to timber cruising came naturally, and at nineteen he moved to Minnesota where he developed a reputation for uncanny accuracy. Tall and lean, weather-hard and wiry-strong, dressed in suspendered pants, scuffed boots, and a wide-brimmed hat that provided protection from hail, rain, snow, sun, and ticks falling from trees, Helmer became a familiar sight, sauntering into the woods on cruising excursions. His accuracy was matched by endurance, enthusiasm, and loyalty to his employer. Helmer's nephew, Leo Guilfoy, liked to tell of the time when, working as compassman for Helmer on a Latah County cruise, Guilfoy suddenly stopped, noticing a bear and cubs ahead. "What's the matter with ya?" Helmer asked.

Pointing to a cub part way up a nearby tree, separated from its wary mother, Guilfoy replied, "I'm not goin' by that thing."

"Aw hell," Helmer chastised, "Give me the compass." And he proceeded to walk between the mother and cub, talking to them at the same time as he continued on an exact line, estimating timber. "Boy, could he travel in the woods, Holy Moses," Guilfoy conceded.

It is little wonder that Deary, having heard of his reputation, sought out Helmer, for while Deary was a short, stout Mutt to Helmer's stringbean Jeff, they were both earthy and tough, shared a love of hard work, and were shrewd businessmen. Appropriately, both have towns named after them, located only three miles apart in eastern Latah County, near the forests they frequently traveled together.[23]

After receiving Helmer's help, Deary took glowing reports of Latah County timberlands to the Northland Pine Company's directors' meeting in May 1901. The directors authorized him to spend $100,000 in timber purchases, and he returned to Idaho. In July the state advertised a 13,000-acre Latah County timberland sale with the caveat that purchasers remove trees within twenty years. Deary was interested but faced competition in Idaho and reluctance in Minnesota, where Northland's directors authorized him to expend the $100,000 only on lands unencumbered by the twenty-year law. Deary tackled the Idaho problem first.

Henry Turrish, representing a Lake States syndicate operating under the name Wisconsin Log and Lumber Company, provided Deary's competition, and Warren E. McCord, whom the Browns consistently beat in the race for Clearwater timber, was one of the firm's principals. The thirty-six-year-old Turrish was an exceedingly handsome man well acquainted with all aspects of logging. First employed as a lumberjack in one of the Weyerhaeusers' Wisconsin camps, he later learned milling and eventually became a successful Minnesota timberland trader, shrewdly and profitably investing his limited personal wealth. Turrish was there when the Idaho timber rush began, with the financial backing and full support of McCord and other investors.[24]

Deary and Turrish worked a limited field, crossing paths frequently. To hold down prices and save aggravation, the two reached a gentleman's agreement to share large timberland purchases equally. The accord, nonbinding and unwritten, required a new handshake with each deal. So, prior to the state sale, Deary convinced Turrish to cut Northland in: if Turrish made the purchase he would offer half of the stumpage to Deary.

Confident he had solved the problem of competition in Idaho, Deary now turned to Northland's directors who were still dissatisfied with the twenty-year rule. On July 5 he wired Drew Musser for Northland's $100,000. In Deary's mind, the Turrish agreement cut only one way: if Turrish bought, he would share with Deary. Deary had not agreed to share with Turrish if he bid successfully, and he had not entirely given up hope that $100,000 might be enough to purchase the whole lot for Northland. To convince his Great Lakes friends that the purchase was necessary even with the twenty-year restriction, Deary added an ultimatum: "I am going to have half of this timber if they [Wisconsin Log and Lumber] buy, and have made arrangements with other people in case that Northland Pine Company should turn me down."

Frederic Bell, representing the Laird-Norton group, and Drew Musser skeptically opposed purchasing lands regulated by the twenty-year rule. But other Northland stockholders outvoted them. "We will have to take our chance on having the timber removed within the next twenty years," argued Charles Weyerhaeuser. Deary had made his point, and Musser, Bell, and Fred Kehl rushed to Idaho, $100,000 in hand, to attend the state sale. They asked Turrish not to bid, thinking the state would drop or extend its twenty-year regulation if it could find no timberland buyers, but Turrish refused to budge. The Northland group then hoped to outbid him, but did not have a chance. Turrish purchased 400 million feet of Latah County timber for $105,000.

True to his word, Turrish immediately offered Northland an option on half the timber. Deary was disappointed at not owning all the stumpage but, believing half was better than none, returned to St. Paul to cajole Northland's directors into buying. While some harbored lingering reservations, he had little difficulty in winning his case. Charles Weyerhaeuser considered the overture magnanimous, "as we were out of it, and Mr. Turrish did not need to make that offer." And even Drew Musser, after viewing Latah County's rich timberlands, thought the company should buy as Idaho's white pine were "the straightest, soundest, smoothest . . . thinest [sic] barked, and most free from rot" of any he had seen. At a special August 1901 meeting the stockholders unanimously authorized Deary to purchase half the Turrish timber, and increased the company's indebtedness to $400,000, providing him with the financial backing to undertake even larger investments. The deal firmly established the Weyerhaeuser associates in both the Clearwater and Latah county areas. No longer was there debate over the comparative merits of the South versus Idaho. The decision was made; Deary had free reign to pick up as much Idaho timber as possible.[25]

The 1901 state timber purchase set precedents for the Weyerhaeuser syndicate's other Latah County timberland acquisitions. For one thing, the group wanted secrecy so local residents would not hold out for high prices, realizing Weyerhaeuser could afford most any purchase. They also feared Weyerhaeuser's name would attract other timberland investors, increasing prices. As a result, the directors anguished over what name to use in recording the state sale. They first considered Frank Thatcher, James Norton's son-in-law and the Laird-Norton Company's attorney, but decided he was too closely identified with the Laird-Norton group and might be recognized. They then considered procuring the stumpage in Samuel Prentiss's name, William H. Laird's son-in-law and vice president of the Second National Bank of Winona, Minnesota, but, though Prentiss was unknown in lumber circles, the associates decided that any Winona timber purchaser would be taken as representing the Laird-Norton Company. Finally, the directors signed the papers in the name of Dr. Eben P. Clapp of Evanston, Illinois, son-in-law of Matthew G. Norton. To confuse matters further, the legal work was recorded with only his initial rather than a first name, and his address was listed simply as Cook County, Illinois.[26]

The other precedent set with the state's sale of 1901 might charitably be called cooperation, but more frankly, collusion. Either way, the practice was legal and not uncommon in timberland purchases. Lumbermen petitioned to have certain timber tracts auctioned, and the Idaho Land Board authorized stumpage sales when such demand arose. The state set a minimum price on the stumpage, with the petitioning firm consenting to pay all auction expenses even if no sale was made. Large timberland purchasers then agreed that only one firm would bid at auction, thus acquiring timber for the pre-established minimum. The winning bidder then divided the tract with other interested parties after the sale. The Northland Pine Company most frequently collaborated with the Wisconsin Log and Lumber Company, but sometimes other firms entered into the accord, with lands divided into several parcels. "I expect there will be about six bidders in the field so our portion will not be as large as I would like to have it," lamented Deary about a sale in 1902. Deary gained a reputation as a facilitator of such arrangements, becoming "quite a factor in settling disputes and outlining policies to be followed."[27]

Idaho officials and local residents hardly discouraged such deals, welcoming the big timber companies' money. As a result, Northland amassed vast tracts of state land. By 1903 the Weyerhaeuser group owned stumpage on over 40,000 acres of state land in Latah and Shoshone counties, purchased at an average of less than five dollars per acre.[28]

With state timber purchases under control, Deary started consolidating holdings by purchasing timberlands from homesteaders. He and Turrish again agreed to help one another acquire lands inexpensively. Since the Northland Pine and Wisconsin Log and Lumber companies virtually controlled the state's timberlands in Latah and Shoshone counties, there was little danger of other companies interfering by buying scattered settlers' holdings. With no other potential buyers to fret about, Deary and Turrish squeezed homesteaders, convincing them to sell cheaply. The settlers had two options: sell at the price offered, or become small, isolated homestead islands in a forest sea owned by wealthy lumbermen. Since most settlers in the timber took homesteads on speculation, planning to sell eventually, they made their decisions easily.[29]

Deary kept extremely busy purchasing stumpage, and as early as August 1901 considered moving his family to Spokane. The death of his eight-year-old daughter from scarlet fever in September at the family's Minnesota home delayed the move, but Deary determined to return West soon after the funeral. The family tragedy convinced him that he needed his family close to his work as he was equally loyal to both, and in 1901 they moved to Spokane. William Deary remained in the Inland Empire the rest of his life.[30]

J. B. Kehl, Deary's long-time partner, felt that Deary, operating independently in Idaho, assumed too much authority over Northland's destiny, and Deary's increasing influence within the Weyerhaeuser group caused bitter feelings between the two. In 1902 Kehl accused the general manager of being inattentive to his cruisers' estimates, and of paying too much for timber. Deary exploded, firing two letters to Kehl, charging him with handcuffing the company's aggressive timber purchasing policy. "By the way of a friendly tip," Kehl retorted, "I would remark to you *that it will pay you mighty well* to treat me respectfully." But the Mussers, Weyerhaeusers, Lairds, and Nortons came down on Deary's side, and Kehl gradually lost influence.[31]

A sometimes petulant person who paid too much attention to detail, John Kehl lacked William Deary's vision. He played a significant role in the Northland Pine Company's original move to Idaho, but when the Weyerhaeuser associates formed the Potlatch Lumber Company in 1903, Kehl was demoted from president of Northland to a director of Potlatch, a move that clearly disappointed him.

Deary, on the other hand, continued to gain esteem as the other directors heartily supported his expansionism. Although the older generation—Frederick Weyerhaeuser, Peter Musser, the Nortons, and Laird—never lost enthusiasm for new purchases and ventures, it was the second generation—Charles Weyerhaeuser, Drew Musser, Frank Thatcher, and Frederic Bell—who really spearheaded the Idaho move. This group had extreme confidence in William Deary, who first ensured them of a strong foundation based on land, then guided them into manufacturing, railroading, and town building in Idaho's forested empire.

By 1903 the Northland Pine Company had outlived its usefulness in Idaho, and stockholders dissolved its holdings into a new, larger entity with a capitalization more appropriate for the visionary plans of Deary and his colleagues of the second generation. Thus the Northland Pine Company became the Potlatch Lumber Company, a corporation with leaders prepared to take it through a dizzying period of expansion, permanently affecting the economic development of a whole region.

CHAPTER THREE

The Potlatch Lumber Company

A NEW COMPANY

It took less than a year for William Deary to tire of Northland Pine Company's joint purchasing agreement with the Wisconsin Log and Lumber Company. Henry Turrish could not match Northland's financial clout and lacked Deary's zealousness for acquiring timberlands. Besides, Deary did not completely trust Turrish's firm. "I dont [sic] find it a very easy matter to carry on this kind of a deal and work in harmony with everybody," he confessed to J. B. Kehl in August 1902. "The Northland Pine Co. at some time may have some selfish designs and it has caused a great deal of explaining about prices and pieces that should be divided and should not be divided." By September Deary detected friction between Turrish and W. E. McCord and suggested to Northland's directors that the time had come to buy out Wisconsin Log and Lumber, leaving a clear field in Latah County for Northland.[1]

By the winter of 1902-03, other company directors also advocated consolidation. Northland and Wisconsin already controlled over 100,000 acres of timberland in the Palouse, Potlatch, and Elk River basins. Efficient management and continued expansion required centralized direction. Early in 1903 officials from both companies agreed to form a new firm, merging all their Idaho properties. One-fifth ownership went to Henry Turrish, and the remainder to the four groups originally forming the Northland Pine Company: Deary and Kehl; the Mussers; the Laird-Nortons; and the Weyerhaeusers. Northland Pine received $930,000 for its Idaho holdings, and Wisconsin Log and Lumber, which owned much less, approximately one-fourth that amount.[2]

Having agreed to form a new company, it remained to select a name and choose leadership. The word potlatch simply means giving in the Pacific Northwest's Chinook Jargon. Potlatch ceremonies, where one Indian group invited others to feasts and provided them with presents, were important activities in Northwest Coast cultures. Though full-fledged potlatches were not a part of the social life of Inland Empire Indians, these tribes did often gather at significant fishing areas, particularly during salmon runs. While there, they frequently traded, danced, and gave gifts. Understandably, early white observers considered these festivities potlatches. One location for such gatherings was along the banks of a stream Lewis and Clark had first labeled Colter Creek. This river rises in the Hoodoo Mountains near the source of Latah County's other significant waterway, the Palouse River. Where the Palouse flows west, its counterpart strikes due east and then cuts sharply south, gaining in force as it gathers in many smaller tributaries, including Moose, Brush, Boulder, and Cedar creeks. The stream flows forty-two miles before converging with the Clearwater River just south of the Latah County line. At some point this waterway's name changed from Colter Creek to Potlatch River. The combined holdings of the Northland Pine and Wisconsin Log and Lumber companies included lands along both the Palouse and Potlatch rivers. Since a local lumber company already carried the name of one, Great Lakes owners tagged their new firm with that of the other, and the Potlatch Lumber Company was born.[3]

With the name chosen, the question of company leadership remained. The position of general manager was the most important, for he would make crucial day-to-day decisions for distant directors. There was little doubt about who would fill the general manager's slot. William Deary had reservations about his own capabilities, writing to Frederic Bell in 1902, on the eve of Potlatch's incorporation, "The lumber business is something that I do not know anything about and if such a company was organized it would take a man that would want to have a great deal more experience. . . . I have always kept out of the manufacturing for the reason that I do not know anything about it." But Northland's directors did not share Deary's concerns. He was, they believed, the type of tireless, hard-driving leader they required.[4]

Deary, of Irish stock, born in Quebec, spoke a full-flavored Irish-Canadian brogue nearly impossible to decode at first hearing. He talked slowly, but never with hesitation, being a shrewd, quick, decisive thinker. Deary had little if any formal education, having begun work in the woods at age thirteen. He knew all aspects of logging from the time a tree was cruised until it rested in a sawmill pond. When he became general manager of Potlatch, however, he understood little about lumbering from that point on, sawmilling and marketing being foreign to his experience. But he asked hundreds of questions and was an intelligent, quick learner blessed with a marvelous memory.

Deary was an outdoorsman who never quite adjusted to office life. Robust and powerful as a logger, he at times ballooned to over 300 pounds after becoming a manager. With a size 17-1/2 collar, Deary was a short-necked, bulldog of a man who always charged through the woods with incredible endurance despite his weight. Tireless and impatient, he once traveled from Spokane to Palouse hoping to catch a train to the company's new millsite ten miles upstream. Having missed the train and being unwilling to wait for the next, Deary commandeered a handcar and a Potlatch worker, threw off his hat and coat, and started pumping uphill in blistering sun. The two had not gone far when Deary stopped and spoke deliberately to the other in his characteristically earthy language: "I ain't mentioning any names, but there's some son-of-a-bitch on this handcar that ain't keeping up his end of it. Let's try it again." Try again they did, each working equally this time, and Deary reached the millsite long before the next train arrived.

Deary was the absolute ruler of an empire he had largely created. He resented orders directed from afar by stockholders who were not nearly as familiar as he with the situation in Idaho. He lost patience when Kehl tried to oversee his actions, and, with the exception of Frederick Weyerhaeuser, bristled when other directors meddled. "He . . . seems to resent what he thinks is interference with his management," his assistant Allison Laird wrote in a confidential letter. He believes "he is doing the best he can, understands the situation better, and does not need outside suggestions. . . . He is by temperament a man who will stand and fight alone . . . sparing neither friend nor foe when he thinks he is right."

Though he disliked direction himself, Deary demanded that his own orders be rigidly obeyed. His fiats were law, decreed bluntly, to be followed unquestioningly. Perched upon a prized possession—a small gasoline-powered rail car topped with a buggy seat—Deary frequently speeded along railroad spurs surveying the company's timber holdings. Although the light car could be easily shuttled off the tracks when a train approached, Deary would suffer no such indignity. If he met a log-laden, mill-bound train it could "damned well" back up to the nearest siding, allowing the general manager to pass.

At times the quick-tempered Deary was overly harsh with employees. W. E. Hearn, who worked four years under him, described the general manager as "generous when he felt he could be, [yet] he could be very severe. He had the habit of firing a man without giving notice, but on the other hand, if he liked a person . . . or liked his work, he could be very generous with him." Sometimes compassionate, other times insensitive, Deary's was a many-sided personality. Once, observing an employee working a horse too hard, he jumped up from his office desk, ran across the yard and immediately dismissed the man. "Get the hell out of here," he bellowed. "We don't want men like you here. You're through. . . . Turn the horse loose. He knows enough to go back to the barn. . . . That's more than you know." He unsympathetically listened to laborers' complaints about working conditions. Insect-infested bed rolls, stenchy bunkhouses, and meals off tin plates had sufficed when he worked in the woods and he saw no reason why they were not adequate still. Niceties such as napkins had little utility except "to blow your nose on."

Many refused to work long under such an autocratic manager, but Deary gained tremendous respect among most of those who stayed. He treated laborers as equals, shared earthy stories with them, and tendered a hard-working example. He required his men to undertake no more then he demanded of himself. He selected assistants carefully, then staunchly supported them as long as they worked earnestly and honestly. A person might make mistakes; Deary understood that as part of the learning process and defended his assistants' decisions even when they were wrong.

Though he did not interfere once he charted the course his assistants were to travel, his greatest managerial fault was an inability to delegate authority. Despite pleas from co-workers and company directors that he relax, relinquishing some control, Deary steadfastly and single-handedly shepherded nearly all the details required for operating the company's many activities. This inability to share authority caused overwork and helped bring on an early death, but before that time the strength of Deary's personality left an indelible imprint on the Potlatch Lumber Company. For years after he died, Potlatch continued to reflect his influence; it was clearly the company Bill Deary built.[5]

Selecting a company president proved considerably more difficult than deciding upon a general manager. At first, J. B. Kehl opposed creation of a new company, believing Northland Pine could adequately purchase and manage all of the Idaho timberlands that were needed. Once the Potlatch Lumber Company was incorporated, though, he hoped to continue as president. Drew Musser believed Kehl "a very good man in a great many ways, a man of honor in whom we can place the utmost confidence." But Kehl controlled only one-fifth interest in Potlatch while the long associated families of Lairds, Nortons, Mussers, and Weyerhaeusers held three-fifths. "It is not to our 3/5 interest to give the office of president and general manager to a 1/5 interest," Musser wrote F. S. Bell at Laird-Norton. Further, Kehl and Deary did not always agree on matters, and Musser believed Deary needed more freedom than he might receive under the "censorship" of Kehl.[6]

Henry Turrish, as president of the other firm that merged to form Potlatch, believed he had a claim on the presidency, but he, too, controlled only one-fifth of its stock. Furthermore, Charles Weyerhaeuser, recalling the Idaho rivalry between his family and Turrish's former partner, W. E. McCord, divulged that "I do not like the crowd with which [Turrish] has been associated in a business way. In my judgment most of them are inclined to be a little tricky."[7]

Weyerhaeuser hoped one of the older generation, such as William Laird, Matthew Norton, Peter M. Musser, or his father would accept the presidency, but the elders had already decided that their children would spearhead the move West, and all refused. Finally, the stockholders selected Charles Weyerhaeuser as president, a position he held for twenty-seven years. Because of his name and experience in all aspects of logging and manufacturing, Weyerhaeuser was acceptable to everyone. Even John Kehl admitted that Potlatch needed "a young man for that place, [and Weyerhaeuser] can fill the bill better than any one in the Company."[8]

Charles, thirty-seven when assuming the presidency—tall, handsome, powerful—was Frederick Weyerhaeuser's most athletic son. His hand was permanently cupped from catching too many baseballs at prep school in Andover, Massachusetts, where he was remembered more for athletic exploits than classroom endeavors. Weyerhaeuser was outgoing and gregarious, with a booming, happy voice. According to family tradition he could trade anybody out of anything. "He'd go off with a knife and come back with a bicycle," recalled his nephew. He treated employees as equals, never displaying superiority. William Maxwell, Potlatch's comptroller and auditor, remembered that Weyerhaeuser, on his frequent Idaho trips, always quietly stopped by a receptionist's desk if he had forgotten someone's name. He would ask about him and his relatives, then greet the employee by first name, inquiring about other family members. "He just made all of us feel that he was taking a personal interest in us," Maxwell reminisced.

However, like Deary he did not believe in "coddling" workingmen, and advocated ten-hour work days long after many in the industry had switched to eight.

A prolific letter writer, Weyerhaeuser spiced business correspondence with humor, gossip, and details about recent travels and family affairs. He often sent multiple copies of letters to different people, adding personal notes to each. "You must have been in a writing mood," his brother John once understated after receiving five letters in a single day. Charles was a life-long Republican, Mason, and supporter of the arts. Unlike the skills of his brothers John and Frederick, Charles's leadership abilities have gone largely unrecognized. He has been underrated. An eternal optimist and business visionary, Charles frequently guided the family into new—and profitable—ventures, winning his father's appreciation for his aggressive style.[9]

The company appeased Henry Turrish by naming him vice president and demoted Kehl, in disfavor because of his petty arguments with Deary, to a directorship. Remaining positions went to others from the principal shareholding families. R. Drew Musser became treasurer, continuing his long association with Charles Weyerhaeuser, while Clifton Musser, Drew's second cousin, became a director and was to serve Potlatch longer than any other original board member.

The Laird and Norton families had few sons. Matthew G. Norton's two boys died as young men before becoming active in the family's concerns, while his brother James's only son never married and had no interest in business. The son of their second cousin, William H. Laird, died in infancy. But while these Laird and Norton names did not survive, capable sons-in-law supervised the family's business affairs.

Frederic S. Bell, husband of Laird's eldest daughter, became secretary of the Potlatch Lumber Company. He began working as an attorney with the Laird-Norton group in 1881 and a year later, at age twenty-three, married Frances Laird. Tall and graceful, alert and intelligent, well-mannered with prep school polish, Bell epitomized the English gentleman. He loved golf and contributed generously to local civic causes. Yet he ruthlessly drove bargains and worked employees long and hard. He was often brusque and businesslike with subordinates, just as he was charming and friendly with family and associates. A perfectionist, Bell watched every detail, keeping meticulous records. From 1917, when Matthew Norton—the last survivor of the three patriarchal founders of the Laird-Norton

Company—died, until his own death in 1938, Bell was the Laird-Norton Company's president, directing it into diversified investments, increasing the family's wealth long after its Winona sawmill had closed. During this time Bell directed most of his energy toward the family's western concerns. He remained as Potlatch's secretary until 1929 and served as director almost until his death. He was also a director of the Boise Payette Company in southern Idaho, and was both president and the first chairman of the board of the Weyerhaeuser Timber Company.[10]

Frank Hill Thatcher became the other original Potlatch Lumber Company director. Born in 1859, Thatcher graduated in law from Northwestern University and joined a prosperous Aurora, Illinois, firm headed by Albert Hopkins, long-time United States Representative and Senator. In 1891 he married Edith, James Norton's youngest daughter, and would have been content to remain in his lucrative law practice. But nine years later, Rudolph McBurnie, another Norton son-in-law, died suddenly of a ruptured appendix. McBurnie had supervised many of the family's business matters for the now blind, seventy-five-year-old Norton. Norton's son William had no desire to enter the business, so Norton urgently pleaded with Thatcher to move to Winona and take over.

Frank Thatcher was a nervous, high-strung thoroughbred who "walked with a quick snap." An incessant worker with a keen eye for legal detail, he nearly single-handedly supervised all the paperwork surrounding the 1903 merger that formed the Potlatch Lumber Company. He threw himself into his new work, heedless of his own health and at times inconsiderate of employees. His intensity led to a premature death by heart attack in 1921. Before then, however, he—more than any other person except Deary—shaped the Potlatch Lumber Company.[11]

Once the directors had determined the new company's name and leadership, they turned to completing necessary legal paperwork. On March 7, 1903, they officially organized the Potlatch Lumber Company in Augusta, Maine, capitalizing it for three million dollars. Frank Thatcher scurried to Augusta for a whirlwind week of activities. State law required the presence of three directors for official signing ceremonies, including the president and treasurer. So, for a brief time Thatcher stood in as Potlatch's first president, and Augusta attorneys C. L. Andrews—the first "treasurer"—and H. M. Heath signed on as temporary directors. Within weeks, the stockholders voted for new directors and officers, and later in March the Northland Pine and

Wisconsin Log and Lumber companies conveyed all of their assets in Idaho to Potlatch. With millions of dollars behind him and few competitors left in the field, Deary now prepared to lead the new company even more aggressively into the future.[12]

PURCHASING MILLS AT PALOUSE AND COLFAX

Northland's directors long debated the merits of timberland speculation versus lumber manufacturing. Wary of Idaho's twenty-year limit on removing state timber, the Musser and Laird-Norton interests at first opposed sawmilling in the Inland Empire. In addition to the time constraints, Latah County's small rivers provided unpredictable and inadequate log transportation, which would necessitate heavy investment in railroad construction. On the other hand, Kehl, Deary, and the Weyerhaeusers always favored manufacturing, believing the lumber market strong enough and Idaho's timber good enough to justify the additional expenses. By the time the Potlatch Lumber Company was incorporated, the manufacturing adherents had converted the skeptics. The question now was not whether Potlatch would mill lumber, but how much it would saw and where.[13]

Having decided to manufacture lumber, company officials could purchase existing mills, build new ones—or both. If Potlatch were to acquire an existing plant, the Palouse River Lumber Company, the region's largest, offered the most attractive option. This mill had greatly expanded after the fire of 1898, and, under president George W. Peddycord's resourceful leadership, landed several lucrative contracts—such as supplying lumber for campus construction at the state college in nearby Pullman, Washington. By 1902 Peddycord was planning to triple the mill's capacity. Northland Pine Company's directors, concerned about this increased competition, began making overtures to purchase the plant.[14]

In the fall of 1902 Charles Weyerhaeuser approached Eugene Carpenter of Minneapolis's Carpenter-Lamb Company, which held a $161,000 purchase option on the Palouse River Lumber Company's mill and timber holdings. Carpenter-Lamb decided to forego this investment to buy pinelands in California instead. This opened the door for Northland. Weyerhaeuser hired Eugene Carpenter to serve as a negotiator so Peddycord would not know the purchase offer came from the Weyerhaeuser syndicate. He authorized Carpenter to offer $125,000, a sum Peddycord brusquely refused. The Palouse company owned 20,000 acres of timberland, the mill, horse teams, and logging equipment. Peddycord now considered even the originally discussed $161,000 figure to be inadequate since another firm had offered $200,000 in the interim. No deal was struck, and Northland's directors shelved the idea of purchasing the Palouse company while they worked out details regarding the incorporation of the Potlatch Lumber Company.[15]

In February 1903 Deary had Bill Helmer cruise the Palouse company's timberlands. He found them considerably richer than Carpenter-Lamb had estimated. Peddycord remained eager to sell, but only at a comfortable profit. Deary reopened negotiations, this time dealing directly with Peddycord, who bargained fiercely. Always ready to embark on new projects, Deary proved unwilling to haggle over a few thousand dollars. After all, the Palouse River Lumber Company purchase was only a small cog in his grand scheme. Late that month Deary and Peddycord reached an agreement: Deary purchased the Palouse company for $265,000 in the name of the new Potlatch Lumber Company. In addition to rich timberlands, Potlatch got a small but nearly new manufacturing facility including a sawmill, planing and molding factory, two-story warehouse, numerous ancillary buildings, and all the necessary operating equipment.[16]

Signatures on the bill of sale had barely been blotted when Deary began remodeling the plant. He organized a "small army of men" and by April all buildings sported new red paint. He constructed brick dry kilns, a larger storage shed, and an electric light plant that enabled the mill to run evening shifts, doubling its daily cutting capacity to 100,000 feet. Never accused of thinking small, Deary considered these mere stop-gap alterations. He hired William A. Wilkinson of Minneapolis, perhaps the nation's premier sawmill architect, to help plan more extensive remodeling. The two envisioned a new box factory, steam plant, and enlarged planing mill. Altogether, Deary proposed spending an additional $35,000.

Potlatch's directors were stunned. By this time they were seriously considering constructing a new, larger plant and believed the heavy investments at Palouse unjustified. "We hardly know what to say to you as to these improvements," an exasperated Frank Thatcher wrote Deary. "You . . . know that we . . . have felt very strongly against making over mills. . . . We knew you contemplated making some changes this winter . . . but we did not anticipate that you had in mind putting in as much as the $35,000 into your mill. If left to us, we do not believe that we would think of putting that much

into the mill." But the decision was not left to the directors. As
Thatcher admitted, Deary was the one "on the ground and . . . we
should defer to your judgment in many of these things." But he urged
Deary to proceed cautiously. Deary, believing he had already exer-
cised sufficient caution, carried on with the improvements. This story
would be repeated: Potlatch's directors occasionally attempted to influence William Deary, but in the end nearly always gave him free
rein to follow his instincts.[17]

The Potlatch Lumber Company also purchased another sawmill
in the area, but this time the purpose was more to remove a source
of irritation than to meet the company's manufacturing needs. When
Deary bought the Palouse River Lumber Company, he did not obtain exclusive Palouse River water rights. William Codd, a Colfax
sawmiller since 1877, had a prior claim. Like George Peddycord,
Codd considerably improved his mill at the turn of the century, and
opened a lucrative market by making boxes for fruit orchardists along
the Snake River. Also, like Peddycord, Codd hoped to sell his mill
and timberlands to Potlatch for a tidy profit. Deary began negotiating
with Codd as soon as he sealed the Palouse deal, but he felt Codd
asked too much. Thinking the small Colfax mill to be of little value,
Deary refused to pay Codd's price. He would regret the decision,
for Codd was a wily businessman who eventually got his way, out-
maneuvering the giant timber firm.

In the fall of 1903 Deary organized a number of Latah County
timber camps in preparation for a log drive to the revamped Palouse
mill. Codd also worked a woods crew, planning to utilize the same
stream. In fact, Codd deliberately began his drive at the same time
as Potlatch, realizing the confusion would cause the larger firm considerable delay and aggravation. That it did, for Deary had to construct a sorting mechanism so Codd's logs could float on by Palouse
to the mill downstream in Colfax.

Codd irritated Deary in other ways, too. He paid more for timber
than Potlatch, easily obtaining enough material to run his mill at
full capacity, thus dampening the local market for Potlatch's product. Even more annoyingly, Codd paid higher wages and allowed
his workers to unionize, something Deary abhorred. As a result,
lumberjacks[18] struck the Potlatch Lumber Company in the fall of
1903, demanding wages equal to Codd's. In the midst of its first working season, Potlatch faced its first labor confrontation.

In November 1903 a group of eighty discontented lumberjacks
holed up in the hamlet of Princeton, threatening men still working in

nearby Potlatch camps. Refusing to negotiate with the union, Deary hired strikebreakers and reduced wages. Deary's uncompromising stand prevailed, for the laborers had mistimed their strike. By the time the confrontation began, Potlatch had already gathered enough logs to run its Palouse sawmill for a season. Deary merely had to wait out the situation, and it did not take long. By month's end the number of harassers in Princeton had declined to fifteen, and Potlatch's first strike was over.

While laborers caused Deary little concern, Codd did, for it was clear this shrewd downriver competitor would allow Deary little rest until Potlatch had purchased his holdings. Deary decided to eliminate Codd before another season began. The Potlatch general manager prepared "to arrange it so that [Codd] will be put to considerable trouble in getting his logs by us" on the Palouse River, but the action proved unnecessary for Codd wanted to sell as much as Deary hoped to buy. Deary and Codd merely needed to agree upon a price, which they did in September 1904. Potlatch purchased all of Codd's timber, cutover lands, sawmill, and water rights for $115,000, considerably more than Deary had hoped to pay.

Potlatch operated the Colfax sawmill until 1907, driving logs to the plant along the Palouse River. By then, Potlatch's aspirations in the Inland Empire had clearly outgrown the small mills at Palouse and Colfax. The company no longer needed the Colfax mill, and it no longer wished to rely on the unpredictable river for transportation. It closed the mill at Colfax after the 1907 cut, bringing thirty-six years of sawmilling there to an end. The next year saw the final Palouse River log drive.[19]

THE WASHINGTON, IDAHO AND MONTANA RAILWAY

The Washington, Idaho and Montana Railway Company made Palouse River log drives obsolete. Northland Pine Company's directors always knew that the area's streams afforded inadequate transportation. The debate over whether or not to manufacture lumber actually centered on the region's inferior waterways. Both the adherents of sawmilling and its opponents realized that, in addition to acquiring or constructing sawmills, the company would also have to build a logging railroad or, less likely, lure an existing railroad company into its timber holdings. Those arguing against manufacturing viewed this additional construction as so costly that sawmilling in Idaho would never generate profits. Those favoring milling believed Latah County's resources were rich enough to absorb the extra expense. By deciding to purchase the Palouse River Lumber Company and begin milling, the directors had also opted for a railroad.

The company's first two sawmilling seasons dashed any hopes that the Palouse River might provide an adequate means of log transportation. In the summer of 1904 Deary was forced to lay off the Palouse mill's night shift and cancel lumber orders because the river was too low to float logs to the plant. The company faced even worse problems in 1905 when an extremely dry spring left the river so low that three-quarters of the logs decked the previous winter were unable to pass downstream. The company clearly needed a railroad if it were to continue sawmilling.[20]

As early as 1901 Northland's directors had recognized that manufacturing and marketing inevitably necessitated a railroad along the Palouse River, connecting with existing rail lines in either Garfield, Palouse, or, less likely, Moscow. John Kehl, who always advocated manufacturing, was also the first to champion railroad construction. "To be sure," he wrote the Laird-Norton Company in 1902, "[we will need a] railroad to get into the Potlatch basen [sic], but you can log very much cheaper by rail than any other way, besides as far as the timber is cut off setlers [sic] will go into the land & improve it."[21]

The company at first hoped to entice existing firms into extending rail lines into the timber, saving Potlatch the expense of construction. Deary talked at length with officials of the Oregon Railway and Navigation Company, a Union Pacific subsidiary, and in the summer of 1903 seemed on the verge of convincing them to build along the Palouse River. The company's officers expressed themselves "as being very anxious to get into our territory." Negotiations collapsed shortly afterwards, however, as the OR&N rethought the line's potential profit. In September 1903 Potlatch's directors, resigned to building their own road, hired a surveyor to plan a route and estimate expenses.[22]

In the winter of 1903-04 word leaked out that Potlatch would construct a railroad, triggering a frenzy among town boosters who vied eagerly for the lucrative terminus. Every community booster in the Palouse knew how railroads had transformed Spokane from a backwater town into the most significant trading center between Seattle and Minneapolis. The era of regional railroad construction in the late nineteenth and early twentieth centuries spurred a time of dreaming, when boomers ignored the probability of lackluster, permanent, small town existence to contemplate a Palouse or a Garfield or a Moscow becoming the next Spokane. Town promoters fervently believed that their communities held glorious growth opportunities, and even the possibility of capturing a shortline logging railroad initiated wild competition. Besides, this railroad, though short, was to be bankrolled by the Weyerhaeuser storehouse of cash. That kind of money, properly utilized, could make fortunes for many adroit entrepreneurs.[23]

The most likely terminals were Garfield, which offered the closest direct route to Latah County timber, and Palouse. Both of these Washington communities already had outside rail connections affording transcontinental routes for the lumber company's manufactured products. Palouse also had the advantage of being the site of the company's mill. A less obvious case could be made for Moscow, Idaho, for while that town also possessed rail connections, it was farther from the company's timber holdings. Boosters, however, are adept at overlooking disadvantages and, thanks to the resourcefulness of the ubiquitous C. O. Brown, many Moscow residents fully expected their community to become the railroad's terminus.

In 1899 Brown and some prominent Moscow businessmen had organized the Moscow and Eastern Railway company.[24] Brown hired a Union Pacific surveyor to mark a line into Latah County's timber. Beginning at Moscow, the route headed east and north, traversing Palouse countryside for eleven miles before reaching trees. Then the survey pushed through the county's forested belt, ending near Bovill, unsurprisingly close to where Brown, his son, and son-in-law held timber homesteads. With the road surveyed, Brown, in his typically persistent fashion, promoted it to Lakes States financiers. He found no one interested in building the line, and when he died in 1902 it seemed that the railroad scheme expired too. But actually the Moscow and Eastern just sat dormant, coming out of hibernation when the Potlatch Lumber Company publicly announced it would construct a railroad.[25]

By early 1904 rumors were rampant that Potlatch would build not only a railroad but also a larger sawmill. It seemed clear that its existing small plants at Palouse and Colfax would be unable to cut all of the logs generated by the company's vast timberland holdings. Moscow, priding itself as "The Queen City of the Palouse," the region's largest town and home of the University of Idaho, possessed promoters as ambitious as any. They prepared to land the new mill, and since the Moscow and Eastern was already surveyed, this appeared to be the logical railroad to feed its saws. Realistically, Moscow's chances were slim, and its promoters' efforts a little quirky. The editor of the Palouse *Republic* wondered how this town hoped to become a logging railroad terminus: "The Moscow correspondent has again jumped over the traces and stretched his legs at full length to find something to say concerning the proposed road to be built into the timber belts of the Potlatch Lumber Company." Like others in Moscow, he seemed to have taken leave of his senses.[26]

William Deary was probably as surprised as the *Republic*'s editor at Moscow's attempt to attract the railroad. It is doubtful he ever seriously considered Moscow as a rail terminus or millsite, but he was in the midst of a political battle and well understood the advantages of inter-town rivalries. Deary's lobbying to have Idaho's twenty-year logging requirement on state lands either removed or extended had unleashed a storm of controversy. While many welcomed big business to the region, this was also the era of progressivism, conservationism, and muckraking journalism, and writers frequently chastised Deary for attempting to remove a law established to protect state lands from high-rolling timber speculators. As Moscow was always a key community in North Idaho politics, Deary held out the logging railroad carrot to persuade town businessmen it was in their interest not to oppose his lobbying. "I am sure I can get the support of the business men of Moscow," he confided to Bell, "and if they oppose it I am going to tell them that if they do anything to prevent our getting the extension we will immediately build a railroad to our two mills in Washington . . . and that Moscow will lose the chance of having the railroad."[27]

Moscow's businessmen did not oppose the time extension,[28] and believed they had a reasonable chance to land both the large mill and the rail line. Deary did nothing to discourage this enthusiasm, using it to gain leverage in Palouse City, which is where he really wanted his line to commence. "We have good inducements from the people of Moscow and along the [Moscow and Eastern] route," Deary calculatingly informed prominent Palouse businessman J. K. McCornack. "They have offered right of way along with considerable land with timber on it as bonus. . . . Now if we start from Palouse, we do not ask for any bonus . . . from the people along this route, but will say if they are favorable and feel like taking hold and getting right of way for us, we shall be pleased."[29]

It might not have actually been an ultimatum—Deary had probably already decided Palouse was the most logical terminus—but the message certainly spurred the activity he hoped for. McCornack called a meeting of the Palouse Businessmen's Association, read Deary's letter, and was greeted enthusiastically when he announced that Potlatch's only requirement for obtaining the railroad was to provide a free right-of-way and depot grounds. "Give them the right of way?" the town's mayor asked incredulously after the meeting. "Of course we will. There is not a man here who will not do all in his power to secure the road." The Palouse *Republic* gushed over the town's potential should it get the new rail connection, mocking county seat Colfax and other neighboring communities: "Simply, it will make a good fat town of ten thousand people. We will have cheap lumber for building, fuel for generation of electric power for manufactories, and many other things which a county seat would sell its eyes, its patrimony and several other inheritances to have."[30]

Palouse businessmen raised over $10,000 to purchase the right-of-way while the town newspaper continuously derided its more "straight-laced" neighbors—especially Colfax and the college towns of Moscow and Pullman. Palouse was not above building its metropolis upon the muscular backs of laboring men, and the community did "not have to depend upon the possible student or court witness to make a town—aye, a city." "The esthetic people of Moscow certainly had no real desire for anything which savors so much of things earthly as railroads and sawmills," it ridiculed on another occasion. By May 1905, just two months after Deary's letter to McCornack, business leaders from Palouse presented the right-of-way to the Potlatch Lumber Company. The line would begin in their town.[31]

Deary clearly indicated during this time that he expected such largess from Palouse. "The right of way through the City of Palouse is to be turned over to us free of any charge along with the depot grounds," he enthusiastically reported to Frederick E. Weyerhaeuser in March 1905. However, in December Potlatch's directors instructed Deary to return the money used to purchase the right-of-way to the Palouse Businessmen's Association. Charles Weyerhaeuser, recalling unpleasant experiences when the Pine Tree Lumber Company accepted similar gifts in Minnesota, wanted no such problems in Idaho. "It was not our intention that the business men of your city should *give* us the right of way," Deary wrote McCornack when returning a check for $10,179.90. But he spoke only half truthfully, for his intentions were not always so generous. Nonetheless, the Palouse *Republic* considered the action "an unexampled and hitherto unheard of precedent in railroad right-of-way matters." Regardless of Deary's original designs, the company had maneuvered a public relations coup.[32]

With the terminus selected, Deary now needed to obtain property for the road out of town. The line would parallel the Palouse River for about eighteen miles, then cut south and east, eventually reaching the Bovill area. Upon completing this section, the company would push on farther across the mountains into Montana.

Deary had considerable difficulty acquiring reasonably priced property, as the whole country by now knew that the "Weyerhaeuser syndicate" backed the road, and property owners demanded handsome settlements. "We are not only being robbed by the people from whom we are securing right of way but they are simply holding us up with a gun," Deary complained. "Land that should be worth no more than $10 per acre they are holding as high as $100, and it is pretty hard for us to improve matters much as it is hard to get appraisers who are not picked from the populace farmers." Deary persuaded the Palouse Businessmen's Association to secure some land—as it could purchase in names not associated with Great Lakes millionaires—and then sell the property to Potlatch "at far better terms than we ourselves could." At other times, though, landowners forced Deary to pay gun-at-the-head prices. Utilizing the services of the Businessmen's Association and purchasing land directly, Potlatch eventually acquired the property required for the road.[33]

Potlatch's directors incorporated the railroad in March 1905 as the Washington, Idaho and Montana Railway Company. Deary had hoped to call the line the Palouse River Valley Road, but other Potlatch officials, believing their railroad would eventually stretch into three states, preferred the grander appellation. They named Frank Thatcher president of the new firm and Deary general manager. Together the two paid meticulous attention to construction, desiring to make theirs a prototypic logging railroad.[34]

Construction crews broke ground in May and drove the first spike in August 1905. Though the hard-driving Deary grew impatient with the line's contractors, constantly accusing them of being laggardly, work progressed quite rapidly. By late September tracks stretched eleven miles upstream, and on March 16, 1906, the first load of logs reached the Palouse mill via the line.

Despite its name, the WI&M never reached Montana. In 1910 the Milwaukee Road constructed a line south from St. Maries, Idaho, to Bovill, giving the Potlatch railway a transcontinental connection at both its eastern and western terminals. Now other railroads at last became interested in the route. The Northern Pacific, concerned about this new connection, offered to purchase the WI&M. The Weyerhaeusers and Mussers wanted to sell, but the Laird-Norton group vehemently opposed the idea, and Potlatch retained control. Thatcher, by now quite enamored with railroading, received half-joking ridicule from some associates that his real ambition was to construct a transcontinental line. Truth is, the WI&M was well-built, the first substantial logging railroad in the Rocky Mountain region. Thatcher and Deary insisted on the finest equipment, and the WI&M claimed the largest railroad shops in the Inland Empire outside of Spokane. In addition to hauling logs and lumber, the line carried passengers, agricultural products, livestock, mail, and other commodities. It also gained considerable national attention because it went through some unusually named towns: Wellesley, Princeton, Harvard, Yale, Stanford, Vassar, Cornell, and Purdue.[35] The road continued as a subsidiary of Potlatch until 1962, when the Milwaukee Road purchased it. The WI&M fed the Potlatch Lumber Company mills, helped settle a region, and brought a boom to Palouse City. It was an indispensable cog in the grandiose project that was Potlatch, but it was also expensive, adding to the lumber company's numerous financial burdens.[36]

PALOUSE BOOMTIME

Palouse City's future looked rosy in 1904: the Weyerhaeuser syndicate had bought the town's sawmill and was constructing a railroad. Palouse's population mushroomed; new businesses started; large buildings were built; the town boomed.

The Washington, Idaho and Montana Railway would carry timber products in and out of Palouse while it opened up a large agricultural region and reawakened interest in Latah County's mining districts, which Palouse residents believed were underdeveloped only because of high transportation costs. "To Palouse as the western terminus, all of this vast and undeveloped region must and gladly will pay tribute, because this is the strategic point," crowed the *Republic*. "Palouse must inevitably become not only a town, but a city of pretension."[37]

In 1905 Palouse received more good news when financiers of the Spokane and Inland Empire Railroad, an electric line, decided to transect the community. As one newspaper advertisement boasted:

"The Railroads are a coming / And now Palouse is Humming / The Boom is on!"[38]

Boom it did. Within two years Palouse changed dramatically. In addition to the expected saloons serving a larger working force, the town welcomed a brewery, music shop, one of the largest pottery plants in the region, numerous stores, a new city hall, jail, schoolhouse, hospital, and Young Men's Christian Association hall. C. A. Hart even delivered fresh fruit door-to-door. By 1905 the Palouse Light and Power Company provided electricity twenty-four hours a day, and that same year the city banned outhouses in favor of flush toilets. Citizens beautified the town, too. City officials forced brothels off Main Street and replaced the town's plank sidewalks with cement, brick, and stone. In the summer town workers dumped straw in the streets to reduce dust, and the *Republic* encouraged landowners to gather garbage, groom lawns, and in other ways dress up the community: "Prospects . . . for a town of 5000 population within two years . . . should spur every property owner on to an effort to beautify his premises and make the town attractive to people of good taste who may be seeking to locate. The Republic will give from time to time reasons why it pays from a financial standpoint to beautify every inch of ground that you can in your town."[39]

Palouse's bank deposits rose 100 percent; town population surged. Even so, Palouse residents fumed in 1905 when they discovered that their municipality was rated only the third largest in Whitman County, lagging behind Colfax, the county seat, and Pullman, which deigned to count college students. But the *Republic* reassured readers that theirs was a true boomtown, in contrast to the nearby college community: "Pullman correspondents loudly boast of 'busy scenes' on the streets there because a road roller is perambulating up and down some of the town lanes. It does not take an extra job like a little macadamizing to create 'busy scenes' on Palouse streets, which are always busy with everyday traffic."[40]

Palouse realized its boom came courtesy of the Potlatch Lumber Company, and in the company's intoxicating days of expansion, Potlatch could do no wrong. When the company purchased the Colfax sawmill, the *Republic* hailed this as a move enabling Palouse to become the principal manufacturing center for William Codd's timber. When Potlatch improved the mill in Palouse, the *Republic*'s editor waxed ecstatic: "The fact is that the Potlatch Company proposes many things beyond the ken of jealous outsiders."[41]

Had the *Republic* not been blinded by its enthusiasm, it could have foreseen emerging company policy that threatened Palouse's boom. Control of Palouse River water rights caused the first split between Potlatch Lumber and other Palouse businessmen. Prior to construction of the WI&M, Potlatch utilized the river to float logs. Though the company constructed splash dams to increase the river's flow, even then the success of river drives was always problematical. During low water years in 1904 and 1905, Potlatch needed all the head obtainable. But others also legitimately claimed some of the river's flow, particularly Palouse's Voltz and Metcalf flour mill.

In the summer of 1904 Voltz and Metcalf enlarged their water-powered, four-story mill, installing new machinery and adding more space in anticipation of increased profits with the fall harvest. The mill generated power from water stored behind a dam upstream from the Potlatch sawmill. Potlatch hoped for a substantial fall river drive in 1904 to provide sufficient logs to operate their mill throughout winter. However, the streamflow was so low that Voltz and Metcalf refused to open their dam to allow logs to pass, stating that they needed all available water to power the flour mill. Deary offered to pay $25 a day to have the dam opened; Voltz and Metcalf demanded $75 an hour. Deary, cantankerous when bullied and never one to sit idly for long, had employees commandeer the dam and stationed guards on it to see that the gates remained open, allowing logs to pass. Outnumbered but not without resources, Voltz and Metcalf filed a lawsuit and obtained a restraining order prohibiting further interference at the dam.

Potlatch's directors admired Deary's bold, if illegal, action. Even attorney Frank Thatcher believed the general manager had been justified and cautioned against offering too-generous compromises to the flour millers' attorney: "He has started the litigation and has attempted to rob you by an exorbitant demand for letting you through and he is therefore in no position to expect anything but his mere legal rights."

Deary negotiated with Voltz and Metcalf throughout the winter, but believing he held the upper hand, showed no disposition toward a philanthropic settlement. In the first place, Potlatch's upstream splash dams could regulate river levels, thereby decreasing streamflow so much as to prohibit flour milling. Secondly, the WI&M would shortly make river drives unnecessary. Finally, another Palouse firm began building an electric flour mill. This plant, not dependent upon waterpower, would considerably depreciate the value of the Voltz and Metcalf property, making them more willing to compromise.

"I am not doing anything with the flour mill party at present," Deary candidly wrote Charles Weyerhaeuser in March 1905. "I think that it will be wiser to buy this party out after a while."

Finally, in July 1905, Voltz and Metcalf decided to deal. Deary made two offers, both contingent upon their dropping litigation. First, he would install electricity in the mill, eliminating the need to utilize waterpower. Alternatively, he would purchase the mill outright. Faced with competition from the recently constructed modern mill, Voltz and Metcalf sold. The Potlatch Lumber Company became flour millers in August with a $20,000 purchase. Potlatch converted the mill to electricity, operating it until 1917 when the Palouse Milling Company bought the plant for $15,000.[42]

Between the flour mill's small, but consistent, operating profits and plant depreciation, Potlatch did quite well. But this was not undertaken as a money-making venture. A local business had interfered with company plans, and Potlatch solved the problem with superior finances, in this instance satisfying all parties. The deal actually prodded the Palouse boom for it allowed the town to keep both its flour and sawmills. Deary's offer to either install electricity or purchase the mill was magnanimous, considering his leverage, though his ethics in seizing the dam were questionable. But the giant company had served notice of its willingness to flex economic muscles to attain goals not always in harmony with local needs. Most other Potlatch business deals would likewise be technically legal and responsible, if not always sensitive to local desires. What was good for Potlatch Lumber was not always good for the area, as Palouse residents were to discover.

As early as spring 1903 Potlatch's directors realized that they needed a larger mill to process logs from the company's timberlands— especially if Deary were unsuccessful in getting the state to revoke its twenty-year cut law. Quietly the general manager bought up property at several possible millsites. By late 1903 rumors that the company planned to construct a huge new plant swept the Palouse region. Moscow's businessmen hoped to lure the mill, providing Latah County with its most repeated legend. The account varies with the teller, but details remain basically the same. Potlatch Lumber Company directors were meeting in Moscow, discussing possible millsites, when Bill Deary entered the room after an all day trek through wet woods. Removing shoes and socks by the stove, Deary heard someone asserting that Moscow presented the best mill location. Jumping up barefooted, he approached a large map spread on the directors' table and bellowed in his thick brogue, "Gentilmen, there isn't enough water in Moscow to baptize a bastard! The mill'll go here," punching a hole in the map precisely where he was purchasing property along the Palouse River.

The directors never seriously considered Moscow as a millsite and doubtless never discussed such serious matters with Deary away in the woods, but the story nonetheless summarizes the case against the college town. In February 1904 Deary publicly confirmed rumors that a new mill would be constructed in Latah County. In May, he sold the company's Moscow office, writing Thatcher that "I do not believe property in that town will amount to much in a few years." Still, hope reigned in Moscow, and as late as February 1905 community residents dug wells at the site they proposed for the big mill. By April, however, Potlatch's directors had virtually confirmed that the mill would front the Palouse River, about ten miles upstream from Palouse. Moscow's loss seemed Palouse's gain. "It is safe to say that when the mill is built and the Potlatch Company begins full operations the pay roll will reach at least $1,000,000 per year," gleefully reported the *Republic*. "Palouse will be the center of activity and every part of the great industry, whether it be located here or up the river, will be tributary to this point."[43]

By September 1905 new rumors hit the region. Not only would Potlatch construct a sawmill, but also a complete town—a town with "large store buildings [to] carry complete stocks of all kinds of goods needed by its employees." This news should have quieted Palouse's boosters, but the *Republic*, failing to see anything foreboding in such nearby competition, hypothesized "that Palouse . . . will profit by the extensive operations of the Potlatch Lumber Company."[44]

Deary and Frederick Weyerhaeuser assured Palouse residents that their sawmill in Palouse would operate permanently, and the *Republic* continued to discover positive benefits in the company's plan for expansion. Some claimed the new town would hurt Palouse, but the newspaper and other Palouse boomers had a different interpretation. "At its mill and in the woods this company will employ about 4,000 men, from which Palouse will directly benefit as the banking and business point," confidently predicted a Palouse Businessmen's Association publicity brochure issued in 1906.[45]

Construction of the new mill and town did temporarily heighten the Palouse boom. The Palouse mill cut all lumber for the construction site, and the town filled to overflowing. Palouse had done all it could to lure big business. Town residents provided railroad right-of-way, helped Deary with land purchases, and in other ways sought to please the Weyerhaeuser syndicate. No one could have asked for a more favorable press than that granted by the *Republic*. But communities that thrive with big business often die that way, too. In the prosperous excitement of 1905-06, Palouse boosters did not see the coming bust. Their town's boom, though dramatic, was short-lived. As early as 1905 Charles Weyerhaeuser suggested dismantling the Palouse sawmill and moving its machinery to the new plant. Because Deary insisted on new equipment, the suggestion died. Clearly, though, company directors were already anticipating the day when their small Palouse mill would be superfluous. Palouse residents basked in their boom for another few years, but the lumbering history of their town was clearly ending while that of another was just beginning.[46]

ALLISON LAIRD

William Deary was overworked: supervising the building of a railroad, the construction of a town, the erection of a sawmill; lobbying the state legislature to remove its twenty-year regulation; buying stumpage; superintending lumberjacks; and managing the Palouse and Colfax sawmills. This was too much even for a man with legendary endurance. As early as 1903 the company's directors recognized that Deary needed assistance. Two years later they sent him Allison White Laird.

Allison Laird was the second of three sons of John and Charlotte Jarvis Laird. Had his father not been so restless, A. W. Laird would have been born wealthy. As it turned out, although Allison was long active in Laird-Norton company affairs, he never held a central leadership position.

John Laird, born in Pennsylvania in 1825, taught school awhile but moved west as a young man. After scouting many embryonic towns along the Mississippi River, he eventually followed his older half-sister, Catherine Goddard, to LaCrosse, Wisconsin. Catherine operated a boardinghouse to supplement her husband Abner's meager salary as a teacher. One of her boarders in 1851 was an original claimholder in the new community of Winona, Minnesota, thirty miles upriver from LaCrosse. Luring Abner with promises of a free town lot and appointment as postmaster, the boarder persuaded the Goddards to become pioneer residents of the community.

A malaria and cholera epidemic scourged the struggling town in the summer of 1852, killing Abner and two Goddard children. In desperation, Catherine asked her half-brother John to come help the family. Moving from LaCrosse to Winona in August 1852, John C. Laird became one of the town's earliest residents. He farmed, started Winona County's first livery stable, and participated in local politics and civic affairs. More importantly for Winona's future, he and Catherine convinced other family members to follow. Younger brother William Harris Laird arrived in 1855 at the age of twenty-two.

William Laird, an aggressive risk-taker, convinced his two older brothers—Matthew and John—to form a partnership known as Laird & Brothers, lumber retailers. Their lumberyard, which opened in May 1855, was an impressive and immediate success. In 1856, the Lairds' cousins, James L. and Matthew G. Norton, emigrated to Winona and joined the partnership, forming Laird-Norton & Company, which quickly became the area's largest lumber dealer. The company started its first sawmill the following year, but then hit hard times.

The timing of the expansion was bad, coming just prior to the Panic of 1857. That depression, together with the Civil War that followed, brought seven lean years, and by then only three partners remained with Laird-Norton & Company. Matthew and John Laird, impatient with lumbering's dwindling profits, tried different ventures. Their departure, temporarily expedient, was an economic mistake of the first magnitude. The Laird-Norton Company became one of the nation's largest lumbering concerns and made its owners wealthy. John Laird was left out. While two of his sons, Will Hayes and Allison White, participated in the firm's dramatic growth, they stood on the periphery, never as part of the family's central core of decision makers.[47]

Named for his uncle William Allison White,[48] A. W. Laird was born in Winona in 1863, where the Laird and Norton families had long been active in banking, holding leadership positions in many of the city's financial institutions. In 1882 Allison Laird started work with the Second National Bank of Winona. By the turn of the century he was cashier, had personally supervised construction of the bank's new building, and was characterized by Frank Thatcher as "one of the leading bankers" in Minnesota.

In June 1905 Thatcher and Frederic Bell asked Laird, nearly forty-two years old, to leave his secure banking job and move to the Palouse country with his wife Anna and daughters Charlotte and Elizabeth to help oversee the family's interests in the new Potlatch concern. Laird was less than enthusiastic about leaving his hometown for a rustic life in the West. He was Winona's city treasurer, a member of the school board, and a director of both the YMCA and Congregational Church, "right in his prime," according to Thatcher, "pleasing and attractive in appearance, possessing a fine temperament and disposition and an affable way that makes him probably the most popular man we have in Winona." Despite his reservations, Laird agreed to give Potlatch a try.

Allison Laird knew nothing about lumbering when selected as Potlatch's assistant general manager, which explains his hesitancy over the mid-life career change. But he possessed just the skills William Deary lacked. Potlatch directors needed someone to keep financial records, audit books, and oversee payments, the sort of details Laird handled so well but Deary had little patience for. Thatcher and Bell induced Laird with a $3,000 annual salary and a large block of Potlatch stock. After meeting the Weyerhaeusers in St. Paul and receiving their approval, Laird moved West.[49]

Though only seven years younger than Deary, Laird always regarded the general manager as a father figure. Upon Deary's death in 1913 he wrote, "The past week has been one of great anxiety . . . in connection with the death and burial of one of my best friends. He . . . seemed to have a father's or a big brother's interest in me during the nearly eight years we . . . worked together. I only know I tried to show my appreciation by a faithful loyalty." Deary and Laird were an unlikely pair. Where Deary was short, squat, homely, coarse, and rugged, Laird was tall, handsome, and educated—"a finished gentleman." But the mismatched duo meshed into an effective management team. Deary supervised logging and milling; Laird directed financial affairs, oversaw town activities, handled many of the firm's public speaking engagements. Deary returned Laird's friendship. The general manager was often testy with his office staff, always in a hurry to accomplish more, impatient with those unwilling to dedicate their lives to the good of the company. In Laird he found a man who shared his temperament. "He is growing more dictatorial," noted Laird of Deary in a confidential 1911 letter to Thatcher, but "he still treats me splendidly and has never jumped on me like he does on most of our men."[50]

Laird arrived in Palouse in September 1905, finding the town "wide open . . . with plenty of saloons and plenty of temptations." The company's upriver camp, where mill and town construction was just beginning, was rustic and "rough." Laird threw himself into his work, handling finances, learning lumbering, helping Deary however he could. "I like my new position very much and am enjoying the country," he wrote to a Winona acquaintance. "So far as work is concerned there is no end of it in sight and I shall have no chance to get very lonesome or to pine for a chair on my good front porch." This gentleman adapted to western life better than he or his Winona friends had believed he would. Like Deary, he remained in the Palouse country until his death, helping to direct Potlatch affairs for twenty-five years.[51]

By 1905 the Potlatch Lumber Company was incorporated, company officials had decided to manufacture lumber in the Palouse, and the management team that would lead the firm through more than two decades was in place. Construction had begun on the company's railroad, sawmill, and town. Large-scale lumbering had come to Idaho.

CHAPTER FOUR

Largest White Pine Sawmill in the World

CHOOSING A SITE; DESIGNING A MILL

The Palouse River was too small, its flow too erratic to supply a huge sawmill with logs. This was not the Chippewa River valley. Still, the river's basin obviously offered Latah County's choicest millsites, and Potlatch Lumber Company directors wanted to secure the region's best available land. They sought a considerable chunk of real estate, roomy enough for a mill and associated buildings, immense lumberyards, and employee housing. William Deary, backed with ample money, could not decide upon the best building location. He solved the dilemma by purchasing every piece of property remotely suitable for a sawmill and townsite.

At first the purchases came painlessly. Upon buying 700 acres eleven miles upstream from the eventual location of the mill, Deary assured Frank Thatcher the property was a bargain that could later be profitably sold even if the plant went elsewhere. But area residents, aware of the Weyerhaeuser syndicate's wealth, boosted prices once they recognized that Deary was Potlatch's land buyer. Cheap purchases came no more. Some local settlers even speculated in property, then held out for generous profits. When squeezing out homesteaders for isolated timber tracts, Deary had been patient, waiting for landowners to accept his offers once they realized no better terms would be forthcoming. But now he was in a rush to begin mill construction even if it meant spending extra money. Less than a year after his inexpensive 700-acre purchase, Deary notified Thatcher that he was buying 140 acres elsewhere, nearer to what would be the eventual mill location, and of his plans to purchase even more property there: "The two big pieces on the bottoms are going to come pretty high, and in fact all this land came high. . . . The . . . parties say it does not make any difference to them whether we will build a mill or not."[1]

Deary continued to buy despite what he considered to be exorbitant prices, and by 1905 the company owned virtually every piece of flat land in Idaho adjacent to the Palouse River. Its directors now had to select their site. The decision was not easy, causing frustrating delays in construction. Two locations had promising potential. One was about ten miles upstream from Palouse where Rock Creek merged with the river; the other eleven miles beyond that, at the junction of Flat Creek and the river, near the present town of Harvard. Rudolph Weyerhaeuser, Charles's brother, preferred the upper site. It was closer to Potlatch's timber and farther from the community of Palouse, which would provide the company's new town with more breathing room and a better chance to attract resident shoppers. Deary believed that only the lower site was spacious enough to construct the plant he envisioned. In April 1905, after the general manager escorted Charles Weyerhaeuser, Henry Turrish, William H. Laird, and Cliff Musser on an inspection of the sites, all agreed that Rock Creek was the superior spot.

Deary was ready to proceed with land clearing at Rock Creek when Frederick Weyerhaeuser, demonstrating his singular influence in the syndicate's affairs, once again opened the matter for discussion by "surpris[ing] us all by saying that if he were building a mill for himself he would use the [upper] site." For another month the directors debated, with Deary aggressively arguing the case for Rock Creek. At one point he peevishly wrote Charles Weyerhaeuser that it would take four months longer to prepare the upper site for construction, "but time does not appear to be of any importance with us as we have already let about one and a half months go by." Finally, on June 12, Frederick Weyerhaeuser withdrew his objections, and the stockholders wired Deary to ready the Rock Creek location.[2]

Even before deciding upon the final millsite, the directors had hired William A. Wilkinson to supervise construction. Wilkinson, who had worked with Deary previously in revamping the Palouse mill, had a national reputation and did not come cheaply. Charles Weyerhaeuser offered $7,500 for his services, but Wilkinson held out for $10,000 "and we could not budge him from his price." Wilkinson quickly unveiled an audacious scheme, presenting a proposal for a $300,000 manufacturing facility at the directors' meeting of February 1905. Though some Potlatch officials were surprised by such grandiosity, after considerable discussion they approved his general ideas and cost estimates.[3]

"After we had decided the question of location I supposed there was nothing further to rise with reference to the sawmill," wrote Frank Thatcher in July 1905. As it turned out, the company had much left to discuss, and debates over the mill's size led to more maddening construction delays.[4]

Differences of opinion arose primarily over the number of saws to be used in the new mill. Wilkinson's plans listed four band saws and one gang saw. Band saws, continuous strips of toothed metal, operate like a perpetually moving belt powered by flywheels above and below the log. Because they take smaller kerfs and create less waste than circular saws, band saws had begun replacing the older circular devices in the late nineteenth century. Gang saws, by contrast, hold several parallel blades which cut logs into boards in a single pass. Usually logs are first squared on the head rig—a carriage upon which a log is placed that moves back and forth, forcing the butt of the log into the stationary head-saw, either band or circular. Once the log has been trimmed, it is mechanically pushed into the gang where it is quickly and inexpensively cut into boards. Sawyers did not get top quality lumber from gang saws, as manipulation to get the best possible grades from a log was impossible. But they got boards speedily, and in the days of abundant old growth stands of large trees which yielded mostly clear lumber, gang saws were both popular and profitable.[5]

Frederick Weyerhaeuser always carried the most weight at directors' meetings and from the beginning had reservations about Wilkinson's grand design. The company patriarch wanted to add an extra band saw to the one-band mill at Palouse, increasing capacity there while reducing the proposed new mill to a two-band with one-gang operation, or to one with three bands and no gang. This would have virtually insured a permanent mill at Palouse, but other company officials disagreed with Weyerhaeuser, believing that facility was too far from the timber and too outdated to justify the expense of enlargement. However, Weyerhaeuser had "a knife in his boot" against the single large mill, being convinced it would cost much more than constructing a smaller plant and revamping the Palouse factory. As Deary, hoping for a large, new facility, noted, "I would much rather that this opposition came from some other party."[6]

In June 1905 when Potlatch directors met Deary in Palouse to discuss the mill, they seemed to finally agree upon the original four-band, one-gang proposal. Frederick Weyerhaeuser either remained after that meeting or soon returned to Palouse, for he met separately with Deary and, surprisingly, convinced the general manager that the mill size should be reduced. Deary now also opted for a two-band, one-gang mill. With the two most influential officers advocating a smaller plant, delays mounted, greatly exasperating the Laird-Norton interests. "I do not see how we could expect to take care of our State timber with such a mill," argued Thatcher, wary of the twenty-year cut limitation, "and I fear if we should build one of that kind it would not be long before we would be planning to increase its capacity." Charles Weyerhaeuser, likewise annoyed, asked Wilkinson to visit his father and persuade him of the need for the larger mill. Wilkinson succeeded in softening the elder Weyerhaeuser and Charles, recognizing that quick action was essential before his father again changed his mind, called the board together to make a final decision on the mill's size. With Deary absent in Palouse, the directors voted unanimously for the large mill. No Palouse improvements would be made, effectively dooming that community as a future sawmilling center.[7]

Only one other major design consideration remained. By 1905 electricity was replacing steam and waterpower as the energy source in many industries. Frederick Weyerhaeuser's son-in-law Sam Davis, enamored with the electric street railway system in Rock Island, Illinois, was a forceful advocate of electricity. He encouraged the use of individually powered electric motors at the new sawmill instead of a single shaft and belt system. This would make Potlatch a lumber industry pioneer. But the directors were unwilling to lead. "I would like to let the other fellow do the experimenting," replied the elder Weyerhaeuser. Wilkinson also believed the time inopportune for an electric facility: "Sam seems to be rather an optimist on the subject of time for the complete electric saw mill. I am looking for great developments along this line, but intend to be conservative on this as I have been in the past." As a result, the huge Potlatch sawmill was belt driven and steam powered, "probably the last large one built with full shaft delivery of power," recalled Frederick Weyerhaeuser's son. It was, in some ways, outdated before it began.[8]

Potlatch's directors stood on a precipice in the summer of 1905. Behind them were years of experience with steam powered mills, years of dependable operation and prosperity. Ahead lay the future: electrically driven motors providing mills with hitherto unknown flexibility. The directors peered over that ledge but chose a conservative course. They would later regret their decision.

MILL CONSTRUCTION

In 1947 Charles L. Billings, general manager of Potlatch Forests, Incorporated, drove into the Bovill woods to inspect a small sawmill his company had recently purchased. There he found eighty-five-year-old Tom Jones bullcocking—performing menial tasks at the plant. Seventy-two years earlier, Jones had left home to bullcock in a Great Lakes logging camp. Between those times he held an astonishing array of occupations inside and outside of lumbering, and had made and lost a considerable fortune. His life had come full cycle. "On the return trip I thought about Jones and his . . . career long and hard," Billings wrote his board of directors. "His history proves something, I suppose, but I'll be darned if I know what."[9]

T. P. Jones was one of the strong, hardworking Minnesotans Deary brought West to tame Idaho's forests. He married Marjorie Campbell, whose family worked for many years for the Weyerhaeusers in Cloquet, Minnesota. Jones, also a Weyerhaeuser employee, was among the first wave of Lakes States supervisors sent West to work for Potlatch. He was a personal friend of Frederick Weyerhaeuser, often entertaining the lumber baron on fishing expeditions in Idaho. As the Potlatch Lumber Company's first logging superintendent, Jones was forceful, short-fused, impatient, and stubborn. Up early, to bed late, he was on the move all day. "He is the most active man I ever saw," remarked one Potlatch lumberjack. "He is just as apt to drop in on us at midnight as he is in the afternoon." Jones's unusual supervision techniques, as well as his tendency to stay "with his decisions longer than [with] his men," caused some disenchantment. "He could sure as thunder bawl you out and give it to you," remembered Frank Rowan. But he had a compassionate side, too, as Rowan recalled: "Let somebody get hurt, and by God, he took care of 'em." Jones moved to Bovill shortly after the WI&M railroad reached that remote hamlet in eastern Latah County. He was the town's first mayor and operated from there during his time with Potlatch.

Like many in his profession, Jones grew restless. In the 1920s he left the company when an oil boom hit Shelby, Montana. There he presided over the Potlatch Oil Company, convincing many former co-workers, including Phil Weyerhaeuser, Frederick's grandson, to buy stock. Potlatch Oil never flourished, shareholders lost money, and Jones returned to Bovill to live his final years. His wife had invested considerably more wisely, but refused to provide T. P. with tobacco money. So, late in life, Jones once again returned to the woods, bullcocking for a Potlatch operation.[10]

In April 1905, however, Jones's fortunes looked considerably brighter, and Deary, convinced he would eventually persuade Potlatch directors to locate their sawmill at Rock Creek, ordered his logging superintendent to begin clearing that site. Jones and crew moved in, becoming the future town's first residents. Through drenching spring rains they cut logs, cleared brush, leveled land, and built a few temporary shacks to ease life somewhat. With logs felled at the site and a few boards cut at Palouse, they threw together a bunkhouse, boardinghouse, community kitchen, small office, barbershop, and store. Construction was crude; buildings cheap. Deary wanted them just weathertight enough to keep rain and snow off, and the hovels had few other amenities. As the buildings would be temporary, used only during construction, Deary saw no reason for extravagance. But by early August, Jones's shanty camp looked somewhat liveable and Deary wrote Wilkinson to come take up residence and begin supervising the mill's construction.[11]

Wilkinson had hoped to begin earlier but was continually stymied by the directors' indecision concerning plant size and location. He finally reached Idaho in September. The construction would consume his time for a year, as he supervised development of one of the world's largest sawmills on what had been a wild, peaceful, flat piece of river property just months earlier.[12]

The Palouse sawmill produced lumber for the new mill's construction. The plant had never been busier, and the workload taxed the small facility. Other orders were ignored as the mill concentrated all summer on cutting and stockpiling construction material.[13]

Another Potlatch crew toiled on construction of the WI&M, laying rails from Palouse to the new millsite, thereby easing the transport of building supplies. On September 30 the connection was completed and the line ceremoniously dedicated when Frederick and Rudolph Weyerhaeuser, along with J. B. Kehl, transferred their private car at Palouse to the WI&M tracks and continued on to the rustic construction site.[14]

At the camp they found a bustle of men laboring amidst the odor of new-cut pine, expanding the site to accommodate the dozens of construction workers arriving weekly. Wilkinson occupied a wooden, two-room shack that he shared with Deary when the general manager stayed all night. Other skilled workers—mechanics, blacksmiths, carpenters—tacked together similar huts on the muddy flat, paying the company nominal rents for the privilege of private housing. Some, including Charles Weyerhaeuser's brother-in-law—in Idaho gaining firsthand lumbering experience—lived in tents. But most stayed in bunkhouses.[15]

The work force grew steadily: 175 men in early November; over 250 by December. They came mostly from nearby communities, as Potlatch did not want to pay to transport Lakes States laborers to Idaho. Yet, even though the company ran large local newspaper ads calling for hundreds of workers, and notified inquirers that "men can get work here at most any kind of common labor," the supply did not always meet demand.[16]

Primitive living conditions, aggravated by a wet fall in 1905, lay behind the reluctance of some to hire on. "It rains every day but the boys have grown ducks feathers on their backs and keep right at it," wrote Wilkinson. As if squishing through mud, straining all day in wet clothes, sleeping with strangers in musty, cold bunkhouses, and living away from families in a camp populated exclusively by men was not discouraging enough, construction workers also contended with an inadequate water supply. The camp's first water was a foul tasting, bad-smelling broth that some complained was not even fit for laundry. Wilkinson finally laid a pipe from the WI&M water tank to the bunkhouses and hired a man and horse to deliver water to those living in shanties and tents. It was hardly refreshing spring water, but at least it was drinkable.

The men could get their hair clipped and faces shaved at a shanty-shack barber's hut, and they shopped at a wooden commissary stocked by the WI&M. At Thanksgiving they celebrated, feasting on local game birds, chickens, and turkey, complemented with cranberry sauce. Many men escaped to families or to Palouse at Christmas, returning after a couple of days to resume construction.

Life was about all that could be expected in temporary facilities at a ramshackle construction site, but workers soon found that a little liquor helped. Some clever entrepreneurs quickly grasped the profit potential of supplying a thirsty work camp with alcohol. Upright businessmen applied to Deary to open saloons, but were refused; those less scrupulous simply carried whiskey to the camp, dispensing grog from the backs of wagons. Deary clamped down on the unsolicited sales, though for a time he tolerated drinking if confined to individual shacks after working hours. When one man pushed the limits of such privilege by inviting others to share his booze, Deary exploded: "If you want to stay on this work, you throw out whatever whiskey you have about your house, or else take your teams and get out of there. . . . Do either one or the other of those two things, and do it mighty quick." Company officials considered hiring a policeman to enforce liquor regulations, but took no action because they wanted someone who was also willing to work on construction in order to prevent "an officer [from] loafing around when he is only needed about once a month." They found no one interested in the double assignment.[17]

After completing the temporary housing, construction workers turned to permanent buildings, starting with a machine shop. When finished in November 1905, Wilkinson proudly sent a photograph of it to company directors, labeling it "The first permanent building [and] rather a land mark to start from."[18]

By the time the machine shop was done, Wilkinson had crews working on a blacksmith shop, powerhouse, and railroad roundhouse. Sawmill construction also began early in the fall of 1905. Crews uncovered a gravel bed underlain with hard-pan directly below the sawmill's proposed location. Wilkinson insisted on basing the mill upon this firm footing, necessitating a deeper, more expensive foundation than originally anticipated. Workers set fourteen-foot-deep concrete piers into the hard-pan in October, then waited a month for them to dry. Finally they were able to lay a floor and raise the frame. In late December they completed the basic sawmill structure, crowning their work with a cupola. Wilkinson noted that the mill "presents a very substantial appearance and the trusses and wood-work look very well from the inside."[19]

Indeed, the millsite's wooden structures were truly impressive. Fourteen-by-sixteen inch posts, fourteen to eighteen feet long, supported similar-sized cross sills and bridgetrees. The Palouse mill churned out over 550 of these monster pieces for the sawmill alone. In place, they supported over 150,000 feet of ten- and twelve-inch flooring. In other buildings at the site, floors were often constructed mosaic-fashion, the butt ends of two-inch lumber laid to form intricate patterns. In many places cribbed walls of double-rowed two-by-fours were stacked over forty feet high. Wood was not precious in 1905, and Wilkinson used it freely. Even storage sheds looked cathedral-like, the interiors not so much resembling warehouses as architectural advertisements extolling the virtues of natural wood. These storage structures had vast expanses of open beam, unpainted wood supports with mosaic floors, bordered by cribbed two-by-four walls—all weathering over the years to a beautiful cedar-red. The entire millsite covered over 200 acres, with dozens of buildings.[20]

In retrospect, the speed at which the huge plant took shape seems astonishing, but at the time Wilkinson was continually frustrated by inclement weather and an inability to retain workers. The spring of 1906 turned out to be as wet and miserable as the fall of 1905, slowing progress, and just when Wilkinson hoped for a summer push to complete construction, laborers began leaving for more lucrative employment on harvest crews. Still, Wilkinson's men began work on storage sheds, loading dock, green chain, planing mill, planing mill powerhouse, log pond and dam, five dry kilns, and miscellaneous smaller buildings, while continuing on the sawmill proper and main powerhouse. In March workers painted the sawmill and in June erected the tall powerhouse smokestacks that became the plant's landmark. Deary hoped the mill could open in July, but the laborers' exodus to the harvest fields delayed sawing for two more months.[21]

Although wood construction predominated, the planing mill was steel-framed, and a good number of other buildings, including the machine, blacksmith, and locomotive repair shops, railroad roundhouse, dry kilns, and the two powerhouses were constructed of brick. Most of it came from the Potlatch Brick Company, a business officially independent of the Potlatch Lumber Company, and brick construction at the millsite launched what would eventually become a major international concern.

German mason Ben H. Terteling had immigrated to the United States in 1859 and settled in Kansas. When his neighbor Stephen Southwick moved to Idaho, Ben followed in a wagon train in 1884 and helped start the town of Southwick in northeastern Nez Perce County. Typical pioneer entrepreneurs, Ben and his sons Pete and Joseph tried many occupations, including masonry in Lewiston and cattle raising in Southwick. When disastrous winters in the 1880s bankrupted the family's cattle business, the Tertelings left Idaho but returned in 1890 when Pete and Joe opened a brickyard.

The brothers persevered through the 1893 depression, and in the early 1900s Joseph established another brick plant just south of Palouse City in Washington. In 1904 George Peddycord, newly rich from the Potlatch Lumber Company's purchase of his Palouse River Lumber Company, organized the Palouse Brick and Tile Company and hired Joe as manager. Begun during Palouse City's heyday, the plant soon employed thirty-five men, and the Palouse *Republic* felt further expansion was inevitable: "The end is not yet. The magnificent bodies of clay accessible and the rapid development of the country, will in time cause the growth of the industry to a point where perhaps hundreds of men will be on the pay roll. It is safe to say that Palouse as a manufacting [sic] town is just in her infancy."

Once again the editor ignored the consequences of the new town and mill construction just ten miles away. In July 1905 Deary contracted with a Spokane company for over a million bricks to be manufactured at the Potlatch construction site. When fewer than 100,000 were ready by early October, further delaying construction, the lumber company took control of the kilns and looked for someone else to undertake brick manufacturing. The millsite and town would have a number of large brick buildings, and the firm supplying the lumber company's needs could expect a lucrative future.

The Palouse Brick and Tile Company satisfied this need during the fall of 1905, but early in 1906 Potlatch hired away Joseph Terteling to supervise its own brick production. In October 1906 Terteling and two other men[22] incorporated the Potlatch Brick Company. Within six months the firm was marketing throughout the Palouse region in addition to supplying the brick needed to complete Potlatch buildings. Terteling prospered, buying out the facilities of his old boss George Peddycord. He absorbed the Palouse Brick and Tile Company, moving its equipment to Potlatch. The Palouse *Republic* predicted that the transfer was only temporary and that the Potlatch firm would again operate at Palouse. But that was wishful thinking. The brick company's relocation was just one of many indicators that Palouse's short-lived boom was nearing an end.

From these beginnings, Joe Terteling and his sons expanded into other construction markets, moving their business headquarters to Moscow, then to Spokane, and, in the 1930s, to Boise, Idaho. There they supervised the growth of one of the West's largest construction firms, international builders of highways, irrigation canals, dams, railroads, tunnels, and air bases. By the time Joseph Terteling died in 1940 his family business—begun as a manufacturer of brick in Palouse City and Potlatch—had sophisticated equipment and hundreds of employees. The company did $65,000,000 worth of defense contracting during World War II alone.[23]

By late August 1906, brick, steel, and frame structures sat side-by-side at the millsite. Less than eighteen months after T. P. Jones's logging crew whacked brush and cut trees from the area, a major industrial complex stood ready for operation. What, just a short time before, had been the location of "Old Whiskers'" log cabin, a peaceful spot in still relatively untamed Idaho woodlands, was now the site of a plant Potlatch officials touted as the world's largest white pine sawmill, the biggest manufacturing facility any members of the Weyerhaeuser syndicate had been associated with. For five years William Deary and Henry Turrish had aggressively acquired timberlands. Now company directors prepared to fire up the plant that would transform logs from that property into boards and lath and railroad ties and other usable products. The Potlatch Lumber Company was about to embark on a whole new venture, dramatically changing not only the operations of a company, but the development of a region.

"THE BIG MILL . . . IN FULL OPERATION"

A warm breeze blew over the Palouse, swaying evergreens near the Potlatch millsite. It was Monday, September 3, 1906. W. A. Wilkinson, William Deary, and Allison Laird barked orders to workmen hustling in and out of the sawmill—adjusting machinery, checking belts, oiling, cleaning, inspecting. The three were nervous. Today they were to start the plant for its first test run. They were pleased with the mill's layout. They had built it the way lumbermen would want it built: no compromises made; no corners cut. It was constructed to rend lumber for 50 years and more, until there were no more accessible trees to fall and buck and transport and slice into boards. But there is an uneasiness that comes at such times. It begins in the stomach, causes the heart to race, brings a blockage to the throat. It is at once a tenseness, tempered with the surging adrenaline of excitement. Deary, Laird, and Wilkinson must have felt it on that warm September day. Would the eighteen hundred horsepower Corliss steam engine start? Would its twenty-four-foot flywheel turn? Would the plant's labyrinth of leather belting rotate, delivering power to machinery?

As workers scuttled in and out and around the plant, Wilkinson, Deary, and Laird waited. Their hopeful anticipation was moderated with memories of sweat and toil and delays, with worry about what they would do and how much longer they would have to wait should things not work. Finally, Deary called Ida Dion, the company's timekeeper, from the office. Standing before a bank of gauges and levers in the engine room, she yanked down a switch and the huge Corliss engine lumbered into operation. The flywheel turned. Workers stopped, gazing appreciatively at the plant's maze of whirring belts, then went on about their tasks, for this was just the first of many tests, and there was much yet to be done. Saws were not even in place. But Deary, Wilkinson, and Laird were relieved. They could easily connect saws to power sources. They knew they could now invite company directors and newspaper reporters to a mill opening in a few days. The plant was at last ready for inspection.

Testing continued throughout the week. On Saturday, September 8, at 5:05 p.m., with saws in place, the first log—a carefully selected white pine—rolled into the mill. It was cleanly cut and slabbed. This white pine would continue on through the conveyors and edgers and trimmers, to the drying yards and the planers, into the hands of a skilled carpenter, until it was finally shaped into the desk A. W. Laird sat behind for years, directing the company's fortunes.

On Tuesday, September 11, with all testing completed, the Potlatch Lumber Company presented its new factory to the world. Charles Weyerhaeuser was there. So were Drew Musser, Frederick Kehl, and John Humbird. The Palouse *Republic* sent a reporter, too, author of the longest story his newspaper had ever run, two full pages, topped with a banner headline. "After . . . days of preliminary testing," he reported, "the big mill . . . was in full operation and turning out lumber as though the ground on which it is located, no more than a stubble field ten months ago, had never known anything else than the vibration of the mill's machinery in restless operation." The machinery that began vibrating that day in September 1906 continued rumbling with few alterations for seventy-five years, until August 14, 1981, when the final shift finished its day's work.[24]

Two dams, one just below the sawmill and another upstream, afforded the company control of the river, allowing for two log ponds. The pond immediately adjacent to the mill had a holding capacity of five million feet of logs, while the upper one held twelve million. The WI&M railroad fed logs felled by Potlatch's woods crews to the ponds. A large crane unloaded the logs from flatcars. When the lagoon froze during the first winter's operation, the company converted the part closest to the mill into a hot pond kept open year-round by utilizing exhaust steam from the mill. Calk-booted log pond workers, the sawmill's equivalent of river pigs, maneuvered logs to the bull chain which transported them into the mill. Logs over six feet in diameter were peaveyed to one side, dragged on shore, and ax-hewn to a size the mill could handle.

The bull chain conveyed logs into the three-story, 276-foot-long sawmill, nearly a football field length of sawing capacity. The first level, a confusion of whirring belts, pulleys, and shafts, transmitted power from the engine room to the saws above. Millworkers enjoyed bringing guests here. Employees got used to the maze of movement; visitors never did. "If I took you on a tour around there," noted Arthur Sundberg, who spent a lifetime working in the plant, "you'd be ducking and squirming and you'd be scared to death before you even got started." Workers especially liked conducting visitors to large moving belts and holding up their hands to watch blue-flamed static electricity pop from fingers.

The mill's third floor contained the filing room and a long observation gallery permitting a bird's-eye view of activities below. Saw filers were among the plant's most skilled and highly paid workers, sometimes referred to as the "dentists" of the operation, keeping the mill's miles of steel teeth in condition. Actually "filing room" is a bit of a misnomer as few files were used, machines doing most of the sharpening. But each blade required skillful hand testing and adjusting, and most saws in the mill had to be sharpened after each shift, and sometimes more frequently than that.

Below the filers, taking up the entire second floor, was the sawmill proper. Workers moved throughout this 276-by-104-foot area unencumbered by posts, the building being supported by a unique Wilkinson-designed truss system. "So different is this truss from any other," noted the Palouse *Republic*, "that it is not given in engineers' manuals, and seemingly is unknown in the engineering world."[25]

Bull chain-transported logs entering the second floor from the pond below were cut to desired lengths by endless belt-driven chain saws. Here scalers estimated the approximate number of board feet that could be expected from the logs. The logs then went to one of the four headrigs. The headrig consisted of a continuous-loop band saw and a piston-driven, steam-powered carriage that ran back and forth on steel tracks. The sawyer, perched on a stationary seat slightly above the carriage, controlled this operation and was one of the mill's most important men, for he decided how each log would be cut, trying to get as much select lumber as possible from it. His judgment largely determined profits and losses. "It is not unusual for a sawyer to have to quit after a year or two and find other employment, because of nerve strain," noted Dewey LaVoy, who withstood the pressure for many years as a headrig operator at both Potlatch and Elk River.[26]

A new layer of wood is built around the trunk of growing trees each year. If trees grow close in thick stands, they strain upward in competition for light. Eventually, light-starved lower branches die, falling off. Until they drop, these branches protrude through the annual wood layers, creating knots. After they are gone, a smooth layer of wood is deposited each year. The art of sawing consists of making the most of these knot-free outer layers, getting as much clear lumber as possible, thus increasing profits. The sawyer read the day's orders chalked on a blackboard in front of him, ran the carriage back and forth a few times to blow water out of the steam lines, then started the shift. For the most part, a good sawyer could run the carriage back and forth continually without stopping, "turning logs on the fly" as the carriage shot back to make another swipe through the saw; "hooking logs in the tail," timing it so a new log rolled off the loader just as the empty carriage returned from its last cut.

In the early days, two carriage riders assisted the sawyer. The dogger clamped logs onto the carriage with toothed "dogs," holding them in place with levers. The setter, receiving instructions from the sawyer by hand language as voices were inaudible in the mill, set and turned logs for cutting boards into various thicknesses. The dogger and setter stood on the carriage, bracing themselves as best they could. After making a cut, the carriage shot back to start over again, and this herky-jerky motion could throw a man off the rig if he was careless. On rare occasions, a carriage could escape control, smashing into the bumper at the end of the track, injuring the carriage workers. Good sawyers smoothed the ride, but even so, uninitiated carriage riders often complained of upset stomachs until they adjusted to the constant motion.

Some logs were merely squared or slabbed on two sides at the headrigs and then were conveyed on power rollers and transfer chains to the mill's gang, a sawing machine carrying over four dozen parallel blades that quickly reduced a log to a pile of boards. When first opened, the Potlatch mill could cut 350,000 feet of lumber in a ten-hour shift.

Sawn lumber passed from the band and gang saws to the edgers. No matter how carefully boards were cut, it was usually necessary to square them into standard widths, the task of the mill's edgermen. Each edger had two or more saws, boards being squared simultaneously on each side. The first job for many mill workers was "picking edgings" behind the edger. Considered one of the plant's least skilled tasks, edging pickers generally watched others for a few minutes on the day they hired on, then stood up to a platform with rollers on both sides, boards and edgings flying down each, and picked the edges off, throwing them into a waste transfer while dodging the boards as they went by to the next production point.

That point was a busy one, the trimming area, where the boards went through one of two trimming tables. Each trimmer table had saws every two feet. The trimmerman, sitting above, controlled all the saws on the table. He could bring up one saw, or two, or even, if the board was particularly defective, all of the saws, cutting it into two- or four-foot lengths for lath stock or waste disposal. The trimmerman cut out defects, squared ends, and lopped off boards to their proper length. It was a job particularly hard on eyes — watching for rot and knots in the thousands of boards that passed through daily.

Next, boards slid along a transfer chain to the green chain, a covered but unwalled 400-foot-long structure jutting to the west of the mill. Endlessly rotating chains carried green boards to the large crew working there, sorting freshly cut lumber. Each crew member worked one or several species and sizes of lumber and had a certain area to work in. All wore heavy leather gloves and leather aprons to protect themselves, because they pulled lumber off the chain and slid it against their bodies before piling it on transfer cars. "Can you feature if you worked on this green chain and pulled two-by-twelves, sixteen feet long all day?" marveled Lee Gale. "You had to be a pretty tough character to handle that type of thing — especially green lumber. It's heavy."

Green chain workers pulled lumber from the transfer table and stacked it onto small cars, the entire area around the green chain being criss-crossed with narrow gauge tracking. Horses towed loaded cars away from the chain, laborers replacing them with empties. The loaded carts were hooked into trains and sent to different parts of the yard, hauled over the plant's thirty-seven miles of tracking by small electric locomotives.

In the earliest days, the mill had only five dry kilns, and very little lumber was kiln dried. Rather, it was transferred to one of two large lumberyards. Here rail crews dropped off carts in the yards' numerous alleys labeled "4 East," "6 West," and the like, a veritable cityscape of causeways. Horses then dragged the loads to locations where piles were to be made, and men with eyes for symmetrical lines unloaded and stacked the lumber, piece by piece, one man standing on the cart handing lumber to a partner on the stack. It took practice and skill to heap lumber twenty feet high, each layer divided by board stickers placed crossways to allow air circulation, the whole pile built with a slope to let water run off. Stackers took justified pride in standing at one end of an alley, sighting down rows of lumber piles, each one just the same, not a hint of variation. At one time up to 120 million board feet of lumber might be in these stacks, "air drying" in wind, rain, heat, and snow, an unpredictable seasoning method in days before kilns.

After the air-dried lumber "cured," sometimes with a considerable amount of warping or end checking, piles were unstacked and reloaded onto railway transfer cars. In its first years, the company shipped a considerable amount of this lumber directly. Most, though, went to the planing mill for surfacing and finishing. The planing mill was even larger than the sawmill: 130 feet wide, 312 feet long, made of steel and iron, its only wood being a mosaic floor. It had twenty-six planing machines lined up in a row, each connected with belts and pulleys to a central power drive, and each exhausted with large pipes carrying away shavings. Each planer contained high-speed cylinders with rotating knives that could surface a board on two or four sides, or produce pattern stock such as shiplap or moldings. Several men worked on the planers. The set up man adjusted the machine according to the type of stock desired. A feeder fed the rough lumber into the planer. In the plant's early years, when all lumber was high quality, all grading was done at the sawmill. Later, graders were added at the planing mill, and marked each planed board as to grade. The lumber had been rough-graded at several points prior to this, but this was the final grade prior to shipment, and the planing mill graders had a particularly important task, for customer satisfaction depended upon their quick but accurate judgment. Next, the boards went along a transfer table where they were removed by off-bearers and piled according to species, length, and grade, ready for shipment.

Rough boards zinged through the planers so fast the mill could finish 500,000 feet of lumber in a ten-hour shift. The surfacers gave off such a high-pitched whine that many planing mill workers gradually lost their hearing. In winter, the planing mill, open on both ends and windy, was one of the plant's most miserable work sites, men standing in place all day pushing icy boards into planers, or marking them, or piling them. "You do that for ten hours a day in freezing weather and I'll tell you, you take an awful beating," Sundberg understated.

Once surfaced, the boards were again stacked onto narrow gauge railcars and pulled by horses either to the 512-foot-long dressed lumber shed – capable of holding five million feet of lumber in relatively clean conditions – or directly to the loading dock for shipping. The loading platform was probably larger than any other sawmill dock in the world. It could accommodate fifty railroad cars at once. Here the lumber was unstacked a final time, loaded into boxcars – with men inside the cars required to wear special slippers to keep lumber clean – and blocked up to prevent shifting and damage while in transport. Workers loading boxcars, like lumberyard stackers, were gyppos – crews paid by the piece rather than the hour. People living close to the mill often heard boards slapping into boxcars late at night and early in mornings, times when the rest of the mill was quiet, as men loaded as much as possible, working for larger checks.

Shipping office crews oversaw dock activities, keeping lumber moving. Boards not shipped directly from the planers were placed in the dressed storage shed and rotated regularly, older stock shipped first, replaced by freshly planed lumber so the product did not accumulate and get dirty, lessening its value.

There were other plant operations as well. Before plasterboard, lath was a major product, and Potlatch had a lath mill on the west side of the sawmill. Here it turned out quarter-inch by two-inch unplaned boards used in plastering house walls. A long tie dock jutted from the north side of the sawmill. Ties and timber cut inside the mill were shipped from here for use on the WI&M and other railroads. A box factory, which produced wooden box stock that was sent all over the United States, was connected to the planing mill. The blacksmith and machine shops, locomotive repair building, railway roundhouse, hose-cart houses, and miscellaneous structures completed the site.

Two steam generating plants powered the factory. The main powerhouse, 150 feet long, was surmounted by two 180-foot-tall smokestacks. Here sawdust and other waste was burned to produce the plant's steam power. If the mill produced insufficient sawdust, edges and slabs were chopped up, or "hogged," and burned for fuel. Planing mill shavings were also carried to the powerhouse through a mile-long pipe system, pushed along by two ninety-inch fans, the largest ever manufactured to that time. The main powerhouse had twelve boilers, each capable of generating 150 horsepower. All this energy siphoned into an 1,800-horsepower Corliss steam engine attached to a flywheel twenty-four feet in diameter. The wheel rotated a leather belt five and a half feet wide, 130 feet long, three cowhides thick. The plant produced enough excess steam to thaw the log pond and provide heat for many of the town's houses and public buildings.

All sawmill machinery drew power from this single drive belt. The main belt protruded into the mill's lower floor, and through an intricate system of belts, countershafts, gears, and pulleys, it energized saws, conveyor belts, and green chain. All countershafts had to run precisely diagonally from each other, unlike electrically powered machinery that can be placed in any convenient location. "It was really a stupendous piece of engineering," noted Arthur Sundberg. A smaller powerhouse sat near the planing mill, housing a 750-horsepower Corliss engine and six boilers. It activated over a mile of belting that kept the planers moving and provided heat for dry kilns.

Even though the powerhouses utilized large amounts of sawdust and hogged fuel, the mill still produced tons of waste. "There was a tremendous amount of choice stock that just went to burn," recalled Lee Gale. Slabs, edgings, and defects were collected in the mill on transfer conveyors. Some of this material was retrieved for use in the lath mill or was sold for fuel. Most, however, was slashed into shorter lengths and conveyed to a huge wigwam burner. The Potlatch burner was one of the world's largest, forty-five feet in diameter, 140 feet high, with an interior wall of half-a-million bricks and an exterior panel of heavy plate iron.

It took about 500 men and thirty horses to operate the plant when it was at full production. Nearly 500 sheep roamed the yards in spring and summer keeping grass trimmed. Two whistles regulated work. A big whistle, heard for miles on a clear day, blew at 5:30 in the morning, awakening the town. Then a smaller warning whistle sounded at ten minutes before starting time, with the big whistle signaling the commencement of the workday shortly afterwards. The whistles also stopped people for lunch, warned them to come back an hour later, and signaled shift's end. Townspeople adjusted their schedules to the mill's, its whistles marking each day's timetable.

The whistles were less active in the company's first years than later, for there was no need to signal breaks. Men labored ten hours, leaving their work sites only for lunch. "There was no such thing as a break," Sundberg recalled. "You had ten hours work and that was ten hours work! And the only break you got was if you had to go to the john. And if you went there too often, you got that slip. You went and got your time and you was done." Though managers discouraged long visits to restrooms, in the days before running water employees were not overly tempted to tarry there anyway. Toilets were board shacks built over holes with two-by-fours for seats. Water buckets with community dippers dotted the plant. Waterboys, who kept the many buckets filled in summer and broke ice in winter, were the company's youngest employees, sometimes starting when less than twelve years old.

Winters were harsh, especially for those working the green chain, lumberyards, planing mill, and loading docks. In prosperous times the company operated all winter, regardless of temperature. Men wore wool underwear, wool socks, wool mittens, wool shirts, wool pants, and ear protectors. At lunch a few lucky ones scurried into one of the warm powerplants, until the crowd got too large. Others sat on cold lumber stacks, ate frozen sandwiches, and tried to thaw coffee in one of the steam discharge barrels.

Winter or summer, workers contended with noise so loud it prohibited talk, especially inside the saw and planing mills. Crews became proficient at sign language. "They would tell stories and they would joke and they would swear and they'd do everything," reminisced Sundberg. "There was characters that worked there that carried on a conversation all day long. Just with their hands." Gus Demus, a Greek, recalled that sign language allowed him to make friends before he could speak English. But the sign code was not infallible. One time a worker chewed off part of another's ear in a fight after he misinterpreted a hand signal comment about his sister.

Working conditions created many other chances for injury. Men were often hired on the spot and put into production without training. Saws and equipment ran with no protective guards; band saws sometimes broke, scattering sharp steel throughout the plant; open belts and pulleys caught clothing. It was not that company officials were unconcerned with safety. Deary once chastised mill superintendent Mark Seymour after a serious injury: "Upon examining the works I have concluded that it was gross neglect on our part to be so careless . . . and it must never be repeated again. . . . I have gone over the mill . . . and have made some recommendations which I wish carried out. . . . It is rather inconsistent to carry so much insurance and not be more careful than we are in guarding against accidents." But this was a time before safety standards, when workers largely discovered risks for themselves. Many were injured; some were killed.[27]

Some employees stayed with Potlatch a lifetime; others did not remain long enough to draw pay. It was not an easy occupation. Emmett Utt stuck it out longer than many, riding a headrig carriage, eventually advancing to sawyer. But he finally left the plant to become a farmer:

> God darn it, I never seen no millionaires ever come out of that damn mill. I didn't get to be a millionaire farmin' either, but you're kind of workin' for yourself, and you don't have . . . a boss lookin' down your neck all the time. When you get through doin' a day's work you can look back out and see what you done. Down at the sawmill, you just look at the log deck and it's full of logs, and you work on that deck all day and you go back the next morning and it's still full of logs. . . . It just don't seem like you get anywhere.[28]

CHANGES AT THE MILL

The company periodically improved its plant, though the basic configuration remained unchanged until it was dismantled in 1983. The first major remodeling came in the mid-1920s, spurred by marketing difficulties. Potlatch's equipment at that time squandered much, saws trimming off large chunks of wood. In the earliest days, these slabs and edgings were simply burned, an enormous waste. The company tried marketing some of this poor lumber, often with pieces of bark still clinging to boards, but discovered that many sales outlets refused to handle the inferior product. Both burning usable, low grade lumber and including it in shipments with higher grade lumber, which sometimes degraded the entire load, were expensive alternatives. Consequently, Potlatch spent over a million dollars improving its box factory in order to use some of the low quality boards. It developed a remanufacturing plant where poor quality but still usable lumber was re-ripped, re-trimmed, and re-graded until it was marketable. At about the same time, the company also began a gradual process of converting the planing mill to electricity, installing faster machines, and doing away with the secondary steam power plant.

Potlatch built more lumber storage sheds in the 1920s, and over the years increased its dry kiln capacity, growing from five kilns in 1906 to thirty-six twenty years later. The kilns brought more visible change than any other alteration. With lumber moving directly from green chain to dry kiln, there was no longer a need for acres of "air-drying" lumberyards.[29]

In the early 1940s, the plant underwent another major face-lift. Workers removed miles of narrow gauge track, over 370 tons worth.

Proceeds from sales of this scrap enabled the company to gravel-fill the yard and purchase gasoline-powered straddle bugs and forklifts. Potlatch retired its last work horse and electric yard locomotive in 1944. While these changes were not as visible to passersby as the elimination of the outdoor lumberyards, they did streamline operations, reduce expenses, speed production – and eliminate a number of jobs.[30]

Despite these improvements the plant was aging. By 1946 company officials believed it would take at least $200,000 more to satisfactorily renovate the operation, and for the first time they seriously considered abandoning the mill rather than investing further in it. In 1931 the Potlatch Lumber Company had merged with the Weyerhaeuser syndicate's Edward Rutledge Timber Company in Coeur d'Alene and the Clearwater Timber Company in Lewiston, forming Potlatch Forests, Incorporated. Potlatch was now just one of three PFI units, and some stockholders believed it uneconomical to continue operating all three mills. In 1946 Frederick K. Weyerhaeuser, grandson of the founder, wrote to his cousin George Jewett, another Weyerhaeuser grandson and PFI's president: "The problem facing Potlatch Forests, Inc. at this time is very serious in view of the low return and rapidly rising costs. . . . Rather than invest $200,000 more money at Potlatch [unit] why not abandon that investment and make new investments necessary at Coeur d'Alene?" Jewett had Potlatch general manager Charles Billings study the advantages and disadvantages of eliminating the Potlatch unit and enlarging the Coeur d'Alene facility. "I have been conscious of certain sentimental pressures to maintain that operation," he wrote, but admonished Billings to ignore these and "have your reasoning in black and white." Billings did just that, finding that producing comparable output by remodeling the Rutledge mill would cost half a million dollars more than if the Potlatch unit was revamped. As a result, the company invested $340,000 improving the Potlatch plant in 1947, primarily by adding new capacity to turn out by-products, including laminated arches, curtain rods, and other diversified products. The Potlatch unit had weathered the first of several threats to its existence.[31]

Another landmark of the millsite disappeared in 1950 when workers dismantled the waste burner. A paper mill had been installed at the Lewiston unit in the late 1940s and now, rather than burning lumber scraps as waste, the company installed a chipper and hauled wood chips to Lewiston for paper production.

The company retired the main powerhouse's ninety-five ton steam engine on July 23, 1952. It had required very little maintenance other than its annual overhaul in forty-six years of service; had seen only two cowhide belts strung across its twenty-four foot flywheel. Engine room men took paternalistic pride in watching the old machine work, knowing it would perform dependably every day. It could have continued churning out power for a good number of years. But the steam operation required thousands of feet of belting, hundreds of bearings, and numerous clutches, gears, and couplings, all needing extensive maintenance at a time when labor costs were steadily rising. Plant manager James J. O'Connell opted to replace steam with individual electric motors on each machine. The conversion took two years, but finally in the 1950s the Potlatch mill progressed to the power source W. A. Wilkinson and Frederick Weyerhaeuser had refused to install so many years before.[32]

Company officers voted for another streamlining in the early 1960s. Outwardly, the plant's appearance changed little, although a new office building was constructed on the grounds and unit managers moved from the downtown structure they had occupied since 1917. Most changes, though, were nearly invisible—mostly new equipment added to improve efficiency. A log barker, edgers, chippers, trimmers, planers, automatic lumber stacker, and other modern equipment entered the plant. Because of new environmental concerns about use of the Palouse River, the company also abandoned its log storage ponds and began utilizing a dry log deck, with logs hauled by truck rather than train. Trucks gradually replaced virtually all train service at the mill, both bringing in raw materials and shipping out manufactured products.[33]

That was Potlatch's last major remodeling. In the 1970s the company changed the mill from one cutting a variety of dimensional lumber to one specializing in two-by-fours, a gamble that paid off while the housing market remained strong. But when house construction declined, the mill closed, forcing the unit's 200 employees—down from the days when it took 500 men and thirty horses to operate the facility—out of work. The shutdown on August 14, 1981, was termed "temporary" at first, but permanent closure came less than two years later when a corporate official from San Francisco made the announcement in a five-minute oration to employees. The mill and ancillary buildings were dismantled, leaving nothing but cement foundations, the only reminders that here, at one time, stood the largest white pine sawmill in the world. "When you spend the majority of your working years in a plant, and you're familiar with an operation . . . and the dedication that people put into their jobs, and now you see it all quiet and torn down and disappeared, it leaves you with a strange feeling," remarked Lee Gale as he looked out upon the former millsite from his house in 1986. "I just can't describe it."[34]

CHAPTER FIVE

Building a Company Town

A COMPANY-OWNED TOWN

Lumbering and hard drinking: The words evoke pictures that seem uncomfortably compatible, conjuring a stereotype. But the stereotype is based upon unfortunate fact—visions of lumberjacks "blowing in" after long months in isolated logging camps; of sawmillers' rowdy saloon behavior at the end of work days. Though the image is at times overdrawn, alcohol did curse the lumber industry, frequently causing absenteeism or tardiness and reducing productivity. Timber entrepreneurs feared liquor for good reason, and Potlatch Lumber Company officials hoped to limit its destructive potential. This concern largely influenced their decisions regarding the type of town to construct for workers near their large sawmill: an open, incorporated community; or a company-owned and managed village.

From their earliest operations, Potlatch officials tried to limit the debilitating effects of alcohol. While constructing the Washington, Idaho and Montana Railway, William Deary constantly pressured Latah County's commissioners to deny liquor permits along the line. He was aided by a state law prohibiting new saloons within five miles of a railroad. However, an establishment operating six months prior to railroad construction even if within the five-mile limit, was entitled to a license renewal. In order to block as many new taverns as possible, the company kept its construction plans secret. It then quickly entered an area, moving workers rapidly up and down the line, foiling the efforts of would-be saloon keepers to establish businesses prior to the six-month deadline. As a consequence, the Latah County areas opened by the railroad were considerably drier than normal in a region catering largely to lumberjacks.[1]

While concerned about alcohol throughout their operating area, Potlatch officials worried most about liquor in the immediate vicinity of their new community. The town of Onaway was founded in the 1880s as a stage stop between Palouse City and the Hoodoo mines. Isolated in northwestern Latah County, it showed little growth

potential until the Potlatch Lumber Company decided to build its
mill and town nearby. Recognizing its possibilities to house Potlatch
workers, John Henry Bull in December 1905 filed for a townsite plat
and began offering lots for sale. Deary feared that this intrusion on
his northeast flank would open the way for liquor sales in a location
easily accessible to his workers.[2]

Time and again, Deary used Potlatch's political clout to prohibit
the dispensing of liquor in Onaway. In April 1906, after hearing
repeatedly from Potlatch's general manager, the Latah County commissioners refused a license for a proposed Onaway saloon. The rul-
ing disappointed the town's promoters who felt a saloon "would insure a fat revenue from the laboring men across the hill." Because
of the considerable money at stake, Onaway businessmen persisted
in their licensing quests, and Potlatch just as stubbornly fought them.
When Onaway entrepreneurs attempted to obtain a saloon permit
the following year, Deary and Laird circulated a petition among area
voters protesting the move and presented it to the county commissioners who again denied the request. In 1907 Potlatch employees
caught an Onaway druggist selling liquor "red-handed" and had him
arrested. The company similarly uncovered bootleggers in nearby
Princeton, and Potlatch officials informed the Palouse *Republic* that
they would "be persistent in . . . efforts to prevent bootlegging
to . . . employees." At one point Potlatch hired private detectives,
dressed them like lumberjacks, and infiltrated upriver towns trying
to locate bootleggers.[3]

Despite the vigilant efforts to prohibit nearby alcohol sales, some
Potlatch officials—particularly Deary, C. R. Musser, and F. S. Bell—
remained pessimistic about the company's chances of success. Largely
for this reason, they argued that their new town should be open and
incorporated. Musser did not believe a company town would attract
the best people, and thought constructing such a community just
to control liquor was nearsighted. "We are all broad enough to know
that we cannot entirely control the morals of our employees," he wrote
Frank Thatcher. He instead suggested an open town with a company-
owned saloon where "we could limit the number of drinks a man
could have."[4]

Like Musser, Bell felt an incorporated community would draw a
better class of people, lessening chances for "extremes of violence."
As he noted to Thatcher, "I believe the town will be healthier and
more wholesome from the addition of this [better] element, and from
their assistance in creating and maintaining local spirit and good

order." He also did not think it advisable to restrict liquor sales, as that would make it more difficult to procure and retain laborers in the isolated community.[5]

Deary even more adamantly advocated an open town. His reasoning, too, largely revolved around alcohol. Despite his many attempts to control liquor sales in the adjacent area, he remained skeptical about the probable success of such efforts:

> I do not believe we will be able to keep the saloon element far enough from us so that we will not be annoyed by liquor and it may be better to have a town with a regular government and let them bear the expense of improving and keeping up the town. . . . At the present time . . . I will vote in favor of an open town.

A few days later, Deary outlined all his reasons for opposing a company town in a letter to Thatcher. First, the company could never eliminate saloons in the area even if it rigidly controlled the town proper. Second, the company could recoup expenses incurred in purchasing the mill and townsite by selling town lots. Third, Potlatch would save considerable money if it did not pay for town necessities such as sewer and water lines. And fourth, "I think we would have no difficulty in retaining the absolute control of the town government" anyway.[6]

Thatcher, however, firmly championed the company town concept, insisting that liquor "is only one of the reasons I do not wish to have the town thrown open to the public. I really cannot say that it is even the principal reason . . . for I have many other reasons why it seems preferable for us to be the absolute owners and controllers of our own property." He eventually converted Deary, convincing him of the advantages of company ownership. Surprisingly, the liquor question lay behind Deary's shift; gradually he came to see benefits in controlling booze, due to his experiences with dry millsite construction crews. "Considering the number of men we have employed and the little trouble we have had this winter in regard to lost time or any disturbance caused by liquor," he wrote Thatcher, "I feel more in favor of the plan of controlling the town ourselves." By March 1906 the directors had decided upon a dry company town, even though some still doubted their ability to successfully implement the experiment.[7]

Though liquor dominated the discussions, other factors contributed to the decision to build a company town. The directors constructed

Potlatch at a time of growing awareness that satisfied workers would increase productivity. They believed that one of the best routes to contentment came by constructing pleasant physical surroundings. "One of the most important features in the industrial life of the last decade has been the rapid development on the part of . . . employers . . . of a growing interest in the welfare of their employees," noted the United States Bureau of Labor in 1904. "It has been recognized more and more fully that the establishing of cordial relations between employers and employees invariably results in a greater industrial efficiency on the part of the workman. . . . Among the most important of all work done in this particular direction . . . is the provision for improved and sanitary . . . living conditions." The Bureau developed an elaborate exhibit at St. Louis's Louisiana Purchase Exposition in that year depicting the advantages of various model workers' communities. At the same time, the popular press highlighted the beneficial effects of company towns, such as the Colorado Fuel and Iron Company's successful reduction of rowdiness, drunkenness, and poor health among employees in its community. True, some writers railed against company town life, particularly its paternalism, but Potlatch officials knew of many places where employer-employee relationships improved and productivity rose following construction of company towns.

Pullman, Illinois, was their prototype. Deary frequently revealed to local reporters that they modeled Potlatch after Pullman. George Pullman's company town attempted to encourage dependable, ambitious workingmen. The Pullman Strike of 1894 showed that he had not attained the ideal, and his company town was dismantled by the turn of the century. Still, Potlatch officials, inspired by his vision, believed their town could mimic the good of Pullman while eliminating the bad.[8]

While Bell and Musser steadfastly argued that an open town would lure quality workers, most company officials agreed with Allison Laird that strict control of housing, schools, hospitals, and alcohol "will give us conditions of life which will be attractive to the better element of laboring men" — a stable, sober working force that would increase profits. Though Potlatch's company town was not unique, it was, as Laird admitted, "something of an experiment," an experiment not only in town building, but also in constructing a particular type of social order. Potlatch officials felt they could engineer a community that was more than buildings and streets, one that would draw the best workers and, having enticed them, tender them a way of life so attractive they would remain.[9]

Though company officials repeatedly denied that they profited from their town, the community did make money, and this monetary potential also helped convince the stockholders of the benefits of company ownership. "Unless some unforeseen problems arise," wrote Laird shortly after the directors decided upon a company town, "we will be more than satisfied with the investment . . . for I believe that it can be made to pay a fair interest on the investment."[10]

Having chosen company ownership for their community, the directors now contemplated a name. Some supported "Thatcher," but Frank Thatcher objected. "Potlatch" was chosen with little discord, as it seemed natural to title the community after the company. C. R. Musser, though, despised the appellation, believing a town in such beautiful environs deserved a more euphonious name. He was the only one voting against "Potlatch" when the directors selected the label in July 1905.[11]

Prior to constructing Potlatch, the company's officials had little experience in town building. The Laird-Norton group had been involved in developing a mill town at Hayward, Wisconsin, in the 1880s, and the Weyerhaeusers had built company stores and houses in Cloquet and elsewhere. All the firms had constructed logging camps. But Potlatch was of a different scale, and company directors encouraged William Deary and Allison Laird to seek outside assistance.[12]

Deary and Laird looked, of course, to the Pullman experience, but that Illinois community was a metropolis by Potlatch standards, a city of nearly 13,000. Pullman inspired, but the two managers needed practical examples if they were to transform the Rock Creek property into a livable community. Deary visited McCloud, a lumber town in the northern California pine forests, while Laird circulated letters of inquiry—to company store operators in Arkansas and Minnesota, to a California logging community for house plans, to a New Jersey company town for water system details. With this information at hand, Deary, Laird, and the Potlatch directors began laying out their town.[13]

The directors first thought to build on the flats immediately east of the millsite, providing workers with convenient mill access. Deary discouraged the idea, however, believing these shallows poorly drained and unhealthy. Attention then shifted to two hills a short distance farther east. Bell and C. R. Musser wanted all of the original housing built on the larger north hill with circular streets that would

provide variety in lot shapes while they allowed houses to take full
advantage of warm southern exposures. Management houses would
be built at the top of the hill, with employees living on lower slopes.
Eventually, if more housing were needed, additional dwellings could
be built on the south hill.

Deary and Laird worked with this design for a few months, but
decided to change the layout significantly. The south hill, farther
from the plant, would be quieter, and prevailing winds would carry
mill smoke to the north. All in all, the south hummock would be
a more pleasant living space. They would construct management
houses there. The north hill, directly east of the sawmill, was also
more convenient for workingmen walking to the plant. The company's engineer then convinced Deary it would be less expensive to
grade precise north-south and east-west streets than to build in an
arc. This would also create smaller, uniform lots. Musser disliked
the monotonous yards this street system produced, but Laird assured
him that "we very carefully considered the matter of difference in
size of the lots and the general opinion seemed to be that with people
in this country they were inclined to take better care of a smaller
lot than a large one."[14]

By November 1905 the directors had made most of the major decisions concerning construction of the town. Potlatch would be a
closed community, owned and operated by the lumber company, with
no liquor permitted. Houses would be constructed on two hills,
separated by a business district, company managers isolated from
laborers. With these decisions made, it remained to actually construct
the ideal working-class town the directors envisioned.

THE ARCHITECTURE OF A COMPANY TOWN

C. Ferris White landed the contract to design the Potlatch Lumber
Company's consummate community. It was a unique architectural
opportunity, a chance to plan an entire town. While many houses
would be similar, limiting creativity, they would provide tidy profits since they could be built quickly after the original designs were
developed. Business and public buildings and some larger homes,
on the other hand, would be individualized, giving White an opportunity to exercise his imagination.

Clarence Ferris White was twenty-three when he moved from
Chicago to Spokane in 1890, after fire had destroyed the latter city.

The conflagration, coming just when Spokane began its mercuric rise as a railroad center and supply headquarters for the Coeur d'Alene mining district, helped create a substantial city out of a frontier trading community. With its former ragtag, hastily constructed frame buildings razed by flames, architects could remake Spokane in an image more suitable to the metropolis boosters believed it would become. Spokane's heyday between 1890 and 1910 witnessed work by some of the Pacific Northwest's finest architects who earned lucrative commissions by designing substantial and ornate houses and business buildings. White's most famous contemporary, Kirtland K. Cutter, was a Spokane bank employee when the fire occurred. Realizing there was more money to be made designing buildings than working in a bank, Cutter put his art school training to use, hung out a shingle, and became an architect. Though he was a novice, Spokane desperately needed such services, and Cutter learned quickly, becoming one of the Northwest's preeminent designers.

Those same pecuniary desires lured White to the city after six years of architectural apprenticeship in Chicago. In a field so open that a former bank clerk could readily find work, White easily landed contracts. He formed a partnership with an established architect, C. B. Seaton, and the two planned some of the Inland Empire's most prominent landmarks, including the Spokane exposition center, the state normal school at Cheney, and Spokane's *Review* building, headquarters of the city newspaper, at the time the most impressive building in the Inland Northwest. White also spent a good part of the early 1890s in western Washington where he and Seaton also maintained offices. He returned to Spokane in 1896, earning a comfortable living but never achieving the lasting acclaim of more famous contemporaries. Though designing over a thousand buildings, his work is largely forgotten today. Ironically, after the turn of the century, White supplemented his architectural earnings as a partner in a wrecking firm, razing rather than constructing buildings. He returned to the West Coast in 1915 and died at Everett, Washington, in 1932.[15]

While Cutter planned millionaires' mansions, the Potlatch Lumber Company hired White in 1906 to build its more humble community. White contracted to plan over 200 buildings in two years. The agreement entitled him to earn 5 percent of the town's total construction expense. In exchange for this fee he provided building specifications and supervised on-site construction.[16]

White arrived in Potlatch in January 1906, finding mill construction well under way and twenty-eight small houses already built.

E. J. Davis, the company's master mechanic, settled into one of these cottages a few days after White's initial visit, becoming the first person to inhabit a permanent Potlatch house. "My wife is here and we were the first to occupy a house in the new town site of Potlatch," he wrote on January 23. "We were chivarred [sic] here for the first time. I did not set out the wine for this is a temperence [sic] town, and the boys took cigars and the ladies candy." By the end of January half a dozen families lived in town. Even after engaging White, A. W. Laird employed a north Idaho carpenter to plan and build some small cottages, as the company wanted to settle as many people as possible before the mill began operating and Laird did not believe White could entirely meet the demand by himself.[17]

White discovered a rustic Potlatch community when he arrived in January 1906. "You had better bring a good pair of stout high rubbers that will stick to your feet unless you want to stick fast in our mud and stay here," Laird had warned. White immediately began drawing plans that would transform Potlatch from a rough construction camp to Latah County's second largest town. Within a month, his crews had built forty cottages, and by spring over 100 workers' houses perched on the north hill while men labored on the south hill's management homes. "The progress," reported the Palouse *Republic* in April, "is almost beyond belief. It is not unusual to see . . . mushroom towns that grow up in a night, built of tents and rough lumber; but to see a town . . . where every building is substantial grow up in practically but a few weeks . . . shows marked mental capacity and executive ability on the part of the men who planned . . . the mammoth project."[18]

Residents moved in faster than houses could be finished, forcing some to hole up in tents and temporary shacks. "Potlatch . . . is making more rapid growth than any town in the history of the state," reported the Pullman *Herald*, and Deary and Laird pressed White to complete construction quickly. "We are not trying to build Rome in a day," one tired worker wrote when ordering lumber supplies from Palouse, "but sometimes I think that Potlatch is wanted complete over night."[19]

There was an appearance of anthill activity that spring and summer of 1906: while Wilkinson supervised one crew assembling the sawmill and power plants and storage sheds, readying for a September start up, White oversaw the construction of more than 200 homes—a town big enough for 1,500 people. The transformation from wooded lot to a sizable community housing one of the world's largest sawmills was truly as remarkable as the normally exaggerating local newspapers made it out to be.[20]

Most of White's working-class houses on the north hill followed a few basic designs, with similar house types generally clustered so that one block might contain all five-room houses, another all six-room houses, and so forth. Alterations in porch, door, and window placement helped relieve neighborhood monotony. Workers' houses ranged from three to seven rooms, with construction costs of under $450 for the most modest, to over $2,000 for the most elaborate. All houses were of wood frame construction, usually with rustic horizontal wood siding, or a combination of rustic and wood shingle sheathing. They had stone foundations and shingled gable or hip roofs. Originally, few had indoor toilets, using instead detached outhouses at the back of each lot along the alleys. All houses had east-west axes with front doors facing the streets. Most had porches and wooden front boardwalks. The smaller houses were one story, while larger ones were usually a story and a half with occasional two-story structures. A typical floor plan for one of the larger six-room homes had a kitchen, parlor, dining room, and bedroom downstairs and two bedrooms upstairs.[21]

White quickly drafted the working-class house plans, and work crews immediately began construction there. The south hill, or Nob Hill, homes rose considerably more slowly. Not only were these homes larger and more ornate, but many managers insisted upon helping with the designs of their houses. They first selected their lot location, then worked closely with White to plan details. Anna Laird, for example, though still living in Winona, forwarded sketches for her new home in March, then in June planned interior decorations, insisting upon larch woodwork, blue paint in the living room to match the rug she would bring West, a green dining room, yellow guest room, tan kitchen, and yellow bathroom.[22]

While north hill houses sat in orderly rows, with larger ones generally higher on the hill, Nob Hill homes enclosed a central grassy park. Lots here were larger; house types more varied. The ten original management houses had seven, eight, or nine rooms and cost between $2,347 and $6,342. Excluding the Deary and Laird homes, the town's most expensive, the average Nob Hill house cost $3,060 to build. The Mark Seymour home at 415 Larch Street had eight rooms and cost $3,105. Since all management homes were individualized, this cannot be called typical, but it does serve to exemplify south hill house types.

Mark Seymour, a forty-six-year-old Laird-Norton Company
employee when he transferred West, was the Potlatch sawmill's first
superintendent. He began as a saw filer for Laird-Norton, gradually
working up to become superintendent of the company's Winona mill.
Seymour came to Potlatch with Frank Thatcher's strong recommendation: "He does his work without any fuss or noise, has splendid
control and influence over men and never has had a particle of trouble
with them since he has been in our employ."

Along with Deary and Laird, Seymour had first choice in house
sites. For some reason, he selected a lot a block away from Nob Hill's
central park, the only original management house not bordering that
open space. His two-story frame home had a stone foundation with
rustic horizontal siding covering the lower floor and wood shingles
on the upper. Its gable roof was shingled and, like all Nob Hill houses,
was well lighted, having twenty windows. The house was nearly
square, thirty feet by thirty-two feet, with a veranda running the length
of the front and a small porch in back. A dining room, kitchen, living room, and parlor comprised the main floor, while four bedrooms,
a small bathroom, and numerous closets made up the second. Like
all management houses, Seymour's had an indoor toilet, one of the
major distinctions between the south and north hill homes. The
heating systems differed, too. Workers' houses had stove heat. Nob
Hill homes had radiators, with some, such as Deary's and Laird's,
being heated with excess steam generated at the mill and some, like
Seymour's, heated with hot water boilers. The Seymour home contained nine bronzed radiators capable of maintaining the house at
a cozy 70 degrees even when outdoor temperatures dipped to zero.
Seymour moved into the house on August 7, 1906, one month before
the mill opened. He was the first person to occupy a Nob Hill home.[23]

Lumbering communities attract bachelors, normally transients who
drift into an area when hiring is good, stay awhile, then move on.
They were often the mainstay of the forest products industry, and
though more prevalent as lumberjacks than sawmillers, no large mill
could expect to operate without a considerable number of unmarried men. While Potlatch directors hoped to build an ideal community
appealing to stable family men, they realized that company profits
depended upon providing living quarters for bachelors as well. Low
on the north hill, on Pine and Fir streets, they constructed several
boardinghouses for single men, reserving working-class cottages for
those who were married. These were two-story frame structures with
shingle roofs, rustic siding, and stove heat. Designed by White, the

boardinghouses had a basic pattern. The lower floor usually housed a kitchen, dining room with long community tables, a stove or two, washroom, closets, storage space, and pantry, with a few bedrooms off to the sides, out of the way. The second floors had small, usually nine-foot-by-ten-foot bedrooms radiating from central hallways, with community bathrooms and wood stoves at each end. Some of the boardinghouses did not have kitchens or dining rooms, with the men taking their meals at a central facility.[24]

By the time the Corliss steam engine powered the mill into operation in September 1906, the town's population had reached 1,000. Residents lived in 140 multi-colored family dwellings and a number of boardinghouses. Construction was imperfect, particularly on workers' homes. The company rushed construction so much that crews often built with green lumber, making it necessary to later reset doors and windows, and plug floor gaps. Moreover, many construction workers had no previous carpentry experience. Nonetheless, the houses were generally sound and solid.[25] In fact, some Potlatch directors complained that the structures were too expensive and too well-built. Nonetheless, construction continued, with 201 houses completed by 1907. Though still a "rather crude" place as Laird admitted, Potlatch by then resembled a real town and Deary and Laird ordered all temporary shacks and tents removed. "I do not want any more shack business and would like to have you notify everyone that are working around our plant and who are living in a shack that they must either move in a house or into a boarding house," Deary directed Seymour at the beginning of the year. The company would add other houses during boom times to come, but by the end of 1907 Potlatch had attained its basic configuration.[26]

COMMUNITY AMENITIES

Houses alone do not an ideal community make. "Their idea," noted long-time Potlatch resident W. J. Gamble, "was . . . that you should have good schools, . . . you should have a company store where [people] can buy things at a fair price." He might have added that company directors also believed that churches, hospital, hotel, bank, jail, opera house, and other amenities were necessary to help recruit and keep quality workers.[27]

Churches and schools were the most vital. Wherever people gather, ministers seem soon to follow, and Potlatch was no more than a work camp when men of the cloth first sloshed through its streets preaching the Gospel. By early 1906 traveling Presbyterian, Methodist, Lutheran, and Catholic ministers held regular services there, sermonizing in several languages. Congregations gathered wherever there was room: outdoors; in boardinghouse dining rooms; in the company store. Both workers and ministers wanted better facilities, and in May 1906 Potlatch directors instructed Deary to construct two churches at company expense, one for Catholics, another for Protestants.[28]

Deary was unusual among leading turn-of-the-century lumbermen. He was one of the few Catholics in a field dominated by Protestants. Because of his influence, Potlatch's first church was St. Mary's Catholic, dedicated in September 1907 with Deary's daughter among the first to take communion. The frame structure on Spruce Street cost $4,000 and, with its Gothic arched windows and bell tower added later, was a classic example of small-town religious architecture.[29]

Company directors refused to support a myriad of Protestant denominations, but did consent to construct a Union Church if various congregations would agree to worship together. Most of the town's Protestant residents accepted the offer, and the result was a united parish of over twenty denominations. "Among the benefits of such a plan," noted the Palouse *Republic*, "will be the absence of the tiresome and somewhat dogmatic doctrinal sermon."[30]

Early in 1908 workers completed construction of the first Union Church, a small two-story frame building. At the time, the congregation had only fifty-three members and the church, with a seating capacity of 200, was quite roomy. The Reverend C. R. Scafe served as its first minister. Scafe also operated his own small printing plant, widely advertising his church's services in the Potlatch vicinity. As a result, the congregation grew rapidly. By 1911, 450 students attended the Union Church Sunday school, more than were enrolled in Potlatch's regular schools. By then the building was overcrowded, and Scafe had to turn many away. In 1912 the company constructed another Union Church on the corner of Sixth and Cedar streets, the largest worship house in Latah County. Built of brick and wood, it was one of the most expensive buildings in town, costing $17,000. The sanctuary, enclosed with varnished cedar and highlighted by arched stained glass windows donated by A. W. Laird, the congregation's first chairman, seated 1,000 and was used for many community events, including school graduations. The building also housed Sunday school rooms, a social hall, study, and kitchen.[31]

Scandinavian Lutherans were the only Protestants in town not satisfied with the united church concept. Late in 1906 they organized their own congregation, the Scandinavian Evangelical Lutheran Church, with pastor Ole Holden preaching in both English and Norwegian to twenty-five members. In 1908 parishioners secured a building site from the company. Although Potlatch refused to build another church, hoping to discourage further splintering of the united congregation, it did discount lumber prices for the building's construction. The one-story frame structure, completed in 1908, later became Grace Lutheran Church, the only early building in town not erected by the company.[32]

Laird and Deary believed a school was as important as churches for attracting stable workers. "Nearly all applications which we receive from family men who desire to come here ask what will be the school facilities for their children," noted Laird when encouraging directors to release funds for construction of a school building.[33]

The directors agreed, but construction in Potlatch had grown increasingly expensive with numerous cost overruns, and Laird had to agonize through several delays before the school was built. Deary at first contemplated a handsome brick structure, but finally decided upon an $8,000, eight-room frame building designed by White. "Now this may not be the best thing to do," the general manager conceded. "It may be better to put up a good school . . . of brick, but it will be much more expensive and much slower to get in readiness for occupancy."[34]

Though frame construction was economically expedient, building delays could not have been much greater had a more substantial structure been erected. Originally planned for an opening in October 1906, Potlatch's 200 students had to meet in temporary quarters until fall 1907 when the school was finally completed.[35]

Although company officials considered church and school facilities the most essential, they realized residents required other services as well. In 1907 they constructed a small hospital just off Sixth Street, and in the 1920s would build a larger medical facility. They erected a log jail while Potlatch was still a construction site, then replaced it in 1908 with a frame jailhouse. In 1905 they constructed a one-story building capable of storing over a thousand tons of ice. When the unheated upper mill pond froze in winter, ice blocks were cut, hauled to the ice house, packed with sawdust, and kept for town use throughout summer.[36]

Many other town amenities were clustered in the community's most imposing structure, the Potlatch Mercantile, or company store, designed by C. Ferris White. This two-story brick edifice on Sixth Street was actually two buildings in one: a brick wall divided the larger merchandising section on the west from an eastern portion housing a bank, post office, confectionary, pool room, and opera house. White originally planned to utilize the entire structure for commodities, but company officials felt "the store building looks too large [with] too much temptation to overstock," so they had him partition it. As it was, the Potlatch Mercantile, or "The Merc" as it was fondly known, opened in 1907 as one of the region's largest stores, with two full floors and a basement stocked with everything from groceries to clothing to hardware goods.[37]

White designed two other substantial buildings during the initial construction period, both bordering Sixth Street. The two-story frame hotel across from the Merc had indoor plumbing, steam heat, men's and women's toilets, a ladies' lounge, large dining hall with a kitchen, and over twenty guest rooms. Even the rough-hewn Deary acknowledged it was "an elegant first-class place."[38]

The WI&M Railway depot marked the town's western edge, separating the community from the millsite beyond. It was Potlatch's most handsome building, a narrow, nearly 100-foot-long frame structure with two stories, shingle roof, and over sixty windows providing natural light. Finished in June 1906, it was the first major town building completed. In addition to serving as the depot, for a time it also housed the lumber company's administrative offices with Deary, Laird, and other managers directing affairs from its second floor.[39]

Buildings—houses, school, churches, store, hotel, jail, hospital—helped Potlatch Lumber Company officials meet their goal of designing a community attractive to a stable, dependable work force. But just as a town is more than houses, so too is it more than buildings. Further planning was required to mold Potlatch into the type of community company officials believed would help generate profits.

After the other directors vetoed the proposal of F. S. Bell and C. R. Musser for graceful, curving streets circumnavigating Potlatch's hills, Deary's engineers laid out boulevards in precise north-south, east-west directions. The plan was functional if not imaginative. Innovation was also little evident in the first proposal for street names. Those running east and west were given numbers beginning with First street on the southern edge of Nob Hill and ending with Tenth on the northern border of the working-class district. Sixth street happened to fall on the valley bisecting the north and south hills. In a less orderly lexicon this might have been designated Main, as it was the community's commercial area, but the directors were nothing if not systematic. Rather than destroy their methodical arrangement, "Sixth" served as "Main." Though company directors agreed to the sequential numbering of east and west streets, they rejected Deary and Laird's original idea to name north-south routes after presidents—Washington, Adams, Jefferson, and so on in order of election—in favor of a nomenclature more fitting to a sawmill town. Beginning on the community's western edge and running uphill to the east, these streets received names of trees—Fir, Pine, Larch, Cedar, Spruce, Oak, Elm, and Maple. By putting together the first letters and eliminating Fir, local residents used the acronym to mean "Potlatch Lumber Company Seems to Own Everything Maybe," a convenient way by which they remembered street layout.[40]

The main roads—part of Pine, part of Sixth, and the mill entrance—were planked. In days when timber was cheap and seemed inexhaustible, planking effectively combatted dust and mud. It also supplied unique sounds. "I can still hear them horses agoin' over them plank roads," remembered Arthur Sundberg, "and after awhile the spikes would get loosened up . . . and them planks would rattle. . . . You take a team trotting in the wagon, and them planks'd rattle and you could hear 'em all over." Although Potlatch streetlights were installed in 1907 as part of the original construction, most town road surfaces remained primitive dirt affairs until the late 1920s when major routes were finally oiled.[41]

The company also encouraged town beautification. All lawns were leveled and seeded to grass, and officials ordered hundreds of trees to line the streets, replacing the natural growth removed by T. P. Jones and crew. Because nature's plantings would have looked unruly in a town designed for orderliness, these were supplanted with numerous varieties of deciduous trees—chestnut, maple, elm, locust, and others—spaced precise distances apart on nearly every block. Extra plantings graced the community's first park near the railroad depot.[42]

Finally, company officials planned for life's necessities. The inadequate water supply that plagued construction workers continued to be a bother. The company solved the situation by drilling two deep artesian wells and pumping water to a million-gallon concrete reservoir high on the north hill. Even this supply was sometimes inadequate, and until the 1920s Potlatch supplemented this pure artesian source with filtered water from the Palouse River. Pressured by state and federal health officials, the company finally drilled an additional well in 1926 and disconnected mains from the river. Pipes delivered water to each house and building, every working-class house having two faucets receiving cold water, one in the kitchen and one outside. Nob Hill homes had more outlets with both hot and cold water. Directors originally hoped to construct a sewer system at the time water pipes were laid, but cost overruns forced them to adjust their plans. Only business buildings, manager's houses, and a few north hill homes received sewer lines, forcing workers to use outhouses. All structures, though, had electricity, with a turbine in the sawmill's power plant generating more than enough energy to provide electric lighting throughout town.[43]

In 1905 Potlatch Lumber Company officials set out to build one of the largest sawmills in the world, surrounded by a well-planned community. Two years later, C. Ferris White and construction crews had fashioned a unique community in Idaho's wildlands. Working-class cottages and boardinghouses dotted the large north hill, with management homes to the south, both overlooking the plant. Traversing the valley bisecting these hills—the only place in town where managers and workers readily mingled—was Sixth Street, lined with most of the public places and commercial buildings needed to transform a housing development into a community. Over and under Potlatch's precisely laid streets were trees, water, steam, and sewer pipes, street lights, and electric power lines providing residents with the essentials of town living. In less than two years the Weyerhaeuser syndicate had built one of the West's largest lumber company towns.

CHAPTER SIX

Potlatch and Environs

TRANSFORMING A REGION

Large newspaper ads, unique in Palouse area history, appeared in March 1905:

> 500 MEN WANTED AT ONCE
> The Potlatch Lumber Company needs
> 500 or more men.

Most Palouse towns—having struggled through thirty or so years of pioneer development; through depression and drought and heavy snows and rain-destroyed harvests; through crop and livestock experimentation determining an agriculture suited to this strange country; through booster campaigns luring businesses and railroads and settlers; through the emotional roller coaster of anticipation as mines and clay potteries and brickyards and other extractive industries moved in and tried the land yet never quite found enough material to make a place boom—most of these towns, after three decades of sweat and toil, still did not contain 500 men within their boundaries, let alone have that many employed. Then almost overnight a new business emerged, providing jobs, spending money, and creating wealth in unheard of dimensions in the Palouse. By November 1905 Potlatch employed nearly 850 men—working in the woods, on mill and town construction, and at its two sawmills. By the time the large Potlatch mill opened, the company was receiving hundreds of job inquiries monthly. This infusion of dollars to build a town, sawmill, and railroad could not fail but to dramatically alter the development of such a rural region.[1]

Potlatch affected the area's growth in many ways. Some changes were dramatic while others were subtle, almost inconsequential individually. Taken together, however, they combined to reshape an entire region. After fifteen years in the Palouse, the Potlatch Lumber Company operated fifteen logging camps; cut 175,000,000 feet of lumber and paid nearly a million and a half dollars in wages annually;

and purchased $350,000 in supplies each year from Inland Empire businesses. It accounted for one-sixth of all the wages paid by all of Idaho's industries, and dwarfed every other entity in Latah County in the amount of taxes paid.[2]

But it was not just salaries and taxes that transformed lifestyles, and Potlatch's impact was felt in places other than Latah County and Idaho. For the first time, residents throughout the Palouse had an abundance of easily obtainable, inexpensive lumber. They also had access to the company's architectural designs, so that by 1915 they could purchase the plans and building supplies to construct a four-room, $281 bungalow; $45 grain tank; $282 barn; $116 chicken house; or even a $2,200 schoolhouse large enough "for 85 scholars." Instead of cutting and hauling their own firewood from Idaho forests, they could now buy wood from Potlatch, which sold 25,000 cords annually. They might pay for their lumber and fuel wood by selling to the company some of the 200 pounds of butter it purchased daily, or some of the equally large amounts of poultry and eggs. They could shop at the Potlatch Mercantile, one of the largest, best-stocked, lowest-priced stores in the country, making it unnecessary to travel to Moscow or Spokane for major supplies.[3]

Yet most alterations brought by Potlatch were even more dramatic than these. One of the most significant was the virtual elimination of small-scale lumbering in the area. Though Potlatch purchased only two mills, most of the other regional sawmills closed, unable to compete with the Weyerhaeuser giant. Even without these small local mills, area residents gained greater access to lumber because of Potlatch's string of sales yards throughout the Inland Empire. As early as 1903 the company established retail outlets at Pullman and Uniontown, selling lumber, fence posts, cordwood, flooring, and shingles. By 1905 it ran a dozen retail yards in the region, all managed from Palouse City under the enterprising leadership of John Kendall, a former Laird-Norton Company retailer. By 1908 Kendall oversaw thirty-three yards, one in virtually every small Palouse town. "The map of Whitman County showing the location of Potlatch yards looks like a case of small pox," boasted the sales department. Though the lumber company moved its main office from Palouse to Potlatch in 1906, Kendall continued to direct retail sales from Palouse until 1916, when the company transferred his headquarters to Spokane. At that time Potlatch began purchasing retail yards in other parts of Washington, and in 1931 Potlatch Yards, Inc., became a completely independent corporation.[4]

Potlatch always marketed outside of the region, of course, shipping most of its product east. Retail yards in towns like Endicott, Rosalia, Genesee, Washtucna, Tekoa, Oakesdale, and Farmington played only a minor role in the company's overall commercial plans. It was not for this local market that the Weyerhaeuser associates had constructed one of the world's largest sawmills. But to area residents, the retail yards were extraordinarily important, places where they could purchase all of their lumber supplies at reasonable cost, and often on credit. The Palouse country was not a rustic region of log cabins and ramshackle houses when Potlatch arrived. Many of the area's finest frame buildings had been constructed long before 1903 from lumber milled locally or imported. But Potlatch's lumberyards made inexpensive materials readily accessible to the masses and altered the local architectural landscape more than any other development. Now residents had ample, cheap lumber supplies – and even free architectural plans – to construct not only houses, but also barns, chicken sheds, and a wide variety of other ancillary buildings that could transform a place from simply a house into a comfortable home.

Many people using Potlatch lumber were new residents of the region lured by glowing reports of farming opportunities on the company's cutover lands. The first Palouse dwellers settled in the prairies where land was rich and easily tilled. An acre of prairie could be broken in a couple of days; it took over a month to prepare a similar-sized piece of cutover land for farming. By the 1890s, though, the grasslands had largely been settled and promoters recognized that continued growth required enticing people into Idaho's timber country. "Farmers steadily came to occupy the lands of the open plains until they were all taken and then the settlers . . . began to push into the foothills of the mountains," noted one area publicist in 1892. "The pine lands . . . proved to be as rich as the prairies when cleared of timber. . . . Thus, farming, which was once supposed to be limited by the line of the pines east of the Palouse Country, is practicable and profitable for fully thirty miles eastward as fast as the trees are taken off."[5]

Of course, it was seldom as easy as the boosters suggested. "Quite a job a-makin' one of these farms," noted Dick Benge of the stump country. "She's a hard, hard way. . . . Of course now they got the dozers, not much of a job . . . to clear a piece of land. But where you do it all with a team and powder, blocks and lines, that's different." Walter Fiscus moved to the wooded country of northwestern Latah County in 1900, settling near relatives who had eked a living

out of that unforgiving land for sixteen years. Here they cleared small
patches for a garden and sold cordwood in Palouse City. They earned
and grew enough to survive, but never enough to prosper. The ground
was unusable until stumps were uprooted, and removal was slow and
laborious. Farmers sometimes dynamited the trunks, sometimes pulled
them, sometimes covered them with wet straw and burned them for
a week or so until they were sufficiently weakened to be grubbed
out. Even after removing the stumps one by one, a process taking
years on a homestead-sized piece of property, they had not won the
battle for survival, because over the years the trees had taken much
from the soil, while their acidic needle droppings returned little. Settlers needed to build up the land with several years of low-profit crops
like alfalfa before it became more than economically marginal
farmland. Fiscus came to the country and remained, but for many
others the task was too much and they quickly left, unable to subsist
in the "rich pine lands."[6]

Still, publicists foresaw a great boom when Potlatch arrived, for
the big company would remove trees, thus easing land-clearing and
encouraging settlement. "A few years ago it was thought that . . . pine
stump land . . . was worthless, but late developments have proven
that for growing timothy as well as for many other profitable purposes it is unequaled," announced the ever-hopeful Palouse *Republic.*[7]

The lumber company likewise anticipated benefits from its cutover
property. As early as 1902 J. B. Kehl had envisioned profitable land
sales, and the company began preliminary marketing in 1905. But
Potlatch's early merchandising was low key, partially because people
only reluctantly bought such land while free timberland and prairie
homesteads were still available. Further, once the large trees were
removed, settlers had less incentive to buy, for selling wood was one
of the few ways they could expect to make money while developing
their farms. Allison Laird assured a prospective purchaser that "our
cutover lands are fine for agriculture, nothing better in the country
when the stumps are out." But that was also a large part of the problem: stump removal was arduous, unprofitable work. Lumber company officials learned it would take time before they could expect
profits from their cutover lands.[8]

As homestead land disappeared and population increased, people
were forced to settle in less desirable areas, and by 1910 Potlatch
began aggressively marketing its cutover lands. Rather than emphasiz-
ing negatives the company highlighted positives: "Located as this
land is, on the very edge of the great treeless prairies of the Inland

Empire, there is a constantly increasing demand for cord-wood, fence posts and rails, so that what small trees are on the ground form a source of immediate financial returns to the settler and his work pays a large enough profit . . . to go a long way toward removing the larger stumps."

In earlier times of free and plentiful land people would have by-passed these rugged cutover properties, fully aware that Potlatch's assurances were exaggerated. But inexpensive western land was now scarce, and Potlatch, enticing people with handsome, widely distributed brochures with titles like *A Home and Prosperity* and *The Fertile Logged-Off Lands of Latah County, Idaho*, had little difficulty finding buyers. Here, if you believed the texts, the climate was ideal, the land rich and moist. With railroads providing access to markets, everyone was able to live comfortably. Buried deep in the flyers were a few warnings: "We do not want you to come with an exaggerated idea of the possibilities. . . . This is not a Paradise." But potential purchasers need not be overly concerned, for this seemed about as close to Paradise as one could come, and even if, for some unlikely reason, a person could not live off his cutover purchase, the company's "lumber operations in the neighborhood afford openings for labor at all seasons at current wages." Of course this was doubly good for Potlatch which not only profited from land sales, but also guaranteed itself a steady supply of local labor.[9]

The company offered reasonable terms. Forty, eighty, and one-hundred-sixty-acre tracts sold for $2.50 to $10.00 an acre, with one-tenth down payment required and the remainder payable in ten years at 6 percent interest. Land-hungry settlers eagerly bought, and Potlatch opened a whole new territory as it pushed back the Latah County forests, significantly increasing the region's population.[10]

In just a few years the presence of Potlatch had dramatically altered the lifestyles of Palouse area farmers, creating markets for their produce, seasonal jobs, inexpensive places to settle, and cheap lumber for construction. Glen Gilder, a Harvard farmer, commented on the change Potlatch brought:

> [It] give 'em a market, give 'em a closer town, . . . give 'em a railroad up the valley. It give 'em a job if they needed it. Yes, . . . it did a lot of good. . . . Lloyd Moles and I were working together one night and he said, "You know, there isn't hardly anybody within twenty miles of here that hasn't pulled themselves out of some kind of a tight [spot] with a job with Potlatch." And I think he's right. It brought a lot of advantages to the country.[11]

No less extreme was the company's impact on towns of the region. Not only did Potlatch provide town dwellers with the same job opportunities and lumber supplies, it actually created several communities where none had previously existed, and forever changed a couple that had been founded long before the timber company arrived.

BOOM AND BUST IN AREA TOWNS

It was a textbook case of boom and bust. No town did more to accommodate the Potlatch Lumber Company. No town was more enamored of the big firm's potential. No town sparkled so brightly with the influx of its dollars, nor did another collapse so completely because of it.

In 1907 Palouse, Washington, giddily rode the crest of Potlatch's boom. The town grew; people got work; businesses opened. Palouse residents jeered at their less fortunate neighbors. "English sparrows have appeared at Moscow," mocked the Palouse *Republic*, "and a . . . man who was over the other day says the specimens are the only real live things seen in the Idaho town this year."[12]

Within a few years things soured. Businesses left; population dwindled; houses and buildings stood vacant. Now the *Republic* chastised even those in its own town who derided their overbuilt, opportunity-less community: "A knocker is a two-legged animal with a corkscrew soul, a waterlogged brain and a combination backbone of jelly and glue. Where other people have their ears he carries a tumor of decayed principles. . . . After God had finished making the rattlesnake, the toad and the vampire he had some awful substance left from which he made the knocker."[13]

When purchasing the Palouse sawmill and beginning its railroad from that town, the Potlatch Lumber Company gave every indication that it intended to remain there permanently. Local residents believed these were just the opening salvos of a long-term investment. Even after Potlatch constructed its large mill farther upstream, Palousers thought the company would enlarge and permanently maintain the facility in their town. Potlatch officials announced plans to double the Palouse sawmill's capacity, even while building the Potlatch plant. Though the improvements had not yet materialized two years later, the *Republic* remained optimistic. "There are indications that the mill here will be enlarged," the paper reported in August

1908. "One reason for an enlargement . . . is that the company has only eleven years longer to cut timber on a vast acreage of state land, and the quantity of timber on this land cannot be cut and sawed by the present capacity of the existing mills within that period. . . . When it comes to a business necessity the Weyerhaeusers are not of the kind to let it slip by without prompt action."[14]

Certainly the Weyerhaeuser associates were aware of the need to cut state lands quickly and did not propose to let a business opportunity slip by, but that did not mean they were unwilling to bypass Palouse. Talk of enlarging the Palouse mill ceased in 1909 when company officials announced instead that they had purchased the Trumbull wayhouse, a popular sportsman's center near Elk Creek in Clearwater County, Idaho, just east of the Latah County line. Here they planned to construct another large sawmill and town, later known as Elk River. In retrospect, Palouse boosters seem to have been unobservant. Just as the construction of Potlatch should have foretold problems, so too the Elk River plans should have alarmed them. But those in the middle of prosperity often view the future with blinders, and Palousers eagerly awaited Elk River's construction. "That Palouse will benefit greatly by the additional activity in the timber district goes without saying," confidently predicted the *Republic*. "This will always be the gateway to the great beehive of industry to our east and with men coming and going daily, the amount of money from the district that will find its way into the tills of the Palouse business houses will not be a little."[15]

Once again, the *Republic* was right – in the short run. The boom that began in 1903 peaked in 1910. In that year the town constructed more concrete sidewalks, banned livestock from its streets, enforced laws against brothels, built a new library, and organized clean-up days. Business houses filled. The Businessmen's Association mailed 5,000 brochures extolling the town's virtues to people throughout the country and received many enthusiastic replies. Palouse also adopted a town yell befitting the ongoing boom: "Push, Pal! Pull, Pal! Palouse, Pal!"[16]

But after a year of enthusiastic cheering, the boom quieted and a downward slide began. Actually, the bust was a long time coming, though when it finally arrived it did so dramatically. It started with the construction of the mill and town at Potlatch. Though the *Republic* insisted that "Potlatch cannot be regarded as a rival, but an auxiliary center of industry," it truly was a competitor. There was no reason for Potlatch residents to travel ten miles to Palouse, for theirs was a self-contained community with its own bank and shops. Further, there was no store in Palouse as well-stocked as the Potlatch Mercantile, and the new town stole much of Palouse's outlying regional trade. The new community also gradually absorbed Palouse businesses. The lumber company closed its Palouse offices in 1906, taking with it many employees; the Potlatch Brick Company bought out and moved the Palouse brick plant.[17]

Still, as long as its mill remained, Palouse weathered these blows and continued prospering, for the entire countryside rapidly gained population and most small trading centers thrived. But the area grew too fast for its own good. Though population zoomed, the number of available farms remained relatively stable. Neither could the lumber industry, the region's other major economic base, expand rapidly enough to absorb the onrush of people. Consequently, Palouse area towns almost invariably reached population peaks in 1910 that they would not attain again for decades, if ever. In that year the region appeared, on the surface, to be a land of opportunity. But in fact new residents found the local economy could not support such rapid growth. With improved roads and automobiles easing travel to larger, better-stocked stores, many trading centers dwindled between 1910 and 1920, and some disappeared completely. Palouse City would have gradually declined along with the rest, despite the Potlatch Lumber Company's actions. But its bust was more dramatic than most others because of Potlatch, the good times ending just as abruptly as they had begun.[18]

Potlatch started its Elk River sawmill in April 1911. With the Potlatch and Elk River facilities now running, it did not reopen its Palouse mill that season—the first time in over three decades that the sound of saws went unheard there. Company officials did not formally announce the mill's closure, and the Palouse *Republic* remained hopeful that it would reopen. The plant had good machinery, and even though Palouse was somewhat distant from the forests, Potlatch owned the railroad and "the additional cost of bringing the logs down here would be so small as not to be taken into consideration."[19]

But such optimism was unfounded. Potlatch officials never did publicly discuss a permanent mill closure, something that rankled Palouse residents for years. Instead, the company just left town. By November 1911 the mill's permanent closure, though still unannounced, was apparent to all—its machinery was removed; plank roadways taken up. For years Palouse boosters had encouraged the company. Lumbering made the town grow and seemed the key to its future. But now the *Republic* bitterly denounced sawmill towns and the company which had, without notice, deserted the community:

> These things have caused some . . . Palouse residents to remark that the loss of the mill will kill the town. Not so. Temporarily it will hurt some, but it was to be expected that as the uncut timber receded further and further away it was inevitable that Palouse would not be a profitable place to saw lumber. . . .
>
> Possibly Palouse has expected too much from the sawmill. Its running of later years has been fitful and uncertain . . . which has had at times injurious effect. New men and families would move into town when the mill commenced . . . and many would move out when it closed. . . . If the mill goes out . . . possibly something in the way of manufactures of a more permanent character and capable of growth instead of decay may be secured. . . .
>
> Let it be borne in mind also that a town situated in the center of a fertile and productive agricultural country will not perish. Agriculture is permanent and dependable. . . . Not so . . . a lumber town built in a gulch, or on stony sterile land. It will spring up quickly, grow fast, flourish and be prosperous for a time, until all the timber around it has been felled and sawed and hauled away, and then it will fall into decay. We here in Palouse may never have a fear of this kind.[20]

The *Republic* did its best to maintain high spirits. It encouraged town beautification and the development of a community band; railed against mail-order houses which drained money from the community; espoused the virtues of diversified farming as opposed to large monocultural wheat farms, since smaller farms meant greater population for the region; encouraged good roads, believing they would lure people to Palouse, not realizing they also eased the travel of shoppers going elsewhere; invited the development of a pottery, creamery, poultry business, and other small industries. In some ways, the *Republic* became more realistic. No longer did it look to big business as a savior. "For years [Palouse] citizens . . . believed that the salvation of the town lay in securing some big manufacturing industry," its editor wrote in 1916. "In other words, there could be nothing accomplished unless the outside world came to the rescue and furnished the money and enterprise." Now, he thought, it was time for Palouse to rely on its own devices.[21]

By 1916 Palouse boosters realized that their heady boom had ended. The community simply did not have the geographical setting or natural resources to entice a permanent major industry. The town gradually shrank, but it did not disappear, finally stabilizing as a quiet agricultural center. Handsome, large, but often empty brick buildings stood as testament to the Palouse that once was.

Just as gradually and very quietly, the big business that brought the boom divested itself of Palouse assets. "After we quit manufacturing in Palouse, the town seems to have naturally died and property values have shrunk terrifically," noted W. D. Humiston in 1916 when explaining the company's unsuccessful efforts to sell its Palouse property. A. W. Laird had experienced similar difficulties five years earlier: "We have been trying to sell some of our houses and lots in Palouse but property there is practically unsalable even at sacrifice price." Potlatch owned several vacant lots, some houses, the sawmill, and the flour mill. It offered property at bargain prices, on long installments, sometimes including additional land at no cost just "to get rid of it" so it would not have to pay further property taxes. "I see you want to throw in another quarter section for nothing," wrote Thatcher to Laird about one proposed transaction. "This used to be good business in South Dakota and . . . we . . . leave it to you to say whether it is a good thing to do with . . . Palouse." The company eagerly accommodated prospective buyers. When a packing house sought to purchase the sawmill, Laird asked $25,000. He quickly lowered his price to $15,000 when the potential buyers balked, and Charles Weyerhaeuser told him to be even more lenient: "I would prefer to except [sic] $10,000 for your Palouse Mill Site . . . rather than to lose the chance of selling it."[22]

By 1917 Potlatch had unloaded all of its Palouse property except railroad land, often at a considerable sacrifice. The bust the company had brought destroyed any opportunity for profits from real estate sales. Even after pulling out, Potlatch continued to have an impact upon Palouse development. A few Palouse residents still found employment with the lumber company. In the 1920s there were enough to warrant running a workers' bus between the two towns. But by 1917 the Potlatch Lumber Company had left Palouse for good. From then on its role would be minor, and Palouse truly was on its own.[23]

Whereas Palouse was an established community of considerable size when Potlatch arrived, Onaway was a tiny place with a few frame buildings, barely larger than its stage stop origins. Palouse was, for a time, a real boomtown. Onaway never realistically had a chance to become one, but that did not stop enterpreneurs from trying.

When John Henry Bull platted the town in 1905, after learning that Potlatch would build its mill nearby, he felt he could prosper by selling lots to employees of the lumber company. But just as William Deary blocked Onaway's liquor dispensers, so too did he foil the town-building efforts of Bull and others. He first purchased a vast amount of property, more than enough for the new townsite and mill. This gave him the luxury of ample space for buildings without relying on facilities in neighboring towns. Several individuals owned the remaining land around Potlatch, and, like Bull, competed for potential profits. When one landowner threatened to sell lots to workers unless the company paid a hefty price for his entire property, Deary would have none of the blackmail, writing the man's attorneys: "Wish to state that we do not wish to purchase this property at any price. If Mr. Jordan desires to go ahead . . . I most certainly wish him and his associates all possible success, but so far as platting a townsite . . . is concerned, will say that it would do no good, for the reason that this company will not employ any men who do not live in the town of Potlatch. . . . Those purchasing [lots] will have to look elsewhere for employment."[24]

If the company refused to hire non-Potlatch residents, Onaway had no real reason to exist, and land speculators soon lost interest in the place. After thwarting these initial enterpreneurial efforts, the lumber company believed Onaway posed no serious threat to Potlatch and gradually relaxed its policy, hiring millworkers from throughout the region. At that point Onaway did grow some: an unplanned, sprawling little community just over the north hill from the meticulously laid-out Potlatch. It became a refuge for people willing to work at the sawmill, but desiring to own their own houses. It was especially popular with Italians who felt they were denied access to Potlatch's better housing. Onaway never experienced Palouse's boom, but neither did it collapse. It remained a relatively quiet community whose peacefulness was occasionally broken by barroom rowdiness when saloons finally gained a foothold. Though it never grew like John Henry Bull and others had hoped, it did survive, owing its existence primarily to its larger neighbor.[25]

Palouse and Onaway antedated the lumber company, but several regional towns – in addition to Potlatch – owed their existence to the Weyerhaeuser syndicate. Most of these were formed by the Washington, Idaho and Montana Railway, which influenced the region in other ways as well. After ten years' operation, nearly 180,000 passengers had ridden the railroad between Palouse and Potlatch. Almost 40,000 more had traveled the whole line, between Palouse and Bovill. The road also carried mail, supplies, and agricultural products. As the Palouse *Republic* reported, "When it is considered that the W.I.&M. practically opened up a new territory, where the settlers were few and far between, the volume of passenger business . . . is rather remarkable. The coming of the road made possible the development of one of the rich sections of the northwest, and where prior to 1906 there was nothing but timber or burned over land, there are now hundreds of productive farms."[26]

Many of the railroad "towns" were only names on a map, rail stops with little if any development. Three WI&M communities, though— Harvard, Deary, and Bovill—became permanent Latah County towns.

Harvard, about eleven miles upstream from Potlatch, would have been Potlatch had Rudolph Weyerhaeuser had his way, for this was the spot he long favored for the mill and town. Once the shareholders chose the lower site, this WI&M railstop almost became Canfield, after Homer Canfield, a local landowner. But Canfield himself preferred the name "Harvard" as a fitting rival to nearby Princeton. Mines, logging camps, and farms in the surrounding area stimulated the growth of the small burg with its hotel, post office, store, livery stable, and a few other businesses. Even so, Harvard was never more than a tranquil trading center. That was not the case with the two new towns farther along the line.[27]

When railroad surveyors marked the WI&M route as far as the future town of Deary in 1905, homesteaders already occupied the area. Settlement came early here by northern Latah County standards, as homesteaders farmed the region's meadows as early as the 1880s. But the appearance of the railroad's surveyors incited the earliest moves toward community development. Andrew Carlson was the first to take advantage of the line's potential by establishing a wayhouse catering to construction crews. Since this was the heart of a considerable agricultural community, William Deary decided to build a depot here. Potlatch Lumber Company officials soon purchased homestead land around the depot and platted a town they named after their general manager. Already overburdened with the company's many other affairs, Deary and Laird chose to "relieve this office of a great deal of attention to detail [in] . . . looking after the sales of lots at Deary." They sold half the company's Deary acreage to Hugh P. Henry and F. C. McGowan, at a tidy profit. McGowan and Henry, former employees of the lumber company, formed the Deary Townsite Company, and in September 1907 sold the town's first lot. Within a few years Deary was flourishing with a flour mill, brick company, creamery, bank, school, doctor, and all other necessary amenities. McGowan and Henry energetically advertised both locally and in the Midwest: Come to Deary, where living is cheap, cordwood is plentiful, and water is pure, said the ads. And for a time people came, but a fire in 1923 destroyed most of its business district. By then the lumber company's nearby logging activity had slowed, and roads and autos took much trade to Moscow. Deary settled into its permanent role as small-town center for the outlying agricultural area.[28]

About ten miles beyond Deary the WI&M terminated near a resort for outdoorsmen operated by Hugh and Charlotte Bovill. Nestled in Idaho's wildlands, the Bovill Hotel sported linen tablecloths and fresh-cut flowers. Hugh Bovill, the youngest of sixteen children of an English lord, was prevented by primogeniture from inheriting property, and sought his fortune in America. In 1901 he found his Paradise in northeastern Latah County and settled there with his family. The Bovills established a wayhouse and, though they did not grow wealthy, loved the region and apprehensively viewed the swelling number of timber cruisers using their facilities. Apparently, Bovill at first refused William Deary's application for a railroad right-of-way, but then succumbed to the inevitable. The WI&M reached his isolated hotel in 1907, and in that year a new town, named for him, was incorporated. The Bovills remained only a few more years, growing more and more disenchanted as the community's population increased. Bovill quickly became Latah County's third largest town, after Moscow and Potlatch. It was a rough place with "no dearth of saloons," catering largely to lumberjacks from Potlatch's numerous logging camps. Bovill's boom subsided in the 1920s as prime timber was logged from nearby forests. It became a quiet village of a few hundred during the Depression of the 1930s, and never recovered to its boom-days peak. New logging methods utilizing trucks instead of trains, and woods workers who commuted from distant towns instead of living in logging camps, eliminated the necessity for such a community. Like Deary, though, Bovill continued as a small trading center for neighboring farmers.[29]

Finally, there was Elk River, about twenty miles beyond Bovill in Clearwater County. It also owed its existence to the Potlatch Lumber Company, even though the WI&M never reached that far east. The rise of Elk River sealed Palouse's fate. Rather than revamping the Palouse mill and hauling logs there by rail from increasingly distant logging sites, Potlatch officials resolved instead to construct a new plant in the heart of their richest timberlands. Many years later Charles L. Billings, the company's general manager, would refer to this decision as "our own unfortunate experience."[30]

Elk River replaced yet another sportsman's hideaway, Trumbull's wayhouse. Though lacking the Bovill Hotel's elegance, Trumbull's was a fabulous fishing refuge, with tales of Elk Creek angling luring people from all parts of the country to this wilderness spot. Here Potlatch officials elected to erect a new mill, once again hiring designer William Wilkinson. By 1910 Wilkinson had become an electricity convert and at Elk River built the world's most streamlined sawmill, "The most modern that human capacity has yet produced," touted the Palouse *Republic*.[31]

Each machine was electrically generated, giving the plant greater flexibility than Potlatch's. With only three band saws and no gang, Elk River had only half Potlatch's capacity and employed about 250 men. But it cut lumber more efficiently, and company officials planned for it to operate longer, believing it would require less modernization.

Around the mill the company constructed a town for over a thousand people, complete with stores and school. But Elk River bore little resemblance to Potlatch, for the company retained no control of houses or businesses. The first town lots were sold in October 1910, and the mill began cutting half a year later.

William Deary wanted to hire Andrew Bloom, a friend from the Lake States, to manage the new plant. Bloom, a large, soft-spoken man with a jutting jaw employed at the Weyerhaeuser syndicate's Edward Rutledge Timber Company in Coeur d'Alene at the time, had reservations about transferring to Elk River: he knew little about manufacturing. Deary, familiar with that problem having had the same reservations himself a few years earlier, nonetheless had confidence in Bloom's ability to learn on the job, and gently persisted. Bloom finally accepted Deary's offer. Relying on his sawmill superintendent to help him through the early years, he learned much and developed into an able manager. He also had a tremendous influence in the community, encouraging town beautification and discouraging rowdiness by threatening to dismiss troublemakers from the mill. It was not his fault that Elk River failed.

The Elk River plant ran smoothly during its first few months. Then in late October the snows came, and kept coming. By early November

Elk River lay buried and residents were unable to dig out until May. The mill closed for seven months. Some company officials optimistically characterized the winter as a fluke; others, like Frederic Bell, feared the worst. He sent an emissary to the site in the spring of 1912. His report: "A gloomy view of the possibility of doing business at Elk River, incredible depths of snow and so much moisture that lumber will never dry."[32]

Having invested heavily in their Elk River facility, Potlatch officials had few options except to wait and hope that the first winter's experience was atypical. It was not. The snows came a bit later in 1912, but still the plant had to shut down for five months. The pattern recurred again and again. As one Elk River resident reportedly joked about conditions there, "You can't depend on the sleighing in July."[33]

In 1927 the Weyerhaeuser group opened a new, larger mill at Lewiston for its Clearwater Timber Company, finally cutting the rich lands scouted years earlier by Charles and Nat Brown. For years, some of the Weyerhaeuser associates had advocated merging their northern Idaho companies as a step toward profitability. Spurred by the Depression of the 1930s, the Rutledge, Potlatch, and Clearwater operations consolidated in 1931 under the name Potlatch Forests, Incorporated. With larger mills at Coeur d'Alene, Potlatch, and Lewiston, PFI's snow-bedeviled Elk River plant became superfluous, an ultramodern testament to an ill-conceived idea. The operation closed; the plant was dismantled. Employees scattered to Lewiston and elsewhere in search of work.

It is hard to imagine a community harder hit by the Depression than Elk River. Businesses ceased; houses were sold or given away and moved from town. Population dwindled to a couple of hundred die-hards who had invested in Elk River's future during better days. They stayed only because prospects did not seem bright anywhere. As the Depression waned and crews again went to work in the surrounding woods, Elk River revived a bit, stabilizing as a small, isolated trading and sportsman's center—which is probably what it would have naturally become had lumbermen not viewed Trumbull's wayhouse as a potential manufacturing center. Timbermen's dreams, however, prevented Elk River's gradual, spontaneous growth. Instead it boomed overnight; collapsed almost as quickly. It was a place, like many in the Inland Empire, forever altered by the Potlatch Lumber Company.[34]

"A HARD DRAIN ON THE STOCKHOLDERS"

The Potlatch Lumber Company had a symbiotic relationship with the region. The timber giant brought significant changes in lifestyle to town dwellers and farmers alike. But the region also affected the company, the Elk River fiasco being just one example of realities in Idaho altering directors' expectations.

Reality set in early. From its first day of operation, Potlatch cost stockholders more than anticipated. Labor was high; shipping costs exorbitant; construction expensive. With no dependable waterways, the directors had to build a railroad. Price: one and a half million dollars. It took $600,000 to construct the sawmill. The choice of a company-built town cost $400,000. Even before the Potlatch mill manufactured its first board, the company's original capitalization of three million dollars was virtually depleted. By 1908 stockholders had advanced five million more, and the loans would continue.[35]

The never ending expenses caused grumbling, which irritated William Deary. "I know it has been a hard drain on the stockholders but they should not have undertaken anything so big or they should have provided some way so that the work could have been done cheaper," he wrote Charles Weyerhaeuser. For example, "I think . . . that it was a great mistake for people who never built a railroad . . . to go into so big an undertaking, and especially in a country that is as rough and expensive to build in as this."[36]

Great Lakes lumbermen flocked to Idaho at the turn of the century, believing the state's white pine provided more lucrative opportunities than the Douglas fir forests in western Washington and Oregon. Time and again, though, the Idaho environment wore them down.

For lumbermen familiar with the gentle hills of the Lakes States, Idaho's mountainous terrain posed unique challenges. Some areas simply were not workable, and extracting logs from accessible slopes, often covered with heavy snowfall, proved time consuming and costly. Further, timber was scattered and species mixed, with cruisers seldom finding dense stands of a single kind of tree. Deary and Laird, who always followed a policy of "cutting clean as we go," often bogged down the Potlatch sawmill with runs of small fir, tamarack, and cedar logs which frequently cost more to manufacture than they returned, and always caused marketing problems for the sales department. In 1922 company directors voted to experiment with selective cutting, but Laird ignored the order and Potlatch continued to clear-cut, often unprofitably, for another decade.[37]

Because of a comparative lack of rain, costly forest fires—such as the catastrophic 1910 conflagration—were more frequent in Idaho than in many other logging regions. Company officials formed the Potlatch Timber Protective Association, one of the nation's first, soon after they began operations, but repeated fires destroyed timberlands and occasionally stopped work as woods crews and sawmill workers were recruited to fight the blazes. The region's timber also was highly susceptible to insect pests such as pine and fir beetles, tussock moths, and spruce budworms.[38]

Idaho's isolation similarly contributed to the disappointing returns. With the region's small population, laborers were often hard to find. Furthermore, wages were high, especially in comparison with the South, which provided keen competition for the products Potlatch shipped east. The small population also meant that there was little in the way of a local market. In 1905 Deary optimistically predicted that "this . . . territory is going to grow so rapidly that the demand for our poor lumber will be fully equal to the supply." Anticipating this strong appeal, Potlatch strung retail yards throughout the Inland Empire. But the market was unpredictable at best, and always tied to the profitability of each year's farm crops. Besides, Potlatch began sawing at about the time regional population peaked, not at the beginning of a growth period, as Deary had prophesized. By 1910 many places actually began a long period of losing residents.[39]

Of course Potlatch officials never expected to grow rich from the local trade, but Idaho's geographical isolation prohibited them from reaping profits where they had planned. One of the company's first shipments went to Chicago, Minneapolis, and other centers near the Great Lakes. Once the large Potlatch plant opened, Paul Lachmund, Maxwell Williamson, and other sales department employees expanded the marketing area, aggressively seeking buyers from coast to coast. They had great expectations for the developing states of Montana and the Dakotas, and for the lumber-depleted regions of Minnesota, Iowa, Wisconsin, and Michigan. To an extent they successfully reached these markets. In 1907, 53 percent of all Inland Empire lumber was consumed nearby, with the remainder going east. When local demand stopped growing, Potlatch and other firms filled the gap by selling elsewhere. By 1923, less than 27 percent of lumber manufactured in the region was sold locally.[40]

Yet even though Potlatch and other Inland Empire firms of necessity weaned themselves of dependence on the local market, their success elsewhere was never what they had hoped for. Railroad freight costs from Idaho were exorbitant, a problem exacerbated by frequent railcar shortages. "The big cloud in the sky," bemoaned Potlatch assistant general manager Walter D. Humiston during World War I, "is the fact that our shipments are so small owing to the almost total failure of the car supply, that we are not getting enough money from current sales to meet the large pay rolls. We have the men and the orders and now all we want is the cars." A car shortage during wartime might be expected, but Potlatch seemed to be permanently plagued by this crisis, both before and after World War I.[41]

Potlatch's marketing difficulties, bad from the beginning, grew worse when the Panama Canal was completed in 1914. That watercourse enhanced the value of timber products from western Washington and Oregon, while placing Idaho's lumber at a tremendous competitive disadvantage. It now cost one-third less to ship products by boat from the West to East coasts than it did to transport them by rail. Already facing increasing pressure from the South with its lower labor and shipping costs, Potlatch and other Inland Empire firms now lost an advantage to another timber-producing region because of the canal. Investing in the Douglas fir forests of Washington and Oregon had seemed speculative at the turn of the century, with many Great Lakes lumbermen opting instead to move into the pinelands of Idaho. Now, stymied by climate, terrain, and isolation, the operations launched there with such enthusiasm faced long struggles for survival.[42]

In 1916 David T. Mason, later one of the nation's leading forestry consultants, undertook a study of the major timber firms in the Inland Empire. He found that in 1909, the region's best year, these companies had net earnings on total investments of slightly more than 3 percent, and that by 1914 the firms actually showed deficits. "These companies, cutting over 60 percent of the timber cut in the Inland Empire each year, which are the largest and best managed companies representing the cream of the whole situation, have on the average failed to earn enough to pay 6 percent on the debt," he wrote. "The consensus of opinion among the lumbermen appears to be that the investment . . . should yield about 12 percent." Further, after completion of the Panama Canal, Mason found that "conditions up to the middle of 1915 were becoming worse so rapidly as to threaten serious damage to the interests of the industry and the public alike." Clearly, this was not a region in which fortunes would be made quickly.[43]

The discontent of Potlatch Lumber Company stockholders started early and continued to fester through many disappointing years. Begun with unrealistic presumptions and an almost total misunderstanding of local conditions, the company never met its shareholders' expectations. Their displeasure eventually led to the consolidation in 1931 of the northern Idaho Weyerhaeuser firms. By that time it was apparent that just as Potlatch had dramatically changed the region where it operated, so too did that region force Potlatch directors to substantially alter their business methods. History is not played out in vacuums. The story of Potlatch shows that what is often referred to as "local" history is not simply a narrow, provincial past. Rather, each region develops as the result of many interrelated local, regional, national, and international forces. Palouse City's boosters and Potlatch Lumber Company's directors, among others, might have planned differently had they better understood how these many complicated elements always combine to shape local destinies.

CHAPTER SEVEN

Providing Essentials in a Company Town

IDEAL WORKINGMEN

George Pullman's model company town included more than neatly arranged houses and conveniently located commercial buildings. The physical setting helped enhance worker satisfaction, but Pullman knew it took more than buildings to please people. Similarly, Potlatch Lumber Company officials aimed to provide employees not only with an attractive town, but also with basic essentials geared to draw high quality workers. People moving to Potlatch found that their needs had been anticipated; that providing necessities was part of the Potlatch plan.

Maneuvering to obtain contented wage earners began even before people arrived in town. Unbeknownst to them, potential employees were screened to bar undesirable elements from the community. This procedure regulated both the work force and the town, for only employees and their families could live in Potlatch. At times, such as when the mill operated at full capacity and the company needed a ready and large crew, screening procedures slackened. Generally though, Potlatch officials believed they knew exactly the type of person that would both do a good day's work and become an integral part of a peaceful community.

First, ideal workingmen should be married. Family men, considered more stable than bachelors, would help eliminate the transiency that often plagued lumber companies. Realizing that their large work force would require some bachelors, Potlatch officials built a number of boardinghouses for them. But bachelors were the last hired, first fired. "I would suggest that you get rid of as many single men as possible and replace them with familied men . . . men who would be apt to be with you when you have . . . need for them," William Deary candidly advised mill superintendent Mark Seymour during a 1907 slowdown. Single men could not rent houses, preventing these from becoming "bachelor hang-out[s]," or . . . place[s] of carousel [sic]."

Boardinghouses were adequate enough, and if the unmarried men disliked these accommodations, they were free to leave.[1]

Second, the consummate workman was American or northern European. Potlatch did much of its hiring through Spokane employment agencies and always placed top preference upon obtaining "white men," an appellation they did not apply to Greeks or Italians, let alone Japanese. One bureau serving Potlatch, the All Nations Employment Agency, boasted on its letterhead "Scandinavian Labor is Our Specialty." "As you are aware, this class of men are appreciated all over the continent for their ability, willingness and steady work," the company's manager wrote Seymour. Seymour needed no persuading. He frequently requested All Nations to send mill workers — Norwegians, Danes, and Swedes preferred. When Spokane's Northwestern Employment Agency notified Seymour it could not hire Scandinavians quickly enough and might "have to send more Greeks, if you are in a hurry for them," Seymour replied that he was rushed and "if you cannot get White men for Common Labor you may send five or six good Greeks or Italians."[2]

Finally, men stood better chances of finding employment if recommended by someone Potlatch officials knew. In fact, in the town's early years no one could rent a house unless "vouched for by some foreman." Consequently, many Potlatchers arrived from the Lakes States where they had previously worked for Weyerhaeuser, Musser, and Laird-Norton firms and were now seeking greater opportunity in the West.[3]

Inevitably, some undesirables slipped through, and Potlatch managers devised ways to rid themselves of unwanted residents. Since expulsion without warning was illegal, company attorneys drew up eviction letters, and Allison Laird instructed townsite superintendent G. W. Morgan to file the forms "so that whenever it becomes necessary to notify any tenant to vacate, you may follow the proper form, according to Law." Blunt eviction notices went to people disobeying company regulations, such as this one sent in 1908:

> The Potlatch Lumber Company have in their possession evidence which makes it imperative that you vacate the house on Fir Street. . . . Unless this notice is heeded in a reasonable length of time, the Company will take forcible and lawful action in the matter.
>
> As to the reason, there is no occasion for our going into details, as you are well aware of it.[4]

Despite efforts to screen employees, Potlatch was forced to hire a good number of men who did not meet its ideal standards— bachelors, "non-whites," and those who came with no recommendations—in order to meet its large labor requirements. Most of these men ended up being valued employees, and the extreme action of eviction was seldom required. Realizing they would occasionally need to hire such people, Potlatch officials developed ways to fit these workers into their plans for an ideal town. One accommodation method was the teaching of "Americanization" and elementary English at night school. First begun by the Union Church, these classes were soon sanctioned by the company, and eventually became company-sponsored. For years Greeks, Italians, Japanese, and Scandinavians— both men and women—began their naturalization process by attending evening classes taught in Potlatch by Ruth Hall, who also instructed a couple of generations of Potlatch first graders.[5]

Company officials also physically segregated less desirable residents from more preferred ones. Though some bachelors did sublet rooms from families up town, many lived isolated from married residents along Pine and Fir streets in boardinghouses built just for them. Greeks, Italians, and Japanese were also sequestered at the foot of the hill in small cottages and boardinghouses, areas known as "Jap Town," "Dago Town," and "Greek Town." Most Greek employees were bachelors, living in boardinghouses. There were also Italian bachelors, but these workers were frequently married, occupying the town's smallest family dwellings. The Japanese also had a boardinghouse where both men and women resided. "There wasn't any of the Greeks or Italians or the Japs that lived in the town itself," noted Arthur Sundberg. Similarly, those who were not Greek, Italian, or Japanese could not live in those sections of town.[6]

The company insisted that ethnic groups preferred segregation, and there was some truth to the claim. Each nationality had its own customs and idiosyncrasies which were more easily followed if the group was left alone. The Japanese, for example, always used their own laundresses, gardened, and took daily communal baths in a large outdoor tank. Italians enjoyed making wine when they believed they could do so and not be detected. The immigrants valued the comradeship of life amidst fellow expatriates. And since many sent a portion of their wages to families back home, they also appreciated the lower rents charged for their modest housing.

Still, company insistence that these groups favored segregation was largely an excuse for isolating them from the community's "better" element. "In those unselfconscious days we thought they preferred to stay down there," recalled Edgar Renfrew, reflecting the town's prevalent attitude in an earlier time. But Mike Stefanos, a Greek, insisted that many lived like this only because of a lack of options: "There's nothing you can do. . . . You got to stay some place. They didn't have anything else to go and stay. You can go to Onaway, . . . but hell, that's too far."[7]

Some Italians did escape to Onaway after the company relaxed its policy of hiring only Potlatch residents. Most Italians, Greeks, and Japanese, though, remained in their corners of Potlatch. There they added to the flavor of a small town rich in ethnic diversity, and contributed dependable labor to the company. Some enjoyed the work and the town, staying years and making lifelong friends among residents of all ethnic backgrounds. Many more, though, were highly transient. All were victims of a subtle racism, seldom overt or hostile, but one obviously marking these "non-whites" as low in the community's social and economic structure, lower than their co-workers and neighbors farther up the north hill, and several rungs below the managers on Nob Hill, none of whom were ever Greek, Italian, or Japanese.[8]

ESSENTIAL SERVICES

Some Potlatchers did live better than others, but every resident had access to basic services, and these amenities helped create a community many believed was an ideal place to live and raise a family. The school system provides a prime example of Potlatch's good life, and Allison Laird was largely responsible for its excellence.

As Deary gained confidence in Laird, he delegated him increasing authority. Though the general manager always closely supervised company business affairs, he granted Laird considerable latitude over town development. As a result, the Potlatch community was shaped more by Laird than any other company official, and his imprint was especially noticeable on the schools. If company officials knew little about town building in 1906, they knew even less about running a school, and it is a tribute to Laird that Potlatch's educational system gained a reputation as one of Idaho's finest.

At first, officials were unsure whether they could operate their own school or if they would have to join an existing district. Laird was convinced the company should run its system, giving Potlatch officials absolute control over hiring and firing of teachers. Such leverage would provide another method of keeping undesirables from town. More significantly, it would facilitate the employment of exemplary instructors, something Laird believed important, as a superior school would be an incentive for attracting dependable, familied employees. Furthermore, he felt that operating the institution would be cheaper than supporting a public school "taxed for all it was worth by the people of this district so that we would be compelled whether agreeable or not, to pay a good large tax."[9]

As soon as attorney William Borah determined that a company-operated school was legal, Laird began working with Latah County officials to organize the system. County school superintendent Clara Ransom Davis sympathized with the company school concept and assisted Laird in clearing political obstacles. Some neighboring districts opposed the new school, fearing a large Potlatch institution threatened the existence of their districts. But, with Davis's support, the county commissioners granted the company its own system—independent district number 94—in the summer of 1906. Davis appointed Laird, F. C. McGowan, and Loring Corner to the first school board. After this initial formality, the company named its own board, and Laird served as its most influential member until his death.[10]

The board's first duty was hiring a staff. F. C. Reese became principal, coming to Potlatch from Clifton, Arizona, a town heavily populated with working-class families that adjoined the mining company town of Morenci. Potlatch officials always sought ideas elsewhere when developing their community, and no doubt thought Reese brought just the experience needed to get their school started. Four teachers—Ursula Owen, Edith Purdy, Emily Montgomery, and Anna Morris—all unmarried women, completed the first-year staff.[11]

Laird believed in hiring the finest teachers available, and Potlatch attracted them more easily than most small communities. One incentive was high pay. Potlatch instructors were always paid above the state average and frequently earned wages comparable to those in much larger communities such as Spokane. In addition, rents in Potlatch were low, enabling teachers to keep more of their earnings. In 1921 the company constructed and furnished a two-and-one-half story, ten-room house on Oak Street for single women teachers. It also maintained an eight-room "family house" on Sixth street that was usually leased to married teachers. Consequently, Potlatch faculty found housing accessible and inexpensive.[12]

Teachers also found Potlatch a receptive community. "It was always quite an event when the new teachers came to town," remembered Elsie Renfrew. Laird encouraged instructors to actively participate in community events, to become part of the town rather than staying isolated from its life. Women faculty were automatically made members of the Polida (*Po*tlatch, *L*atah County, *Ida*ho) Club, a group consisting of teachers and selected town women who met monthly during the school term and presented community plays and other entertainments. The club provided a means of fellowship while involving teachers in town activities and serving as an inducement to women teachers contemplating a move to Potlatch.[13]

As a result of these benefits, the community's schools had good instructors and an enviable reputation. Potlatch pupils regularly scored higher on standardized examinations than other Latah County students, and the school's graduates who attended the University of Idaho traditionally earned among the best performance records. Potlatch was frequently innovative in vocational studies, with shop and farming classes, a school garden, and probably Idaho's first training in printing. In 1914 manual arts students built the Union Church parsonage with materials supplied by the company. While residents attended school free, those living outside Potlatch paid tuition. Yet with the school's exemplary standing, many rural parents willingly incurred the extra expense.[14]

Just as important as schooling was medical care, especially since sawmill and woods work were dangerous occupations. One of the company's first actions upon commencing Inland Empire operations was arranging for medical services. In 1904 Potlatch contracted with Dr. Ernst T. Hein of Palouse to care for all its employees. Though some, particularly lumberjacks, did not appreciate Hein "as he was very strict, made them get into the bath tub and scrub themselves off clean . . . and some of them were not used to that," he remained a Potlatch doctor for nearly twenty years. The company withheld one dollar per month from each worker's pay, turning the sum over to Hein. In return, the doctor performed all necessary medical treatment for Potlatch's hundreds of laborers. He constructed a hospital in Palouse, with the company transporting sick or injured employees to the facility.[15]

As logging operations moved farther from Palouse, the company needed facilities closer to its mills and camps. Potlatch took over the Bovill hospital built by the Milwaukee Railroad in 1910, and also established a hospital at Elk River. Both were operated under contract by the Western Hospital Association of Seattle in exchange for the mandatory one dollar per month fee that Potlatch received from its workers.

Hein, still under contract, now primarily served the town of Potlatch. In 1907 the company constructed a small, one-story frame hospital in town, just off Sixth Street, where Hein sent a resident physician. Though it was hardly a model of modern medical facilities, at least Potlatch residents no longer had to travel ten miles to Hein's larger Palouse hospital.

Over the years the company's medical plan came to include illnesses not related to work, and allowed treatment for employees' families. Though this was a considerable improvement, Laird still worried that the company was not doing enough, particularly for Potlatch residents. The town's tiny hospital was totally inadequate. The company suffered several bleak economic years, but 1923 was its best to date. Encouraged, officials authorized renovation of the mill and construction of several new houses. Laird felt the time opportune to construct a larger hospital, and the directors granted permission.

Rather than build a new structure, the company remodeled a boardinghouse on Pine street, transforming it into a community hospital with four multi-bed wards, a dozen private rooms, operating and x-ray facilities, kitchen, and office space. At the same time, Potlatch canceled its arrangement with Hein, contracting with the Western Hospital Association to maintain the facility. With the opening of the larger Potlatch hospital, Hein's facility in Palouse went out of business and became a lodge hall, one more economic loss to the newer town upstream. Western closed the Bovill hospital, moving Dr. Frank Gibson to Potlatch where he teamed with Dr. Joseph W. Thompson. Both served the town for many years. The Palouse *Republic* claimed Potlatch now had "a modern and fully equipped hospital," but actually Gibson and Thompson were quite isolated and frequently had to improvise. Gibson's son recalled that his father, working in conjunction with the town blacksmith, once fashioned a steel-plated lower jaw connected to a helmet-like plaster of paris headgear to repair the mouth of a man injured at the mill.

When Western Hospital in 1944 requested a considerable increase over the monthly dollar-per-employee fee it had received for years, the lumber company dropped its contract, arranging for individual doctors to provide services to town residents. The Potlatch medical facility in the old boardinghouse shrank from a hospital to a doctor's office. Furnishings and equipment were sold. The company negotiated with Moscow's Gritman Hospital to provide care, and supplied ambulance service to that facility. By then ambulances could rush patients from Potlatch to Moscow in twenty minutes over paved highway. Like much of small town life, the Potlatch hospital succumbed to a transportation revolution. For nearly forty years, though, the hospital had been an integral part of the company town, serving both employees and their families at reasonable cost during a time when many communities its size were without medical facilities.[16]

Potlatch residents lived in close-set frame houses, connected by board sidewalks and plank streets, overlooking a huge sawmill holding thousands of feet of stacked lumber. Fire was never far from their minds. Jobs, not to mention lives, depended upon preventing it. Potlatch officials carefully considered fire control when planning their mill and town. They placed over forty hydrants at the mill with thirty more in town, all painted in easily distinguishable red or yellow and all connected with ample water supplied from the mill's ponds and the town's reservoir. They built nine firehouses at the millsite and two more up town, each equipped with two-wheeled, hand-pulled hose or chemical carts. They installed alarm boxes throughout the plant and community, each linked to a siren. They kept the plant under twenty-four-hour surveillance, even when not operating, with watchmen making continuous rounds to detect fires. They placed large barrels filled with sand, "shur-stop" fire bombs, and hand extinguishers in key locations throughout the millsite. They kept sheep munching and men cutting and burning and spraying all spring and summer to keep down tinder-dry grass. As fire fighting technology advanced, they converted a logging truck into a fire engine and eventually purchased more modern vehicles.

To utilize all of this equipment, virtually every man in town became a volunteer fireman. Some, the first-line regulars, were more active than others and had periodic, specialized training. But officials directed everyone to drop everything if the fire siren—which "blew as loud as the whistle on the liner *United States* when it's out in midstream"—sounded. Potlatch's first major social function, held in November 1906, was a gala firemen's ball. Attended by nearly everyone in town with a special WI&M train transporting others from the surrounding area, it served as an indication of the significance of fire protection to the community.

Maxwell Williamson vividly recalled an early fire alarm and rushing from his mill office to the scene:

I heard that fire whistle and then they gave the code. We stood
there scared to death, listening to hear from the code where the
fire was. We'd all been told to immediately drop everything and
grab a hose-cart. So, we listened to the code. It repeated, and
my Lord! it was a station at the far end of the lumberyard, with
a breeze blowing toward our direction, which could have cleaned
out the whole lumberyard. My gosh, I ripped off my coat and
shirt. We ran out and grabbed a hose-cart. Everywhere there were
hose-carts. You never saw so many hose-carts in your life. Mill
men were running in every direction.

Down through a runway, down through the middle of the yard,
clear down to the end of the yard. My God, it must have been
half a mile! The dust churned up in our faces from everybody
ahead. I could hardly see the wheels ahead of me. I was really
pulling.

When we got down there, who should come out from behind
the yard but Mr. Deary—great big round face, wide with laughter.
"Boys, you did a damn nice job—now you can go back to work."

Most of the time, the siren did signal tests and drills. Later, in
fact, officials blew it weekly as an equipment check. Potlatch had
few large fires—a few houses burned, the ice house was destroyed,
the American Legion cabin was damaged. In later years blazes consumed the Union Church and Mercantile. But fire was definitely
on the mind of community residents. "Every time I'd hear the whistle I'd think," 'There goes the town'," recalled Edgar Renfrew. The
company probably provided no community service more significant
than fire protection.[17]

While dozens of men tended to fire control, Potlatch needed only
one policeman—a town constable who doubled as a county deputy
sheriff. There was a certain amount of crime in Potlatch, especially
fights among workmen and youth vandalism. Generally, though, the
policeman's main duty was to "harrass bootleggers and occasional
noisy drunks." Still, police protection was one more of life's essentials provided by the company.[18]

Schools, hospitals, police, and fire protection were basic necessities.
But company officials believed other amenities, not quite so essential, were also required for a good life. Some of these the company
provided; others were supplied by independent organizations and
businesses with the company's sanction.

PROVIDING COMFORTS

The Potlatch State Bank, organized at Allison Laird's insistence, served town residents until 1940. Though technically separate from the lumber company, Potlatch controlled a majority of the bank's stock, and the institution was part of the company's plan to provide Potlatchers with a comfortable lifestyle.

The bank weathered a few crises during its lifetime. In 1922 some fast-talking "oil men" tempted bank cashier John Bottjer, a family man of "good character and clean life," into purchasing Texas oil stocks. As these ventures soured, Bottjer tried recouping his losses with investments in Montana oil companies. To cover increasing losses he embezzled bank funds by forging bogus loans. By 1924, when state examiners routinely audited the facility, Bottjer had stolen over $140,000, the largest bank defalcation by an individual in Idaho history to that time. Once discovered, Bottjer pleaded guilty and was sentenced to fifteen to sixty years in the state penitentiary.

Laird, the former banker, was highly discomforted by the scandal, sheepishly writing his directors that "it will be difficult for you to understand how stunned we all are and with what chagrin I am filled to feel such a gross embezzlement could be carried on under our eyes." Despite the financial loss and the embarrassment, company officials recognized it was important that town residents retain confidence in the facility, and immediately authorized payment of $150,000 to cover losses. The bank survived, and within two years was again paying dividends. Company directors never hesitated in their decision to save the institution, believing such a service was essential in a proper town.[19]

Less than ten years later the bank again faced difficulties. By March 1933 over 5,000 American banks had failed within three years, victims of the Great Depression. Lines of customers grew at nearly every bank, people withdrawing cash to store in coffee cans, under mattresses, almost anywhere, believing any place safer than the local savings facility. Michigan's governor launched a national trend when he proclaimed a "bank holiday," temporarily closing institutions there. By presidential inauguration day on March 4, over thirty-eight states had declared such closures, and one of Franklin Roosevelt's first actions upon entering office was to announce a national bank holiday. On March 2 depositors had made a mild run on the Potlatch State Bank, withdrawing $6,700. The lumber company again moved swiftly to allay fears, obtaining an immediate loan of $25,000 from the Weyerhaeuser Timber Company to secure holdings.

Many banks in nearby communities never re-opened after the bank crisis of 1933. Others were absorbed by larger institutions. But Potlatch State Bank continued to enjoy the trust of its depositors, who saw in two instances that lumber company officials would move quickly to insure their savings. The bank seemed as safe as the Weyerhaeuser syndicate itself, and even during the hard times of the Depression that was reassuring enough for most Potlatch residents. The bank even showed a slight gain in 1933, and profits continued to rise gradually during the remaining years of the decade.[20]

By the late 1930s the lumber company was seeking to rid itself of many non-forestry interests. It had always run the Potlatch State Bank more as a service to town residents than as a major money maker, and when Idaho First National Bank of Boise expressed an interest in purchasing the institution, company directors responded eagerly. Potlatch insisted that twelve-year cashier George Anderson be retained, and expressed the hope that Idaho First would maintain a branch in Potlatch. The Boise institution agreed to the requests and on May 11, 1940, the Potlatch State Bank, with deposits of over a million dollars, became a unit of Idaho First. While town residents retained local banking services, this sale represented Potlatch's first important step in divesting itself of its company town.[21]

Some company directors, particularly Frederic S. Bell, believed contented workers required a library. The Potlatch library began in 1908 as a public reading room in the basement of the Union Church, primarily serving as a place where the town's many bachelors could spend their leisure time. In 1914 the Union Church's pastor, N. M. Fiske, instigated the idea of a more formal library and immediately received the support of Bell, who contributed both money and books to the newly named Potlatch Free Public Library. For many years the new Union Church housed the facility. At first Reverend Fiske and the town's Catholic priest guided the library, but townswomen soon championed its cause. Mollie Humiston, wife of the lumber company's assistant general manager, was the library board's chairman for over fifteen years. When the Humistons moved from Potlatch in 1932, Alta O'Connell, wife of the new Potlatch unit manager, replaced her, also serving a long tenure. Jessie Metcalf was town librarian for more than a quarter century.

These influential local women, along with Bell, convinced Potlatch officials to contribute monthly stipends to the library. In 1930 the company also provided a building, and the library moved into the frame structure that had served as the community's first hospital.

With the exception of a few difficult years during the Depression, the company gave a monthly donation, allowed rent-free use of the building, and paid the librarian's salary, until it sold the town.

Bell served as a library benefactor until his death, regularly contributing money and books. In 1927 he, Mollie Humiston, and Anna Laird persuaded Mrs. Charles Weyerhaeuser to host a library benefit concert, an event that raised over $1,000. When the company temporarily withdrew library funding in 1932, Mabel Kelley, longtime secretary for the lumber company, acting on behalf of the library, debated with herself for several days before finally asking Bell for help. "If I have presumed too much, please ignore this letter," she hesitantly wrote in outlining the institution's plight. "You did just right when you wrote me about the needs of your library," Bell responded, enclosing a check for $100. When Frederic Bell died, his son Laird took a similar interest, personally matching every dollar raised locally for the library.

A library was not part of the original company design for a contented work force, but Potlatch directors soon saw its benefits and ended up supporting it for nearly forty years. During that time the facility became an integral part of the Potlatch plan.[22]

In a self-contained society devised to provide all life's requirements, a sound body was as important as a sound mind. Baseball was Potlatch's first organized sport. The town fielded a team in 1907 and regularly competed with neighboring communities for many years. Former player Charles Weyerhaeuser encouraged the sport, and the company constructed a fine diamond and grandstand on the flat near the mill. Many small towns enthusiastically supported baseball in those early years of the twentieth century, but Potlatch's affinity for the game always seemed remarkable. By 1913 the community boasted four different teams. When other towns quit playing during bad winter months, Potlatch players simply adapted the game to an indoor gymnasium and played through the storms.

In 1914 American and National League baseball all-stars toured the world promoting their sport. While on a West Coast swing in October, the teams were to compete in Spokane, and Maxwell Williamson, long-time Potlatch patriarch of athletics, requested that they detour south for an additional exhibition at the company town. The result was one of the best-remembered episodes in Potlatch's early history.

The all-stars' manager, wary of playing in such a small community, required a $1,000 guarantee with an option of taking 80 percent of gate receipts, whichever he felt would bring him the greatest revenue. Williamson agreed to the terms and met the teams—with baseball legends Grover Cleveland Alexander and Connie Mack among them—in Spokane, traveling with them in their private railroad cars to Potlatch. When the players pulled into the depot that morning of October 26, the mill was closed, for company officials realized they could not field a work force on such an eventful day. The streets were nearly vacant. The business manager immediately opted for the $1,000 guarantee, confident that such a sleepy village could not produce a sizable audience or large gate receipts.

By game time he realized his mistake. There at the immaculate ball park were new bleachers and grandstands. There, in the middle of the centerfield fence, stood a ninety-foot cedar flagpole, personally selected for this historic occasion by T. P. Jones. And in crushed the fans, people from Potlatch, Palouse, Deary, Bovill, and places in between. "My mouth watered when that [game] went through here," recalled J. S. Starr.

The National League won 12-1 and the satisfied crowd witnessed a small episode of Potlatch history. Gate receipts totaled nearly $3,000. The ball players' loss was Potlatch's gain, for the profits purchased an electric player piano that was used regularly at community dances, a reminder of one town's love of baseball.[23]

Max Williamson had arrived in Potlatch in June 1909 seeking new opportunity, having wearied of tallying lumber at an Iowa mill. He worked as assistant sales manager for the Potlatch Lumber Company, lived on Nob Hill, and remained in town until 1923. Locally he is most remembered, though, for encouraging recreational development in the town. Not only did he arrange a major league baseball game, but he also inspired the formation of the Potlatch Amateur Athletic Club, perhaps the community's most prominent organization. Along with company auditor Fred Gleave, Williamson convinced Allison Laird that the town needed a sporting facility. Laird converted the basement of a combination livery stable/theater into a gymnasium, hired a director, bought wrestling mats, punching bags, and other apparatus, and made the Potlatch gym "one of the most completely equipped in the Inland Empire."[24]

When the gym burned the day after Christmas in 1915, Williamson immediately urged Laird to rebuild. Having seen the benefits of organized recreation, Laird was sympathetic. "The boys and men who belong to the Potlatch Athletic Association have already approached me, asking if something is likely to be done to give them any place where they may exercise and follow with a shower bath," he wrote Thatcher shortly after the fire. "The Athletic Club has been a real live organization. . . . [It] takes the place of what would be an industrial Y.M.C.A. It seems to minister to the want which is resting in the breasts of a good many young men for some taste of club life."[25]

If an athletic facility would appease residents and encourage good workers to stay in town, company directors were all for it. In 1916 they constructed Potlatch's largest frame building, the town gymnasium, a two-story structure eighty-five feet long which cost $15,000. In the view of the Palouse *Republic*, it was "undoubtedly the most comprehensive plant for social and amusement purposes ever built outside the larger cities in the northwest." Besides having a full-sized, maple-floored basketball court, the gym contained lounges and club rooms, an office, showers, and locker space. By the time the facility opened, the Athletic Club, with Williamson as president, had grown to 400 members.[26]

The gym became a significant social center, a place not only for sports but also for plays, dances, card parties, and other gatherings. It even had a reading room. In 1918 the company added some of the finest outdoor tennis courts in the region, and for years Potlatch hosted the Idaho State Tennis Tournament. Though originally intended as a facility for working men, within a few years women actively participated in athletic events, and by the mid-1920s women's evening gym classes were better attended than men's. In 1925 the company authorized remodeling of a second floor room into a women's club room.[27]

Having seen the value of physical fitness, the company hired top quality physical education directors to staff the gym, often from the University of Idaho or Washington State College. It also furnished the facility with modern equipment and encouraged participation in exercise classes, inter-departmental athletic competitions, and town ball clubs. During the early years of the Great Depression it eliminated athletic funds. But by 1937 the company was once again supporting the club, and for a while membership increased. By then, though, times had changed, and the Athletic Club never again was the community force it had been in the teens and twenties. Good roads and automobiles enabled Potlatchers to travel to nearby universities to view athletic contests, and to take recreational outings away from town. Still, the gymnasium remained a prominent community center until the company sold its town, a place where residents gathered for physical fitness and relaxation.[28]

Perhaps no company town entity is more widely known—or misunderstood—than the company store. The term "company store" often conjures negative images characterized by overpriced goods and credit schemes forcing employees into constant debt. Tennessee Ernie Ford fixed this stereotype with his popular 1950s version of "Sixteen Tons":

> Sixteen tons, what do 'ya get?
> Another day older and deeper in debt.
> Saint Peter don't 'ya call me 'cause I can't go,
> I owe my soul to the company store.

Others remember growing angry with Ma as she helplessly confronted the company store clerk about overpriced goods in John Steinbeck's *The Grapes of Wrath*. There were unreputable company stores, just as there were undesirable company towns. But the negative image seems overdrawn in most cases, and certainly was in Potlatch, where low prices prevented anyone from "owing their souls" to the establishment.[29]

The first Potlatch store was a wooden commissary constructed on the flat by T. P. Jones's crew. It dispensed clothes, groceries, patent medicines, and other supplies to construction workers. George W. Marshall managed the commissary, coming to Potlatch after working for Charles Weyerhaeuser in the Pine Tree and Northland Pine companies. Marshall had no previous merchandising experience. Having differed with Deary over store management, he resigned in the spring of 1907 and was replaced by A. A. McDonald, who developed "the Merc" into a million-dollar business.[30]

Within three months of being named manager, McDonald supervised the commissary's move into a new facility, one of the largest store buildings in the Palouse country. The brick structure, 100 by 105 feet, had three full floors of merchandise divided into several departments. Though the departments changed slightly over time, Potlatch residents could always purchase virtually all of their necessities at the Mercantile: groceries, clothing, furniture, drygoods, jewelry, hardware, drugs, shoes, china, glassware, and toys. Eventually the Merc sold farm implements and automobiles. Services, such as cobbling, a fully furnished sewing studio where townswomen could fit and make dresses, and a beauty salon, were also available.[31]

In addition to the store, the Merc's manager supervised a large warehouse, a produce cellar capable of storing enough fruits and vegetables to fill twenty-five railcars, and a 640-acre ranch east of town. The company purchased the ranch in 1908, intending to establish a "model stock farm." Within a year, ranch hands were overseeing the daily slaughtering of cattle, hogs, and chickens, providing the Merc with meat. The farm produced oats, wheat, barley, and hay, and here the company also fed its work horses. For nearly thirty years the Merc received fresh meat from its own farm, but when the ranch began losing money in the 1930s, the company sold it.[32]

Immediately upon assuming control of the store, McDonald embarked upon a personal goal of registering a million dollars in sales annually. To generate that kind of income he needed a broader patronage than Potlatch lumber camp dwellers and town residents, so he began the merchandising campaigns that made the store locally famous. McDonald needed little excuse to hold gigantic "Sales Days," often sponsoring five or six a year. There were spring sales, summer sales, after harvest sales, fall sales, and the annual Christmas sale when Santa Claus arrived on the WI&M and handed out candy and presents to every child stopping by the store. "People like to trade at our store because it is always bright and busy; never dull; never listless or other than thoroughly attractive," McDonald boasted in one of his frequent newspaper advertisements.[33]

Certainly the place was "always busy" on Sales Days when customers might be treated to free lunch, a free dance, free movies, gift drawings, or free stud service from the ranch's prize bulls and stallions. There was always free horse feed, and sheds were provided for people to park their rigs under in bad weather. With those inducements the sales, usually two-day affairs, became major activities anticipated not only by town residents but also by people throughout the Palouse region. McDonald ran multi-page advertisements in area newspapers and tacked posters to crossroad signposts throughout the countryside. The Sales Days frequently drew hundreds of horse teams and at times over 4,000 people to town. Arthur Sundberg remembered how they were:

> Well, this McDonald . . . was a typical P. T. Barnum. . . . He was full of blarney from one end to the other. . . . He'd advertise a big sale. And he advertised it clear from Spokane to Lewiston . . . and, maybe one time he'd say he had free haircuts or maybe the next time it'd be . . . free candy for the kids or something. . . . Well, then the Sale Day come here'd come the people and actually they'd come as far away as Rosalia with horses and buggies and wagons and maybe some of em'd take two, three

days for the trip. . . . The hillside, over here on the north side
of town . . . well, from there clear over—almost to Onaway . . .
that hillside'd be just thick, just full of wagons and teams, tied
out there. And, of course, the town was full of 'em. And the
streets down there—you couldn't drive through for people and
teams and stuff.

And old Mac he'd stand there and his belly'd bounce up and
down and he'd laugh and he'd talk and he'd trade and he'd trade.
He'd swindle some of them people just something terrible, and
oh, they liked it, they just really soaked it up. There was nobody
in the world like Mac![34]

McDonald demanded discipline from Merc employees, requiring
that his clerks strictly follow the regulations he established to please
customers. There were no excuses for tardiness; all shelves, counters,
and show cases had to be dusted daily; customers were to be treated
promptly and with courtesy. Under McDonald's tutelage the Merc's
profits steadily rose, aided with the coming of automobiles. "It was
a case of everybody headed for the big sale at Potlatch," noted the
Palouse *Republic* in 1915. "The extensive use of automobiles broadens
the range of those sales materially and the effect is easily seen in the
increased crowds that attend." By the time he left Potlatch in 1920
to take up ranching in Montana, McDonald had reached his goal
of million-dollar sales years. "Under Mr. McDonald's management,
the Potlatch Mercantile Company store . . . has grown from an ordinary commissary . . . into one of the largest and best appointed
department stores in Idaho," the *Republic* accurately reported.
Acknowledging his good work, the lumber company presented
McDonald with a $500 bonus upon his resignation.[35]

A. W. Douglas replaced McDonald, coming to Potlatch from
Arkansas where he had managed another lumber company store. In
1923 Alec Walsh became manager. He was followed by A. G.
Ferguson, William Thompson, and Milo King. Only Walsh showed
glimpses of McDonald's flamboyance. He reinstituted the Sales Days,
developed the Merc's familiar slogan "Everything to Eat, Wear and
Work With," advertised widely, and staged gimmicks to attract
crowds—such as bringing a "famous artist extraordinary" to Potlatch
for a few days and setting him up on public display in the store's
show window. The other managers, though less flashy, were competent. In fact, the Merc made steady profits, even during the Great
Depression, until it burned in 1963 in one of Potlatch's most spectacular fires. But it lost its stature as a major regional retailer when

the showy Walsh and McDonald left. The automobile and improved roads, while providing a temporary business boon, eventually drew people to more modern stores in Moscow, Pullman, and Lewiston, and the Merc increasingly catered to a Potlatch clientele. It was the last nonlumbering concern in town to be owned by the lumber company. Despite numerous efforts to sell the store, Potlatch could find no buyers, and the Merc was still company-controlled at the time it burned, long after the rest of the town had been sold.[36]

The Merc prospered because it was convenient and well-stocked, with competitive prices. Potlatch employees were never coerced into shopping there. Normally, the store sold for cash only and discouraged credit. This seems to have been done both because company officials believed extending credit was an unsound business practice and because they were sensitive to the criticism about company stores keeping employees in eternal indebtedness. "We firmly believe that a man does his best work when free of credit entanglements," wrote Potlatch unit manager James O'Connell in 1939. During hard times, such as the worst years of the Great Depression, the company did relax its no-credit policy. During some periods it also issued scrip between monthly pay days. This could be used like cash at any Potlatch business, including the Merc, with the amount advanced by the coupons being debited from monthly pay.

Some people did complain about the Merc. An anonymous "Friend of Justice" wrote Rudolph Weyerhaeuser in 1936 that "We citizes [sic] of Potlatch are fed up with this gang of theives [sic] operating under the name of Potlatch Mercantile Company. . . . We poor devils can hardly live the prices at store are awful and if you get behind $15 or so you get a dirty insulting letter from Old Scroge [sic] (Alias) Ferguson . . . so he can show a big profit." Most town residents, though, were proud of their community store. It generally served them well. "The Merc fascinated me," reminisced Ray Harris. "I loved to watch it operate and improve year by year. No wonder one of the town's residents was unimpressed when, on a trip to Chicago, he was shown through Marshall Fields. 'It's just bigger than the Merc,' was his reaction."[37]

Potlatch officials soon realized that even a large company cannot provide everything required for satisfactory community living. So, while the company supplied essentials, it depended on others to offer some services. Though it constructed and furnished the Union and Catholic churches, the congregations were responsible for hiring their own pastors and paying their own bills. They carried on their religious work without interference from the company. Similarly, an independent telephone company provided Potlatch with service and, of course, the community had a federal post office.

Many autonomous merchants operated in Potlatch, generally working from company-owned buildings. At different times Potlatch had such businesses as laundries, a confectionary, pool hall, blacksmith shop, beauty shop, barber shop, creamery, and bakery—all managed by independent enterpreneurs leasing company property. The Potlatch Garage, managed for many years by Felix Stapleton and housed in a brick building near the Merc, was privately run, as was the hotel across the street.[38]

The People's Theater on Pine Street, with a seating capacity of 250, was completed in 1917 after the town's original theater burned. Here local thesbians presented plays and theater managers showed movies. Seeing the need for such entertainment, the company constructed the building but leased the business, allowing theater managers to operate independently. Occasionally company officials interfered if they believed certain shows were unacceptable. In 1940 O'Connell objected to a film entitled *Sin*, particularly because of the way it was advertised in Moscow. "We do not take it upon ourselves to guide the morals of the adults living here, but do have a keen interest in the morals of the younger people," he wrote. "Your ad, appearing in a paper which has a wide circulation in this territory, makes Potlatch appear as though it tolerated shows such as advertised—and that it was too rotten for Moscow, so it would be shown in Potlatch." Defending his action, the theater manager pointed out that "the form of advertisement used is sensational but if you advertise it as a medical picture approved by the board of health . . . not many would come." Nonetheless, he agreed in the future to "try and run the theatre in a manner that will meet with your approval."[39]

Either through services it provided directly, or through leasing businesses, the Potlatch Lumber Company insured that its town was self-contained, having all the essentials necessary for comfortable living. But the company was, after all, in the business of making money from lumbering. In order to relieve its managers of much of the daily detail of running the town, company officials established a townsite department to oversee community activities.

THE TOWNSITE DEPARTMENT

The townsite superintendent surely was one of the busiest people in Potlatch. In 1908, for example, George Morgan, the first superintendent, scheduled meetings in the lodge hall; hired a hotel manager; purchased hospital equipment; watched vacant houses to prevent vandalism; parceled out garden plots; supervised the town constable; decided which residents rented what houses; furnished free lumber to people building chicken coops; and directed workers who repaired broken windows and faulty plumbing, patched leaky roofs, replaced sidewalks, painted and wallpapered houses, and placed monuments on cemetery graves.

Thirty years later, the townsite department was just as active. In that year it remodeled the beauty shop and put a new floor in the Merc; refinished desks at the bank; moved a small school building to a new location; built an addition to the high school; installed furnaces in several houses; poisoned rats; sprayed trees; reconstructed the hotel; painted the exteriors of fifty-seven houses; papered, painted, and calsimined sixty interiors; rebuilt house foundations; replaced a water main and all of the town's window and door screens; and constructed a block and a half of new sidewalk. When people were born they were usually delivered at the Potlatch hospital, maintained by the department. When they died they were buried under markers made at the department's shops, in the cemetery which was also maintained by the department in the days before the community cemetery association was formed. Between birth and death, virtually every other aspect of a Potlatch resident's life was touched in some way by the work of the townsite department.[40]

If a family needed house repairs, they contacted the department, which mended the structure at no charge to tenants. The department also followed a maintenance schedule established for each building so that renters were sometimes surprised by crews arriving unannounced for repairs. "You'd wake up at seven o'clock in the morning and hear a terrible racket," recalled Edgar Renfrew, "and you'd go out and there'd be a bunch of guys shingling your house . . . or somebody'd be painting it and they wouldn't even tell ya' what color they were going to paint it. Just whatever happened to be the next color in the can, why that'd be the color they'd paint your house. On the other hand, your house was always in good repair."[41]

Department workers spent much of their time beautifying the town. While crews maintained public spaces, townsite superintendents expected residents to care for their own surroundings. The department encouraged participation in spring cleanup days, occasionally awarding prizes for the best-kept yards. When such incentives did not bring results, the department took stronger action. "This is to advise you that the yard . . . where you now reside is badly in the need of being cleaned up," superintendent George Hudson wrote a tenant in the early 1950s. "Unless this is done within the next ten days, we will have to ask that you vacate the property."[42]

The department also contracted for garbage disposal, and provided "honey wagon" service for houses with privies. Sundberg recalled Potlatch's special outhouses:

> You take rural living, used to be that they would dig a hole . . . and then they'd build a little building on top of that. . . . And then they'd generally put in a crescent or a star . . . in the door to indicate what it was. . . . [In Potlatch] on the end of the wood-shed . . . was this little privy building. . . . But instead of having a hole in the ground it had a drawer. . . . Well, then they had a contractor that come around . . . and he would empty all these . . . and cart it off. . . . So you see, they were a little bit more modern than the average rural person![43]

The townsite department also enforced rules prohibiting "indiscriminate spitting on the floors and baseboards" of the opera house; encouraged residents to keep dogs in their yards; and tried to minimize late-night street noise.[44]

In addition to making repairs and keeping the community neat, the townsite department supervised many essential services. In the early days employees delivered ice to residents by horse and wagon. They also graded streets, but despite their best efforts were seldom able to keep ahead of the mud. The department maintained the lines providing running water and the wires bringing electricity to each house, as well as the pipes conveying steam generated at the the the mill to heat some Nob Hill residences and downtown buildings.[45]

To accomplish its numerous tasks, the company granted the department a sizable budget. But from the beginning, Potlatch officials hoped its town would generate at least minimal profits from rents. Company directors often publicly stated that the town made no money, as if to imply that they wanted to provide workers with a healthy social atmosphere regardless of cost. The statements were erroneous. While the company did want an ideal community, its shareholders were unwilling to sacrifice profits for idealism. Rents were generally low and service good, but company stockholders fully expected – and received – a reasonable return on their investment in a company town.

George Morgan did his best to keep all houses rented and performed his numerous tasks with the smallest crew possible, maximizing profits and setting a pattern his successors would follow. Townsite budgets are unavailable for the company's early years, but existing records show that even during the Great Depression of the 1930s the department showed profits. In 1931 revenues exceeded expenses by $45,000, and during the department's worst year in 1934 profits were still nearly $28,000. These gradually rose to $54,000 in 1942. In 1946, when some company directors requested a study determining the advantages and disadvantages of moving from Potlatch and concentrating sawmill activities in Coeur d'Alene and Lewiston, general manager Charles Billings pointed out that Potlatch divestiture would cost nearly $90,000 a year in profits from the townsite and Mercantile alone. It was a persuasive argument, and the company decided to retain its Potlatch facility.[46]

Shortly after Billings's report, though, townsite profits began a steady decline. By 1949 revenues exceeded expenses by only $15,000. Post-war increases in labor costs and the deterioration of frame buildings that were approaching fifty years of age combined to cut profits. Even though the company substantially raised rents in 1947, the slippage continued. The trend was clear. Within a few years the townsite would cost more than it made, and company officials began laying plans for selling its community.[47]

The great social experiment was coming to an end. It was not a victim of failure, for the company had demonstrated that it could retain a contented work force, one that toiled diligently with little labor strife. Rather, the experiment expired because it could no longer pay for itself. When launched with so much idealism in 1905, the town was a significant component of the operation known as the Potlatch Lumber Company. By the 1950s, both the town and mill were playing progressively smaller roles in the total operations of the larger company then called Potlatch Forests, Incorporated. Of course, even the company's original directors had wanted to make money from the town. But they might have been more tolerant if these profits dwindled, for they believed there was intrinsic value in providing comfortable accommodations for employees. By the 1950s, a younger generation then in control of company destinies had lost much of this vision. Rather than looking with affectionate pride upon one of the West's largest company towns, these officials increasingly viewed it as an anomaly. Important company decisions were no longer made in Potlatch, and owning a town was acceptable only if the arrangement proved cost effective. It was a frill easily disposed of when profits waned. By mid-century, the days of the company town were limited as Potlatch officials began seeking the best way to rid themselves of an unwanted burden.

When H. W. Wilkinson—the mill designer's son—took this photo of Potlatch in April 1906, permanent residents were already living in the town, the depot was completed, and a temporary village of tents and boardinghouses stood close to the mill construction site. *(LCHS #12-1-2)*

For nearly eighty years, until it was dismantled in the 1980s, the huge Potlatch sawmill dominated the landscape at the company's town. *(LCHS #12-3-19)*

A Washington, Idaho and Montana Railway train steams past the mill's acres of drying lumber stacks on its way to Palouse. *(Courtesy Lee Gale)*

This photograph of the largest log train in the world was staged as a publicity gim-
mick, but slightly shorter versions rolled into the Potlatch plant regularly, delivering
logs felled by Potlatch lumber crews to the mill's log pond. *(LCHS #25-3-22)*

The Averill sawmill at Elberton, Washington Territory, was one of the earliest in the Palouse region. It was typical of many small-scale lumbering concerns that were driven out of business by the arrival of the Potlatch Lumber Company. *(Courtesy Roy Chatters)*

In 1911 the company opened another mill in the heart of its timberlands, and constructed the town of Elk River for its mill workers. The community was served by the St. Paul, Chicago and Milwaukee Railroad. *(Courtesy Lee Gale)*

The Elk River sawmill was electrically driven, and was one of the country's most sophisticated mills when constructed. But because of harsh winters in the area, the plant was an economic disaster from the start. It was permanently closed during the Great Depression. *(Courtesy Lee Gale)*

Several towns grew up along the route of the Washington, Idaho and Montana Railway in Latah County. Potlatch company directors named this one Deary, after their general manager. *(LCHS #4-1-1)*

The company purchased the site of Hugh and Charlotte Bovill's sportsman's hotel and made it the terminus of the Washington, Idaho and Montana Railway. A thriving community, Bovill, arose there, catering to the area's lumber workers. *(LCHS #2-2-2)*

Prior to the construction of the Washington, Idaho and Montana Railway, all logs cut in Idaho were carried to mills via the Palouse region's waterways. This scene of Palouse shows the Palouse River covered with logs waiting to be manufactured in one of the community's mills. *(Courtesy Roy Chatters)*

Allison Laird meets with company patriarchs Frederick Weyerhaeuser and P. M. Musser at a Potlatch lumber camp. *(Courtesy Allison Decker)*

Frederick Weyerhaeuser's oldest son, Charles, served as president of the Potlatch Lumber Company from its founding until his death in 1930. Underrated as a corporate executive, he was an aggressive and visionary leader of the timber family's concerns. *(Courtesy Weyerhaeuser Company Archives)*

Frederic Somers Bell spearheaded the Laird-Norton families' move to the West. He was the first secretary of the Potlatch Lumber Company, and president and first chairman of the board of the Weyerhaeuser Timber Company. Bell and his son, Laird, were largely responsible for building Potlatch's library. *(Courtesy Weyerhaeuser Company Archives)*

Walter D. Humiston came to Potlatch in 1907 as the company's land agent. He later advanced to assistant general manager, and oversaw Potlatch's innovative early efforts in forest products research. *(Courtesy Florence Woods)*

Hard-working William Deary, Potlatch's first general manager, was the person most responsible for shaping the lumber company's development. *(LCHS Individual file "D")*

Matthew G. Norton, one of the three founders of the Laird-Norton Company. *(Courtesy Weyerhaeuser Company Archives)*

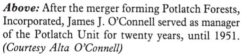

Above: After the merger forming Potlatch Forests, Incorporated, James J. O'Connell served as manager of the Potlatch Unit for twenty years, until 1951. *(Courtesy Alta O'Connell)*
Right: William Helmer was Potlatch's chief timber cruiser for many years. The town of Helmer in Latah County is named for him. *(LCHS Individual file "H")*
Below: Long-time company clerk Mabel Kelley helps train new clerk Louise Nygaard in 1950. *(Courtesy Louise Nygaard Rosenholz)*

Potlatch Lumber Company loggers, circa 1906. *(LCHS #25-3-47)*

Potlatch Lumber Company horse logging crew. *(LCHS #25-3-41)*

This steam engine is transporting logs from the woods prior to their transport by train to the mill. *(Courtesy Lee Gale)*

Logging crew gathered at Potlatch's Camp 6, one of the company's numerous logging camps in northern Idaho's woods. *(LCHS #25-3-77)*

Preparing for meal time at a Potlatch Lumber Company logging camp. *(LCHS #25-3-79)*

Log pond workers from left to right: Henry Panky, unknown, Charles Rambo, unknown, Floyd Layton, Harvey Shaffer, and George Bird, seated. They are shown here maneuvering logs to the bull chain, which carried the logs into the mill, 1909. *(Courtesy Pearl Shaffer)*

The mill's gang saw, with over four dozen parallel blades, could quickly reduce a log to a pile of boards. *(Courtesy Lee Gale)*

Greenchain workers. *(Courtesy Potlatch Corporation)*

The headrig sawyer—assisted by a dogger and setter who rode the carriage—had one of the mill's most responsible and highest paying positions. *(Courtesy Lee Gale)*

Some of the plant's most skilled and highly paid laborers worked in the saw filing room on the third floor of the mill. *(LCHS #12-3-32)*

Small, electric battery-powered locomotives transported lumber over miles of tracking at the Potlatch mill. *(LCHS #12-3-77)*

Washington, Idaho and Montana Railway engine No. 1, pulling passenger cars, stands in front of the Potlatch depot. *(LCHS #12-3-1)*

Potlatch Lumber Company shay engine. *(Courtesy Lee Gale)*

Finished lumber stacked and ready for shipment from the mill. *(LCHS #12-3-42)*

These workers are posing in front of some of the Potlatch mill's 150,000 feet of high quality white pine airplane stock produced for the American war effort during World War I. *(Courtesy Lee Gale)*

With most former employees either off to war or to higher paying defense industry jobs on the West Coast, the company hired its first women mill workers during World War I. After the war, men returned to their jobs and women were not again hired for mill work until World War II. *(Courtesy Lee Gale)*

Although the threat from Wobblies was more imagined than real, Potlatch—like many other Idaho towns—formed a Home Guard during World War I to help protect the community from subversives. *(Courtesy Lee Gale)*

Dressed up for the camera, a group of unidentified Potlatch residents pose in front of one of the working-class houses. *(Courtesy Lee Gale)*

Company directors considered a good school essential for the town. Teachers and pupils posed in front of this temporary building in 1906, prior to construction of Potlatch's first permanent school building. *(LCHS #12-6-1)*

Anna and Allison Laird in 1911. First as assistant general manager, and then as general manager of the company, Laird oversaw the construction of the town, and supervised community activities. *(Courtesy Allison Decker)*

Union Church, Potlatch

The Potlatch Union Church served numerous Protestant denominations. It was also a popular town meeting place, and hosted school graduation ceremonies. The building burned in the 1950s. *(Courtesy Kathryn Vowell Fader)*

The Potlatch town band. *(Courtesy Lee Gale)*

Potlatch High School girls' basketball team, 1924-25: G. Arneson, Lucetta Lindsay, Elaine Horning, Marie Cunningham, Lena Cunningham. *(Courtesy Lucetta Marr)*

No activity in the early history of the town unified the community more than baseball, and for many years the town had several teams. *(Courtesy Lee Gale)*

Mollie Humiston, shown here with her son, Julian, *(middle)* and Don and Ed Thompson, was the town's leading civic organizer. Among her many community endeavors was service with the Red Cross. *(Courtesy Josephine Thompson Cox)*

Elmer Coffman, Almeda Cone, Felix Stapleton, and Eileen Puckett inside the Stapleton Motors showroom, circa 1939. *(Courtesy F. J. Stapleton)*

Charlotte Cada, Eleanor Larkin, and Violet Cada pose with an unidentified man inside the Potlatch Mercantile. *(Courtesy Eleanor and Jack Larkin)*

The Potlatch Mercantile catered to more than just townspeople. For example, it had a separate building that sold implements to nearby farmers. *(Courtesy Pearl Hanson)*

The Potlatch Mercantile, the company-owned store, was one of the largest in the Palouse region. Its competitively priced merchandise and frequent, well-advertised sales drew customers from a wide area. *(Courtesy Pearl Hanson)*

In 1921 the company transported two large boulders to the front of the gymnasium and fitted them with a bronze plaque memorializing William Deary, first general manager. *(LCHS #12-9-11)*

The company constructed this building in 1917 to serve as its main administrative headquarters. When the town was sold in the 1950s, it became city hall. *(Courtesy Potlatch Corporation)*

This Nob Hill house was constructed at a cost of $3,746 and was for many years the home of Walter and Mollie Humiston. When this photograph was taken, Arlie Decker, Allison Laird's son-in-law, lived there. The Humistons later moved into the former Deary house next door. *(Courtesy Allison Decker)*

The living and dining rooms of Potlatch's largest management house, as it appeared in the mid-1920s. At the time of this photograph this was the home of Walter and Mollie Humiston, although it had been constructed at a cost of over $6,000 for William Deary's family. *(Courtesy Julian Humiston)*

A house in the working-class neighborhood. *(Courtesy Lee Gale)*

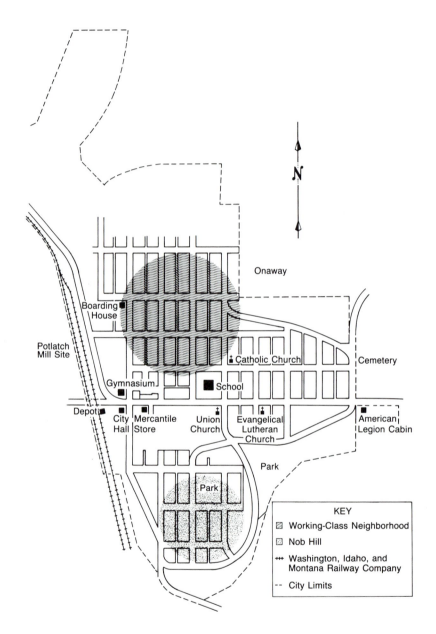

N

Onaway

Boarding
House

Potlatch
Mill Site

Catholic Church

Cemetery

Gymnasium

School

Depot

City
Hall

Mercantile
Store

Union
Church

Evangelical
Lutheran
Church

American
Legion Cabin

Park

Park

KEY

▨ Working-Class Neighborhood

▧ Nob Hill

+++ Washington, Idaho, and
Montana Railway Company

-- City Limits

Potlatch, Idaho, is situated on two hills overlooking the former site of the Potlatch
mill. The south hill—Nob Hill—was reserved for managers; it was quieter and away
from prevailing winds that carried mill smoke over the town. Workers lived on the
north hill, closer to the mill. Preparing to divest itself of Potlatch and in order to
beautify the community, the company added two curving streets on the town's eastern
boundary in the 1950s.

Life in a Company Town

A DIVERSITY OF LIFESTYLES

"Life in Potlatch was different," noted Ray Harris, who knew the place well. The town kept time to the rhythm of the mill, waking with the morning march of workingmen to the plant; taking noon lunch when the sawmill paused at mid-day; preparing for evening activities at the night whistle when sometimes, if the plant operated at full capacity, the homeward-bound day shift walking up the hill met the plant-bound swing shift going down. Potlatch residents slept in company houses, attended company schools, walked on company sidewalks, kept company yards, shopped in the company store. This was not Moscow or Palouse or Garfield. Life here was different for everyone who lived it. Yet there was diversity within the community. How one lived depended upon nationality, age, sex, income, marital status, and house location.[1]

The largest houses on Nob Hill equaled most of the better residences in surrounding communities. Though Nob Hill residents did not own their homes, they lived as comfortably as anyone in the region and better than most. Houses here, with their steam heat, indoor toilets, handsome woodwork, built-in cabinets, and running water, bordering an immaculate park, were an attraction, and most south hill residents, drawing good pay and living well, stayed many years. Certainly life for the managers was not without stress, as they were under considerable pressure to increase mill production and profits. But on this hill, with its commanding view of the plant and countryside beyond, the household problems were different from those of other residents. One of Allison Laird's greatest domestic concerns was his inability to find a live-in servant at reasonable cost, a situation causing his wife Anna to continually be "pretty well tired out." He wrote Frederic Bell of his frustrations: "It is hard to get a girl. The Dearys pay $35-$40 a month for one and as the Lairds are *supposed* to be as rich, they ought to do as much and that, fact or fiction, makes it harder than ever for us as we cannot afford the luxury of those wages."[2]

Servants were seldom on the minds of bachelors residing in boardinghouses with their small shared rooms, taking meals while sitting on stools around community tables, eating off plain white graniteware. Here the major concern was not comfort but making the most money possible and moving on to a better place. Few stayed in Potlatch for any length of time.

Between these extremes were the families living in north hill houses. Here the quality of life depended largely upon how far up the hill a family lived, the more desirable houses generally being near the crest. There was regular turnover on the lower streets, many people moving from town within a few months or years after arrival. Others, such as John and Anna Scott and Fred and Gladys Schnurr, spent decades in Potlatch, first taking whatever housing was available low on the hill and gradually progressing up to more desirable accommodations.[3]

During prosperous times, up-hill progression proved difficult. Housing did not open up, as people stayed in town to take advantage of steady work. In some of these years—particularly 1910, 1916, and 1923—the company erected additional cottages to house the overflow. At other times company managers allowed workers to construct shacks on the town's fringes. Though such privately owned structures were not officially approved, the managers unofficially permitted this ramshackle housing during peak periods to insure an adequate work force. These shacks, however, could hardly pass as desirable privately owned dwellings, and one of the leading causes of Potlatch transiency was the unwillingness of many residents to live in houses they did not own.[4]

In fact, one of the major characteristics distinguishing Potlatch from its neighbors was the impermanence of its population. True, many people moved in and out of nearby "stable" towns more often than is generally accepted, and just as surely Potlatch, like more traditional communities, had families who remained for generations. Still, Potlatch's population was more impermanent than most towns of similar size, particularly during its first years. "We were a town of young men who came to seek [our] fortunes and learn the lumber business in a hurry, and [we] . . . didn't last long," recalled William Maxwell. "Most of the ordinary laborers and the clerical type stayed two or three or four months and then were gone." In 1909 townsite superintendent George Morgan notified William Deary that "there have been a great many removals . . . but fortunately people have come in equally as fast and I have been able to fill the vacated houses as quickly as we could get them in shape." Though most pronounced early, transiency was always a Potlatch trait. Men "just come in, shift in, and then out they'd go again, after being here awhile," remembered one long-time resident.[5]

A variety of factors fed the transiency. Many of Potlatch's bachelors were typical lumber trade drifters who seldom spent much time at any one place. Others were frustrated with poor housing and an inability to move up to better, so left the community. Some disliked Potlatch's working conditions, while others moved on when work was slow. Many wanted to own their own homes. And some left because they were uncomfortable with Potlatch's social stratification.

"There was very little class distinction. Everybody got along, and practically everyone was known by his first name," stated A. N. Frederickson. This was true to some extent. Potlatch did not have the tremendous gulf between very wealthy and very poor that existed in cities or even in some nearby communities. Some of the mill's skilled laborers earned more than the lower echelon company officials who directed them, which blurred class distinctions. Most Potlatch stockholders, some of whom were wealthy, lived elsewhere, and their representatives, people like Deary, Laird, and O'Connell, were known by everyone, and on a first name basis with many.[6]

Still, social distinctions persisted. Japanese, Italians, and Greeks seldom mixed with the rest of the community, and other residents rarely entered their part of town. Ray Harris was one who did travel there, on a milk route that took him through all parts of Potlatch. He remembered these ethnic enclaves as being distinctive, the people somewhat exotic, and the Japanese especially as "appreciative of any courtesy or recognition we natives showed them." This area was "sort of a ghetto" as Malcolm Renfrew recalled it, life here bearing little resemblance to that in other parts of town. But there was also stratification among the "white" ethnic groups. Many Norwegians and Swedes kept to themselves and attended native-language services and social functions in the Lutheran Church. "I don't think I ever knew a Lutheran," Renfrew noted. Oftentimes even members of the same religion did not mix. "They've had a Catholic Church here . . . ever since the town started," noted Arthur Sundberg. "And you take all these Italians, . . . you'd never see one of 'em go to the Catholic Church . . . because these other snooty women that went to church there . . . didn't want to mingle with 'em." Hostilities among ethnic groups were infrequent, though. "The one thing that stands out to me about Potlatch probably as much as anything else, was the Duke's mixture of so many nationalities living, working, and schooling with so few problems among them," wrote Charles Talbott, Jr. Although Potlatch's was not a heavy-handed oppression, those on its lower social rungs knew a division existed between classes.[7]

Everyone recognized Nob Hill as the town's elite section and most other residents kept away. This reinforced a segregation between blue and white collar employees. Some women's clubs were composed entirely of Nob Hill wives, and the town's managers at times held social functions without inviting other community members.[8]

Residents of the north hill's more desirable streets, like their Nob Hill counterparts, usually were quite stable. Because they were old-timers with well-paying jobs and lived in large houses, they were almost equal in stature to Nob Hillers. Company managers worked the reins of this social honor, rewarding good workers with better housing when it became available, thereby minimizing turnover among desirable employees.

Potlatch had many more bachelors than most neighboring towns, and they comprised a distinct subgroup. Much of Potlatch's social life, which revolved around school activities and women's clubs, excluded bachelors. Aside from interaction with workers at the plant, these men, unless they sublet space from a family, lived and kept to themselves, spending most of their time in Potlatch unknown by others living uptown.

Though not an egalitarian utopia, Potlatch had equalizers. "Children in school took part in everything without any painful social distinctions," recalled one resident, and the Amateur Athletic Club gymnasium served all sexes, classes, and age groups. Here Italian boys might box with management children; bachelors might visit in the lounge with married people; Nob Hill women might exercise next to someone from the north hill; and everyone could participate in the frequent community dances.[9]

Several other things about Potlatch distinguished it from similar-sized communities. Although male-dominated work forces prevailed throughout America in the first half of the twentieth century, in Potlatch household incomes were almost exclusively earned by men. Women and children only rarely worked outside the home, since there was little opportunity for them in the mill, and the town had few other employers. Some women worked at the Merc and on the company clerical staff. Some single women taught. A few Japanese women took in laundry. A very few women were nurses, maids, boardinghouse cooks and waitresses, or post office workers. Some supplemented family income by subletting rooms to bachelors. Potlatch's women, though, were primarily childraisers and housekeepers. Because few worked outside the home, and a good number on Nob Hill retained servants and thus had leisure time, the town had an active women's social and civic network. The community was always receptive to charity drives, largely because many of its women had the time and interest to organize fundraisers. Many aspects of the ideal working environment company officials sought were possible only because the town had a large number of women with the time to coordinate community activities and improvements.

Although it was a town largely populated by single-income families, Potlatchers fared quite well economically in comparison to their neighbors. Renting was cheaper than owning a home, and utilities were considerably less in Potlatch than in surrounding areas. Goods purchased at the Merc were competitive with, and often less expensive than, those sold at other stores, and there were few frivolities for a person to squander wages upon. As a result, a considerable percentage of townspeople saved money or sent regular payments to family members left behind in the old country.[10]

Another characteristic distinguished Potlatch as much as anything from surrounding towns: with the exception of parents living with their children, there were few old people or widows there. If a man died or became too ill or disabled to work, the family was asked to leave in order to open up housing for employees. Similarly, the company forced retirees to leave. Management was not uncaring and provided as much time as possible for people to vacate. During slack times at the mill, when there was little demand for housing, nonemployees might actually stay in town for several years. Still, this was never a permanent arrangement. "The housing situation in Potlatch has finally reached the stage where we are unable to take care of the key men employed here," wrote Potlatch manager James O'Connell in 1937 to a family that had lived in town for several years during the Depression even though it was no longer affiliated with the company. "I have put off as long as I possibly could, the unpleasant duty of asking those not employed by the company . . . to vacate to make room for those we feel are entitled to first consideration." Despite the company's general understanding, these evictions were often traumatic, especially for long-time Potlatch residents forced to retire in a new community, away from familiar surroundings and old friends.[11]

The company's tight control over the community prevented much of the crime frequently associated with lumber centers. Potlatch experienced a few fights, especially in the Greek and Italian sections, and even a rare murder, such as the death of Jim Makaia in 1911 after a severe beating. The town doctor was stabbed by a deranged patient in the 1920s, and a Japanese janitor was brutally beaten in the 1930s. These violent acts, however, were exceptional. There were also occasional disruptions to the moral atmosphere the company attempted to maintain. At one time a teacher developed a romantic fondness for a high school senior whom she later married, but not before she was forced to leave town. At another time a bachelor fathered the child of a high school student and was similarly expelled. All in all, though, life in Potlatch was secure, consistent, and safe—sometimes in contrast to neighboring communities. "We don't really have much scandal to remember," noted Edgar Renfrew. "It was a pretty decent town. . . . [The company] set standards for the town. If there was somebody came . . . that they didn't like, the guy didn't have a job, he didn't have a house to live in, and he didn't have credit at the store. Therefore, it was a pretty select group in the town. It was a pretty highly structured society. . . . It was unlike any other town that I have ever heard of."[12]

Some aspects of Potlatch life were similar to those in any village. This was, after all, a small town, and its people entertained themselves in ways common to all such places, with a familiarity unique to small communities. "I remember one time I called the operator," a resident reminisced. "I gave her the Garber number and the operator says, 'Well, alright, I'll ring it, but Helen is over at the Gambles.' I said, 'Well, alright, ring Gambles.'" Alta O'Connell remembered that town functions usually featured a room full of women all wearing the same hair style, for everyone went to the same beauty shop. In winter the air filled with the shouts of children sledding or riding bobsleds down the steep slope from the reservoir to downtown. Or adults might hear the laughter of kids ice skating or playing hockey or crack-the-whip on the Palouse River. In summer these same youngsters, like children everywhere, searched out their favorite swimming and fishing holes. Overall, though, living in Potlatch was considerably different from residing in most small towns. It was a lifestyle good for some and not so good for others. The difference was largely dependent upon a person's nationality, income, and marital status.[13]

SOCIAL ACTIVITIES

Seen from Allison Laird's perspective, requirements for Potlatch residency were simple: cleanliness, neatness, orderliness, and keeping rent, utility, and Merc bills paid. The company periodically issued rules and regulations and residents who disobeyed were evicted. Most dictums required neat houses and yards or prohibited alcohol, but there were other regulations as well. If children misbehaved frequently, parents were threatened with dismissal—a rule "applied more rigorously to the millworkers than to the children of the managers," recalled Malcolm Renfrew. Another rule prohibited prostitution. Though "a carfull of ladies from Spokane" might on occasion spend the weekend in Potlatch with the company looking the other way to appease single employees, prostitution threatening to enter the more respectable parts of town was strictly taboo. As a 1910 visitor observed: "No women of questionable character are allowed at the hotel and should a waitress or chambermaid show signs of departing from the path of virtue she is at once discharged and has no recourse but to leave town."[14]

Management edicts pertaining to cleanliness and health were common. The company regularly asked for assistance in keeping trash and rubbish picked up. The townsite department periodically conducted mass poisonings of rats and earwigs. The "honey wagon" regularly cleaned outhouses. Despite these efforts, Potlatch was not the most sanitary of towns. In the days when house sewage simply drained outside and ran freely, it was often something of an adventure to walk down alleyways or through yards, especially those on downhill slopes. "You would have to tiptoe your way," recalled Edgar Renfrew. Lew Young moved his family out of town from their Cedar Street house to escape the constant presence of yard sewage.[15]

Occasionally diseases proliferated, some epidemics no doubt resulting from the lack of sanitation. Scarlet fever and diptheria plagued the community in its early years, and jaundice was widespread in the late 1920s. Not infrequently, red flags and posters appeared on Potlatch houses marking quarantined residences. The biggest scare occurred in 1907 when health officials detected smallpox in Potlatch, Onaway, and Princeton. Schools closed, public gatherings were suspended, and several houses were isolated. Laird fumed when he discovered that a family suspected of smallpox was mingling with neighbors. "Numerous complaints are coming in that no kind of quarantine is being enforced against the Smiths, who have the smallpox," he wrote the town constable. "It is also claimed that one of their neighbors in that row of houses . . . also has the smallpox but are not quarantined. We know positively that people are going in and out of these houses and that the children are playing in the yard and on the street. We shall expect you to use your position as an officer of the Law to enforce a strict quarantine."[16]

Most of the time, however, company managers not only permitted but encouraged public gatherings, and Potlatch had a diverse array of civic and social organizations. The list of clubs, in fact, was so lengthy that it seems unlikely anyone could have gone without joining something had they the desire to do so.

The town's earliest clubs spun off its three churches— groups like the Swedish Ladies' Missionary Society, Ladies of the Union Church, Catholic Church Altar Society, and Christian Endeavor. Then in late 1906 residents established a local lodge of the Royal Neighbors of America, giving parties and sponsoring dances and community events. Numerous other locals of national fraternal organizations followed: Odd Fellows, Modern Woodmen of America, the Scandinavian Lodge, Elks, Masons, Ladies of Eastern Star, Rebekahs, Neighbors of Woodcraft, Moose, and, after World War I, the American Legion and Legion Auxiliary. The Legion Cabin, built on the east edge of town in the late 1920s as a memorial to Potlatch men who died in World War I, was a large log structure built of timbers donated by the company and hand-hewn by skilled volunteer axmen. When completed, it became nearly as important as the gymnasium as a place of social gatherings. With the exception of the Legion, lodges met in the hall above the bank on Sixth Street, renting space from the company at a nominal fee. With so many active organizations, one of the townsite department's most pressing tasks was maintaining a meeting calendar to avoid room conflicts.[17]

Other national organizations were also popular. The Loyal Legion of Loggers and Lumbermen was stronger as a social organization than as a workers' bargaining force in a town run by a company philosophically opposed to unionization. A Ladies Loyal Legion was also present. The Red Cross gained strength in the period around World War I by recruiting clothes, food, and money for American servicemen and needy Europeans. Camp Fire Girls and Boy Scouts were popular, the latter being especially encouraged by the company, which donated a large piece of land east of Potlatch for a regional Scout camp in 1938.[18]

Many groups formed out of specific local needs. The Polida Club served to attract women teachers and gave public presentations of plays and performances. The Card Club met in the lodge hall, gym, and people's houses to play bridge and pinochle. The Umbeewee and Bachelor Girls of Potlatch clubs gained popularity by hosting progressive dinners. The Potlatch Mothers' Club, organized in 1927 to "give mothers the help they need in teaching children the best use of their minds," was one of the town's longest-lasting groups. The Stitch and Chatter Club, Neighborhood Birthday Club, Royal Banner Club, Zipper Club, Mistletoe Lodge, and Linger Longer Club were among the groups providing various entertainments for women, while the Gun Club, Craftsmen's Club, Potlatch Golf Club, Men's Glee Club, and the town band—active in Potlatch's earliest days with several concerts a year—appealed mostly to men.[19]

During the day, while the plant's machinery whined in activity down the hill, many Potlatch women participated in an intricate social network. They might attend club meetings, sew for the Red Cross, play cards, or host luncheons, such as the "progressive 500 party" given by Mrs. John D. Morrissey in 1914, her home being "profusely decorated in nasturtiums and roses." In fact, such entertaining often took the form of social obligation, as Elsie Renfrew recalled: "They had bridge parties, and I hated to play bridge, but that was part of living in Potlatch. You had to do your share of entertaining."[20]

In the evenings Potlatch came alive for both men and women, especially on Friday and Saturday. Some activities were small—dinners with friends; cards in the boardinghouses; serenading by the Union Church choir. Others were community-wide events, with dances being especially popular. In the early days dances were held in the opera house, but they later shifted to the gym or the American Legion cabin.

Entertainers traveling the Inland Northwest, such as the Williams Colored Jubilee Singers who gave concerts of "first class plantation songs and melodies," added Potlatch to their itinerary, for the town soon earned a reputation as a community of "goers." In 1908 George Morgan described the opera house facilities and its popularity to one entertainer:

> The hall is used nearly every night in the week. . . . We are sorry to say that both [December 11 and 12] are taken, and there are no two nights open in succession.
>
> We have a good large stage, piano and plenty of seats that can be arranged so you can have reserved seats. The seating capacity

> . . . is about 600 and the population of the town is from 1200
> to 1400. Good shows usually draw a good crowd.

Performers from the two nearby universities and area towns—especially Palouse—also frequently played Potlatch. Lecturers and politicians made regular stops, such as the 1910 campaign appearance by Governor James Brady, when crowds filled the opera house to its doors and "men of political experience . . . state[d] that they had never attended a political meeting that equaled it in enthusiasm." Former company attorney William Borah frequently launched his campaigns at Potlatch during his thirty-four years in the United States Senate.[21]

Local talent provided much of the community's entertainment. Grade and high school students held regular programs; young musicians gave recitals. Townspeople presented talent shows, comic operas, and plays. Community-wide banquets were popular. One of the first, held in September 1907, celebrated the first anniversary of the mill's opening and became an annual event during Potlatch's early history. High school athletic contests—particularly basketball—also brought the community together. An especially strong team, such as the 1925 unit with 5'3" star Phil McGreal, not only had home support but developed a following for away games unusual in the days before good roads. When the team played the state tournament in Moscow that year, Potlatch's principal arranged for a car to transport student spectators. The fans demonstrated their loyalty by patching thirteen flat tires before wearily arriving at the game site.[22]

In the 1930s many community functions shifted to the Riverside pavilion a few miles out of town. In addition to dances, families might rollerskate or attend special all-day summer events hosted by local organizations. These often featured rodeos, races, speeches, ball games, and a host of other entertainments for all ages.

In the early days when the mill closed only on Sundays, weekend activities centered around the churches. Later, when workers had both Saturdays and Sundays free, other social events gained in popularity. Potlatch residents might take part in community swim meets or golf and tennis tournaments sponsored by the Athletic Club. Or they could join friends at Riverside or picnic at the pine grove. Young people often gathered at the upper mill pond for parties. In the 1910s, a photo of the pond was attached to a card with the following message, and sent to many in the town:

In this picture you will see,
the spot we love the most.
The general line of fun will be
a big marshmallow roast.

A company-wide picnic was for decades an annual summer highlight.
Sometimes these were held at the Palouse city park; at other times
at nearby Laird Park. Often, though, the company planned more
elaborate outings, encouraging mill and woods workers to mingle.
In 1927 and 1930 Helmer hosted the picnic. All Potlatch operations
closed, and special WI&M trains transported workers and families
to the small town for a day of baseball and feasting and an evening
of dancing. Over a thousand people attended in 1930. In later years
the company generally held the picnic on Labor Day and sponsored
bingo, pie-eating contests, softball, races, horseshoe pitching, and
other games, with winners receiving prizes from the Merc.[23]

Holidays were special times of gathering, and in a town as socially
active as Potlatch almost any holiday served as an excuse for celebrating. There might be masquerade parties on Halloween, costume
balls on St. Patrick's Day, a "barn dance" with a turkey prize at
Thanksgiving, or American Legion ceremonies on Memorial Day.
The town's special holidays, though, were July 4th and Christmas.

The mill generally closed on July 4th, sometimes for two days,
and the Athletic Club sponsored activities that drew not only
townspeople, but also residents from neighboring communities. There
was nearly always a dance or two, as well as a couple of baseball games,
with the Potlatch team crossing bats with players from nearby towns.
Usually there were picnics, speeches, contests and, of course, fireworks, which proved quite impressive to the town's younger residents.
Gordon Gleave remembered when his uncle let him light the town
fireworks one special year: "Imagine, at my young age, being in on
the pleasant task of setting off a hundred or more large Roman candles,
sky rockets, pinwheels."[24]

Christmas was a time not only for community gatherings but also
for merchandising, and the Mercantile's more aggressive managers—
particularly A. A. McDonald— never missed an opportunity to make
this the year's biggest holiday. Santa Claus usually arrived on the
WI&M a few days before Christmas. He was met at the depot, and
then marched through town blowing his horn, calling all children
to follow him to the Merc where he gave away bags of nuts and candy.
At other times he delivered the candy door-to-door, somehow knowing

just which residences housed youngsters. No matter how the treats were distributed, McDonald made sure the young people knew the Merc had lured Santa to Potlatch, and the store held its grandest sale of the year when the old man was in town. The school sponsored Christmas pageants and traditionally there was a community Christmas tree, brilliantly lighted, in front of the gym. Potlatch often had an outdoor evening musical program and caroling, and in later years the company hosted a large bonfire on the ballfield, with singing and visiting. During hard times, some of the town's more affluent people distributed Christmas baskets to needy residents.

A vital social life was an important aspect of the company's desire to make Potlatch an ideal community. If there was a gap between social activities, the company moved to fill it, encouraging the Athletic Club and its many functions, hosting company picnics, or lining up baseball games. Generally, though, the company left social affairs to the town's many clubs, churches, and organizations. "Socially Potlatch is all right," Drew Musser assured Charles Weyerhaeuser in 1907. "Last week there was a banquet and a dance and this week there is a play and a masquerade. The more I see of things here the better I am pleased."[25]

Social activities might range from having ice cream or a soda with friends at the Confectionary after school, to playing billiards in the pool hall after work, to visiting neighbors, to attending a gala community-wide event. Throughout its history as a company town Potlatch was a social place. There were groups to join and activities to attend. Some of the clubs were snobbish. It is hard to imagine a transient Greek laborer participating with Allison Laird and other members of the Potlatch Golf Club in the general manager's favorite sport. Nonetheless, activities, both formal and informal, organized and spontaneous, were many and diverse, and there was generally something for everyone.

"THINGS . . . CHANGED SO"

Potlatch survived nearly fifty years as a company town, and each year brought changes. The type of life people led depended as much upon when they lived there as upon the social class they belonged to.

As a new town in a lightly populated region, things in Potlatch during its early years were rustic. "Life here is somewhat crude and will be for awhile yet," Laird warned a prospective emigrant from

St. Paul. "We are somewhat removed from the kinds of entertainments furnished by the city and a man must be somewhat sufficient unto himself and . . . in love with his work to be contented long in a place like this." The turnover of residents that always plagued Potlatch was especially troublesome during its early years, when amenities were few. "Those who come to us from the East, find after they get here, that they did not expect to put up with quite so much lack of Eastern comforts as they find in this locality," Laird lamented.[26]

Some residents, especially clerical workers and managers, came from the Great Lakes region where many had lived in cities like St. Paul or in long-established, sizable communities. Others arrived from the surrounding region or other rural areas. Consequently, it took Potlatchers some time to straighten out whether theirs was a small city or a densely populated farm, as early controversies over maintaining livestock demonstrate. After townsite superintendent George Morgan seeded his lawn in 1908, he complained to Laird about his neighbor's chickens running loose in his yard: "It was not my intention . . . to provide a rich scratching ground for . . . chickens, but rather to improve the looks of my place, and as I understand it this is the desire of the company. . . . Are chickens to take precedence over our lawns and gardens?" When several people complained of a resident's bellowing cow and calf, the company made the owner move them out of town. When a farmer's hogs continuously ran loose in the community, Morgan threatened to impound them.[27]

Though the company attempted to keep animals controlled, it did for several years encourage some livestock ownership among community residents, renting them space in the company-owned "cow barn," and selling them hay. It also provided a place for horses in the days before automobiles, and one of the community's most imposing structures was its large "horse barn." Eventually, however, the company acceded to the wishes of the town's majority and discouraged livestock ownership, although it continued to allow some animals within town limits, especially the rabbits and chickens raised for food during hard times.[28]

In 1916 the Potlatch Mercantile began selling automobiles, and from that time on there was always a car dealership in town. Automobiles greatly altered lifestyles in Potlatch, just as they did everywhere. As families acquired cars, many modified the woodsheds behind their homes into garages. More significantly, automobiles and paved roads made it possible for residents to travel out of town for entertainment, and to shop in stores other than the Merc, especially after Potlatch was connected with Idaho's major north-south highway. In 1919 residents petitioned to have that highway extended from Moscow into Potlatch. Construction began within a year, but it was not until 1925 that state highway crews, working with mules and fresno scrapers, graveled Sixth Street. This finally eliminated the mud problems that had plagued townspeople for twenty years. In July of that year the community, which knew "what it means to be stranded in a sea of mud and virtually isolated," celebrated completion of the highway with a "Heap Big Potlatch" featuring a parade, free refreshments, and a dance. By the early 1930s when crews paved Sixth, Pine, and a few other streets, Potlatch had made its transition from a rustic, rural community to a modern one.[29]

The good roads that virtually every burgeoning community sought did more to alter small towns than any other technological advancement. Potlatch gradually changed from a self-contained community to one looking outside for much of its entertainment, recreation, business, and shopping needs. With good roads and automobiles, people easily motored to Moscow, Pullman, Spokane, and other communities. They could take weekend camping or fishing excursions away from town, and they were no longer tied to Potlatch on Friday and Saturday nights.

These changes came almost simultaneously with the Great Depression, when the company cut back on its support of nonessential activities like the Amateur Athletic Club, the town's greatest provider of social entertainment. Organizations not directly supported by the company also suffered because dwindling incomes forced a decline in membership and activity. The early 1930s also saw a major change in Potlatch company leadership. Such members of the old guard as Allison Laird and assistant general manager Walter Humiston were replaced by new officials "who were running things on a cost basis, not on a basis of what's good for the community. . . . [They] lacked the personal interest in people that had been there before."[30]

As a result the number of town clubs gradually dwindled and regular community-wide functions virtually disappeared. While neighbors continued to neighbor, relationships generally grew less intimate and people more distant socially. There was no longer the pressure to make friends in town, for if you did not get along with Potlatchers you could now drive to Moscow, Palouse, Harvard, or elsewhere to visit. Since it was not necessary to limit recreation to activities in town, many people backed away from local group involvement, and Potlatch lost much of its vitality. Elsie Renfrew moved to Potlatch in 1923 and left in 1937. Though she could not pinpoint all the changes that had happened during her years there, it was apparent things were different in the 1930s than they had been just ten years earlier: "It was a very busy place those first years. . . . The last years we were there were very different from the first ones. . . . Things had changed so. It was just like having been in two separate towns."[31]

Radio and—in the very last years of Potlatch's existence as a company town—television also decreased social activities and networks among people. Families now more and more frequently remained inside their own homes for entertainment. While some community activities like dances, parties, and card games suffered, a few flourished despite the onslaught of technological changes. If anything, interest in high school sports increased, as good roads made it possible for boosters to attend games both at home and on the road. More than any other activity, high school athletics became the focal point of community involvement. The ballfield and gym supplanted the dance hall as a place where managers and workers alike mingled for a couple of hours in the evening, drawn by an event of mutual interest.

One cannot generalize about life in Potlatch. Some aspects were very different from living in other small towns, and remained so throughout Potlatch's history as a company community: the inability to own housing; the company's insistence upon cleanliness and orderliness. Other things were thoroughly typical of small-town life: neighborliness; club activity; interest in high school sports. Some social activities were confined to certain classes and some characterized Potlatch only for brief periods. Finally, over-generalization is impossible because Potlatch existed as a company town during a period when rapid technological change coincided with extreme social upheaval. One-third of Potlatch's history as a company town was spent adjusting to world wars and economic depression. It is tempting to characterize town life during these disturbances as atypical, but when one out of every three years is spent coping with the constraints imposed by international politics and economics, it is difficult to label these times "unusual." Nonetheless these years differed significantly from those that preceded and followed them, and World Wars I and II and the Great Depression profoundly altered the lifestyles of Potlatch residents.

CHAPTER NINE

Two Wars and a Depression

WORLD WAR I

Potlatch was eight years old when a Bosnian revolutionary assassinated Archduke Francis Ferdinand, heir to the Hapsburg empire, in Sarajevo on June 28, 1914. Though a small community, Potlatch was internationally sophisticated. Its people knew the map of Europe; many had come from there. Still the event passed largely unnoticed in the lumber community. After all, Balkan crises were common. Within a month, though, Potlatchers, like all Americans, recoiled at the chain reaction of events hurtling Europe into an international war. The assassination detonated a series of actions no one seemed to want, but all proved incapable of avoiding.

Potlatch residents followed war news in the Palouse *Republic*, relieved that America remained untouched. When they thought much about the conflict, they tended to side with the Allied cause, for there were many Japanese, Italians, and English among them; few Germans or Austrians. But they were a group eager for neutrality and not at all sure exactly what the war was about.

After Germany began unrestricted submarine warfare, the United States finally entered the hostilities in April 1917. Americans had to shift quickly from a neutral state to one of belligerence. To promote this transition, government propagandists set out to win people's hearts and minds. America would fight for the lofty goals of freedom and democracy, making this a war to end wars. Support of that effort, together with unbridled patriotism, was essential, and the government found few slackers in Potlatch.

The war that began in far-away Bosnia suddenly became intensely personal: neighbors, sons, and friends were now off fighting. Potlatch never tired of patriotic speeches during America's nineteen months of combat. Its people raged at alleged German atrocities; welled with pride after American victories; cried during renditions of the national anthem. The town supported its boys by backing Liberty Loan drives and the Red Cross; by conserving food and observing meatless days. Its residents believed that to do less would imperil soldiers' lives, and the town tolerated no evaders of patriotic duty.

Within a week of Congress' resolution of war, Melvin Brannon, president of the University of Idaho and "one of the most brilliant speakers in the Northwest," launched Potlatch's involvement with a talk "full of red blooded patriotism" at the opera house. Local dignitaries joined in with shorter addresses, and the town orchestra played patriotic tunes. This "monster . . . mass meeting" set the tone for many that followed.[1]

In addition to hosting frequent parades and speakers during the war, the town sponsored fundraisers for servicemen. By Christmas 1917 forty Potlatchers were in the armed forces and the Amateur Athletic Club hosted smokers with proceeds used for tobacco, gum, candy, and toothpaste, which was then sent to each Potlatch serviceman. The seven-pound parcels were carefully packed in wooden containers made at the mill's box factory. The many literary and musical programs, plays and minstrel shows, boxing and tennis matches held during these months not only relieved community tension but also raised money for the soldiers' tobacco fund, or for the local Red Cross, 200 members strong, which sewed and folded bandages for Army and Navy men.[2]

During the war's latter months, when patriotism reached its zenith, the company erected a ninety-foot flag pole by the mill. Each day at seven in the morning and five in the evening the mill whistle signaled three blasts, a huge flag was raised or lowered, and all community residents, whether at home, at work, or on the street, stood, faced the flag, and saluted. It did not help win the war, but it was one small town's way of signifying unity, of reminding itself of many neighbors and relatives gone freedom fighting, of pledging support for the democratic ideals they believed made this sacrifice worthwhile.[3]

Patriotic fervor also spurred Potlatch's support for war financing. Probably few in town had heard of government bonds before 1917. But now residents eagerly awaited each bond drive, competing among themselves and neighboring communities to see who could subscribe the largest amount. Potlatch never failed to reach its quota of sales, and few Latah County towns had a more enviable record in purchasing bonds. The town frequently won the county "Victory Flag" as the first to over-subscribe its quota. Teams of bond sellers canvased the community on foot and the surrounding countryside by automobile. Boy Scouts also sold door-to-door, and Potlatch schools initiated contests between classes to see which could sell the most war stamps.[4]

The Potlatch Lumber Company lost many laborers as men left town to join the service or went to the coast seeking higher paying jobs in shipyards. Their departure led to the mill's most dramatic change, the company's first use of women laborers. Potlatch initially hired young boys to replace the men, but there were not enough to keep the mill operating at full production. By 1918 company officials had shifted work crews to make room in the box factory for women workers. The women not only looked "trim and neat in their suits of khaki colored overalls," but performed admirably. Their work was so satisfactory that the Palouse *Republic* predicted "they will have a permanent place in the operation of the big industry." But, though they did their part for the war effort, women were not asked to remain once the men came home. It would take another worldwide conflict before the lumber company again hired female employees for its mill.[5]

The war required sacrifices, but it was also an economic boon to the company. Potlatch put on as many workers as possible and ran night shifts to complete orders for boxes that were used to ship munitions and supplies, and for lumber utilized in constructing ships, airplanes, and a host of other uses. Although shortages of railcars hampered shipments, the company found enough cars to maintain peak plant operations throughout most of the war.[6]

Much of the company's effort went to meeting the needs of the country's new air force. Western white pine made excellent stock for wing beams in the wooden aircraft then used, and the government approached Potlatch about supplying material. The request forced the company to dramatically alter its logging methods. Clear-cutting would not do, as only the best 200- to 300-year-old clear white pines could be used. Cruisers journeyed into Potlatch's vast forest lands and blazed trees they judged suitable — seldom more than a handful on a forty-acre tract. Loggers cut trails to these giants and felled them. Potlatch bought its first caterpillar tractor to haul the logs to rail spurs, then shipped them to the mill where one band saw exclusively cut airplane stock. The company constructed four special kilns to meet the government's drying standards.

Potlatch produced about 150,000 feet of the special white pine, turning out a good product. "Without question it was the finest Aeroplane Beam stock we have received from any source," commended the purchasing agent for the government's construction firm.

"You should be congratulated on the excellent spirit which your concern . . . showed in producing this material . . . thereby showing that your patriotism is 100%." Unfortunately, because of the time required to produce this unique product, little of it reached airplane production plants before Armistice Day on November 11, 1918. Still, the federal government reimbursed Potlatch for its extra expenses, in addition to paying a good price for the stock. Allison Laird believed the effort had been worthwhile. "It retarded our other work, but there is . . . compensation in knowing that our work was appreciated," he later told a reporter.[7]

The "100% patriotism" demonstrated at Potlatch and elsewhere solidified the nation behind the war effort. But, as is often the case during such displays of unquestioning loyalty, it also unleashed a hysteria that compromised the civil rights of many. In some parts of the country people ridiculed and sometimes attacked German-Americans, and virtually banned German music, food, and customs. In Potlatch, nativism took another bent, a fear that socialists, in the guise of the Industrial Workers of the World – or Wobblies – might sabotage the war effort.

Pacific Northwest lumbermen knew about Wobblies even before the war. Formed in 1905, the IWW organized miners, factory workers, and farm laborers from coast to coast. In the Pacific Northwest woods they mustered laborers to their cause by speaking out against atrocious logging camp conditions. So numerous were the Wobblies in the Inland Empire that a few days after America entered the war the Palouse *Republic* predicted that "the only . . . condition that could interfere [with Potlatch's war effort] would be an uprising among the Industrial Workers of the World employed in the woods."[8]

Logging camps were usually temporary bunkhouses or railcars set up at the end of a railroad spur for a year or two until all nearby timber had been cut and hauled away to mills. Timber company officials hated to invest heavily in such quarters, which generally housed a highly transient work force. Lumberjacks labored in all types of conditions, returning to camps that had no bathing facilities, piling into overcrowded sleeping quarters where the stench from sweat, steam, smoke, and tobacco juice mingled nauseatingly. Hershiel Tribble of Princeton recalled the interior of a bunk car where he worked:

> These people, most of them never took a bath. There was no place for them to bathe unless they went in an ice cold creek. . . .
> They had those big old heavy wool socks on, and they'd be wet from sweat. If they weren't wet from snow and water, they'd be

wet from sweat. They'd hang these on wires above the stove to dry. Some of 'em used tobacco, chewed tobacco, and they'd spit at this sand around the stove, and a lot of 'em wasn't very good shots. They might either aim too low or too high, and hit the stove or the floor. And then with these socks a-stewin' up above the stove, you can think that there must have been a little odor in there. In fact, if you wasn't used to that, and you didn't have a cast steel stomach, I don't know if you'd ever make it full-length of that car and save your last meal. . . . I tell ya, that was wicked.[9]

Bunkhouses frequently had no windows, with doors on either end providing the only ventilation. The poorly lighted shacks were bitterly cold in winter, and laborers carried their own bedrolls from camp to camp, freely transporting bedbugs and lice. "I've gone in to lay down and I felt something crawling on me, and I turned my flashlight on, and I bet I coulda' counted a hundred and fifty bedbugs," recollected Byers Sanderson of Bovill. "I've seen their pillows just dotted all over with blood where they'd smashed those bedbugs. Stink! . . . I'm right here to tell you, the lice and bedbugs were *terrible*! You couldn't stay there but what you'd get lousier than a pet coon." Latah County was not the only place in the Northwest with a Bedbug Creek so named by suffering lumberjacks.[10]

It took woods workers, traditionally an independent lot, some time to gear up for collective bargaining. But IWW organizers had wandered through Pacific Northwest logging camps for over a decade, recruiting members and sympathizers.[11] By 1917 the union believed itself strong enough to call a regional strike, rallying support behind demands for eight-hour days, higher pay, an end to Sunday and holiday work, sanitary food service, bathing facilities, and bedding provided and laundered by lumber companies.[12]

Actually, preliminary skirmishing between labor and management began spontaneously even before IWW officials planned to strike, and the first volley in the bitter Pacific Northwest labor war of 1917 came at a Potlatch camp. In December 1916, 150 lumberjacks near Bovill walked off their jobs, protesting poor working conditions. Allison Laird reacted swiftly. Strongly anti-union, Laird especially abhorred the Wobblies. In November, the Northwest had been rocked by news of a violent confrontation between the IWW and residents of Everett, Washington, where seven people had been killed and over fifty wounded. Laird wanted no such turbulence in Latah County. He ordered warnings posted at all Potlatch camps advising employees that IWW members and sympathizers would be summarily dismissed, "for the protection of the better citizens and our mutual interests." The company also slowed its work schedule, believing it more advisable to cut fewer logs with loyal employees than to hire potential Wobblies.[13]

The Bovill conflict and Laird's anti-union response set off a chain reaction in the Inland Empire. Wobbly organizers quickly infiltrated northern Idaho camps, encouraging lumberjacks to strike in sympathy with the Bovill workers. In January and early February 1917, employees at logging camps of the Milwaukee Lumber Company, the Bolin Match Block Factory, and the Weyerhaeuser syndicate's Edward Rutledge Timber Company walked off their jobs in support of the Bovill action.[14]

Management's reaction came just as swiftly. Employers in eastern Washington and northern Idaho formed a "Loggers Club" to unite against IWW activities. The club promised to clean up logging camps, improve cook shacks, and install showers and steel spring beds. But IWW organizers insisted that the owners did not truly intend to fulfill those promises. Besides, noted the Wobblies, the club refused to address the critical issues of an eight-hour day and higher pay. Wobbly activity intensified. Lumber owners, too, increased their efforts, shifting to a different front.[15]

Led by managers of the Potlatch and Rutledge companies, northern Idaho lumbermen pressed the state's legislature to provide legal assistance in battling the Wobblies. As a result, Idaho passed a criminal syndicalism law, the first of many such statutes enacted in western states to combat the Industrial Workers of the World. According to the new law, signed on March 14 by Idaho's progressive governor Moses Alexander, "Any person who advocates or teaches . . . crime, sabotage, violence or other unlawful methods of terrorism as a means of accomplishing industrial . . . reform . . . is guilty of a felony and punishable by imprisonment in the State Prison . . . or by a fine." Alexander requested that newspapers throughout the state print the law as a warning to Wobblies in Latah and Benewah counties and potential sympathizers elsewhere. Other anti-Wobbly legislation followed.[16]

Action now moved back to the IWW. In March, Wobblies met in Spokane and outlined plans for an Inland Empire strike during the summer. On June 1 organizers assembled again and selected July 1 as the strike date. Long before then, however, spontaneous labor stoppages throughout northern Idaho virtually halted all logging. Anti-management hostility had grown so vehement that even the IWW, perceived as the militant fomenters of labor discontent by lumbermen like Laird, could not maintain control of the situation.[17]

Again, Potlatch was one of the first companies to react. In an effort to keep its camps free of Wobblies, the company announced in April that all employees would have to complete information cards affirming that they were not members of the IWW. Labeling these as "rustling cards," the union called a meeting of woods workers in Spokane, where one of labor's most effective speakers, Elizabeth Gurley Flynn, a fiery soapbox orator affectionately known as "The Joan of Arc of the working class," bitterly condemned Potlatch. She warned that such intransigency on the part of management would unleash in the Pacific Northwest "the greatest drive the labor movement has ever known."[18]

Flynn's prediction eventually proved to be nearly correct, but rather than paying heed, other lumbermen chose to follow Potlatch's lead. By mid-April all northern Idaho companies required employees to carry the cards. Reacting to this hard-line management move, angry laborers throughout the Inland Empire stopped working long before the officially appointed date for the start of the summer strike. By the end of June, Laird reported to his directors that "most of the men left the camps because of sympathy for the strike or because of intimidation. . . . I.W.W. headquarters were established at both Bovill and Elk River and pickets were sent out to the camps to work on the men as they went to and from their work."[19]

The strike action against Potlatch spread throughout the Inland Empire and also to the entire Pacific Northwest. Once again, IWW officials were not so much leading events as they were simply trying to stay abreast of them. Initially, the IWW showed little interest in extending the strike to the area west of the Cascades. But workers there began agitating for action, and the American Federation of Labor laid plans for a walkout. Fearing they would lose their position of leadership among logging crews, the Wobblies called a mid-July strike to coincide with the AFL work stoppage. The two unions successfully closed down 90 percent of logging and milling operations in western Washington.[20]

Wobbly victories, however, were short-lived. With the United States actively involved in World War I, local, state, and federal officials moved quickly to break the union. In addition to white pine, the country's air force even more desperately needed Sitka spruce, a splinter-resistant wood ideally suited to aircraft use. Because the Pacific Northwest contained the nation's only appreciable stand of

Sitka spruce, government leaders insisted that Allied victory depended upon the unobstructed manufacturing of the region's supply. Wobblies faced hostile attacks by area newspaper editors who compared their revolutionary viewpoints to those of the Bolsheviks in Russia. When they overthrew the Russian government in November 1917 and surrendered to Germany, anti-Wobbly propaganda became even more heated: what the Bolsheviks did in Russia the Wobblies could do in America unless they were completely and utterly smashed.[21]

In this volatile situation, newspapermen and others blamed Wobblies for starting forest fires, placing spikes in logs in efforts to wreck sawmill machinery, and other acts of sabotage. They accused union members working on Inland Empire farms of destroying threshing machines and starting wheat fires. Even an anti-unionist like Laird believed these reports highly exaggerated, however, and wrote to Frederick E. Weyerhaeuser in August that "this band of men have certainly held on to themselves so far as damage to property and violent acts are concerned, bad street speaking and picketing being their worst activities."[22]

Still, Laird did not become any less anti-Wobbly. A week after Congress declared war on Germany, Idaho's Governor Moses Alexander had created a State Council of Defense to oversee the state's war effort and named Laird to the Council. There he joined a majority of hard-liners adamantly opposing compromise with the Industrial Workers of the World. Laird did not believe the Wobblies would lead an American socialist revolution, nor did he accept the exaggerated accusations of IWW sabotage, but he did despise the union. Patriotism partially accounted for his concern: any disruption of woods work could potentially hamper the war effort, and wartime strikes should be expeditiously stamped out. Even more than patriotism, monetary concerns moved Laird. Begun with such high expectations, his Potlatch Lumber Company had scarcely turned a profit since the big Potlatch mill had begun manufacturing eleven years earlier. Faced with continuous stockholder pressure to lift Potlatch out of the red, Laird viewed lucrative government war contracts as the prod needed to turn the ledgers black. Conversely, neither strikes nor acceding to union demands for higher pay and shorter work days would aid company finances. "I think we all realize the danger to our industry in the Pacific Northwest if we have to come to this short-hour high-pay basis and have to compete with the southern and northern mills which can continue to operate on a ten-hour basis," he wrote in 1917. Laird believed the answer to his dilemma was to do all he could, both as a powerful lumberman and an influential member of the State Council of Defense, to break the union.[23]

For whatever reason, Alexander appointed a Defense Council more conservative than himself. Early in the spring of 1917 the Council requested that the governor call in federal troops, ostensibly to protect manufacturing plants, but obviously intended to frighten lumber workers away from the IWW. Alexander steadfastly refused to enlist the military, though he sympathized with the Council's other request that northern Idaho communities be encouraged to organize companies of "home guards" to protect their towns from Wobblies. In fact, Alexander wanted to do all he could—short of declaring martial law—to combat the union. In July he temporarily moved his offices from Boise to Coeur d'Alene, and that north Idaho town in effect served as the state capital for the remainder of that difficult summer. From this headquarters the governor stumped the Idaho panhandle, urging communities to fight the Wobbly threat. Not only did he encourage home guards, he also unleashed a vengeful law enforcement crackdown on the union. On July 14 he met in Moscow with sheriffs from thirty-one counties, urging intensified action to break the Wobbly strike. He then went to Bovill, Elk River, and Deary, making equally aggressive pleas.

As a result of these meetings, a group of individuals formed the Latah County Protective Association. The association urged Latah County's sheriff to appoint ten or more deputies in each county precinct; recommended that action be immediately initiated "to arrest such persons as are not employed or engaged in some useful and helpful vocation"; and encouraged the county commissioners to "erect such structures and enclosures . . . as may be necessary to . . . hold such persons as may be placed under arrest because of their being a menace to the peace and safety of the industries, property and people of the county." Residents of Moscow and Bovill constructed bullpens, barbed wire enclosures guarded by townsmen with deer rifles, and the county sheriff and his new force of deputies proceeded to fill them with suspected Wobblies.[24]

Law officers proved especially diligent in their efforts. They raided union headquarters, disrupted union meetings, confiscated Wobbly literature, and sent men to the bullpens on the slightest evidence of violating the state's new criminal syndicalism law. While sheriffs and deputies applied pressure in the logging camps, towns dutifully followed the admonitions of the governor and Defense Council to form home guards. As the community with the state's largest sawmill,

Potlatch had one of Idaho's earliest and most active home protective associations.

The Potlatch Home Guard originated on April 20, 1917, when the military commandant at the University of Idaho came to town and recruited 100 members who promised to drill regularly and keep Wobblies and other socialists from interfering with the mill's important war work. Laird, "one of the most enthusiastic members of the guard," guaranteed that the lumber company would provide $1,000 for necessary equipment, and granted free use of the gymnasium for the group's headquarters. Other company officials joined the general manager in active membership: Max Williamson, Mark Seymour, Paul Lachmund, and Walter Humiston. When the Latah County Protective Association formed a few months later, T. P. Jones served on its Board of Directors. The Potlatch guard exercised regularly and gave frequent community exhibitions. It was, at least in the opinion of the Palouse *Republic*'s editor, "one of the best drilled home defense organizations in the Northwest." Certainly it was a well-practiced, nattily attired group, having its own regulation army uniforms and a goodly supply of Winchester rifles. It participated occasionally in encampments at the Mercantile's ranch. When guardsmen declared that they needed more target practice, Laird provided additional company funds to construct a bridge across the Palouse River to a ten-acre plot of ground that the men used as a rifle range. The lumber company also constructed a clubhouse and built target pits and rifle ranges of various lengths.[25]

The IWW never gained a foothold in Potlatch, but it is doubtful it would have even if the home guard had been less vigilant. Potlatch mill workers had far fewer complaints about working conditions than their lumberjack counterparts. If a few did grumble, the company, in this completely controlled environment, simply ousted the protestors. In the words of Allison Laird, "there has been no trouble amongst the men at Potlatch as it is more difficult for agitators to work here without being found out promptly and bounced."[26]

Within a few weeks, Governor Alexander's aggressive methods effectively broke the strike. "The I.W.W. movement in the Inland Empire blazed a little, sputtered and went out . . . a complete fizzle," commented the *Republic*. "Reports . . . from the Potlatch Lumber company's logging camps are that everything is serene. . . . The I.W.W. leaders have either been taken in charge by the authorities, or have left the district." Although he despised Wobblies, Idaho's governor empathized with the lumberjacks' demands for better working conditions and urged companies to make improvements. The lumbermen, though, were unsympathetic. They complained that they had to adhere to policies followed elsewhere in order to remain economically competitive. The labor struggle begun in the Inland Empire would not be completely resolved until lumbermen there became convinced by activities west of the mountains that certain accommodations to workers were necessary. National attention now shifted from the Inland Empire pineries to the spruce forests of western Washington.[27]

Even though the IWW strike had by this time supposedly been broken, laborers' demands had not been met and workers continued slowdown protests. In October 1917 the War Department sent Colonel Brice P. Disque to investigate the situation and find ways to procure the spruce needed for the war effort. Disque proposed a bold plan with two major components. First, he received permission to organize a special division of troops to serve as laborers in logging camps and mills, insuring production. Twenty-five thousand men eventually worked in this Spruce Production Division, receiving civilian pay while living under military discipline. Next, in an effort to interest industry in his strategy, Disque encouraged organization of the Loyal Legion of Loggers and Lumbermen – the "Four L's" – an unusual conglomeration of labor and management that the Wobblies quickly branded as "a company union." Nonetheless, the Four L's gained strength, displacing the AFL and IWW as the predominant union in Pacific Northwest forests. By war's end the union had over 100,000 members. Many lumber workers joined the Four L's because membership was a prerequisite to employment with some companies. Still, while the press and industry leaders frantically raved about Bolsheviks in the woods, in actuality many lumber workers were as patriotic as other Americans and willingly joined the Four L's for the same reasons their contemporaries bought war bonds. Once Colonel Disque brought the prestige of the military to Northwest woods and appealed to workers' patriotism, most laborers readily rallied behind the cause.

Disque also served as a somewhat reluctant labor reformer. While he acted more from a need to stimulate production than because he opposed abhorrent working conditions, he did persuade the Four L's to advocate eight-hour days, modest pay increases, and improvements in logging camp conditions. Once most of the region's lumbermen accepted those reforms, the IWW lost virtually all of its potency.[28]

Activities in northern Idaho generally paralleled the Pacific Northwest regional pattern. The Potlatch Lumber Company at first viewed improvements in living and working conditions unenthusiastically. Laird told Governor Alexander that Potlatch would reform only when others did. But now, company after company fell into line and the Western Pine Manufacturers' Association, in which Laird actively participated, advocated acceptance of better working conditions. Potlatch relented, although grudgingly. For example, Andrew Bloom spoke out against the company's providing bedding at lumber camps: "As you well know with the present prices of supplies and other commodities it is now impossible to make both ends meet and were we to further increase this expense it would simply mean so much additional wages to the men." Huntington Taylor of the Rutledge Timber Company agreed, but told Bloom they would all have to yield to the inevitable as "there [is] no use trying to make a fight on this unless everyone [is] unanimous." Potlatch did, however, derive some financial benefit from the changes: virtually all Inland Empire lumber companies ordered their bedding through the Potlatch Mercantile, providing A. A. McDonald with "one of the largest single orders ever filled by a mercantile establishment in the northwest."[29]

By May 1918 the town of Potlatch had its own local Four L's, and the union had effectively replaced the IWW in surrounding woods. When University of Idaho professor H. T. Lewis toured Potlatch camps on behalf of the Latah County Protective Association that spring he found few Wobblies, and working conditions much improved from his inspection a year earlier. "In some of the camps the men themselves have taken steps to see that trouble-making wobs' go down the river," he reported.[30]

The town of Potlatch successfully geared up for the war, and weathered the labor strike of 1917. However, the war era had another impact on the community. On January 10, 1919, seventy-year-old Priscilla Ahrens died in Potlatch, a fatality of an influenza epidemic that swept the nation during the war's final months. With military men moving about the country in the fall of 1918, the "flu bug" traveled from place to place. It hit the Palouse region as hard as anywhere, carried by military men training at the college campuses in Pullman and Moscow. Dozens of young men died in those towns, and the disease inevitably spread to adjoining communities. But quick action by Potlatch officials limited its impact. They closed the school, theater, and gym, and quarantined families who contracted the disease. They hired a Spokane nurse to provide educational training and home

care. They discouraged people from congregating except when
necessary; encouraged frequent airing of bedding; and asked residents
to sleep with windows open, following the prevailing belief that the
"bug" could not survive cold temperatures. The town had dozens
of flu cases and a rash of quarantines, but, because of the company's
ability to strictly enforce preventive measures, survived the epidemic
better than most communities.[31]

After Armistice Day the lumber company and its town gradually
returned to normal. The company's labor dispute had been resolved
for several months. Although Potlatch had suffered worker shortages
during the war, production had eventually stabilized, bringing profits. As the Potlatch community celebrated the peace, its people
welcomed the opportunity of again having access to ample supplies
of sugar, meat, and other commodities. The town grandly welcomed
its boys home, and for several years thereafter patriotism welled strong
in the community. On July 4, 1919, the company closed its Elk River
and Potlatch mills for three days so people could attend gala festivities
in Moscow marking the war's end. On the first anniversary of the
armistice, all town businesses and schools closed, and residents
gathered to hear patriotic addresses by Idaho's governor and company officials. Early in 1920 Potlatch veterans formed a local
American Legion post, destined to become one of the community's
most active organizations. The mill moved back to a peacetime operation. Still, town residents did not hurriedly shut out international
affairs. Fundraising drives for war orphans and European relief efforts continued to garner the support of many Potlatchers for several
months after the war ended.[32]

C. J. Robinson never came home from the war, and the American
Legion named its local post after him. His death, along with that
of others from Potlatch and vicinity, was the community's most visible
sacrifice to the war effort. But the conflict brought other, less percep-
tible changes as well. The town broke out in a high-pitched, flag-
waving patriotism when the war began, but the intensity could not
be maintained. By 1920 Potlatch, along with the rest of the nation,
was ready for a return to "normalcy," that elusive, nostalgic desire
for a past that never really was. Normalcy for the Potlatch Lumber
Company had consisted of short, erratic periods of profitable operations, followed by longer terms of depression. And that is exactly
what happened following the boom days of the war. The conflict
brought increased wages and better working conditions to many,
especially those in the woods. But the victory was shallow because

there would be no long-term permanence to their employment during the difficult years of the early 1920s.

Many women who found jobs at the mill during the war hoped to retain their positions, but they were replaced by men returning to the plant. Nonetheless, these Potlatch pioneers had shown that they could do "men's work," and they struck a local blow for women's equality, one of many small advances that, taken together, eventually led to more equal treatment of the sexes.

Finally, many Potlatchers came to regret their treatment of Wobblies, recognizing that wartime hysteria had nullified the civil rights of men often no more radical than they. True, IWW leaders espoused extreme measures, but the average union member merely desired better working conditions and did not deserve incarceration in a bullpen. In the end, it became apparent that lumberjacks were willing to do their patriotic duty to win the war, and that the home guards and law enforcement crackdowns were unnecessary.

Arthur Sundberg was a member of the Potlatch Home Guard, as diligent in his anti-Wobbly beliefs as anyone in town. But years later he credited the union for vastly improving working conditions, and criticized himself and others for the anti-union tensions generated during the war:

> I think . . . I might have been just as gullible as most of the rest of them, because . . . the Wobblies were something new to us, you know. The fact of the matter is, we never had any personal contact with them. And our knowledge of the Wobblies was what we read in the newspapers and what we were told by officials. And there's no reason in the world why a person shouldn't believe what they read in the newspapers. You know, whatever you read in the newspapers was gospel truth. . . . They published facts! That just shows how gullible people are, at least how gullible they were. Fact of the matter is, you know the average American citizen, he was just a plain, hard working person that didn't want to bother anybody else and . . . didn't want to be bothered by somebody else, and all they wanted to do was work every day and just make a living.[33]

THE GREAT DEPRESSION

It is hard to say just when the Depression hit Potlatch. Many residents of the Palouse area later recalled that they would not have known they were in the "Great Depression" had they not read about it. Times had been bad for years. The Potlatch Lumber Company was not immune to the regional suffering, having endured a decade of financial losses in the 1920s, interspersed only occasionally with short-lived gains. Things were so bleak, in fact, that Allison Laird believed the stock market crash of 1929 was a good omen. "Demand for lumber and sales have taken on a very disappointing slump," he wrote company directors a few days after the collapse. "There has been no money available for several months for residential building, due to the speculative stock market. Now that the break has come, perhaps conditions affecting sensible financing may change and help our lumber demand some."[34]

Laird, of course, was wrong. Though the market's downfall did not cause the 1930s Depression, it signaled a deflationary trend lasting for years, the beginning of more than a decade of difficult times. While the New Deal of 1933 brought hoopla, it did not generate a recovery for Potlatch residents. They suffered through financial doldrums after Franklin Roosevelt entered the White House just as they had while Herbert Hoover lived there. But Roosevelt at least gave them hope that things would eventually get better.

As always, the fate of the town hinged upon the progress of the company, and those were bleak times for lumbermen throughout the Pacific Northwest. During the Depression's early years timber companies chronically overproduced. While prices declined, they manufactured ever more lumber in an effort to maintain the same dollar level of business. "It was so bad that some of the . . . lumber in the yard would cost more to pick up and put through the planing mill and on . . . cars than it could be sold for," recalled Phil Weyerhaeuser, who spent these years in Lewiston. Few people could afford to construct houses or buildings, which reduced lumber's demand. Further, lumber companies increasingly had to compete with new wood substitutes flooding the market. Northwest lumbermen eventually realized that their ruthless competition and overproduction accomplished nothing, and by 1932 they dropped their output to less than a third of 1929 levels. The Depression now hit lumber workers as well as business stockholders. At least during the period of unprofitable overproduction laborers had work. Now they were idled.[35]

Though Laird hoped a business upturn would quickly come, it did not. By mid-1930 it was apparent that remedial steps were required if Potlatch was to survive. The general manager began by eliminating the night shift at the Potlatch mill and curtailed remaining employees to a thirty-two hour week. These steps reduced production to about half of normal. The company also finally instituted the selective logging practices that some directors had so long advocated, thus eliminating expensive manufacturing from low quality logs and undesirable species.[36]

Laird hoped that such action would avert pay reductions, but that proved impossible. On January 1, 1931, Potlatch instituted a cut of 5 to 10 percent for all salaried employees, with workers' wages trimmed five cents an hour. Even this failed to bring recovery, and in April 1931 the Potlatch Lumber Company Board of Directors finally approved a plan, long circulated among stockholders, to merge northern Idaho's Weyerhaeuser operations into one larger organization. Thus the Edward Rutledge, Clearwater, and Potlatch companies became Potlatch Forests, Incorporated – PFI – with corporate headquarters in Lewiston. Decisions would now be made on the basis of what was best for these operations collectively, rather than what was best for each individually.[37]

It quickly became apparent to directors of the new company that continued operation of four sawmills would mean only greater losses. Consequently, they permanently closed the Elk River mill and "temporarily" shut down the Potlatch and Coeur d'Alene plants. Only the company's newest and largest facility at Lewiston remained open. Although officials assured Potlatch and Coeur d'Alene residents that they intended to restart those plants when justified by market conditions, the assurances seemed hollow, as hundreds of lumberjacks and mill workers were thrown out of work. The few who remained on the job received another wage and salary reduction early in 1932.[38]

When company officials closed the Potlatch plant in the fall of 1931, they gave employees only a week's notice. The news rocked the community. While the plant stayed down month after month, rumors circulated that PFI never intended to reopen it. "There's nothing deader in the world than a sawmill town when the mill's not running," noted one resident. In such an atmosphere of inactivity, gossip spread quickly. Some in town no doubt distrusted company officials. They had seen at Palouse and Elk River that the shareholders had no qualms about permanently closing plants with little warning. Their own short notice before shutdown had hardly provided ample time for personal planning. The town was ripe for sensationalistic stories, and in the fall of 1932 the front pages of regional newspapers fueled the gossip by announcing that PFI was pulling out of Potlatch permanently, bringing "the final abandonment of the individual identity of the Potlatch Lumber company in its future operations as a member of the Weyerhaeuser interests." Paraphrasing Mark Twain, Potlatch unit superintendent R. E. Irwin replied a week later that reports of the plant's death were "greatly exaggerated."[39]

Despite continued assurances that the Potlatch unit would eventually operate again, things did not quickly improve for either the town or PFI. The company's operating losses of nearly a million and a half dollars in 1932 forced it to temporarily close even the Lewiston mill. It was delinquent in paying taxes in 1933, and had to negotiate agreements with the Washington Water Power Company and the Northern Pacific Railroad to defer payments on bills owed them. Early in 1935, PFI reduced all wages an additional 15 percent. As directors repeatedly wrote to impatient stockholders during these years, PFI "made no earnings . . . and the prospect of such earnings is most discouraging." Indeed, the company lost nearly nine million dollars during the 1930s. Only the vast resources of the Weyerhaeuser syndicate enabled it to forestall insolvency at a time when many lumber firms in the Pacific Northwest failed.[40]

The hard times did produce one positive consequence: a pioneering role by Potlatch in the field of forest products research. Timbermen had paid little attention to research into the possible uses of lumber "waste" when times were good and forests seemed plentiful. But the depression and a growing awareness that American timberlands were exhaustible led to increased research and conservation efforts. In 1931 only about one-third of a tree's total volume was utilized during manufacturing. Finding ways to use shavings, sawdust, edgings, and other waste materials could ensure long-term profits.

The PFI research and conservation effort began at the Clearwater Timber Company even before the merger. Phil Weyerhaeuser and Charles Billings had already instituted that firm's enterprising selective logging program and seriously considered reforestation. This was still a time when most lumbermen, including Phil's uncle, saw limited potential in such methods. "I see little prospect of any reforestation under private ownership, except where timber grows very rapidly and taxes are extremely light," Frederick E. Weyerhaeuser cautioned his young nephew. Still, Phil Weyerhaeuser and Billings proceeded with parts of their plan—temporarily dropping reforestation—and directed loggers to cut only larger trees, leaving smaller ones to mature. To Phil Weyerhaeuser, selective logging and research went hand-in-hand since greater utilization of trees would help conserve forests.

When he became president of Potlatch Forests, he strongly encouraged the company's forest products research effort.[41]

Actually, that research, too, had begun before the merger, when Potlatch Lumber Company assistant general manager Walter D. Humiston made an impassioned plea to company directors in 1928 to provide funds to undertake research. "If something can be produced in a practical manner out of forest and mill waste nobody needs it so much as these inland mills," noted a sympathetic Frederic Bell. The other directors agreed and gave Humiston enough money to travel throughout the country to consult with experts already at work in the forest products research field.[42]

Humiston, a tall, handsome man who parted his hair precisely in the middle, came to Potlatch in June 1907 as the company's land agent. He was primarily responsible for selling cutover properties to settlers, and by 1916 had disbursed over 20,000 acres. Other lumber concerns in the Pacific Northwest noted this enviable record; indeed, they frequently copied Potlatch's hard-selling methods. Company directors also noticed Humiston's good work and advanced him to the position of assistant general manager in 1916. He became a leader in efforts to control forest fires, fungus diseases, and insect infestations, and strongly advocated reforestation. To Humiston, research was just another means of conservation, and he viewed forestry research not only as an avenue to greater profits but also as a way of ensuring long-term timber harvesting.[43]

With the funding from the company, Humiston traveled to the country's most famous wood research facility, the Forest Products Laboratory in Madison, Wisconsin. He also visited with chemists at Dupont headquarters, met with Wilson Compton, Secretary of the National Lumber Manufacturers Association in Washington, D.C., and discussed research possibilities with scientists in Boston and foresters at the University of Idaho. In January 1929 he presented his findings at a directors' meeting in St. Paul. As a result of his report, company officials authorized the expenditure of $40,000 for research, establishing one of the earliest research programs undertaken by a lumber company in the United States.

As the company's first director of research, Humiston quickly pushed efforts on several fronts. He negotiated a contract with a Boston chemical firm, funded a research fellow at the University of Idaho, and set up a lab in the basement of his Nob Hill home, where a recent chemistry graduate of the university undertook experiments.[44]

Humiston oversaw experimental efforts to convert wood wastes to automobile fuels; extract a dentifrice to remove tartar from teeth; produce cattle feed; manufacture wood flour used in making linoleum; derive banana oil from wood fungi; extract clothing dyes; and obtain oils from pine needles. The product for which he held the greatest hope, however, was a "synthetic lumber" made from sawdust and other wood wastes. He envisioned a product that would be practically fire proof, highly durable, extremely dense, and easily worked. It would eliminate many of the objections of architects and insurers to wood, and allow lumbermen to more effectively compete with lumber substitutes then coming on the market.

By 1930 Potlatch had developed a considerable reputation for its research program. "The Potlatch Lumber Co. is one of the first large lumber organizations in the United States to enter this field seriously, systematically and aggressively, with the assistance of a staff of distinguished scientists, and it now looks as though Humiston's dream of being able to profitably utilize his waste, not only once, but two or three times perhaps, may come true," reported The *Journal of Commerce*. But the prediction was premature. Two years later, frustrated at the company's unwillingness to continue funding research, Humiston left Potlatch for New York, where he spent the rest of his life dealing in real estate.[45]

Phil Weyerhaeuser, Humiston, and a few other enlightened officials realized that research was time-consuming and expensive, with rewards not apt to come immediately. Yet to most directors facing economic crisis, financial difficulties were eminently short-term, and long-range research seemed extravagant. In fact, some doubted whether research would ever pay off. "Our experience in the past indicates that the development commercially of any new by-product, no matter how carefully tried out in a laboratory, results in years of strenuous effort and in expense many times over the original estimate," admonished Frederick E. Weyerhaeuser. Having invested money for over three years with little apparent result, the directors did not believe that research would ever lead them out of the Depression, and ceased virtually all funding. Research at the Potlatch unit halted completely. At Lewiston, where engineer Robert Bowling had developed Pres-to-Logs, some work continued, especially as Bowling attempted to perfect his briquettes made from wood wastes. Essentially, though, much of PFI's waste product "research" in the remaining years of the Depression became nothing more than product experimentation and diversification, such as its efforts to market boxed lumber scraps for Home Carpenter Kits, and play blocks for children.[46]

The beginnings made by Humiston and a few other pioneers scattered about the country eventually led to the discovery of particleboard, the "synthetic lumber" Potlatch's research director believed possible. But, while PFI eventually marketed a product in this line, it did not invent it. The research project launched at the Potlatch Lumber Company as a result of the Depression eventually became a victim of those hard times.[47]

The company's embryonic research efforts had little effect on most residents of Potlatch, where the Depression dragged on. The mill remained closed from October 1931 until April 1934, when 220 men again went to work. Even so, the facility ran only sporadically from then to the end of the decade, normally operating about six or seven months a year.[48]

The Depression brought other disruptions to the town. Potlatch no longer received daily train service, as the WI&M cut back to a schedule of hauling freight and passengers only three times weekly. School teachers suffered a 10 percent salary reduction, and vacancies frequently went unfilled for long periods. Company managers eliminated the Potlatch school manual training program. The company also withdrew its financial support of the community library, forcing boosters to sponsor fundraising events and, for the first time, to charge patrons for borrowing books. Potlatch Forests also released the Amateur Athletic Club's physical director, which greatly curtailed gym activities. There were no physical education classes for the schools; the tradition of weekly community dances ceased; and for a time the gym closed completely. During most of the Depression, though, the club limped along as town volunteers provided janitorial service and kept the doors open for recreational use.[49]

Some Potlatch residents blamed the merger for what they perceived as the company's declining interest in the town's welfare. Potlatch was now just one of several PFI cogs. Further, Allison Laird died while officials negotiated the merger, and assistant general manager W. D. Humiston left town shortly thereafter. Now unit managers, answerable to higher authorities in Lewiston, directed the town's activities, R. E. "Jack" Irwin being the first. He came to Potlatch in 1923 to take charge of manufacturing, after having learned lumbering in Wisconsin, Oregon, and with Weyerhaeuser concerns in southern Idaho. At the time, Potlatch manufacturing was suffering under the leadership of C. E. McGibbon, who insisted on marketing

low-quality materials in an effort to increase profits. By 1923 many
sales outlets refused to handle Potlatch products. Company directors forced McGibbon to resign and replaced him with Irwin. When
Laird died, they appointed Irwin unit manager. He lasted only eighteen months, however, before PFI officials replaced him with James
J. O'Connell, who remained on the job until 1951. Many town
dwellers viewed Irwin and O'Connell as "company" men who placed
profits ahead of community welfare. Certainly they did not take the
personal interest in overseeing the town that Laird and Humiston
had. But Irwin and O'Connell managed the town during its most
difficult time, and it would be inaccurate to say that they totally ignored the community's well-being in their efforts to maximize company income.[50]

The corporation did attempt to soften the blow of the Depression
in Potlatch. Laird greatly disliked lowering wages. Consequently,
when he made the first pay cut in 1931 he coupled it with a reduction in house rent. Potlatch Forests followed this policy when other
wage reductions proved necessary.[51]

As another concession to the difficult times, company officials tried
to keep a few men working throughout the Depression—on the
WI&M, at plant maintenance, in shipping stockpiled lumber. During those times when the mill did operate, O'Connell attempted to
distribute work evenly among families, giving preference to married
men and town residents. "I believe you . . . can make changes that
will give work to married men, with large families to support and
living in Company houses without in anyway being a detriment
to . . . efficient operation," he wrote department heads. "It would be
well to stagger their employment rather than to give anyone a full
time job." The company did, however, remain flexible in cases of
individual hardship. When a Potlatch woman pleaded with O'Connell to hire her son, as the family needed extra income for medical
expenses, the manager found him a position even though others in
the family were already working.[52]

The company also relaxed its cash payment policy at the Merc and
extended credit during the Depression. In addition, numerous people
fell behind on their house rent, and PFI officials allowed those debts
to accumulate. Irwin and O'Connell also proved lenient when people
constructed a "Hooverville" in town. A considerable village of tents,
cardboard huts, and flimsy wooden shanties grew up in the forested
grove east of town. These living conditions were hardly comfortable,
particularly in winter. Even though the company officially frowned

on such "private" and untidy housing, the managers looked the other way and allowed these hard-luck dwellers to remain.[53]

Potlatch received various forms of outside relief throughout these years. In the early 1930s the Red Cross dispensed flour, cloth, and other basic necessities to the town's neediest. After the inauguration of Franklin Roosevelt, limited federal aid became available and basic foodstuffs were distributed. The federal agency with the greatest impact by far was the Works Progress Administration, which employed many Potlatch residents at minimal wages in return for work on road construction, bridge building, and other public projects.

Throughout the Depression Potlatch people helped their neighbors. They distributed food baskets and clothing, for example, while groups such as the Women's Society of the Union Church sewed for those unable to provide for themselves. Many in town planted gardens on property the company provided, and for the first time since the town's earliest days, small livestock, such as chickens and rabbits, began to appear in large numbers as people sought inexpensive ways to supply their families with food. There was also considerable bartering in a community very short on cash.[54]

By 1936 the company began its gradual climb from the depths of the Depression. "The outstanding fact in Potlatch is that they are making money," wrote an ecstatic – and surprised – Laird Bell to his father Frederic in October that year. "This is, after all, the first year that we have come near making any money – in fact I thought we never would make anything." Potlatch Forests shipped more lumber in 1936 than in any year since the merger. In 1937 sales jumped again, as did lumber prices. The company showed a profit of $92,000 in 1936 and nearly $190,000 in 1937. Beginning in December 1937 the market again stagnated, and PFI operated at a loss the following year. But by then the worst of the Depression was over. By 1940 PFI began showing the profits that would increase substantially nearly every year into the 1950s. By 1937 it employed 4,500 people, and in both 1936 and 1937 gave substantial pay increases. At the end of the latter year, its wages were higher than ever.[55]

Increased corporate profits also brought better times to the town. By early 1937 Potlatch was again full as people flocked to the community seeking employment. Though the mill operated only periodically, the work was more reliable than in most other places in the region, and people eagerly took it. Those no longer employed by PFI, but who had been allowed to remain in town during the bleak years, were forced to leave so employees could rent the company's houses. When all existing houses were occupied, PFI constructed a number of temporary cottages to help contain the overflow. Though truly "good" times would not come for another few years, Potlatch residents had weathered the worst of the Depression. The dismantling of the shack village in the pines provided a concrete illustration of the change.[56]

Even during the hardest times, many things about Potlatch remained the same. Clubs and lodges stayed active, though membership sometimes declined. Groups hosted dances at the American Legion Cabin and at Riverside. Although it had no paid director, the gym remained open during most of the Depression, and the Athletic Club sponsored community events such as boxing smokers. Potlatchers might attend a card party at the Catholic Church; concerts in the Union Church; watch a Polida Club or high school play; attend a home meeting of the Royal Neighbors; partake in a progressive dinner; or take in a movie at the People's Theatre, where kids for ten cents and adults for thirty could escape into a feature film bearing little resemblance to their own Depression-time experiences.[57]

In some ways the Depression drew the town together. Potlatchers had demonstrated during the war that they would willingly give to worthy causes, and even now they scraped together what they could for various groups. They raised money at dances, card parties, and dinners for organizations such as the Boy Scouts, Camp Fire Girls, the library, and the Athletic Club. The Depression hit Potlatch hard, but the community was not as devastated as some small towns. Those who could afford to save found that their money was always safe at the State Bank. There were no landowners, so Potlatchers, unlike their neighbors, did not have to forfeit property for failure to pay taxes. Rents were lowered and credit was extended. There were few businesses in town, so Potlatch did not suffer the rash of bankruptcies familiar in most small communities. There were few widows or older residents, the people who suffered most in many small towns. Schools remained open, and the town's inhabitants always had plenty of electricity, water, and fuel wood. Town dwellers were even able to joke about their plight. One community play depicted the death of a company manager. While he was being carried to the gravesite he rose in his coffin and asked, "How many pallbearers are working today?" "Six," came the reply. "Well, lay off two," he ordered.[58]

Certainly, those in Potlatch's shack city had a difficult time. But their numbers were quite limited—probably never more than fifty or so. Potlatch had no hobo jungle like the one that went up along the river banks in Palouse every year during harvest time with itinerants sleeping under boxes or burlap, hoping for a job on the farms. Though local residents helped those in need, Potlatchers did not find it necessary to organize a private relief fund as their neighbors in Palouse did. There simply were not that many desperate people in Potlatch. In the evenings Potlatchers pulled up to their radios to hear the reassuring fireside chats of Franklin Roosevelt. The President gave them the comfort of knowing they were not suffering alone. Potlatch residents tightened belts, but they knew from reading local papers or watching newsreels or listening to the radio that they were better off than many. They did not prosper, but as a community, they weathered the Depression better than most.[59]

WORLD WAR II

Prosperity finally came to Potlatch in the 1940s. For the first time in over a decade the mill ran steadily, night and day discharging the lumber needed for another war effort. But this was affluence purchased at enormous cost. "It was a sad event when you saw people leave . . . with their induction notice—your friends and acquaintances," noted Lee Gale. "There were a few that never came back."[60]

The news no doubt spread quickly through town on that Sunday, December 7, 1941. Radios were commonplace by then. One person told another, and soon the entire community listened for information about the Japanese bombing of Pearl Harbor. The next day, many tuned in again as Franklin Roosevelt addressed Congress, and that body responded with a declaration of war. The call to war, the second in the memory of most Potlatch residents, had an immediate impact on the small community.

Potlatch had contributed to the conflict even before this formal declaration. Many of its young men were in the service prior to the Japanese attack, called up during the President's 1940 mobilization order. One, Elmer Hicks, died at Pearl Harbor on board the *Arizona*. Early in the spring of 1942 word arrived that three Potlatch men who had also joined early—26-year-old Edwin Chambers, a mill straddle-bug operator; Robert Trotter, a 28-year-old planer employee; and 27-year-old Harlin Owens, a dry kiln worker—were taken prisoner at Bataan and Corregidor. The story of the three captured the community's attention. It was not that they were alone in their sacrifices.

But they were examples of Potlatch offering its best for the war effort, and their plight galvanized the town. If Chambers, Trotter, and Owens could give this much, others should be willing to do all they could, whether that meant enlisting, buying bonds, gathering scrap, or tending victory gardens. Potlatch eagerly awaited news of the prisoners, for their struggle was now the town's, a communal battle against the enemy. For awhile the three sent occasional letters to families, correspondence shared throughout town, but communication ceased in 1943. Not until Japan surrendered in August 1945 did Potlatchers hear from them again when the Red Cross reported that all three were alive. "Potlatch is rejoicing," remarked Mabel Kelley, plant secretary. Chambers, Trotter, and Owens returned home a few weeks later, thin from three and a half years in Japanese work camps, but as glad to be back as the town was to see them.[61]

No one in the Potlatch vicinity was unaffected by the conflict, and the stories of some area residents provide an example not only of the diversity of this community's commitment, but also a sort of national composite of America at war. There was Alfred J. Larson, a plant employee since 1906 and one of three generations of Larsons working there in 1939. Alfred Larson spent much of the war corresponding with fourteen grandsons stationed around the world in the armed services. There was the A. H. Goodnough family who, in the late 1930s, had bought a forty-acre tract of Potlatch cutover land a few miles east of town. The family had seven sons and a daughter, most of whom worked for PFI in 1941. When the war began, five of the boys joined the armed services while their sister worked on community war bond drives at Potlatch High School. There was the family of Lowery and Daisy Berry of Onaway. They had no children of service age, but the war made a difference in their lives just the same. Daisy went to work at the mill in 1942 and remained for the duration; her husband, an employee since 1917, stayed on to help the plant manufacture its increased wartime quota. To save gas they commuted to work on bicycles. When labor grew scarce, their thirteen-year-old son and fifteen-year-old daughter worked for neighboring farmers, filling wartime employee shortages. Another fourteen-year-old daughter supervised the family's housekeeping and shopping. All three children matured early during those years.[62]

There were others, too, like Donald Hansen and Harold Allpress, who spent most of these years in German prisoner-of-war camps. "Although I've lost 50 lbs., and am suffering from malnutrition, I'm the happiest man alive, cause I'm on my way to the good old USA, home and you," Allpress wrote to his wife after Russian soldiers liberated him in 1945. His letter—like so many others during these years—was shared with the whole town. Or there were those like Virgil Wright, a mill employee before the war who came out of the conflict wearing a uniform heavy with medals won in the Pacific; or Captain Philip Hearn, a bombardier equally well decorated, who flew over fifty missions against the Japanese. Or you could look at the example of Shirley Fiscus, killed early in the war while serving in the Army in New Guinea, his name placed prominently upon the town's "Honor Roll." This outdoor sign, located in the downtown business section, listed Potlatchers serving and dying in the war. Community residents meticulously maintained it, and watched it daily. Dolores Kammeyer's name did not appear on that list, nor was her picture in the Merc's window with those from Potlatch serving in the military. But she sacrificed nonetheless. Kammeyer, one of the few women to ever ride a sawmill headrig carriage, gained national attention when the Associated Press ran photographs and a story about her as an example of women in the war effort. In the spring of 1945 she married Ensign Wendell LaVoy, who was subsequently killed in a plane crash over the Atlantic during the war's closing days, one of Potlatch's last casualties. Or you might look at the Potlatch High School graduating class of 1944, the one with fifteen boys, eleven of whom had made arrangements to enlist even before commencement. Or to Setsua Matsura, a Japanese-American who joined up early and became a highly decorated war hero. Or finally, to the sad sacrifice of Harry Honda. Most of Potlatch's Japanese had left town during the hard times of the Depression. Matsura and Honda had remained. Matsura was young enough to enter the service; Honda, janitor at the Merc, was not. People liked Honda. But when President Roosevelt ordered Japanese-Americans relocated to detention camps early in 1942, Honda disappeared and Potlatch never heard from him again. He had served the town and company well, but his years of service were quickly forgotten in the war fervor following Pearl Harbor.[63]

On the home front, Potlatch responded quickly to the war call, with mobilization, like enlistment, beginning even before Pearl Harbor. Townswomen had been sending packages to war-battered England as part of the "Bundles for Britain" effort for some time. The war declaration, however, spurred more feverish activity, and by January 1942 over fifty men had volunteered to form a unit of the Idaho State Guard. Company A, First Battalion, 5th Regiment

Infantry, Idaho State Guard, appropriately drilled under an emblem of a rifle superimposed on a logger's peavey. By February enough men had volunteered to form an additional unit, and the men prepared to defend the town in the event of attack or bombing.[64]

People in town contributed in various ways. School students collected scrap, using the money earned to buy bonds. They held school dances with admission being the purchase of a savings stamp, and organized auctions with donated gifts going to the student bidding the most for war bonds. In 1942 each of Potlatch's 180 school children spent an average of twenty-seven dollars on war stamps and bonds, a record equaled during other drives in following years. Potlatch graduates serving in the military frequently spoke at assemblies while they were home on furlough, and some of the school's girls formed a writing club to keep every Potlatch serviceman informed of hometown activities.[65]

There could not have been much scrap iron, aluminum, or rubber remaining in town by the end of 1942. Students gathered it; workmen dismantled old trucks and cars after work; the company encouraged all tenants to search houses for every bit of useful material, then sent Townsite Department crews to pick up the salvage. Residents sent Potlatch service personnel continual reminders of the town's appreciation of their efforts. In addition to organized letter campaigns, they shipped Christmas boxes each year and gave parties to every enlistee leaving town and to each one home on furlough. When the Office of War Information encouraged Americans to plant victory gardens so more food would be available for the armed forces, Potlatchers again responded enthusiastically. The lumber company plowed empty plots in the townsite and on the flat where stacked lumber had formerly stood, dividing the property into gardens. The Victory Garden appeal was so popular that winners of spaces had to be drawn by lottery. The townswomen, encouraged by OWI, took renewed interest in canning and preserving food.[66]

Almost continuous pleas to aid in winning the war helped maintain the community's enthusiasm. The company sponsored speeches by decorated war heroes – now on the federal government's lecture circuit – who addressed workers at regular noontime rallies in the mill's lunchroom. The company also showed patriotic movies at the plant and the high school. Workers tacked up a large world map in the lunchroom to better follow events, and during breaks listened to a company-provided radio for up-to-the-minute news. They worked amidst an abundance of posters reminding them that "Production

Wins Wars" and that wood was essential to the Allied cause.[67]

And Potlatchers contributed money. They never seemed to tire of the many fundraising drives, almost as if they had forgotten how poor they had been just a few years earlier. They gave money to the Salvation Army, the United Service Organization, and the Red Cross. They contributed to European relief efforts, the March of Dimes, and the Infantile Paralysis Fund. Mostly, though, they bought war bonds. The government promoted bonds as a means of providing revenues for the defense build-up and of curbing runaway inflation. And the country responded. Potlatch held contests among the Townsite Division, the office crew, and various mill departments for which could purchase the most bonds. There was competition between employees of the Potlatch Unit and their co-workers at Coeur d'Alene and Lewiston. There was competition between Potlatch and neighboring towns. People bought bonds almost feverishly until the war's closing months. When victory seemed assured, they finally refused to contribute more, despite urgings from company and government officials. Before then, however, the special flag signifying that Potlatch had reached its bond quota had flown frequently on the mill's pole, the plant's "Victory" whistle had sounded many times as departments reached their goals, and "Minute Man" banners—PFI's method of informing other employees that a department had "gone over the top" in a bond drive—had adorned most work areas. During rare times when the buying pace subsided, company officials schemed about ways to boost sales. "Will you get together and plan out how you can work on those . . . who have not yet purchased Defense Savings Bonds?" O'Connell wrote his department heads. The company also required that all new employees subscribe for a minimum monthly bond purchase.[68]

Throughout the period, the plant ran at or near peak production. Wood was essential for the war effort. The military used lumber in constructing air and naval bases, troop housing, hospitals, and supply depots. Railroads needed ties for the nation's vital transportation system. Pres-to-logs became an important railway fuel. Ship parts, airplane propellers, and storage bins all required lumber. And virtually everything sent overseas, from food to howitzers, radios to tanks, went packed in wooden crates. Both PFI and the Potlatch Unit set new production records during the early war years.[69]

Maintaining this record production level proved difficult, however. Many employees left for the service; others moved to Washington, Oregon, and California for higher paying jobs in shipyards and defense

plants. The company faced constant labor shortages. "The personnel situation continues to grow worse and before long it may be
desperate," general manager Billings wrote to directors in July 1942.
"We are replacing skilled men . . . with almost anything we can get."
"For the first time in years it was necessary to go out and seek labor,"
noted Jim O'Connell of the Potlatch plant's experience. "After . . .
scouring the country and many long distance calls and wires, a crew
of old men, school boys and others who had no experience was got-
ten together." Among those working on the Potlatch night shift were
University of Idaho students who commuted daily from Moscow after
classes.[70]

By August 1942 it became apparent that the only way to meet production goals was to reintroduce women to the mill after a quarter-
century hiatus. Women had never before worked in the Lewiston
plant, and few PFI managers remembered the World War I experiences at Potlatch or Coeur d'Alene. Consequently, early in 1942,
the company sent an investigator to Weyerhaeuser mills in western
Washington to study the use of women employees. He reported
favorably, with only a few reservations: women should not be used
in highly dangerous areas, because injuries could cause bad public
relations; supervision must be by men because "women . . . straw
bosses absolutely do not work out"; and, while women should be paid
the same as men, they should sign waivers that their jobs would be
good only for the war's duration. Within weeks of his report, all three
plants had hired women. Workers at Potlatch installed a separate
women's restroom and lunch area, and soon women were working
in the Pres-to-log and remanufacturing plants, riding carriage, tending slasher, feeding molders, working on the railroad tie dock, and
serving as janitors.[71]

Unlike the First World War, Potlatch millworkers showed little
fear of sabotage during World War II. Rather than looking for spikes
on incoming logs, mill employees waited to see with what design
logger-artists might decorate stump ends. "V" victory signs were
especially popular, as were caricatures of Hitler and Tojo. Slogans
such as "Hitler's Coffin, Ax the Axis," and "More Production — Log
Like Hell" were also frequently inscribed on the logs. Nonetheless,
the company did take some effort early in the war to protect the plant.
All employees were fingerprinted and were required to carry passes
to enter the main gate. O'Connell authorized construction of several
watchtowers and guardhouses, and encircled the plant with lights.
Armed watchmen, under Army direction, patrolled the plant when

it did not operate. Workmen fitted windows in the power plant with bars, and boarded up or covered sawmill windows with wire mesh. Power plant doors were kept locked and were fitted with peepholes: anyone wishing entrance had to ring a bell. Though O'Connell bragged that getting inside was "as impossible as getting into a lodge of which you were not a member," the precautions were really only half-hearted, and plant employees of the time do not recall that the guardtowers were ever staffed. After the initial shock of Pearl Harbor, restrictions slackened and the plant operated much as it always had, although on a busier schedule.[72]

In May 1943 WI&M employees struck because they did not receive a wage increase when other PFI workers did. After a week the company granted them a pay hike, and Billings, lamenting lost shipments, called the strike a misunderstanding from which "no one gained except the enemies of our country." The strike irritated some servicemen, such as Sig Alsaker, Jr., who wrote home, "I'm afraid if I said what I really think about such strikes in war time the censor would have to cut it out of my letter." But there was none of the hysteria accompanying the IWW strike of the First World War. Some might dislike strikers for failing to perform their patriotic duty, but these were not people feared as saboteurs.[73]

In many ways, Potlatch community life during the war resembled the heyday of the town in the teens and twenties more nearly than it did the years immediately preceding the conflict. Improved roads and automobiles had limited many town social functions in the 1930s as people went elsewhere seeking entertainment. But with wartime gas rationing, Potlatchers again looked close to home for diversions. The town sponsored well-attended dances, bobby sox parties, Christmas caroling, Halloween functions, and community-wide celebrations. In some ways it was a sad period, with many gone to war; but this was also a gay time when the community actively participated in social affairs as a way not only of forgetting, but of congratulating itself for the good, patriotic duty its residents were performing.[74]

It was also, however, a frustrating period. The town had suffered economically for years prior to the war. Now the plant ran steadily and wages were high. But rationing prevented purchases of the goods people had long gone without. At war's end, the community, along with the rest of the country, virtually exploded in a mass of consumer buying, and the plant remained busy filling the lumber needs of a country that at last had money with which to build. The end of hostilities, although a happy time, brought little of the fervor of Armistice Day 1918. Rather, the war's end marked a beginning—a time when people could at last get on with good living. For one thing, victory never seemed in doubt after the first year or so of conflict. As early as September 1944 Potlatchers began planning the town's victory celebration. When treaties in Europe and Asia were signed, they were properly signaled with community church services, a parade, and soundings of the plant whistle. But these were not emotion-charged events. Even more than after the first war, Potlatchers were ready for a return to "normalcy," for this would be a normalcy not only of a nation no longer at war, but also of a return to prosperity too long absent.[75]

Homecomings for armed services returnees began in September 1945—just forty years after William A. Wilkinson began mill construction and thirty-nine after the plant had started operating. Sixteen of those years had been spent in war or depression. It is almost inaccurate to describe these crises as unusual, because for many who lived in Potlatch during those times they simply represented everyday life. Finally in 1945 Potlatchers confidently prepared for good times ahead. Little did they know that within ten years this prosperity would bring the most dramatic change in the history of their community—the selling of the company town itself.

CHAPTER TEN

The End of the Experiment

HIGH EXPECTATIONS; IDAHO REALITIES

When entrepreneurs from the Great Lakes moved into Idaho and organized the Potlatch Lumber Company, they did so with high expectations—expectations for long-term, steady profits. These hopes were repeatedly dashed by the geography, climate, and isolation of the state. During Potlatch's many difficult years, some directors viewed the company's town as an expensive burden. Others believed it an example of enlightened capitalism that should be retained despite the cost. Still others looked upon the community as one of the few money-making ventures in an otherwise unprofitable enterprise. Given this diversity, it is understandable that the directors managed the town differently at various times, depending upon who served in leadership positions. But regardless of who led the corporation, and whether in good times or bad, the community's fortunes were always closely tied to the company's.

Frederick Weyerhaeuser sometimes ruefully stated that naming the Idaho operation Potlatch after the Indian ceremony of giving away treasures was quite appropriate, for the stockholders seemed to continually give to the company's account, receiving nominal dividends in return. Indeed, by the time Weyerhaeuser died in 1914 the company had shown only minimal profits, and many shareholders had already begun a long and loud criticism of executive decisions, including the decision to maintain the town. Ironically, Potlatch retained control of its community for nearly fifty years, few of them profitable. It sold its town only when corporate prosperity finally arrived.[1]

It seemed that each year brought new financial problems to Potlatch. Early in its history, the company suffered from higher than expected construction costs. An extreme shortage of railroad cars, which limited shipments, and a depressed national economy compounded the difficulties. William Deary and Allison Laird attempted to "sit on the lid" by cutting wages and streamlining operations, but they repeatedly had to draw on stockholders for more capital. When some directors—particularly Charles Weyerhaeuser and Drew Musser—complained about the company's lack of profits, Deary exploded. He detested the grumbling, believing he was doing the best that could be expected under the circumstances, and confided to Laird that he would never put himself through the misery of that first year's operation again for any amount of remuneration.[2]

Potlatch enjoyed its first mildly successful years in 1908 and 1909 as building construction accelerated, particularly in the Dakotas and Montana. Its products at last found a ready market. The company had its most profitable year prior to World War I in 1909, putting on a night shift at Potlatch for the first time. The town's population swelled to 1,700 people. Many lived in tents while awaiting construction of additional company houses.[3]

The boom was short-lived, though. In addition to the recurring problem of high freight costs, the great northern Idaho forest fires of 1910 brought further difficulties. While comparatively little Potlatch timber burned, production suffered. Woods operations shut down because of fire danger, and the mill closed so men could fight the flames. The conflagration also had a long-standing impact on company profits. Fire-damaged timber became an insect haven, and the company was forced to construct expensive railroad spurs earlier than planned in order to log trees before the insects destroyed them. With the situation somewhat improved by 1916 Laird wrote Charles Weyerhaeuser that he hoped he would not be "seriously shocked" when hearing the company might be able to pay a 3 percent dividend to stockholders that year.[4]

This modest dividend, however, was hardly what directors had hoped for when entering Idaho, and though it was encouraging, the upsurge was temporary. In 1913 the nation's economy again stagnated, and lumber products, especially those expensively transported from Idaho, had a difficult time finding markets in states to the east. Potlatch's problems were further magnified amid confusion following the death of the company's most influential manager in that year.[5]

William Deary returned to Potlatch from a New York trip in mid-April fighting a cold. Typically, he refused to rest and spent a few days at the office before going to Spokane on business. There he was stricken with what he thought was pleurisy. He took a few days off, then returned to Potlatch. The illness lingered, and a variety of doctors treated him at his home. The physicians frequently disagreed on diagnosis and medication, and Deary gradually weakened. In the end he received regular injections of morphine to fight the pain, and died of internal hemorrhaging on May 7.

All businesses in Elk River and Potlatch closed for memorial services. Potlatch's small Catholic Church overflowed with mourners. The company arranged to run a special WI&M train over Northern Pacific tracks to Spokane. There Deary's wife had his body interred, although the general manager had wanted to be buried in Potlatch. "I knew nothing would please Mr. Deary better than to be carried to Spokane in a special [train] composed of his own equipment," wrote Laird. "He was so proud of 'his' railroad." Many old friends gathered to pay last respects—Laird and Andrew Bloom; T. J. Humbird and F. W. Kehl; Henry Turrish and Charles Weyerhaeuser, among others. They recognized Deary as the company's leader, the man to whom they had always deferred on crucial decisions. "In Mr. Deary's death we have lost a general," wrote Charles Weyerhaeuser, who was genuinely fond of him. "He was about the best organizer and one of the most courageous men that I ever knew, with splendid business judgment. We can never hope to get another man to do the work that he did."[6]

Though Weyerhaeuser questioned whether the company could find another man of Deary's ability, the most obvious place to begin was with Allison Laird. Next to Deary, he knew the operation best. As Deary grew to like and trust Laird he granted his assistant increasing authority. At the same time, Laird educated himself about the lumber trade, frequently writing to relatives and friends in Winona for advice and suggestions. Deary favored Laird as his successor, and Laird did some lobbying on his own behalf after his friend's death. "I do not need to be told I cannot *fill* Mr. Deary's place," he wrote the Laird-Norton Company. "But he leaves a well organized lumber business and railroad business (maybe I have helped some) and . . . I wonder where one could go to find more loyal or better manned institutions than ours. I believe I have my place here." Laird received his wish. The directors appointed him temporary general manager— just "long enough . . . so that you may show your capacity for independent management." Later they made him the permanent manager.[7]

Some company officers questioned Laird's early "independent management" decisions. His actions were made more difficult by a depressed lumber market, and by internal strife among the directors. "It is too bad that you have to go into an unsatisfactory market for your first season of direct responsibility," sympathized Frederic Bell. When Laird elected to temporarily shut down the Potlatch mill during the peak of the 1913 season without consulting the directors, he irritated Charles Weyerhaeuser who felt he was reacting too pessimistically to the economy. The Laird-Norton interests backed the new general manager, however, and Allison Laird rode out the storm. Part of Weyerhaeuser's complaint was based on economic reasoning, but underlying this was a growing concern that his family was losing influence in the Potlatch Lumber Company. William Deary's allegiance had clearly rested with the Weyerhaeusers and Mussers, whom he had known and worked with for years. The new general manager's loyalties were obviously with the Laird-Norton group. Although the Weyerhaeusers, Lairds, and Nortons were long-time partners and friends, Weyerhaeuser opposed turning over too much control to them. He was peeved when the Lairds, Nortons, and Turrish vetoed his suggestion that a man from another Weyerhaeuser operation be brought in as Allison Laird's assistant. Turrish confided that he was "especially unfavorable to an outsider from any of the other Weyerhaeuser plants." Instead of heeding Weyerhaeuser's advice, the directors voted to temporarily eliminate the position of assistant general manager. Eventually, Allison Laird and Charles Weyerhaeuser mended their differences, and Weyerhaeuser became one of Laird's most ardent supporters during subsequent management debates. But Laird frequently disagreed with other members of the Weyerhaeuser family, and during his first few months as general manager did not enjoy the unqualified support of his company's president.[8]

In reality, Allison Laird was unqualified to manage such a large, complex organization. Compounding his inexperience was the fact that he assumed command at a time of economic depression and internal dissension. To make matters even worse, he had inherited an unhealthy organization, one that probably no person could have operated profitably at that time. "Nowhere in the Far Northwest did the Weyerhaeuser group cherish brighter hopes at the beginning of the century than Idaho," remarked historians Ralph Hidy, Frank Hill, and Allan Nevins. Yet nowhere did they meet with more frustration.[9]

Potlatch's problems were many. One year after Laird became general manager, the United States completed the Panama Canal, which proved anything but a boon to Inland Empire lumber firms. Now it cost considerably more for inland mills to ship products east by rail than it did for concerns on the West Coast to transport them by boat. This further lessened the competitive advantage of an area already suffering. In addition, northern Idaho's rugged terrain made logging more expensive than originally anticipated. Some large stands of timber were unharvestable, while others required construction of costly railroad spurs. The large belt-driven Potlatch sawmill was outdated almost from the day it began. The Potlatch and Elk River plants, the town of Potlatch, and the WI&M Railway were very expensive because Deary and Laird insisted upon better-quality construction than was really necessary. Despite many legal and political attempts, Potlatch never did convince the state to rescind its law requiring the harvesting of timber on state lands within twenty years. This constraint forced the company to construct its costly Elk River plant and led to hasty, unprofitable clear-cutting as the firm rushed to harvest state timber within the allotted time period. In the early years, when Potlatch officials felt confident they could persuade the legislature to change its rule, they bought too much state timber, an amount almost impossible to log in two decades. Later, as it became clear the law would stand, company officials became too conservative, refusing to purchase timber even when not regulated by the state's twenty-year policy. As a result, Potlatch suffered in later years because it had an inadequate source of timber. Finally, perhaps no managers could have produced consistent profits, but Deary and Laird were especially ill-suited to the task. "William Deary was a good logger and perhaps was a good woodsman, but he knew very little about any phase of the lumber business after the log arrived at the sawmill," wrote Frederick E. Weyerhaeuser, who did not share his brother Charles's high esteem of the Canadian. "A. W. Laird was a banker by training, and never gained much more than an office experience in solving the problems of the lumber business."[10]

Laird, who like his predecessor was a tireless worker, remained at Potlatch's helm for eighteen largely unprofitable years. In 1914 the company suffered its biggest losses ever to that time. In 1915 production and sales picked up, largely in response to wartime markets. Despite labor shortages, Potlatch experienced particularly successful years in 1917 and 1918, but even after this time of growth, Laird viewed the future pessimistically: "The year 1919 started with a belief in general that business should be good. With the removal of all building restrictions and the apparent prospect of labor shifting back to normal pursuits, it was reasonable to expect good business. . . . It was not to be."[11]

Laird's caution proved justified. The years from 1920 to 1922 were nearly disastrous. The nation again slumped into a depression in 1921 with agricultural areas and the businesses serving them—such as Potlatch—being hardest hit. Until the spring of 1921, Potlatch continued full-scale production, but as lumber stockpiles rose and buyers grew scarce, Laird shut down all woods and mill operations. The company tried to dispose of lumber by selling it at less than production costs. Still, little moved. "It is deadly quiet in Potlatch, Bovill, and Elk River and it will be worse before it is better," he wrote F. S. Bell. Many residents left Potlatch, and others formed committees to assist needy people who remained. For the first time, company directors gave serious consideration to selling the community. Phil Weyerhaeuser strongly supported the idea, believing the company town was unnecessary to the business. Phil's uncle Charles, along with other older directors, vetoed the proposal, convinced that the grand experiment had not yet run its course. But the seed had been planted. From this point, younger company officials would become more powerful and more vociferous in advocating relinquishment of the town.[12]

Laird miscalculated the length of the post-war economic recession. Having closed the mills and depleted the company's reserve of lumber, he was unprepared for the sudden business upswing which came in 1923. "We had orders for 2,500 or 3,000 cars of lumber on our books that we couldn't possibly fill," recalled William Maxwell. "The orders were coming in faster than we could fill them, because we had slowed down a little bit, expecting business to stay quiet for a while after the war. Then it picked up so rapidly." Potlatch's directors authorized an expenditure of over a million dollars to enlarge and revamp the Potlatch mill in order to increase production. They also put on a double shift. The lumber company had an extremely profitable year in 1923, and the town boomed as it never had before. So many people came to find work that it was impossible to house them all, despite the construction of twenty-six new cottages. It was in this year that the shack village on the town's border first appeared. During the depression this became a haven for people unable to afford better housing. But at first, the village grew out of prosperity, not poverty. People moved here because of good times at the plant, when there was no other place in town to live. Louise Klumb Heighes's father came to Potlatch in 1923 and put up a tent for his family so that he could work at the mill. Over forty other men did the same that year. "When housing became available they moved up town. But it was a long wait," Heighes remembered. Rather than discouraging this ramshackle addition, Laird encouraged it because he needed the workers. "In that little pine grove are . . . tents and shacks which we have permitted married men to put up to house them and their families," he wrote his directors. "We piped water down so that they can all go to a common watering place and draw their water for domestic use."[13]

Potlatch remained lively until the early 1930s. Production peaked in 1929 as Laird, like other western lumbermen, sought to stimulate profits by increasing yields. While this policy brought good times for workers, it was nearly catastrophic for the company. Potlatch showed financial losses every year from 1924 through 1929. As assistant general manager Walter Humiston stated in 1928, "The lumbermen of the Intermountain Region are generally operating at a loss or at no profit." By the late 1920s, many directors of Potlatch and other Weyerhaeuser-affiliated operations in Idaho began thinking about merging their businesses so as to cut costs, and, they hoped, pay dividends.[14]

THE MERGER: POTLATCH FORESTS, INCORPORATED

Discussions about merging Weyerhaeuser's Idaho concerns were actually as old as the firms themselves. "I agree with Mr. Thatcher that it is a mistake to organize too many Idaho co[mpanies]," Charles Weyerhaeuser had written to James Norton in 1902. But his warning went unheeded. In the north the associates formed the Clearwater and Edward Rutledge Timber Companies and the Humbird, Potlatch, and Bonners Ferry Lumber Companies. In southern Idaho they organized the Barber Lumber Company and the Payette Lumber and Manufacturing Company. Having failed to convince his fellow directors to incorporate fewer firms, Weyerhaeuser now concentrated his efforts on attempting to merge the northern and southern Idaho interests. His idea gained little support among the companies' other stockholders, however, although the two southern Idaho firms did consolidate in 1913 to form the Boise Payette Lumber Company, the predecessor of the Boise Cascade Corporation.[15]

Serious merger talks began in 1919 as the various companies suffered post-war economic declines. Major stockholders of Rutledge, Humbird, Potlatch, and Boise Payette agreed to discuss the possibility of combining their businesses. But with each director protecting his own interests, the negotiations foundered. Charles Weyerhaeuser still strongly supported unification, but he could not even convince his long-time friend Drew Musser who remained "more opposed to this consolidation than any one else." Suspicions and rumors abounded. When writing Allison Laird about merger prospects, Weyerhaeuser requested that Laird return his letter "as I do not want it in your files." If Drew Musser was the most adamantly opposed to consolidation, certainly Allison Laird challenged him for that honor. As general manager of Idaho's largest lumber company, Laird believed his firm had much to lose and little to gain by any merger.[16]

Talk of consolidation cooled as the companies again showed profits in 1923. But by the late 1920s discussions intensified as many directors came to realize that only drastic managerial changes would avert bankruptcy. In August 1927 the Clearwater Timber Company's huge sawmill at Lewiston started up. The operation was so big that Phil Weyerhaeuser, Clearwater's general manager, wrote to a friend that his characterization of the plant as "colossal" seemed a "very conservative statement." The Lewiston facility dwarfed the Potlatch mill, which for years had been Idaho's largest. Construction of the Lewiston plant had both positive and negative effects upon merger talks. On the one hand, some Weyerhaeuser associates now believed a consolidation was possible. Before the Clearwater company had a mill, it had little to offer to any merger. Further, Phil Weyerhaeuser was now in a position of authority, as was his cousin George F. Jewett, who would shortly become general manager of the Rutledge operation. Like their uncle Charles, Phil and Jewett strongly advocated unifying the Idaho interests. On the other hand, Allison Laird now even more stubbornly opposed consolidation. He had believed Potlatch stood to lose before Clearwater began sawing, since his was then the largest Idaho firm and would be asked to give away the most. Now he feared that Clearwater would completely overwhelm Potlatch. Further, while Laird liked Charles, he remained suspicious of most of the Weyerhaeuser family, and particularly abhorred Phil. The feeling was mutual, with many Weyerhaeusers questioning Laird's managerial abilities. Nonetheless, Laird was influential, and his steadfast opposition delayed the final merger.[17]

The events that finally led to a merger developed late in the troubled year of 1929 when George "Fritz" Jewett sent a "Plan for Consolidation of Idaho Lumber Companies" to primary stockholders in each firm. Jewett outlined some compelling reasons for consolidation: a single company would need fewer executives and administrative staff;

cooperation among firms would eliminate duplication of equipment; larger quantities of supplies and materials could be purchased at a considerable savings. While the ideas had merit, they did not meet with unanimous enthusiasm. Frederick E. Weyerhaeuser wrote to Cliff Musser, "apparently Will Musser feels that Boise Payette has the rosiest future; John [Weyerhaeuser] and I feel that Clearwater has, while Charles [Weyerhaeuser] and Allison Laird think Potlatch has, so all that is left is for the Rutledge Company to merge with itself."[18]

Despite these difficulties, the associates did agree to appoint a committee to investigate merger possibilities. They selected Laird Bell, Frederic's son, as chairman. Bell had little experience in the lumber industry. He had graduated from Harvard in the same class with Franklin Roosevelt and attended the University of Chicago Law School in the class with Harold Ickes, who became Roosevelt's Secretary of the Interior. Bell, a prominent Chicago attorney, was a political liberal surrounded by relatives and associates in the lumber business who were much more conservative than he. But he worked hard arranging a merger, and as a result of his tireless efforts – and perhaps because he was an "outsider" against whom no one held grudges – he succeeded. Certainly he received more cooperation from Allison Laird, who had always considered Frederic Bell his closest confidant, than any Weyerhaeuser could have. Even so, the Potlatch manager remained unenthusiastic. He wrote to F. S. Bell after meeting with the merger committee in September 1930 that he would rather liquidate Potlatch than merge, allowing stockholders to enjoy the high dividends that would result if the company sold its assets.[19]

Shortly into the merger process, discussions concentrated on the three northern firms: Rutledge, Potlatch, and Clearwater. Boise Payette was too far away to make consolidation with it workable; and the Humbird Lumber Company, Weyerhaeuser's only Idaho firm that had shown consistent profits, was about to complete its logging operations and its shareholders wanted to reap their last dividends without sharing them. Bell and the merger committee worked out various details concerning timber allocation, stock divisions, and other matters, and presented their proposal to the three companies' shareholders. On April 29, 1931, the Potlatch Lumber Company stockholders held a special meeting to vote on the proposal. By then Potlatch's leadership differed considerably from when the unification discussions had begun. Charles Weyerhaeuser had died in April 1930 while on vacation in India, and the directors had replaced the long-time company president with Allison Laird's adversary, Phil Weyerhaeuser. Furthermore, Laird himself was not at the special meeting. Earlier in the year, suffering from cancer, he had moved from Potlatch to California. His absence eased the consolidation process. While some Potlatch shareholders did fight the merger, they were easily outvoted. Stockholders of Rutledge and Clearwater also favored consolidation, and with all legal obstacles cleared, Potlatch Forests, Incorporated emerged in 1931. Phil Weyerhaeuser was the first president, and corporate headquarters were located in Lewiston.[20]

Allison Laird died one day after the April 29 stockholders' meeting. His death signaled the end of an era in Potlatch's history. No longer did the Potlatch Lumber Company control its own destiny. No longer was the town of Potlatch as integral to the total corporate operation as previously: rather than being the administrative center of a sizable operation, the small town was now merely the unit headquarters of an even larger business. And no longer did Potlatch residents have Allison Laird, their concerned benefactor, protecting their interests. As the community poured into the Union Church on May 5 to pay last respects to their general manager—town flags flying at half-mast—many Potlatchers worried about their futures and the continued existence of their town.[21]

When the merger brought some immediate unpleasant consequences, Potlatch residents' fears seemed justified. With the loss of much business mail to Lewiston, the Potlatch post office went from second to third class status. One of PFI's first actions was to permanently close the Elk River mill, and many Potlatchers believed theirs would be next. "People . . . got very suspicious about how long Potlatch would last," stated A. N. Frederickson. "It appeared then that its days were numbered, and that it would eventually end up as a ghost town."[22]

While PFI officials did not take as keen an interest in the town as Potlatch Lumber Company's managers had, the merger did help the community survive. Potlatch Unit managers Jack Irwin and Jim O'Connell were not unsympathetic to community affairs. And, as even Laird had admitted, before his death, had it not been for the merger, the Potlatch Lumber Company would have been liquidated, which could have destroyed the town. As it was, consolidation brought a more efficient and streamlined operation, and the Potlatch plant continued to operate another fifty years—almost thirty years longer than originally anticipated by Deary, Laird, and other early officials.

It took nearly a decade after the merger before PFI began showing consistent profits. Wartime demand and rising prices increased revenues during the early 1940s, and post-war sales to newly affluent Americans pushed the prosperity into the 1950s. By that time PFI had considerably diversified its production and was less vulnerable to lumber market downswings. It reeled off profits into the late 1970s. Even so, many directors, particularly those in the Weyerhaeuser family, looked upon the Potlatch Unit as a hindrance to even greater PFI gains. "Is there any reason for prolonging the life of the Potlatch Plant beyond the period of time required to clean up the White Pine tributary [sic] to that plant?" questioned Frederick K. Weyerhaeuser, Phil's brother, writing to PFI general manager Charles Billings in 1939. "Are we permitting ourselves to prolong the life of . . . Potlatch . . . for personal reasons at a net cost to Potlatch Forests, Inc.?" Billings replied that "the answer . . . is clearly No," and the question temporarily became moot as war flared in Europe, bringing a steady demand for materials from all PFI plants.[23]

The issue emerged again at war's end. In 1946 Frederick K. Weyerhaeuser wrote to George Jewett, by then PFI's president, asking for a thorough study of the Potlatch Unit. The company planned to revamp its mill operations at Coeur d'Alene, Lewiston, and Potlatch, but Weyerhaeuser wondered if it would not be better to simply abandon the Potlatch site. He believed decisions about Potlatch were being made because of sentimentality for the community and apprehension about creating a "ghost town," rather than on the basis of cost effectiveness. "The Potlatch operation is a high cost operation. . . . Putting new dollars into Potlatch in order to perpetuate the town will probably not yield as great a return on new investments as if the dollars were invested at Coeur d'Alene or Lewiston," he asserted.[24]

Jewett directed Billings to study the matter, probably to the dismay of some other Weyerhaeusers. Though Billings was a close personal friend of many in the family, particularly Phil, some believed he let emotions override profit motives. "Phil has always been pretty critical of the Potlatch operation," Laird Bell accurately noted. "He has a feeling that the organization is not cost and profit minded enough. . . . On the other hand, Billings is always thinking that everything is going to be wonderful, which merely seems to irritate Phil." Billings wanted to retain all three plants, and, not surprisingly, his study indicated that PFI would lose considerably by abandoning Potlatch. The PFI executive committee found some flaws in Billings's study and stated that the unit's slim profits projected "over a twenty year period [are] of little importance." Nonetheless, following the long-standing Potlatch tradition of granting considerable decision-making autonomy to general managers, they voted to retain the Potlatch plant. The mill was renovated again, and PFI kept control of the town.[25]

Charles Lee Billings, born in St. Paul, Minnesota, in 1888, never lived in Potlatch. But, like Deary and Laird, he was one of the community's most ardent supporters, a fact largely unknown in that town. Billings moved West in 1910, landing his first forestry job fighting fires in Montana. He then worked for ten years with the U.S. Forest Service, taking a little time off to study forestry at the University of Montana. In 1920 he became land agent for the Edward Rutledge Timber Company, attending to taxes, land sales, fire protection, and timber cruising. During his Forest Service work and his later experiences with Rutledge, Billings formulated what was then an unusual forest management policy: through selective logging and reforestation, lumber companies could avoid the "cut and run" trauma that traditionally plagued their industry. Properly managed forests could last forever. When Phil Weyerhaeuser went to Rutledge, the two men began a life-long friendship. Many of Billings's progressive ideas subsequently found an effective voice in the most influential of the third generation of Weyerhaeusers. The two moved together to Lewiston in 1925, Phil as general manager of the Clearwater Timber Company and Billings as his assistant. Billings became PFI's general manager in 1933 when Phil went to Tacoma as vice president of the Weyerhaeuser Timber Company. Billings remained as general manager at Lewiston until his death in 1948. During that time he worked diligently to retain PFI's interests in all three of its mills. While he was alive, the Potlatch Unit and company town would survive. After his death, however, several directors began again to consider eliminating the company's least profitable operation.[26]

By 1950 PFI was booming, earning more than six million dollars that year. Utilizing these profits, the company began a policy of expansion out of Idaho, purchasing land and plants elsewhere. Idaho operations would remain predominant for many years, but the state's role in the total corporate picture was diminishing, and the future of the Potlatch Unit became particularly perilous. In 1950, PFI's executive committee requested another study to determine whether the company should abandon the Potlatch mill. Again, the mill survived, although it was reduced from four headrigs to two. But company officials decided the time was finally opportune to rid themselves of the town. Its aging buildings required considerable maintenance at a time when increased labor costs made such repairs expensive. The townsite department's profits had dwindled every year. Now there was no strong voice speaking out for preservation of the community—Deary, Laird, Charles Weyerhaeuser, and Billings were dead, and Potlatch Unit manager James O'Connell was not opposed to ending the company town experiment. Potlatch had been company-controlled for forty-five years. During most of that time it survived despite disappointing business returns. Potlatch sold its town not during a time of economic difficulty, but during one of its most prosperous periods. It was not that the company could no longer afford its town. Rather, company officials, expanding into newer and larger arenas, did not want to be burdened by ancillary sideshows. Any sentimental compulsion to retain the community had died, a victim of an increasing interest in more cost-effective, efficient operations.[27]

FROM COMPANY TOWN TO INCORPORATED VILLAGE

Frederick Weyerhaeuser knew his children would inherit a lumber empire, and insisted that his sons learn the business from the bottom up. It was a trait the second generation passed onto the third, and Frederick K. Weyerhaeuser, Phil's brother, gained much of his introduction to lumbering with Potlatch. Returning home from active duty during the war in 1919, he worked with the company's retail sales department. In 1923 he and his wife Vivian moved to the town where they remained for over a year. Weyerhaeuser later assumed leadership positions with the family's business concerns, but he never forgot his Potlatch interlude, and must have retained fond memories of the town.

It was Frederick K. Weyerhaeuser who, in 1950, convinced PFI's directors to seriously investigate the possibility of selling the town. He continued to push the idea until the company finalized its decision to sell a year later. His motives were primarily economic, but he also believed it to be in the community's best interest for the company to divest its non-mill holdings there. He insisted that PFI not simply pull out without planning for the town's future. "I would like to see us handle the disposal of the property in Potlatch in a manner best calculated to improve the town," he wrote PFI's president William P. Davis. Norton Clapp, Matthew Norton's grandson and by this time head of the Laird-Norton interests, agreed. "Potlatch . . .

presents an interesting challenge to anyone who is interested in trying to convert a 'company town' into a modern little community that
everyone can be proud of," he wrote. William Davis also believed
the company had an obligation to the community. "I am very happy
that you and Fred are interested in doing some things at Potlatch
that will make it more attractive and a better place to live," he wrote
Clapp. Together, the three would ensure that the transition from
company town to incorporated village went as smoothly as possible.[28]

Though Weyerhaeuser championed the cause that eventually
separated Potlatch from its town, PFI directors had taken gradual
steps to divest some interests there even before voting to sell the entire community. In 1940 they sold the Potlatch State Bank. In 1948
they sold their townsite electric distribution system to the Washington
Water Power Company. In that same year the company quit the
school business, donating all of its school buildings to a new consolidated district. The company also tried, without success, to find
a buyer for its waterworks system. By the end of the 1940s it was
apparent that PFI's directors wanted out of the company town
business. Frederick Weyerhaeuser's motion merely assured that this
divestiture would be done systematically rather than haphazardly over
a long period.[29]

By early 1952 PFI had several employees working on various aspects
of the sale. At that time the company owned 267 houses, two apartments, thirteen business buildings, and two churches. In the fall of
that year the company sent letters to all Potlatch residents announcing that it planned to sell its townsite and offering current tenants
first option to purchase the places they occupied. The company offered buyers ten-year mortgages at 6 percent interest with this
guarantee: in the event PFI was forced to close the mill before houses
were paid off, the company would refund all of the purchaser's money,
less the amount it would have cost to rent. They added this provision to reassure buyers that the company did not merely want to make
a quick profit from sales and then close the mill, leaving new owners
with property of little value.[30]

Under these terms, sales went quite quickly and within a year PFI
had disposed of 177 houses. The remaining ninety houses, though,
moved more slowly, and the company, believing it had "just about
come to the end of the line as far as selling homes on our present
plan," developed ways to encourage sales of the remainder.[31]

At first the company refused to increase rents as it wanted "to give
people every opportunity to buy without any pressure being applied."

When sales stagnated, however, it did raise rents. In June 1954 it sent an announcement of substantial rent hikes to all tenants. Renters were also informed that their houses would be offered to any buyers wishing to purchase them. The letters had the effect company managers desired in that they stimulated sales. But some residents protested the treatment. Sixty-four-year-old Sven Alsager wrote, "If I should be retired at the age of 65, it would not be worthwhile to buy after paying rent for 40 years. . . . A faithful employee should get some consideration." His sentiment was seconded by Charles Talbott who complained that in twenty-two years "I have payed in rent a little over $3700 on this house that cost $700 to build. . . . [The] rent [increase] for this place is worse than Highway robbery for in highway robbery you are permitted to fight back." And H. H. Hanson, manager of the Potlatch Branch of Idaho First National Bank, while agreeing that a "reasonable increase, in our monthly rental, is in order," protested that "a $50 per month increase appears exorbitant." To each such complaint company officials stated that they believed it was necessary that "all Potlatch tenants should receive uniform treatment with respect to any changes that we find it necessary to make" and refused to compromise, except in a few cases where people were planning to retire shortly and move from town.[32]

Although they were more drastic than PFI officials originally hoped would be required, the strong measures worked. By September the company owned only thirty-three houses. It continued to rent these, and in the coming years gradually sold some while razing others and selling the vacant lots. In late summer 1954 the company laid off the last three employees of the townsite department, which had maintained the community for nearly fifty years. The sawmill maintenance crew handled necessary repairs on the company's few remaining town buildings.[33]

Simultaneously with the sale of houses and commercial buildings, PFI made other arrangements for transforming Potlatch from a company town into an incorporated village. It donated St. Mary's Catholic Church to parishioners and also gave the lot on which the Lutheran Church stood to that congregation, as the Lutherans already owned their building. In 1940 the Union Church had become the Community Presbyterian Church, but in 1951 the handsome structure burned. In the following year the company donated land on Nob Hill for a new church, and also built its basement and foundation. Potlatch also donated the library, fire hall, and a fire truck to the community, and hired a landscape architect to improve the town's appearance. The architect's primary recommendation, which would have greatly pleased C. R. Musser and F. S. Bell who always disliked the community's grid-like layout, called for the construction of two curving streets – Ponderosa and Memorial Drives – connecting the community's two residential hills. In addition to relieving the monotony of north-south, east-west streets, this plan eliminated much of the isolation between the two hills by providing three routes between them rather than one. Finally, PFI deeded the pine grove, long the site of temporary housing, as a city park. At the same time, it began working with community residents on a new form of municipal government.[34]

In late 1952 Potlatch officially became known as the Village of Potlatch, no longer controlled by the company but governed temporarily by a five member board of trustees appointed by Latah County's commissioners. In April 1953 the board sent notice to all town residents informing them they were eligible to vote in an upcoming election for city council if they had lived in town three months. It was the first time any Potlatch resident had voted in an election affecting the community's government. Councilmen selected during that first election were Theodore Saad, Milford Jones, Alfred Johnson, Dewey LaVoy, and William Bell.[35]

One of the incorporated community's first ordinances required that all outhouses be removed from the north hill, and by 1954 the town had a complete sewer system. The company continued to pay for garbage collection and police protection, believing the new village could not yet afford these. But it stopped subsidizing garbage services on January 1, 1955, and police services on July 1. Even so, the company still retained a large presence in town. In addition to running the mill, it owned the Merc, a few houses, and some downtown buildings, including the main office, which it had gerrymandered to outside village boundaries to avoid paying taxes. City officials loudly complained about this action. By the late 1950s the company gave in to the demands of the city council and this building, too, became a part of the town. It was eventually turned over to the community and served as city hall.[36]

Potlatch remained a single industry community heavily dominated by PFI and was, therefore, still atypical of most small towns. But in many ways it now functioned like communities elsewhere. A Junior Chamber of Commerce formed, as well as a Potlatch Area Boosters group that undertook civic improvements and, for the first time, encouraged town growth. The Boosters organized the first Potlatch

Community Day celebration in 1953, an event that gradually developed into a regional festival of logging skills. Without the company to pay all expenses, Potlatch now had to compete for businesses with other area towns in order to create a tax base. Potlatch would never experience the boom and bust cycles of a place like Palouse, since the region by now was well-developed and its population stable. Still, the town's boosters worked just as hard to market their community as had their pioneer predecessors in neighboring towns.[37]

The Works Progress Administration's American Guide Series book on Idaho, revised in 1950, predicted that Potlatch "will doubtlessly steadily decline . . . until it is little more than a store and a gas station." The authors would have been surprised had they visited the community in the late 1950s, as one writer did. Rather than declining, incorporation had infused the community with new energy:

> Mrs. Woodrow Nye . . . recalls that the houses were so similar when they moved onto Maple Street six years ago that their daughter . . . couldn't find the right place one day when she came home from play. . . .
>
> [When sold] the rows of houses . . . as uniform as an army cantonment, blossomed out in pinks, greens and blues. Off came the porches; in went the picture windows, full basements and landscaped gardens.

Local building supply stores did a land office business as new homeowners scurried to modernize their houses. By the latter part of the 1950s, with all the former company houses occupied, some people began building new homes on the town's fringes. This constituted Potlatch's first substantial construction since the boom time of 1923. By 1960 Potlatch's population had stabilized at 880 people. While only half the size it had been fifty years earlier, Potlatch was hardly the ghost town predicted by the 1950 guide book.[38]

Potlatch entered its fifty-first year in 1957 as a completely self-governed community. It had never been the "ideal" company town many directors had hoped for at the turn of the century. Neither was the incorporated town quite as handsome as Norton Clapp, Frederick K. Weyerhaeuser, and William Davis might have liked. Many of the beautification measures proposed by their landscape architect—such as creating more city parks and providing a greenbelt around the community—remained undeveloped. Still, the company had not done badly by its town. For nearly fifty years it had seen to every need of the community. When the company decided to end its town experiment, it did not pull out quickly and cause a leadership and economic void. In an effort to seek greater profits and eliminate inefficient operations, PFI's directors had voted to divest themselves of their community. To their credit, they undertook such divestiture in a way which benefited most town residents.[39]

Epilogue

POTLATCH AT EIGHTY

I spent a spring day in Potlatch in 1986. The town was eighty years old by then. Since I first began researching Potlatch's history, I had made the twenty-five mile trip from my house too many times to remember. It had become something of a second home, and I had many friends there. But I wanted this day to be different – a day set aside for observation. I wanted to get an impression of how Potlatch in 1986 compared to my image of Potlatch in 1906.

Initially there seemed to be little similarity. For almost eighty years the mill had been the dominating site upon entering town. In 1986, though, a visitor would probably have to be told there once had been a sawmill on the flat field at the edge of the community. If you look closely you can still see some vestiges of the plant – the loading platform; patches of asphalt not yet overgrown by weeds; some concrete footings. There is even a roadside sign stating "Potlatch: Main Gate Next Right." But the gate leads nowhere except to a small office building. This structure was once dwarfed by the manufacturing plant surrounding it. Now it is all that is left of that huge facility, and the nearby land is not unlike the undeveloped riverfront property William Deary purchased as a potential millsite in the early 1900s.

In 1983 a group of Latah County Historical Society volunteers photodocumented the mill prior to its dismantling. We found the plant to be a virtual time capsule. On August 13, 1981, company officials had suddenly announced a temporary mill closure. Many employees left work that week believing they would eventually return. Yet two years later their work clothes still hung in lockers; tools sat on tables; calendars remained opened to August 1981. Two brief, yellowing notices tacked to an abandoned bulletin board provided a thumbnail sketch of the plant's history that summer:

> June 3, 1981. R. E. Vassar, plant manager, to all employees: Because of the depressed lumber market conditions, Potlatch Unit

will not operate on Fridays until further notice.

August 13, 1981. R. E. Vassar to all employees: The Idaho Department of Employment in Moscow has agreed to process applications for unemployment in Potlatch.

Not until March 1983 did company officials announce the mill's permanent closure. "Future uncertainties in the demand for wood products, . . . unavailability of timber . . . plus the age and configuration of the mill have made this decision necessary," stated Potlatch vice president James Morris. Long before then, however, most Potlatch residents had resigned themselves to the inevitable announcement. "We kind of all expected it," said Kenny Austin, a former employee. "But . . . it kind of jars you."[1]

Rumors of the mill's closure had run through Potlatch periodically since the merger of 1931, and the company had seriously considered shutting down the plant in the 1930s, 1940s, and 1950s. It was not that town residents were surprised by a closure many had long viewed as unavoidable; it was that they were dismayed at the way word came down from corporate executives. The company had a long history of closing mills on short notice, giving employees virtually no time to plan for their futures. They did it in Palouse in 1911, in Elk River in 1931, and in Potlatch in the 1980s. That this had become standard company procedure, however, did not lessen the blow's impact. A 1981 *Lewiston Morning Tribune* editorial summarized many Potlatch residents' feelings:

> When the closing of a mill can mean the closing of a town, a conscientious corporation would work and plan with the citizens of the community, giving them both time and assistance to plan for the future.
>
> A corporate decision on Monday to close on Friday gives them neither.
>
> It is a callous decision and perhaps tells us more than we want to know about how the major corporation in our midst plans to face the tough times ahead.[2]

Seen from the perspective of a Potlatch resident, the short notice seemed callous. Seen from the perspective of company executives in San Francisco overseeing a vast, international, diversified, "Fortune 500" corporation attempting to maintain solvency during a difficult time for lumber manufacturers, closure of an outdated mill made perfect sense. Perhaps the thought never occurred to them that they should provide more notice to the 200 employees scheduled for layoff. The simple fact was that Potlatch, the business, had long outgrown its origins in Potlatch, the town, and by the 1980s operations in Latah County were expendable. There is a story one hears when talking to people in Potlatch today that might or might not be true. But in a short time it has gained the status of folk tradition. Supposedly in the 1970s the town's mayor received a telephone call from an administrative assistant at corporate headquarters in San Francisco wondering if there was any connection between the names of the town of Potlatch and the Potlatch Corporation. To a Potlatch resident, the tale indicates both how small a role the Potlatch mill played in the company's overall operations during its last years, and how little the latest generation of Potlatch corporate officials understand about their Idaho roots.

In fact, the company's growth after selling its townsite was truly remarkable. In 1949 and 1950 PFI began a long-term diversification project by adding veneer, plywood, and pulp and paperboard plants at Lewiston. In 1952 it expanded operations outside of northern Idaho with the purchase of a paper mill in Pomona, California. This diversification and expansion gained velocity in the late 1950s and early 1960s when the company bought vast timberland tracts and mills in Arkansas and Minnesota, along with various types of paper manufacturing plants from coast to coast. By the mid-1960s the firm had forty operations in fifteen states employing nearly 12,000 people. Keeping track of these diverse holdings from Lewiston, with its limited transportation and communication facilities, became increasingly difficult. Consequently, in 1965 PFI moved its executive headquarters to San Francisco.[3]

Growth proved to be just as dynamic in the decade following that move. Potlatch became an international corporation in 1968 by purchasing timberlands and mills in Western Samoa and Colombia. It entered new fields, including real estate development and the manufacturing of factory-assembled buildings. By the end of the 1960s, PFI recorded annual sales of well over $300 million and controlled a million and a quarter acres of timberland in Arkansas, Minnesota, and Idaho. In 1973 Potlatch Forests, Incorporated, became Potlatch Corporation, a name deemed more appropriate for the diversified conglomerate it had become. It now was one of the world's largest manufacturers of timber products, with shares traded on the New York Stock Exchange. Even Bill Deary, who always dreamed on a grand scale, would have marveled at what his efforts had wrought.

In the late 1970s Potlatch, along with other American lumber concerns, hit a difficult period. High interest rates slowed housing construction while a stronger dollar and growing technological ad-
vancements abroad brought increasing competition from foreign firms.
In order to retain a viable business footing, Potlatch trimmed operations. Between 1979 and 1985 it divested itself of over twenty different types of businesses it had ventured into during its heady years
of diversification and expansion. At the same time many of its plants,
particularly those in Idaho where the company had operated longest,
became outdated. Streamlining, modernization, and consolidation
were essential if the corporation was to remain competitive. The large
old mill at Potlatch, originally designed to last only fifty years and
already pushing eighty, was too cumbersome to profitably remodel.
It was the first of several Idaho operations closed down. A business
with a far-flung industrial empire fighting for corporate survival cannot let sentiment rule decision making. Closure of an outdated mill
in an isolated part of Idaho made good business sense, even if it did
cut off a major international corporation from many of its historical
roots.[4]

So now in 1986 the millsite lies bare and the most distinct reminder
that this was once a sawmill town is gone. Potlatch has visibly changed
in other ways, too. With private ownership, virtually all the town's
smallest houses were removed or enlarged. Today, the lowest part
of the north hill, the former segregated home of Japanese, Italians,
and Greeks living in Potlatch's least desirable housing, holds the
town's most modern expansion. Large split-level homes have replaced
the former cottages and boardinghouses there. The Potlatch Mercantile burned in 1963. The site today supports a parking lot and
small shopping center. Across the street, a modern building houses
the Potlatch branch of Idaho First National Bank. Just up Sixth street
the former post office, constructed in 1912, was razed early in 1986.
In its place builders have constructed a small frame building with
a false boomtown front containing a restaurant called the "Li'l
Wrangler"—an effort like so many others in the modern West to bring
economic revitalization by creating an atmosphere of "history" that
never existed. Potlatch was not Dodge City, and not one stick of Idaho
white pine shows on the new building. The structure is out of place,
and one wonders why builders try to invent a past in a community
with a unique and rich history that waits to be told to visitors.

In residential neighborhoods, new siding, asphalt-shingle or metal
roofs, room additions, and picture windows have brought a diversity

that was never present during company town days. Only a few board sidewalks remain, remnants of the time when wood was plentiful and inexpensively combated dust and mud. Many homes and yards are immaculately maintained, but others have a cluttered look that townsite superintendents would not have permitted. The former school building is now an apartment house, and new grade and high schools have been constructed. On Nob Hill a church occupies part of the former neighborhood park.

So Potlatch has changed, just as any living town changes with time, for this is not a museum. Looking more closely, though, one can still find many reminders of the community's past. In fact, so much remains intact that in 1986 the Idaho State Historic Preservation Office nominated forty-four Potlatch structures for inclusion on the National Register of Historic Places.[5]

Trains still stop daily at the WI&M depot, though now they carry no passengers and use tracks owned by Burlington Northern. Potlatch sold its railway to the Milwaukee Road in 1962, which in turn sold to Burlington. Nearby, the remarkably well-preserved former administrative office building now houses city hall. Across the street sits the gymnasium, empty except for small living quarters in front. The name "Town and Country Store" painted on its side, however, indicates the building's adaptive reuse over the years. Out front, two boulders hauled here in 1921 support a bronze plaque memorializing William Deary.

Despite the incursion of the church on the former Nob Hill park, the south hill has the feel that Nob Hill must have always had. The deciduous seedlings Allison Laird ordered in the early 1900s and meticulously and evenly planted are now huge shade trees. Houses here, because they were the best built, are well-preserved. Nob Hill is even undergoing a bit of a renaissance with restoration projects under way on several homes. Across town one can also still find a few examples of unaltered architecture in the workers' houses. And even though most homes here have been extensively remodeled, the north hill still has the feel of a planned community. The town's only remaining boardinghouse, which later served as the hospital, still stands on Pine Street. Now an apartment, it looks much as it always did. Just a few blocks away is the community's only historic brick house. Built by Joseph Terteling in 1916, it is basically unaltered.

The pine grove that once housed the temporary shack village is now a community park. It is still a popular picnic and recreation area, just as it was in the days before cars, when people entertained themselves close to home. Below the park are the WI&M tracks, and below the tracks the Palouse River. Well-worn foot paths course down from Nob Hill to the stream, places where kids and dogs race to find fishing holes and swimming spots just as Potlatch kids and dogs have done for generations. Downstream from the park are the remains of the upper dam, which formerly transformed the river into a log pond. Across from the damsite is a wild, rocky hillside nurturing tall second growth pines. It does not look too dissimilar from the way it appeared when Laird built a rifle range for the Potlatch Home Guard a short distance away during World War I.

Walking out of the park in the other direction, going upstream, one comes to the American Legion Cabin. Now a restaurant, it is still a massive structure little changed from the time lumberjacks hewed its log walls in the late 1920s. Across the highway is the cemetery, with Catholics on one side—an abundance of Italian and Irish names here—and Protestants on the other. The oldest grave belongs to Charles Rafford who died on Christmas day, 1907, "the first member of Evergreen Lodge No. 124, IOOF, to cross the silent river" according to his marker. Not far away is the second oldest gravesite, belonging to seven-year-old Mabel McGreal. Next to her rests Philip McGreal, the Potlatch High School basketball star of the 1920s. Some tombstones are written in Japanese and some in Norwegian. Dominating the cemetery is the tall, ornate headstone of Mark L. Seymour, first plant superintendent, who died in 1925. But his grave is an anomaly. There are no Dearys or Lairds or McDonalds or O'Connells here. They controlled Potlatch, but in the final analysis this was a community of working-class people. The managers managed and then moved on—if not while living, then upon death—and are buried in places their families presumed were more fitting for people of their stature. The Potlatch cemetery is a place for more common folk who called the community home both in life and in death.

Potlatch is still home to ordinary people. One can measure the pulse of this community by taking lunch at the Brown Hut Cafe on Sixth Street. The Brown Hut has six tables and a lunch counter surrounded by walls paneled in pine, adorned with local historic photographs. The conversation is often room-wide, people at different tables just as likely to be talking to others across the room as to those sitting with them. A person unfamiliar with the community gets the feeling of walking in on a conversation that has been months—perhaps years—in progress, complete with inside jokes and references to people and events unknown to outsiders. It takes only a quick glance at people eating in the Brown Hut to realize that the cowboy stereotype projected by the new restaurant next door does not speak to this West. I have seldom seen a cowboy hat in the Brown Hut, even though bareheaded men are in the minority. The preferred head piece is what folks here call "seed caps," though they might just as likely advertise tractors or banks or lumber products as seed companies. One notices something else about men in the Brown Hut, and indeed about men everywhere in Potlatch: they often have fingers missing—a reminder of the sawmill that once provided their employment.

As often as not, if one ate at the Brown Hut in the winter of 1986 they overheard conversation about the Potlatch High School boys basketball team. The Loggers remained undefeated until the season's last game and featured Dan Akins, a six-foot-seven-inch center who attracted college scouts from throughout the region. There might have been a few scouts in the stands the night I squeezed into the Potlatch gym to watch the team play old rival Palouse. The facility was not built with audiences of 1,000 in mind. But this team galvanized the community, and it was not uncommon for crowds larger than the town's population of 800 to attend its games. Entering the gym I walked by pictures of former graduating classes, past the case displaying trophies those earlier students won, into the basketball court where a loudspeaker blasted Tina Turner rock as players warmed up. A few minutes later cheerleaders in green and white urged everyone to stand, the pep band played the school fight song and National Anthem, Potlatch controlled the center jump, Akins scored, the crowd sat, and the Loggers eventually won: ten victories, no losses. It is a drama played out every winter in hundreds of gymnasiums in hundreds of small towns throughout America. Potlatch would finish fourth in the state tournament that season, while Akins would be named honorable mention high school All-American and sign with the University of Idaho basketball team.

At other times in 1986 people in Potlatch spoke among themselves about the $10,000 donation of Malcolm Rossman, a 1927 Potlatch High School graduate, to establish a community scholarship fund; or about the superior ratings the Potlatch schools again received from Pacific Northwest accreditation organizations— carryover honors from the high standards first set when the company ran the school. Residents also debated whether or not a Potlatch teacher had had "romantic" relations with a student. And the town buzzed over the trial and conviction of the former chief of police and his son for dealing in cocaine.

All in all, Potlatch in 1986 is much like any small town. It has much to be proud of and some things to be concerned about. No paternalistic company is in control now to keep things on an even keel. In earlier times, romantically involved teachers and lawbreaking constables would have been forced from town long before rumors had a chance to divide the community. On the other hand, the suspension of company control has brought benefits. It is difficult to imagine, for example, a person donating money to Potlatch Corporation to provide college scholarships for graduates of a company-owned school. The end result of the company's divestiture of the town has been the development of a community not too different — except in physical appearance and historical legacy — from other places of its size.

When the mill closed in 1981, the old theory that Potlatch would become a ghost town resurfaced. But that fear was not realized. While a few houses and businesses changed hands, the community's population remained stable. Several people in town commute daily to the mill in Lewiston. In the summer of 1985 bad news once again struck these and other Potlatch Corporation employees. On July 24 company officials announced that over 1,200 workers — including everyone at the Lewiston sawmill — faced immediate layoffs, another in a long line of corporate decisions passed out with little warning. The company's wood products division had lost nearly $6 million during the first half of 1985, and officials saw no alternative but to make cutbacks in Idaho. Politicians tried to capitalize on the bleak announcement. Some accused environmentalists of creating Potlatch's difficulties. Others blamed the company's outmoded sawmill for the problems; held that increasing Canadian imports were responsible; or censured skyrocketing federal deficits. In the end, it remained for the company and its employees — not politicians seeking advantage in their particular responses to the crisis — to work out matters. In November Potlatch and its workers reached a compromise enabling the company to rehire employees and reopen the Lewiston mill. Members of the International Woodworkers of America agreed to wage cuts saving the corporation $11 million annually, and the company announced it would build a new $35 million sawmill in Lewiston as part of its pledge to the union to modernize the plant.[6]

At the same time that Potlatch negotiated with the union, it fought an expensive takeover effort that could have brought an end to the company. Canadian financier Samuel Belzberg in early November

1985 offered nearly $700 million for Potlatch's stock in a hostile attempt to gain control of the corporation. Potlatch executives staved off the bid, but only after Belzberg had made a tidy $10 million profit when the company bought back his shares in what some viewed as a classic "greenmail" maneuver.[7]

Unlike some major corporations, Potlatch did not grow from tiny beginnings into a huge operation. While the Potlatch Lumber Company of 1903 was small in comparison to the Potlatch Corporation of 1986, in its day the lumber company was large. It had begun on a grand scale. The Weyerhaeusers, Lairds, Nortons, and Mussers were hardly financial novices. Still, even Frederick Weyerhaeuser would have been stunned by a $700 million corporate takeover attempt. The company he and his colleagues organized had grown and diversified to the point that it was hardly recognizable as the concern that started by purchasing the Codd sawmill in Colfax and the Palouse River Lumber Company in Palouse.

While the corporate structure has been completely transformed, Bill Deary or Allison Laird or Frederick Weyerhaeuser would still recognize the town of Potlatch were they to drive through it. The community weathered the company's financial crises of 1985 just as it had the plant closure of 1981. Though the mill is gone and many houses and buildings have been altered, the town still has the unmistakable look of the community that Deary and Laird planned so carefully eighty years ago. Town life has changed much. Now there are regular local elections, property is privately owned, and new businesses have been established. But the Potlatch of 1986 is clearly the descendant of the Potlatch of 1906.

I ended my spring day tour at the small Presbyterian Church built on Nob Hill in the 1950s after the Union Church burned. Church women were sponsoring a rummage sale, and I went inside to have some coffee and visit awhile. The church is ministered by the Reverend Kenneth Onstot, who is also the town's Lutheran pastor. "Economy is the inventor of a lot of things," Ken admits when asked about his dual role. The joint ministry came about when the congregations chose to cooperate by sharing one pastor. Though he has been in town only since 1979, Ken is well aware that while his ministry would be unusual in other towns, it has a long tradition in Potlatch. Here company officials years ago refused to build churches for every Protestant denomination, insisting that a myriad of religious followers worship together under the roof of one church. I was pleased when I thought of how this and many other traditions have been passed on from generation to generation in Potlatch. The origins of the customs might be unknown to some recent residents, but even they can appreciate the fact that these are somehow based upon past community experiences. It is these shared values that provide each town with its own distinctions. Perhaps Potlatch today has more in common with similar-sized small communities located anywhere in the West than it does with the town developed for lumber workers by a paternalistic company eighty years ago. But it still retains certain traditions — as all communities do — making it unique.[8]

I left the church that day and took one last drive around Nob Hill — past the Deary house and the Humistons' and the Lairds' and the Gambles' and the McDonalds' and the Seymours'; down the hill by the Merc's former implement warehouse, now a tavern. I turned onto the highway at city hall. The weathered WI&M depot at the former mill entrance was now in front of me. Off to the side stood the gymnasium. As I rounded the corner on Sixth Street going out of town, I glanced at the two huge boulders in front of the gym which serve as a memorial to Bill Deary. They seemed a fitting, permanent tribute to a massive man, and a massive idea.

Abbreviations

In an effort to consolidate notations, the following abbreviations have been used in the notes.

COL-OH: Columbia University oral history collection transcripts. These interviews were undertaken in the 1950s in conjunction with the writing of *Timber and Men: The Weyerhaeuser Story*. They are presently housed in the Weyerhaeuser Company Archives, Tacoma.

JEWETT: George F. Jewett papers, manuscript group 43, University of Idaho Library Special Collections, Moscow.

LCHS: Latah County Historical Society Library, Moscow.

LCHS-OH: Latah County Historical Society oral history collection. These interviews were conducted in the 1970s and 1980s. A page number following a LCHS-OH citation refers to a transcript page. Most interviews have been transcribed, and all are indexed.

LN: Laird-Norton Company Archives, Seattle. These materials were not completely processed during the time this study was undertaken, so future researchers might find some variation in box numbers. The materials are, however, very well catalogued at the archives.

MG: Manuscript group.

PFI: Potlatch Forests, Inc.

PLC: Potlatch Lumber Company. If PLC is not followed by any other letters, it indicates the materials were used while unprocessed and stored at Potlatch. Most of these records were later donated to the University of Idaho and are now its manuscript group 135, cited as PLC-UISC. Unfortunately, some items were thrown out and others were claimed by souvenir hunters prior to that transfer and are therefore inaccessible to future researchers. The letters LCHS, LN, or UISC following PFI or PLC indicate that these are Potlatch company papers stored at, respectively, the Latah County Historical Society Library, the Laird-Norton Company Archives, or the University of Idaho Library Special Collections.

RG: Record group.

UISC: University of Idaho Library Special Collections, Moscow.

VF: Vertical file.

WEYER: Weyerhaeuser Company Archives, Tacoma.

WI&M: Washington, Idaho and Montana Railway Company.

WSU MASC: Washington State University Library Manuscripts, Archives and Special Collections, Pullman.

Notes

CHAPTER ONE

[1]For an introduction to the geology of the Palouse see D. W. Meinig, *The Great Columbia Plain: A Historical Geography, 1805-1910* (Seattle: University of Washington Press, 1968), especially pp. 3-25; and Roald Fryxell and Earl F. Cook, *A Field Guide to the Loess Deposits and Channeled Scablands of the Palouse Area, Eastern Washington* (Pullman: Laboratory of Anthropology, Washington State University, 1964). Marilyn von Seggern, ed., *Palouse Bibliography* (Pullman: Washington State University, 1983), provides an introduction to the accumulation of scientific literature dealing with the Palouse, while Barbara Austin's "A Paradise Called the Palouse," *National Geographic*, vol. 161, no. 6, Je. 1982, pp. 799-819, provides a more popular examination of the geologic setting. For Palouse prairie vegetation see E. W. Tisdale, "Ecologic Changes in the Palouse," *Northwest Science*, vol. 35, no. 4, 1961, pp. 134-38.

[2]There has long been a local misconception that the Palouse derives its name from the French "pelouse," meaning lawn or sports green. But the original rugged landscape encountered by the area's first explorers hardly resembled a manicured lawn, and it seems likely that any French fur traders' influence over the place name would have resulted in a more accurately descriptive word, perhaps simply and logically "prairie." More recent scholarship shows that the region more than likely derives its name from the Indians who occupied the region. See Roderick Sprague, "The Meaning of 'Palouse,' " *Idaho Yesterdays*, Summer 1968, vol. 12, no. 2, pp. 22-7; C. C. Todd, "Origin and Meaning of the Geographic Name Palouse," *Washington Historical Quarterly*, vol. 24, no. 3, July 1933, pp. 190-92; and Lalia Phipps Boone, *From A to Z in Latah County, Idaho: A Place Name Dictionary* (Moscow: Lalia Boone, 1983), pp. 75-7. For the Palouse Indians see Richard Scheuerman and Clifford Trafzer, *Renegade Tribe: The Palouse Indians and the Invasion of the Inland Pacific Northwest* (Pullman: Washington State University Press, 1986), and Scheuerman and Trafzer, "The First People of the Palouse Country," *Bunchgrass Historian*, vol. 8, no. 3, Fall 1980, pp. 3-18. For the unique agricultural lifestyle of the Palouse see Meinig, *Great Columbia Plain*; Meinig, "Wheat Sacks Out to Sea," *Pacific Northwest Quarterly*, vol. 45, no. 1, Jan. 1954, pp. 13-18; Keith Petersen and Mary Reed, "Latah

Vignettes: Tramways," *Latah Legacy*, vol. 14, no. 2, Summer 1985, pp.
21-4; Kirby Brumfield, *This Was Wheat Farming: A Pictorial History of
the Farms and Farmers of the Northwest Who Grew the Nation's Bread*
(Seattle: Superior Publishing Company, 1968); and Thomas B. Keith,
*The Horse Interlude: A Pictorial History of Horse and Man in the Inland
Northwest* (Moscow: University Press of Idaho, 1980).

[3]For the best sources on the settlement of the Palouse see Meinig, *Great
Columbia Plain*; Alexander Campbell McGregor, *Counting Sheep: From
Open Range to Agribusiness on the Columbia Plateau* (Seattle: University
of Washington Press, 1982); and Selma Yocom, "History of Crops in the
Palouse, 1880-1930," Rural Life in the Palouse, Binder 2, LCHS. Also
see J. Orin Oliphant, *On the Cattle Ranges of the Oregon Country* (Seattle:
University of Washington Press, 1968); Oliphant, "Winter Losses of Cattle
in the Oregon Country, 1847-1890," *Washington Historical Quarterly*, vol.
23, no. 1, Jan. 1932, pp. 3-17; Frank Gilbert, *Historic Sketches of Walla
Walla, Whitman, Columbia, and Garfield Counties, Washington Territory . . .* (Portland: Printing & Lithography House of A. G. Walling,
1882); *An Illustrated History of Whitman County* (W. H. Lever Publisher,
1901); and *An Illustrated History of North Idaho* (Chicago: Western
Publishers, Inc. 1903).

[4]Idaho's white pine is *Pinus monticola*, commonly known as western white
pine or Idaho white pine. It shares many characteristics with *Pinus strobus*,
the white pine of northeastern North America, and was highly valued
by lumbermen.

[5]Throughout this discussion of the forests of the Palouse River drainage
I will refer to various species by their preferred common name. Because
the region's conifers are sometimes known by several common names, the
following gives their scientific names in the order they appear in the
text. Alternate common names are provided in parentheses.

ponderosa pine (yellow pine; bull pine)—*Pinus ponderosa*

Douglas fir (red fir)—*Pseudotsuga menziesii*

lodgepole pine (jack pine; black pine)—*Pinus contorta*

western larch (tamarack)—*Larix occidentalis*

white pine (Idaho white pine; western white pine)—*Pinus monticola*

western red cedar—*Thuga plicata*

grand fir (white fir)—*Abies grandis*

Engelmann spruce—*Picea engelmanni*

subalpine fir—*Abies lasiocarpa*

mountain hemlock (black hemlock)—*Tsuga mertensiana*

whitebark pine—*Pinus albicaulis*

[6]Higher up, eastward beyond the Palouse River's source, came another
habitat region, that of the subalpine fir. Subalpine fir could be found even
in lower valleys but predominated at elevations above 5,000 feet where
it seldom grew tall and on the highest peaks was dwarfed, gnarled,
firmly rooted, and wind tolerant. Other trees here included mountain

hemlock and, especially along crest lines, whitebark pine. These trees never found a commercial market in this region.

[7]I am unaware of any work that has been done to reconstruct the look of northern Idaho forests at the time they were first viewed by whites. Further, there are very few early written accounts of the specific forests drained by the Palouse River. I have pieced this reconstruction together from a variety of sources dealing primarily with neighboring forests of similar climate and elevations. Especially helpful were three publications by John B. Leiberg, a nineteenth century botanist who spent many years studying northern Idaho and other Western timberlands. See "General Report on a Botanical Survey of the Coeur d'Alene Mountains in Idaho During the Summer of 1895," in *Contributions from the U.S. National Herbarium*, vol. 5, no. 1 (Washington: U.S. Department of Agriculture, Division of Botany, 1897); "Present Condition of the Forested Areas in Northern Idaho Outside the Limits of the Priest River Forest Reserve and North of the Clearwater River," *Nineteenth Annual Report of the United States Geological Survey*, 1898, U.S. House of Representatives, 55th Cong., 3d. Sess., Doc. no. 5, pp. 373-86; and "Bitterroot Forest Reserve," *Twentieth Annual Report of the United States Geological Survey*, 1899, U.S. House of Representatives, 56th Cong., 1st Sess., Doc. no. 5, pp. 317-410. The best sources for the forests of the Palouse River area are the field notes of General Land Office surveyors. These exist for surveys from the 1870s through the 1890s and are housed in the Auditor's Office of the Latah County Courthouse. Also useful were: J. A. Larson, "Association of Trees, Shrubs, and Other Vegetation in the Northern Idaho Forests," *Ecology*, 1923, vol. 4, pp. 63-7; Robert Marshall, "The Life History of Some Western White Pine Stands on the Kaniksu National Forest," *Northwest Science*, June 1928, vol. 2, no. 2, pp. 48-53; Johnson Parker, "Environment and Forest Distribution of the Palouse Range in Northern Idaho," *Ecology*, Oct. 1952, vol. 33, no. 4, pp. 451-61; Jean B. and R. Daubenmire, Forest Vegetation of Eastern Washington and Northern Idaho, Technical Bulletin no. 60 (Pullman: Washington Agricultural Experiment Station, 1968); and Harold St. John, *Flora of Southeastern Washington and of Adjacent Idaho*, 3d. ed. (Escondido, Ca: Outdoor Pictures, 1963). I am also indebted to Frederic D. Johnson of the University of Idaho and Thomas R. Cox of San Diego State University for their assistance. The habitats were not as precise as I have drawn them here. There was much overlap in trees and undergrowth between the various zones, especially in the transitional areas at the lower and upper limits of each. Unlike some other regions, the impact of Indians on the area's forests was quite limited. The local populations were small, the villages concentrated along waterways, and the hunting-gathering patterns such that Indian-caused environmental changes in the forest were extremely limited. There may have been a few Indian-set hunting fires, but the majority of fire evidences noted by early recorders were lightning-caused.

[8]For the Walla Walla Council, see Kent D. Richards, *Isaac I. Stevens: Young Man in a Hurry* (Provo: Brigham Young University Press, 1979), pp. 215-26.

⁹*Reports of Explorations and Surveys to Ascertain the Most Practicable and Economical Route for a Railroad from the Mississippi River to the Pacific Ocean*, Sen. Ex. Doc. no. 46, 35th Cong., 2nd Session, 1859, Serial Set no. 992, "Narrative of 1855," pp. 173-76. Though Stevens identified the Indians he saw along the Snake River as Nez Perces, it is possible they were Palouses.

¹⁰Kolecki's report is in John Mullan, *Report on the Construction of a Military Road from Fort Walla Walla to Fort Benton* (Washington: Government Printing Office, 1863), pp. 102-05. The quotation, from the Weiser, Idaho, *Signal*, 1 Je. 1872, is in Robert Wayne Swanson, "A History of Logging and Lumbering on the Palouse River, 1870-1905," unpublished master's thesis, State College of Washington, 1958, p. 8.

¹¹The first quotation is from the Portland *Morning Oregonian*, 24 Apr. 1889. The second is from *The Pacific Northwest, Facts Relating to the History, Topography, Climate, Soil, Agriculture, Forests . . . of Oregon and Washington Territory* (Portland: Bureau of Immigration, 1882), p. 21. D. W. Meinig, "Environment and Settlement in the Palouse, 1868-1910," unpublished master's thesis, University of Washington, 1950, gives a good analysis of Palouse settlement patterns. See especially pp. 39-43, 131-2.

¹²Details on the Colfax mill can be found in several places. See Tom Fryxell, "James A. Perkins and Colfax: The Entrepreneur and His Town," *Bunchgrass Historian*, vol. 11, no. 1, Spring 1983, pp. 4-7; Swanson, "Logging on the Palouse River," esp. pp. 13-20; Thomas Clair Williams, "A History of the Settlement, Organization, and Growth of Whitman County, Washington," unpublished bachelor's thesis, State College of Washington, 1909, pp. 10-13; Gilbert, *Historic Sketches*, pp. 433-9; *Illustrated History of Whitman County*, pp. 104, 146-7; and Edith Erickson, *Colfax, 100 Plus* (Colfax: Edith Erickson, 1981), pp. 37, 226-9.

¹³For early mills in the area generally see *Illustrated History of North Idaho*, p. 582; transcript of oral history interview with Ellen Clark Rickets, 3 Oct. 1960, Cage 2072, p. l, WSU MASC; and Guy O. Brown, "Reminiscences of George T. Miller," unpublished, n.d., VF 1017/231, WSU MASC. For early sawmills in Palouse City see *Palouse Town and Country Study Program: History Report* (Palouse: Town and Country Committee, 1962), pp. 21-3; J. B. West, *Growing Up in the Palouse* (Palouse: J. B. West, 1980), pp. 5-6; and Garret D. Kincaid, *Palouse in the Making* (Rosalia, Wa.: Citizen-Journal, 1979, reprint), pp. 17-19. There was no newspaper in Palouse City at this time, and the exact date the first mill began is unverified. West claims the mill started in 1875; Kincaid says 1878. Early pioneers George W. Reed, apparently a part owner of the mill, and Charles H. Farnsworth, definitely a partner, claimed that the mill began in 1877, while another pioneer, Benjamin Burgunder, remembered there was a mill in the town by at least that date. For these three sources see George Reed biographical sketch, James E. Lindsey papers, Cage 491; story of Charles H. Farnsworth in Fred Yoder, "Stories of Early Pioneers in Whitman County, Washington," unpublished, ca. 1938, Cage 4022, p. 4l; and Burgunder, "Reminiscences of a Pioneer," unpublished, 1920, Cage 1704, p. 15. All in WSU MASC.

[14]For early house descriptions see Yoder, "Pioneer Social Adaptation in the Palouse Country of Eastern Washington, 1870-90," *Research Studies of the State College of Washington*, vol. 6, no. 4, Dec. 1938, esp. pp. 141-2; John Squires interview for KWSC radio, 1938, Cage 1566, pp. 8-10, WSU MASC; Nancy M. Prevost, *Paradise in the Palouse: The Development of a Farming Frontier in Eastern Washington, 1870-1900* (Fairfield, Wa.: Ye Galleon Press, 1985), pp. 15-18; William M. Tierney, "In the Heart of the Uniontown-Thorncreek Country," unpublished master's thesis, University of Idaho, 1932, p. 18; Williams, "A History of Whitman County," pp. 11-12; and "The Homesteaders Come to the Palouse Country," pp. 1-4; and "The Sawmill Changes Building Styles," pp. 7-9, both in *Bunchgrass Historian*, Winter 1975, vol. 3, no. 4.

[15]Quoted in Swanson, "Logging on the Palouse River," pp. 15-16. For descriptions of the difficulty in getting lumber for houses see Brown, "Reminiscences of George Miller," p. 8; "Reminiscences of Bessie Fullerton," in Phoebe Taylor papers, Cage 4177, WSU MASC; stories of Mrs. Sarah J. Wohleter, Emma Ickes, and Levi Wiggins in Yoder, "Stories of Early Pioneers"; and Yoder, "Pioneer Social Adaptation," p. 142.

[16]Palouse *Republican*, 27 July 1895.

[17]The quotation is from the Palouse *Republic*, 2 March 1917. For the relationship between the mining districts and Palouse see Richard C. Waldbauer, *Grubstaking the Palouse: Gold Mining in the Hoodoo Mountains of North Idaho, 1860-1950* (Pullman: Washington State University Press, 1986). For more on the nearby Idaho mining districts see Frank Milbert, interviews 1 and 2, LCHS-OH. For the early growth of Palouse see Palouse *News*, 5 May 1893; *Palouse Town and Country Study Program*; Kincaid, *Palouse in Making*; and West, *Growing Up in Palouse*.

[18]Spokane and Palouse, the local Northern Pacific branch line.

[19]The quotation is from the Palouse *Boomerang*, 28 Sept. 1888. For details on the 1880s growth of sawmilling in Palouse City, see "Wheat Fields of the Columbia," *Harpers New Monthly Magazine*, Sept. 1884, p. 510; Portland *Morning Oregonian*, 24 May 1889; *Palouse City: Manufacturing and Geographical Center of the Great Palouse Country*, a promotional brochure from ca. 1890 in the Paul Bockmier Papers, Cage 94, container 2, folder 18, WSU MASC; Eugene V. Smalley, "Pullman, Palouse City, and Colfax," originally printed in 1892, republished in *The Record*, vol. 31, 1970, pp. 68-77; and Swanson, "Logging on the Palouse River," pp. 26-8, 59.

[20]The quotation is from Brown's diary, 28 July 1893, C. O. Brown Papers, MG 88, UISC. For the Palouse Mill Company see Swanson, "Logging on the Palouse River," pp. 27-31; and Smalley, "Pullman, Palouse City and Colfax," pp. 76-7.

[21]Swanson, "Logging on the Palouse River," pp. 30-1. For details on the 1893 wet harvest and depression in the Palouse country see Lever, *Illustrated History of Whitman County*, pp. 125-7; and *Illustrated History of North Idaho*, pp. 594-5.

[22]Swanson, "Logging on the Palouse River," pp. 31-3, 61-2; Palouse *Republican*, 15 Feb. 1901, 2 Aug. 1901.

[23]The observations and quotations from the Portland journalist can be found in *The Oregonian Souvenir* (Portland: Lewis and Dryden Printing Co., 1892). The Palouse *Republican* quotations are from the 27 May and 6 Nov. 1892 issues. For other descriptions of Palouse around this time see Smalley, "Pullman, Palouse City, and Colfax"; Smalley, *The Fertile and Beautiful Palouse Country in Eastern Washington and Northern Idaho* (St. Paul: Northern Pacific Railroad, 1889); John E. Cochran, "Pioneer Days in Eastern Washington and Northern Idaho," unpublished, 1942, VF 336/214, p. 27, WSU MASC; Paul Bockmier, Jr., unpublished manuscript on Palouse City history, Bockmier papers, Cage 94, container 4, folder 31, WSU MASC; *Palouse Town and Country Study Program*, p. 62; and Colfax *Commoner*, 1 Je. 1888; 27 Jy. 1888.

[24]See story of Charles Farnsworth in Yoder, "Stories of Early Pioneers in Whitman County," WSU MASC; Lyman T. Babcock. "Memories," unpublished, ca. 1947, Cage 395, p. 312, WSU MASC; and Palouse *Republican*, 12 Nov. 1892, 27 Apr. 1895.

[25]Bockmier, "Mr. Lumber," unpublished, ca. 1965, in R. H. Bockmier Papers, Cage 387, p. 5, WSU MASC, contains a good first-person description of the Palouse drives. Also see Byers Sanderson, interview 1, pp. 11-12, LCHS-OH; Swanson, "Logging on the Palouse River," pp. 47-54; *Bunchgrass Historian*, vol. 8, no. 2, Summer 1980, a complete issue devoted to lumbering on the Palouse; and Smalley, "Pullman, Palouse City, and Colfax," p. 70. At times the woods workers were treated quite harshly by Palouse lawmen and citizens concerned with maintaining a certain level of respectability in their community. See Samuel Alan Schrager, " 'The Early Days': Narrative and Symbolism of Logging Life in the Inland Northwest," unpublished Ph.D. dissertation, University of Pennsylvania, 1983, pp. 155-6. For details on log drives on the nearby Clearwater River see *Potlatch Story*, Je. 1961, pp. 2-7; and William K. Dyche, "Log Drive on the Clearwater," *Forest History*, vol. 5, no. 3, Fall 1961, pp. 2-12. The descriptive quotation about log drives is in Robert F. Fries, *Empire in Pine: The Story of Lumbering in Wisconsin, 1830-1900* (Madison: State Historical Society of Wisconsin, 1951), p. 42.

[26]For the Idaho forests as an important way of making a living for early Palouse residents see Lulu Downen, "Voice of the Pioneer," KWSC radio broadcast, 1938, Cage 1566; "Ancestors and Descendants of Daniel Wright Boone," unpublished manuscript, n.d., Cage 1905, pp. 19-20; Rickets interview, Cage 2072; all in WSU MASC. Also see Swanson, "Logging on the Palouse River," pp. 55-6; Thomas Wahl, interview 1; and Rudolph Nordby interview, both in LCHS-OH. Conversely, once wheat farming became established, many area settlers trying to make a living by homesteading in the Idaho forests supplemented their incomes by working on threshing crews in the Palouse prairie. See, for example, William Burkland, interviews 1 and 2; and Hilda Carlson Ruberg interview, both in LCHS-OH.

[27]Eastman's speech is quoted in Charles E. Twining, "Plunder and Progress: The Lumbering Industry in Perspective," *Wisconsin Magazine of History*, vol. 42, no. 2, Winter 1963-64, p. 116.

[28]For the best summary of colonial lumbering see Thomas R. Cox, Robert S. Maxwell, Phillip Drennon Thomas, and Joseph J. Malone, *This Well-Wooded Land: Americans and Their Forests from Colonial Times to the Present* (Lincoln: University of Nebraska Press, 1985), pp. 3-48.

[29]For lumbering in the Northeast see Richard G. Wood, *A History of Lumbering in Maine, 1820-1861* (Orono: University of Maine Press, 1935); David C. Smith, *A History of Lumbering in Maine, 1861-1960* (Orono: University of Maine Press, 1972); Stewart H. Holbrook, *Yankee Loggers: A Recollection of Woodsmen, Cooks, and River Drivers* (New York: International Paper Co., 1961); Thomas R. Cox, "Transition in the Woods: Log Drivers, Raftsmen, and the Emergence of Modern Lumbering in Pennsylvania," *Pennsylvania Magazine of History and Biography*, vol. 104, no. 3, Jy. 1980, pp. 345-64; and Cox, *This Well-Wooded Land*, pp. 51-108. For lumbering's move west and south, in addition to *This Well-Wooded Land*, see James Elliot Defenbaugh, *History of the Lumber Industry of America*, 2 vols. (Chicago, 1906-1907); and David C. Smith, "The Logging Frontier," *Journal of Forest History*, vol. 18, no. 4, Oct. 1974, pp. 96-106.

[30]For some of the better sources on Great Lakes lumbering see George W. Hotchkiss, *History of the Lumber and Forest Industry of the Northwest* (Chicago: G. W. Hotchkiss, 1898); Fries, *Empire in Pine*; Charles E. Twining, *Downriver: Orrin H. Ingram and the Empire Lumber Company* (Madison: The State Historical Society of Wisconsin, 1975); Agnes M. Larson, *History of the White Pine Industry in Minnesota* (Minneapolis: University of Minnesota Press, 1940); Theodore C. Blegen, "With Ax and Saw: A History of Lumbering in Minnesota," *Forest History*, vol. 7, no. 3, Fall 1963, pp. 2-13; and Cox, *This Well-Wooded Land*, pp. 90-188.

[31]For background on Weyerhaeuser and the Mississippi River Logging Company see Ralph W. Hidy, Frank Ernest Hill, and Allan Nevins, *Timber and Men: The Weyerhaeuser Story* (New York: The Macmillan Company, 1963), esp. pp. 1-76; Fred W. Kohlmeyer, *Timber Roots: The Laird, Norton Story, 1855-1905* (Winona, Mn.: Winona County Historical Society, 1972), esp. pp. 82-116; Twining, *Downriver*, pp. 105-15; and Cox, *This Well-Wooded Land*, pp. 159-60. For further biographical detail on Weyerhaeuser also see John H. Hauberg, *Weyerhaeuser & Denkmann: Ninety-Five Years of Manufacturing and Distribution of Lumber* (Rock Island, Il.: Augustana Book Concern, 1957); and *Frederick Weyerhaeuser: Pioneer Lumberman* (Minneapolis: Louise L. Weyerhaeuser, 1940).

[32]Hidy, *Timber and Men*, pp. 50-62; Kohlmeyer, *Timber Roots*, p. 117. Technically, Laird-Norton was known at this time as Laird Norton & Company, later the Laird, Norton Company. Throughout this book I use a hyphen for consistency when referring to this particular company, and to the broader activities of the Laird-Norton families.

[33]Hidy, *Timber and Men,* pp. 103-22.

[34]Hidy, *Timber and Men,* and Kohlmeyer, *Timber Roots,* trace the development of interlocking directorships and the rise of the "syndicate." Also see Fries, *Empire in Pine,* pp. 122-40; Twining, *Downriver,* pp. 210-35; Larson, *White Pine Industry,* p. 236; and Frederick K. Weyerhaeuser and John M. Musser interview, pp. 128-31, COL-OH.

[35]For background on Northwest lumbering before the Weyerhaeuser move, see Thomas R. Cox, *Mills and Markets: A History of the Pacific Coast Lumber Industry to 1900* (Seattle: University of Washington Press, 1974); and S. Blair Hutchison's three-part article, "A Century of Lumbering in Northern Idaho," *The Timberman,* August, September, and October, 1938. For the anticipation with which Northwest boosters awaited the Weyerhaeuser incursion see Robert E. Ficken, "Weyerhaeuser and the Pacific Northwest Timber Industry, 1899-1903," *Pacific Northwest Quarterly,* vol. 70, no. 4, Oct. 1979, pp. 146-54.

CHAPTER TWO

[1]Diary, 20 Apr. 1893, C. O. Brown papers, MG 88, UISC.

[2]The quotation is from Brown's diary, 6 March 1893. Despite the significant role Brown played in the development of northern Idaho's lumbering, little has been written about him. For brief biographical accounts see Ralph S. Space, *Pioneer Timbermen: A History of Clearwater Timber and Timbermen* (Lewiston, Id.: Ralph Space, 1972), especially pp. 3-6; and A. B. Curtis, *White Pines and Fires: Cooperative Forestry in Idaho* (Moscow: University Press of Idaho, 1983), pp. 22-4. Some of Brown's Civil War materials are in SC/BRO-4, LCHS.

[3]Brown's 1893 journey to Idaho can be traced in his diary. The quotation is from the 27 Jy. 1893 entry. Also see 2 Jy. 1893 and 4 Jy. 1893 letters from Brown, while on his trip, to his family, in SC/BRO-4, LCHS.

[4]Space, *Pioneer Timbermen,* pp. 6-12, provides a good summary of Brown's activities from 1894 to 1900. More details can be found in Brown's diary. For biographical sketches of Fohl and Nat Brown, who also played significant roles in the development of Idaho lumbering, see Curtis, *White Pines and Fires,* pp. 16-21, 24-5; Space, *Pioneer Timbermen,* pp. 43-4, 50-5; *The Family Tree,* Apr. 1937, pp. 6-8; and Stewart Holbrook, "Theodore Fohl, Trail Blazer of the Clearwater," *Weyerhaeuser News,* Oct. 1953, p. 19. For a good summary of the long, negative impact of the 1893 depression on Great Lakes timbermen see Twining, *Downriver,* pp. 266-75.

[5]Brown's address on the "Timber Resources of the Potlatch and Clearwater Country" was given 3 Apr. 1896 and was printed in *Idaho: Gem of the Mountains* (Kendrick, Id.: Potlatch Immigration Association, 1896). A copy is in VF 318, UISC.

[6]The quotations are from the Pullman, Wa., *Herald,* 12 Aug. 1899. Also see Space, *Pioneer Timbermen,* pp. 11-12, for a summary of the Scofield episode.

[7]The quotation is from Brown's diary, 30 May 1900. An anonymous, un-dated manuscript entitled "Potlatch Timber Company," RG 7, Box 6, "Potlatch Lumber Company" file, WEYER, provides excellent background on the Brown-Glover-Weyerhaeuser relationship. Also see Space, *Pioneer Timbermen*, p. 12; and Hidy, *Timber and Men*, pp. 250-1.

[8]The quotations are from, respectively, Brown's diary for 24 Aug., 12 Sept., and 18 Sept. 1900. Also see Space, *Pioneer Timbermen*, p. 18. A letter hastily written from Brown in Lewiston to his wife in Moscow on 12 Sept. 1900 provides a good feeling for the tension and excitement Brown experienced during this period. See SC/BRO-4, LCHS.

[9]Brown's diary for the period September 17 to 25, 1900, outlines the story of the night ride. A more thorough account can be found in Space, *Pioneer Timbermen*, pp. 20-4. Space had access to Nat's personal reminiscences of the event.

[10]Quotations and details are from Brown's diary, 16 Oct. through 24 Oct. 1900.

[11]See "Potlatch Timber Company," n.d.; and notes from Frederick E. Weyerhaeuser's Record Book, vol. 4, p. 569, both in RG 7, Box 6, "Potlatch Lumber Company" file, WEYER; and Hidy, *Timber and Men*, p. 251. The Potlatch *Timber* company should not be confused with the Potlatch *Lumber* Company. The Timber Company continued to exist until the 1930s, and was used by the Weyerhaeusers to handle miscellaneous residual activities of their various partnerships, especially trading in Great Lakes region cutover lands.

[12]C. A. Weyerhaeuser to F. S. Bell, 4 Oct. 1902, Northland Pine Company papers, Box 41, LN.

[13]Hidy, *Timber and Men*, pp. 184 (quotation), 208-11. In later years the Weyerhaeuser interests expanded their southern holdings greatly.

[14]Ibid., pp. 211-12; Kohlmeyer, *Timber Roots*, p. 135-6; Fries, *Empire in Pine*, p. 241.

[15]For the impact of railroads and the changes they brought to Pacific Northwest lumbering see Cox, *Mills and Markets*, esp. pp. 287-96.

[16]The quotation is from Frederick K. Weyerhaeuser interview, p. 46, COL-OH. For additional background on the Hill-Weyerhaeuser friendship and the land deal see Hidy, *Timber and Men*, pp. 207, 211-215; Albro Martin, *James J. Hill and the Opening of the West* (New York: Oxford University Press, 1976), p. 465; and Ficken, "Weyerhaeuser and the Pacific Northwest Timber Industry."

[17]For the impact of the Weyerhaeuser/Hill transaction on the Inland Empire and the rapid development of lumbering there after 1900 see I. V. Anderson and E. F. Rapraeger, *Highlights of the Lumber Industry*, Occasional Paper no. 2 (Missoula, Mt.: Northern Rocky Mountain Forest and Range Experiment Station, 1940); Hutchison, "A Century of Lumbering in Northern Idaho," Part 2, pp. 15-16; W. Hudson Kensel, "The Early Spokane Lumber Industry," *Idaho Yesterdays*, vol. 12, no. 1, Spring 1968, pp. 21-31; John Fahey, "Big Lumber in the Inland Empire: The Early

Years, 1900-1930," *Pacific Northwest Quarterly*, vol. 76, no. 3, Jy. 1985, pp. 95-103; Fahey, *The Inland Empire: Unfolding Years, 1879-1929* (Seattle: University of Washington Press, 1986), pp. 188-213; Arlie Decker, "Lumbering Moves West," *The Pacific Northwesterner*, vol. 3, no. 2, Spring 1959, pp. 17-24; and Robert Anthony Perrin, Jr., "Two Decades of Turbulence: A Study of the Great Lumber Strikes in Northern Idaho," unpublished master's thesis, University of Idaho, 1961, p. 33. Lumbering was such an insignificant economic enterprise in northern Idaho prior to the Weyerhaeuser move that it barely warranted mention in the only overview of the economic history of the region to that date. Noted D. E. Livingston-Little, *An Economic History of North Idaho, 1800-1900* (Los Angeles: Journal of the West Publishers, 1965), p. xi: "To be *important* enough for inclusion, the extent or amount of the economic activity had to be significant in relation to the number of people involved or affected. Thus, lumbering . . . is merely mentioned, since it was not until after 1900 that it became economically important." The increase in production in the interior region *after* the Weyerhaeusers and others moved into the area was even greater than the figures provided here suggest. Production in eastern Oregon and Washington, also skyrocketing at this time, was excluded from statistics for the Rocky Mountain region, even though it was a part of the same general expansion.

[18]For the Pine Tree Lumber Company, the Kehl and Deary Company, and the beginnings of the Northland Pine Company see R. D. Musser, "The Northland Pine Company," typescript, n.d., RG 7, Box 19, "Northland Pine Co." file, and "Northland Pine Company: A Corporation that Led Three Lives," typescript, n.d., RG 7, Box 5, "Northland Pine Co" file, both in WEYER; R. Drew Musser interview, COL-OH; Deary to Pine Tree Lumber Co., 22 Oct. 1898; R. D. Musser to M. G. Norton, 28 Oct. 1898; Minutes of Directors' Meeting, Northland Pine Co., 22 Jy. 1899; and, for the quotation, R. D. Musser to F.S. Bell, 4 Nov. 1899, all in Northland Pine Co. Papers, Box 41, LN; Kohlmeyer, *Timber Roots*, pp. 273-83, 287-94; and Hidy, *Timber and Men*, pp. 106-15, 182-88.

[19]For the Canadian quotation see Deary to F. S. Bell, 23 Nov. 1899; for the Texas quotation Deary to Bell, 28 May 1900. For further details on Deary's southern trips also see R. D. Musser to Bell, 21 Apr. 1900; Deary to Bell, 6 Je. 1900; and F. W. Kehl to Laird-Norton, 15 Oct. 1900. All in Northland Pine Co. papers, Box 41, LN.

[20]The quotations are from, respectively, Deary to Bell, 23 Nov. 1899; and Deary to Laird-Norton, 26 Sept. 1900. For an outline of Deary's August-September 1900 western trip see his expense account attached to a letter to Bell, 13 Oct. 1900. All in Northland Pine Co. papers, Box 41, LN. The Idaho investments of the Weyerhaeuser associates were, for many years, among the least profitable the group ever made. Earlier historians of the Weyerhaeuser move west have inaccurately placed too much of the "blame" for going into the state on Deary. For example, Kohlmeyer, *Timber Roots*, p. 291, gives this account of the move: "Deary was sent on another tour of the southern United States and Mexico. . . . At the

conclusion of his second six-month Southern tour, Deary drifted to Spokane where he learned that the state of Idaho planned to dispose of timber in Latah County. . . . Instantly and overwhelmingly convinced of the desirability of Idaho white pine, he communicated his enthusiasm in a decisive [Directors'] meeting held at Little Falls on May 23, 1901." The account is wrong in two areas. First, Deary had already been in Idaho before his second southern trip and did not just happen to "drift" there. More than likely he was strongly encouraged to go by the Weyerhaeusers, who sought confirmation of their own enthusiastic opinions of Idaho white pine. Second, Deary did become enthused about Idaho's prospects, but not "instantly and overwhelmingly" as is clearly indicated by his letter of 26 Sept. 1900 to Laird-Norton Co. Hidy, *Timber and Men*, states "[Deary] and Kehl also visited the Far West and at the [Directors'] meeting of October 12th [1900] reported enthusiastically on white pine stands in Idaho" [p. 183]; and "stockholders of Northland Pine Company . . . accepted William Deary's adverse reactions to investments in southern timber" [p. 209]. Both accounts are only partially correct. Kehl was enthusiastic about Idaho pinelands early on, Deary much less so. It is likely that Kehl, not Deary, was the one encouraging investment at the October meeting, which came just a few days before the Weyerhaeusers' pivotal horseback venture into the Clearwater and Latah county forests. Further, while Deary did not find an abundance of good investments in the South, he did find some, but the Weyerhaeusers decided against making the purchases. Until 1901, when the senior stockholders of Northland had clearly opted for Idaho over the South, Deary remained convinced that potential in the South was greater. The point is significant because there has been a tendency among historians to place too much of the blame for the Potlatch Lumber Company's financial difficulties on Deary. If forming the Potlatch Lumber Company and moving into Idaho were unsound business ventures, the blame much more appropriately lies with Frederick Weyerhaeuser and his son Charles than with William Deary.

21 The quotations are from Musser to Laird-Norton Co., 24 Apr. 1901; and Deary to Bell, 25 Nov. 1901. Also see Deary to Bell, 12 Je. 1901. All in Northland Pine Co. papers, Box 41, LN.

22 For brief descriptions of timber cruising see Fries, *Empire in Pine*, pp. 164-5; Kohlmeyer, *Timber Roots*, p. 124; R. E. Marsh, "Timber Cruising on National Forests of the Southwest," *Forest History*, vol. 13, no. 3, Oct. 1969, pp. 22-32; *The Family Tree*, Jy. 1945, pp. 1-6; and George L. Martin, Jr., "Forest Inventory and Valuation Practices," in Richard C. Davis, ed., *Encyclopedia of American Forest and Conservation History*, vol. I (New York: Macmillan Publishing Co., 1983), pp. 217-22.

23 For biographical details on Helmer see *The Family Tree*, May 1937, p. 8; Jan. 1952, p. 3. The quotations are from Leo Guilfoy, interview 1, pp. 3-11, LCHS-OH. Guilfoy was Helmer's nephew by marriage, his wife being a daughter of Helmer's brother, John. Guilfoy, a Latah County woodsman of considerable local renown himself, frequently accompanied Helmer on cruising expeditions.

24Among the other Lake States investors Turrish represented were Orrin H. Ingram and William Carson.

25For Deary's ultimatum see Deary to R. D. Musser, 5 Jy. 1901. The Charles Weyerhaeuser quotations are in, respectively, Weyerhaeuser to Kehl, 12 Jy. 1901; Weyerhaeuser to Laird-Norton Co., 16 Jy. 1901. Drew Musser's estimation of Latah County's white pine is also contained in the latter. For other details on the state land sale see Drew Musser to P. and P. M. Musser, Jy. 1901; C. A. Weyerhaeuser to Frederick Weyerhaeuser, 8 Jy. 1901; and minutes of Northland Pine Co. special stockholders' meetings, 23 May 1901 and 14 Aug. 1901. All in Northland Pine Co. papers, Box 41, LN. For Henry Turrish see RG 7, Box 10, "Henry Turrish" file, WEYER; and William L. Maxwell interview, p. 87, COL-OH.

26From Northland Pine Company's earliest days in northern Minnesota, the directors kept a low profile. This atmosphere of secrecy continued at least through the first decade of Idaho land transactions. As late as 1911 the Potlatch Lumber Company printed new stationery eliminating company directors' names from the letterhead because listing them "made things smack too much of the so called Weyerhaeuser Syndicate." For the 1911 stationery change see A. W. Laird to F. H. Thatcher, 16 Mar. 1911, PLC correspondence files, Box 2, LN; and for earlier secrecy in Minnesota dealings see Deary to Pine Tree Lumber Co., 22 Oct. 1898, Northland Pine Co. papers, Box 41, LN. For the debate over whose name to take the Idaho state land under see R. D. Musser to Bell, 21 Aug. 1901; and Deary to Bell, 20 Sept. 1901, both in Northland Pine Co. papers, Box 41, LN; and notes from correspondence, Bell to Deary, 5 Sept. 1901; Bell to Musser, 4 Oct. 1901; and Thatcher to Deary, 24 Oct. 1901; all in RG 7, Box 5, "Northland Pine Co." file, WEYER.

27The first quotation is from notes from correspondence, Deary to Laird-Norton Co., 18 Dec. 1902, RG 7, Box 5, "Northland Pine Co." file, WEYER. The second is from R. D. Musser to Bell, 26 May 1902. Also see Deary to Bell, 18 Jan. 1902, both in Northland Pine Co. papers, Box 41, LN; and Kohlmeyer, *Timber Roots*, pp. 292-3.

28Actually, the Northland Pine Company only acquired part of these holdings and Wisconsin Log and Lumber another part. No exact figures for Northland's timber purchases are available. However, in 1903 Northland and Wisconsin jointly formed the Potlatch Lumber Company, at which time the Weyerhaeuser associates controlled all of the purchases previously made by each firm. For Potlatch's state timberland holdings see John Pearson to Thatcher, Jy. 1903, PLC correspondence files, Box 1, LN.

29Deary to Bell, 26 Sept. 1902, Northland Pine Co. papers, Box 41, LN; notes from correspondence, Deary to R. D. Musser, 26 Sept. 1902, RG 7, Box 5, "Northland Pine Co." file, WEYER. There is much correspondence between Deary and individual landowners negotiating over purchase prices in Box 1, Letterbook #1, 1903, PLC-UISC. For the experiences of some local timber homesteaders bought out by large lumber companies see the following in LCHS-OH: Ione Adair, interviews 1, 2, 5; Floyd Lawrence, interview 1; Albert Pierce, interview 1; and Byers Sanderson, interview 3. The efforts of lumbermen to purchase property and squeeze out homesteaders in the northern Idaho woods has been fictionalized in a work by Carol Ryrie Brink, the area's most famous novelist. See *Strangers in the Forest* (New York: The Macmillan Co., 1959).

[30]For the move west see Deary to Bell, 2 Aug. 1901; 31 Aug. 1901; 16 Sept. 1901; 20 Sept. 1901; all in Northland Pine Co. papers, Box 41, LN; and Deary to C. A. Weyerhaeuser, 11 Oct. 1901, Box 38, PLC-UISC.

[31]The quotation is from Kehl to Deary, 2 Nov. 1902. Also see Kehl to Deary, 10 Oct. 1902; and Kehl to Laird-Norton Co., 8 Nov. 1902, all in Northland Pine Co. papers, Box 41, LN; and notes from correspondence, Deary to Kehl, 23 Oct. 1902; 25 Oct. 1902, RG 7, Box 5, "Northland Pine Co." file, WEYER.

CHAPTER THREE

[1]Deary to Kehl, 20 Aug. 1902; Deary to F. S. Bell, 26 Sept. 1902, both in Northland Pine Co. papers, Box 41, LN.

[2]C. A. Weyerhaeuser to Frank Thatcher, 13 Feb. 1903, Northland Pine Co. papers, Box 41, LN; notes from correspondence, F. S. Bell to R. D. Musser, 17 Feb. 1903, RG 7, Box 5, "Northland Pine Co." file; "Memorandum on Stumpage Values of Standing Timber Owned by . . . Potlatch Lumber Company . . . ," Jan. 1919, RG 7, Box 4, "Stumpage Values" file, both in WEYER. For further background on the merger also see Ralph Hidy, "Lumbermen in Idaho: A Study in Adaptation to Change in Environment," *Idaho Yesterdays*, vol. 6, no. 4, Winter 1962, pp. 2-17; Hidy, *Timber and Men,* p. 255; Kohlmeyer, *Timber Roots,* p. 296.

[3]Several local histories state that the present site of Potlatch, Idaho — on the Palouse River — was the scene of Indian "potlatches," and that when the company decided to construct its mill and town here, it naturally chose the name "Potlatch" for its town and company. However, there is no evidence that this was a popular Indian gathering spot, and besides the name "Potlatch" had been selected long before the company chose the site for its town and mill. For potlatches by Inland Empire Indians see Robert H. Ruby and John A. Brown, *The Spokane Indians: Children of the Sun* (Norman: University of Oklahoma Press, 1970), p. 16.

[4]Deary to Bell, 26 Sept. 1902, Northland Pine Co. papers, Box 41, LN.

[5]For the handcar episode and quotation see Maxwell W. Williamson interview, pp. 9-10. Hearn's quotation and the horse story are in "Laboring Men of Potlatch" interview, pp. 34 and 149. Both are in COL-OH. Laird's characterization is in notes from correspondence, Laird to Thatcher, 4 Feb. 1911, RG 7, Box 9, "William Deary" file, WEYER. For further biographical information see William L. Maxwell interview; and R. E. Irwin interview, p. 11, both in COL-OH. The story of Deary's gasoline railroad car is in the only biographical sketch written about

the man, Stewart Holbrook's "The Indomitable Bill Deary and His Gas Flagship," *Weyerhaeuser News*, vol. 23, June 1953, pp. 20-21. Also see A. W. Laird to F. S. Bell, 31 Oct. 1907, Box 2, PLC-LN; Deary's 1902 diary for personal statistics, PLC; and numerous reminiscences in LCHS-OH, especially Arthur Sundberg, interview 3, pp. 120-35; Byers Sanderson, interview 2, pp. 2-4; and W. J. Gamble, interview 2, pp. 9-12.

⁶Musser to Bell, 14 Feb. 1903, Northland Pine Co. papers, Box 41, LN.

⁷Weyerhaeuser to F. H. Thatcher, 13 Feb. 1903, Northland Pine Co. papers, Box 41, LN.

⁸Ibid.; Kehl to Bell, 23 Feb. 1903, Northland Pine Co. papers, Box 41, LN.

⁹The quotation about Weyerhaeuser's trading ability is in F. K. Weyerhaeuser and John M. Musser interview, p. 83, while Maxwell's quotation is in William Maxwell interview, p. 95, both in COL-OH. For the letter-writing quotation see notes from correspondence, J. P. Weyerhaeuser to C. A. Weyerhaeuser, 23 May 1925, RG 7, Box 10, "C. A. Weyerhaeuser" file, WEYER. For further biographical information see Hidy, *Timber and Men*, pp. 33, 106-7, 115, 183-4, 325, 414; and Weyerhaeuser's obituary in the *St. Paul* (Minnesota) *Dispatch*, 15 Feb. 1930.

¹⁰See *The Family Tree*, Mar. 1938, pp. 1-2; and Kohlmeyer, *Timber Roots*, pp. 200, 234, 245-7, 257, 315-6.

¹¹*American Lumberman*, 23 Apr. 1921, p. 98; Kohlmeyer, *Timber Roots*, pp. 200, 296-7; 315. The "quick step" quotation is from William Maxwell interview, p. 88, COL-OH.

¹²The Maine charter, among other advantages, permitted Potlatch to own stock in other companies. See Potlatch Lumber Company's "State of Maine Certificate of Organization of a Corporation Under the General Law," 7 Mar. 1903, RG 7, Box 6, "PLC Miscellaneous" file; "Northland Pine Company," typewritten manuscript, n.d.; and C. A. Weyerhaeuser, "To the Stockholders of Northland Pine Company," 28 Mar. 1903, both in RG 7, Box 5, "Northland Pine Co." file. All above in WEYER. The Northland Pine Company continued to exist after the formation of the Potlatch Lumber Company, but in a completely different guise. In early 1903, Kehl and Deary were replaced as directors and Northland had no further dealings in Idaho, becoming a subsidiary of the Pine Tree and Mississippi River lumber companies, under the control of the Laird, Norton, Musser, and Weyerhaeuser families. It then began manufacturing lumber in Minneapolis, sawing its last log in 1919. As the last of that city's many sawmills to close, its passing marked the end of large-scale Great Lakes lumbering. See Minutes, Northland Pine Company directors meeting, 19 Jan. 1904, RG 7, Box 5, "Northland Pine Co." file, WEYER; Kohlmeyer, *Timber Roots*, p. 287; Hidy, *Timber and Men*, p. 590; and Larson, *White Pine Industry in Minnesota*, p. 235.

¹³See notes from correspondence, Kehl to Deary, 10 Oct. 1902, RG 7, Box 5, "Northland Pine Co." file, WEYER; and R. D. Musser to Bell, 14 Feb. 1903, Northland Pine Co. papers, Box 41, LN.

¹⁴Swanson, "Logging on the Palouse River," pp. 33; Pullman *Herald*, 8 Jy. 1899; R. D. Musser to Bell, 26 May 1902, Northland Pine Co. papers, Box 41, LN.

¹⁵Kehl to C. A. Weyerhaeuser, 2 Oct. 1902; Weyerhaeuser to Bell, 4 Oct. 1902, 25 Oct. 1902; Weyerhaeuser to Carpenter, 23 Oct. 1902; Carpenter to Palouse River Lumber Co., 24 Oct. 1902; Peddycord to Carpenter, 29 Oct. 1902. All in Northland Pine Co. papers, Box 41, LN.

¹⁶Peddycord to Deary, 18 Feb. 1903; Deary to Bell, 20 Feb. 1903; both in Northland Pine Co. papers, Box 41, LN. See also notes from Frederick E. Weyerhaeuser's Record Book, vol. 4, p. 5, RG 7, Box 7, WEYER.

¹⁷The "army of men" quotation is from C. E. Isenberger, PLC, to John Hoag, Pullman, 28 Apr. 1903. Also see Peddycord to James Hinchliffe & Sons, Pullman, 27 Je. 1903; and Isenberger to E. H. Hanford, Oakesdale, 7 Mar. 1904. The first two are from Letterbook #1, the latter from Letterbook #4, Box 1, PLC-UISC. For the Thatcher admonition see Thatcher to Deary, 16 Feb. 1904. Also see Deary to Bell, 29 May 1903; and Deary to Thatcher, 10 Feb. 1904. All in Box 1, PLC-LN. Additional details can be found in Spokane *Spokesman-Review*, 16 Jy. 1903; and Swanson, "Logging on the Palouse River," pp. 33-4.

¹⁸Use of the term "lumberjack" has fallen upon disfavor by scholars of Northwest culture. Walter McCulloch, whose *Woods Words: A Comprehensive Dictionary of Loggers Terms* (Portland: Oregon Historical Society, 1958) is the standard reference on the logging language of the region, states, p. 113, that lumberjack is "a genteel term used by fiction writers who should have said logger if they mean a man working in the western woods." Folklorists Barre Toelken, *The Dynamics of Folklore* (Boston: Houghton Mifflin Co., 1979), p. 53, Jan Brunvand, *The Study of American Folklore: An Introduction* (New York: W. W. Norton and Co., 1968), p. 34, and Andy Bartels, "Folklore vs. Fakelore," *Wash. Board, The Newsletter of the Washington State Folklife Council*, vol. 2, no. 2, Summer 1986, p. 6, agree that the term is inappropriate, something woods workers would never apply to themselves. Unfortunately, these scholars have only studied lumbering in the Pacific Northwest west of the Cascade Mountains and assume that, since the term was not used among woods workers there, it was not used anywhere in the region. At least in northern Idaho they are wrong. In that region, the term was traditionally used among lumberjacks to describe themselves, and it was a term they referred to with pride. It was hardly an invention of "fiction writers," since precious few have written about northern Idaho's woods. The oral history collection of the Latah County Historical Society is rich in interviews with lumberjacks who describe themselves, their co-workers, and their predecessors using the term. Similarly, the valuable oral history accounts gathered and published by Bert Russell of Harrison, Idaho, about lumbermen further north, around Lake Coeur d'Alene, give ample evidence that the term was in wide use there as well. See his *Calked Boots and Other Northwest Writings* (1967); *Hardships and Happy Times* (1978); *Swiftwater People* (1979); and *North Fork of the Coeur d'Alene River* (1984). For a more

detailed discussion of use of the term lumberjack and its appropriateness in northern Idaho see Schrager, " 'The Early Days': Narrative and Symbolism of Logging Life in the Inland Northwest," especially pp. 122-4.

[19]The quotation is from Deary to Laird-Norton Co., 2 Oct. 1903. For additional information on the aggravation caused by Codd, see Deary to Thatcher, 19 May 1904. Strike details can be found in Deary to Thatcher, 2 Nov. 1903; 24 Nov. 1903; and 30 Nov. 1903. Details on the Codd purchase are in R. D. Musser to Laird-Norton Co., 14 Sept. 1904. All the above in Box 1, PLC-LN. For historical background on the Codd mill and the purchase see Swanson, "Logging on the Palouse River," pp. 17-25; and Spokane *Spokesman-Review*, 13 Sept. 1904. Most local histories state that Potlatch immediately closed the Colfax mill after the purchase, but actually this mill helped the company meet its manufacturing requirements until 1907. See Deary to C. A. Weyerhaeuser, 2 Apr. 1905, Box 2, Letterbook #9; and Deary to Kehl, 26 Feb. 1906, Box 3, Letterbook #21. Both in PLC-UISC. Also see Palouse *Republic*, 1 Mar. 1907; 28 Feb. 1908; 6 Mar. 1908; and 17 Apr. 1908. Codd had bought out his former partner, Martin Sexton, in the 1890s.

[20]For water shortages in 1904 and 1905 see Deary to Kehl, 15 Aug. 1904, Box 1, Letterbook #5; C. E. Isenberger to Chicago Lumber and Coal Co., St. Louis, 29 Sept. 1904, Box 1, Letterbook #6; Isenberger to Iowa Canning Co., Vinton, Iowa, 17 Mar. 1905, Box 1, Letterbook #8; and Deary to F. W. Kehl, 13 Mar. 1905, Box 2, Letterbook #9. All in PLC-UISC.

[21]Kehl to Laird-Norton Co., 22 Jy. 1902, PLC, Box 1; R. D. Musser to Laird-Norton Co., 6 Dec. 1901, Northland Pine Co. papers, Box 41. Both in LN.

[22]The quotation is in Deary to Bell, 29 May 1903. Also see Deary to C. A. Weyerhaeuser, 26 Je. 1903. Both in Box 1, PLC-LN. For further information see C. A. Weyerhaeuser to George S. Long, Weyerhaeuser Timber Company, Tacoma, 5 Sept. 1903, RG 1, Box 20, "C. A. Weyerhaeuser" file; notes from PLC director's minute book, 15 Sept. 1903, RG 7, Box 19, "Potlatch" file, both in WEYER; W. J. Gamble, interview 1, LCHS-OH; Keith Petersen, ed., *Railroad Man: A Conversation with W. J. Gamble* (Moscow, Id.: Latah County Historical Society, 1981), p. 3; *The Family Tree*, Dec. 1936, p. 8.

[23]For good discussions of the relationship between railroads and Palouse area boosterism see Meinig, "Environment and Settlement in the Palouse," pp. 118-29; Meinig, *Great Columbia Plain*, esp. pp. 321-64; and Dale Leo Martin, Jr., "Tekoa and Malden: A History of Two Railroad Towns in Eastern Washington," unpublished master's thesis, Washington State University, 1984.

[24]George Creighton, town merchant, was president; Brown was vice president and manager; and Frank Gilbert—whose son Albert C. would later gain fame as an Olympic pole vault champion and inventor of the Erector Set and other "Gilbert Toys"—was secretary and treasurer.

[25]The Moscow and Eastern is a little-known episode in Latah County history, and details on the enterprise are sketchy. See Brown's eight-page

publicity tract about the line, *Moscow, Idaho, January 15, 1900,* in the
Charles Moore papers, LCHS. Also see *History of North Idaho,* p. 598;
Homer David, *Moscow at the Turn of the Century* (Moscow,Id.: Latah
County Historical Society, 1979), pp. 67-8; and "Potlatch and Its Mill
Were Never Meant to Be Created," Moscow *Daily Idahonian,* 50th An-
niversary Historical Edition Supplement, 29 Sept. 1961.

[26]Palouse *Republic,* editorial, 22 Jan. 1904. See *Republic,* 29 Jan. 1904 for
the comparative merits of and rivalry between Palouse and Garfield.

[27]Deary to Bell, 26 Nov. 1904, Box 1, PLC-LN. For animosity toward
Deary and his lobbying activities see notes from Frederick E.
Weyerhaeuser's Record Book, vol. 4, p. 574, RG 7, Box 6, "Potlatch
Lumber Co." file, WEYER.

[28]One reason for their amicability—in addition to Deary's threat—was that
the Potlatch Lumber Company engaged Boise attorney William E. Borah,
soon to become a U.S. Senator, to lobby for modification of the twenty-
year limit before the state legislature. Borah was the son-in-law of William
McConnell who, before the depression of 1893, was Moscow's leading
businessman, and a former governor and U.S. Senator. Although
McConnell was no longer wealthy, he was still prominent in local affairs, and Moscow had adopted Borah as a "favorite son."

[29]Deary to McCornack, 2 Mar. 1905, Box 2, Letterbook #9, PLC-UISC.

[30]The quotations are from, respectively, Spokane *Spokesman-Review,* 10
Mar. 1905; and Palouse *Republic,* 10 Mar. 1905.

[31]The quotations are in two Palouse *Republic* editorials, 17 Mar. and 24
Mar. 1905. Also see the *Republic* for 5 May 1905.

[32]Deary's first quotation is in Deary to F. E. Weyerhaeuser, 20 Mar. 1905,
Box 2, Letterbook #9; the second is in Deary to McCornack, 18 Dec.
1905, Box 4, Letterbook #28. The emphasis is his. Both in PLC-UISC.
For the Palouse *Republic* see 22 Dec. 1905. For Weyerhaeuser's previous
bad experience with bonuses see C. A. Weyerhaeuser to Cliff Musser,
26 Dec. 1905, Box 1, PLC-LN.

[33]The first quotation is from Deary to William E. Borah, Boise, 27 May
1905, Box 4, Letterbook #26; the second from Deary to F. W. Kehl, 13
Mar. 1905, Box 2, Letterbook #9. Both in PLC-UISC.

[34]For Deary's name preference see Deary to C. A. Weyerhaeuser, 6 Mar.
1905, Box 1, PLC-LN. Other officers were Frederick E. Weyerhaeuser,
vice president; F. S. Bell, treasurer; and C. R. Musser, secretary, with
C. A. Weyerhaeuser and R. Drew and William Musser also on the board
of directors.

[35]There has been considerable confusion over these place names. Princeton
was already an established community by the time the railroad came
through. A couple of miles east of Princeton the line ran though property owned by Homer Canfield. The company proposed to name the station there after him, but Canfield protested. He suggested that the name
be Harvard, a likely "rival" for neighboring Princeton. This set the pattern for naming other stations along the line after colleges. Vassar however,

may have honored nearby homesteader James Vassar. See Boone, *From A to Z in Latah County.* In 1935 the WI&M, because of the unusual names of the towns along its line, was featured nationally in the Ripley's "Believe It or Not" syndicated cartoon. See Palouse *Republic,* 13 Dec. 1935.

[36]This summary of the WI&M is based largely on secondary accounts. However researchers should be aware that a massive collection of business records and correspondence relating to the WI&M are at UISC. In addition, LN maintains a substantial group of WI&M papers. For the first train of logs to Palouse see Deary to R. D. Musser, 11 Mar. 1906, Letterbook #21; and for a typical letter of discontent over the slow progress of railroad construction, Deary to Thatcher, 5 Je. 1906, Letterbook #22. Both in Box 3, PLC-UISC. For groundbreaking and the first spike see Palouse *Republic,* 12 May 1905, 11 Aug. 1905. For the WI&M as the first substantial logging road in the Rockies see Jay M. Haymond, "Lumber Industry: Rocky Mountain Region," in Davis, *Encyclopedia of American Forest and Conservation History,* vol. 1, pp. 318-3. Helpful for general logging railroad background are Michael Koch's *Steam & Thunder in the Timber: Saga of the Forest Railroads* (Denver: World Press, 1979); and Arthur Benter, "Lumber Railroads of the Weyerhaeuser Timber Company," *Pacific Railway Journal,* Mar. 1957, pp. 3-16. For the WI&M specifically see Petersen, ed., *Railroad Man*; Kohlmeyer, *Timber Roots,* pp. 300-3; Hidy, *Timber and Men,* pp. 257-8; *Potlatch Story,* Sept. 1960, pp. 8-11; and Fred Bendix, "Washington, Idaho & Montana Ry.: A Western Short Line Serving Princeton, Yale, Harvard, Vassar, Stanford, and Cornell," *Model Railroader,* Sept. 1975, pp. 40-7.

[37]Palouse *Republic,* 23 Feb. 1906. Also see issues of 4 Aug. 1905 and 29 Dec. 1905 for the predicted positive impact of WI&M on the mining region; and Swanson, "Logging on the Palouse River," p. 34.

[38]Palouse *Republic,* 31 Mar. 1905. For further details on the Spokane and Inland Empire see issues of 10 Feb. 1905 and 1 Sept. 1905.

[39]Palouse *Republic,* 12 Jan. 1906.

[40]The quotation is from an editorial in the 18 May 1906 Palouse *Republic.* Descriptions of the Palouse boom can be found in numerous front page stories, advertisements, and editorials from the *Republic* for the years 1904-06. Also see Evelyn Rodewald, "Palouse: Boom and Bust? 1900-1920," *Bunchgrass Historian,* vol. 10, no. 2, Summer 1982, pp. 21-35.

[41]Palouse *Republic,* 5 Feb. 1904. Also see issue of 16 Sept. 1904 for the Codd purchase.

[42]The Thatcher quotation is in Thatcher to Deary, 25 Oct. 1904. Also see Deary to Thatcher, 24 Oct. 1904; both in Box 1, PLC; Thatcher to Deary, 29 Jy. 1905, WI&M papers, Box 62; and A. W. Laird to Bell, 28 Nov. 1917, Box 4, PLC. All above in LN. For Deary's quotation see Deary to C. A. Weyerhaeuser, 23 Mar. 1905, Box 2, Letterbook #9. Also see Deary to John Gray, 26 Jy. 1905, Box 4, Letterbook #26. Both in PLC-UISC. Further details on the Palouse flour mill and controversy can be found in the following issues of the Palouse *Republic*: 2 Sept. 1904; 24 Oct. 1904; 18 Nov. 1904; 25 Nov. 1904; 31 Mar. 1905; 4 Aug. 1905; 8 Sept. 1905; 15 Sept. 1905; 26 Oct. 1917.

[43]For Deary's 1903 potential millsite purchases see Deary to Bell, 29 May 1903; and Deary to C. A. Weyerhaeuser, 26 Je. 1903, Box 1, PLC-LN. Deary's "baptize a bastard" story is repeated frequently in interviews in LCHS-OH. For published versions see Richard L. Williams, *The Loggers* (New York: Time-Life Books, 1976), p. 205; Kohlmeyer, *Timber Roots*, pp. 298-9; and Hidy, *Timber and Men*, pp. 255-6. For Deary's first public statement that a mill would be constructed in Latah County see Palouse *Republic*, 26 Feb. 1904. The quotation concerning Palouse's expected boom following mill construction is in the 28 Apr. 1905 *Republic*. For Deary's disparaging remark concerning Moscow's future see Deary to Thatcher, 19 May 1904, Box 1, PLC-LN. Two letters provide background on Moscow residents' efforts to land the mill as late as 1905. See Deary to Turrish, 9 Feb. 1905, Box 1, Letterbook #7; and Deary to C. A. Weyerhaeuser, 18 Feb. 1905, Box 1, Letterbook #8; PLC-UISC.

[44]Palouse *Republic*, 15 Sept. 1905. The first *Republic* notice of the new town was buried in a story about the WI&M on 8 Sept. 1905.

[45]For the assurances from Deary and Weyerhaeuser see Palouse *Republic*, 27 May 1904; 6 Oct. 1905. The text of the publicity brochure is printed in the issue of 1 Je. 1906.

[46]C. A. Weyerhaeuser to Cliff Musser, 26 Dec. 1905, Box 1, PLC-LN.

[47]When he first moved to Winona, Laird constructed a shanty on an apparently vacant eighty-acre tract near town and thereby became embroiled in a claim-jumping controversy. The original claimholder destroyed his shack, and Laird rebuilt. The persistent claimholder razed the hut again, and when Laird just as stubbornly rebuilt, he found himself in court, facing charges of claim-jumping and trespassing. Laird lost the case, the first jury trial held in Winona County, but still refused to budge, planning an appeal. While away on legal matters in LaCrosse, Laird left Catherine to protect his home. Thinking the time opportune to finally remove Laird, Winona's sheriff rode to the hut, demanding that Catherine vacate. Tenacity ran in that family, however, and Catherine informed the sheriff of her intention to shoot anyone approaching, successfully holding the place until John's return. Laird filed his appeal, but eventually settled matters by purchasing the property. For John Laird and Catherine Goddard see "Reminiscences of Early Days and Incidents in the Life of John C. Laird," typescript, Laird Family Collection, Box 25, LN; *History of Winona County, Together with Biographical Matter, Statistics, Etc.* (Chicago: H. H. Hill and Co., 1883), pp. 310-18; and Kohlmeyer, *Timber Roots*, pp. 19-51.

[48]William Allison White married John Laird's older sister, Elizabeth Ann Laird.

[49]See Thatcher to Deary, 12 Jy. 1905, WI&M papers, Box 62, LN, for an excellent biographical sketch of Laird and the tasks he was expected to undertake for the company. Additional biographical details can be found in "Reminiscences of John C. Laird," Laird Family Collection, Box 25, LN; William L. Maxwell, interview, pp. 32-3, COL-OH; and Kohlmeyer, *Timber Roots*, p. 298.

[50]The quotations are from, respectively, Laird to Laird-Norton Co., 11 May 1913; Box 3, PLC-LN; and notes from correspondence, Laird to Thatcher, 4 Feb. 1911, RG 7, Box 9, "William Deary" file, WEYER. Anna Laird wrote of her husband's hardworking nature upon his death: "My regret is that . . . he could not have been spared to take it a little easier and have had a little more fun. He always used to say—my *work* is fun because I love it—but he took little time for play." Anna Laird to F. S. Bell, 6 Sept. 1931, F. S. Bell papers, Box 2, LN.

[51]The quotations are from, respectively, Laird to Robert Dougherty, Winona, 19 Sept. 1905; and Laird to H. C. Garvin, Winona, 19 Sept. 1905. Both in Box 4, Letterbook #26, PLC-UISC.

CHAPTER FOUR

[1]The quotation is from Deary to Thatcher, 8 Mar. 1905. Also see Deary to Thatcher, 16 Jy. 1904 for early inexpensive land purchases. Both in Box 1, PLC-LN. Also see Moscow *Daily Idahonian*, 11 Jy. 1956; and Mamie Sisk Wurman interview, pp. 7-9, LCHS-OH for further background on Deary's purchases and land speculation along the river.

[2]The first quotation is from C. A. Weyerhaeuser to Wilkinson, 8 May 1905, Box 5; the second from Deary to C. A. Weyerhaeuser, 9 Je. 1905, Box 4, Letterbook #26, both in PLC-UISC. For additional background information on the site from the same collection see Deary to F. W. Kehl, 19 Apr. 1905, Box 2, Letterbook #9; and Wilkinson to C. A. Weyerhaeuser, 22 May 1905; 1 Je. 1905, both in Box 5. Also see R. M. Weyerhaeuser to Thatcher, 7 Je. 1905; Thatcher to R. M. Weyerhaeuser, 10 Je. 1905; and C. A. Weyerhaeuser to Bell, 12 Je. 1905, Box 1, PLC-LN.

[3]The quotation is from C. A. Weyerhaeuser to George S. Long, 22 Mar. 1905. Also see Weyerhaeuser to Long, 3 Apr. 1905. Both in RG 1, "Weyerhaeuser Timber Co. Incoming Correspondence." And see PLC Directors' minutes, 20 Feb. 1905, RG 7, Box 19, "Potlatch" file. All above in WEYER. Wilkinson's son, H. W. Wilkinson, took hundreds of photographs of mill construction while living with his father at the site. These were used for many years as publicity photographs by the company. H. W.'s son, Bud, later gained fame as the highly successful football coach of the University of Oklahoma.

[4]Thatcher to Deary, 8 Jy. 1905, WI&M papers, Box 62, LN.

[5]For descriptions of various saws and changes in sawmills over time see John A. C. Howard, "Trends in American Sawmilling," unpublished research report, University of Minnesota, 1956; Cox, *This Well-Wooded Land*, pp. 64-7, 158; and Fries, *Empire in Pine*, pp. 61-2. Gang saws, in the days when old growth timber was plentiful, were considered an optimum device. In fact, Laird Bell in 1939 wrote about the Laird-Norton group's use of them: "I have found old letterheads of the family business proudly asserting that we were manufacturers of gang-sawed lumber. Why that was a selling argument I can't now see." Gangs went out of popularity

for a time, but came back with the development of more efficient models. With these, clear material from outside of the log was cut into high grade lumber and the remaining cant was then put through a speedy gang saw to quickly and inexpensively manufacture a uniform grade of common lumber from the knottier central part of the log. Swedish gang saws also came into popularity, chewing through poorer quality, small logs without any preliminary squaring. See Laird Bell, *The Mid-West Lumber Cycle* (Princeton: Newcomen Society, Princeton University Press, 1940), p. 24.

[6]The "knife in the boot" quotation is from Deary to Wilkinson, 27 Je. 1905, Box 5; and the latter quotation from Deary to Wilkinson, 23 Mar. 1905, Box 2, Letterbook #9. For further background on Weyerhaeuser's opposition see Deary to Thatcher, 29 Je. 1905, Box 4, Letterbook #26. All in PLC-UISC.

[7]For the quotation see Thatcher to Deary, 8 Jy. 1905, WI&M papers, Box 62. For further background on the debate about mill size and maneuvering to reach an agreement see Deary to Thatcher, 24 Jy. 1905, WI&M papers, Box 61; and Thatcher to Deary, 12 Jy. 1905, WI&M papers, Box 62, all above in LN; C. A. Weyerhaeuser to Wilkinson, 1 Jy. 1905; Thatcher to Wilkinson, 5 Jy. 1905; and Wilkinson to Thatcher, 10 Jy. 1905; all in Box 5, PLC-UISC.

[8]The Weyerhaeuser to Davis quotation is in Hidy, *Timber and Men*, p. 362. For Wilkinson's views see Wilkinson to Thatcher, 20 Jy. 1905, WI&M papers, Box 61, LN. For the final quotation see notes from Frederick E. Weyerhaeuser's Record Book, vol. 4, RG 7, Box 6, "Potlatch Lumber Co." file, WEYER.

[9]Billings to Board of Directors, 31 May 1947, Box 8, PFI-LN.

[10]The "active man" quotation is from *Salesmen's Log*, publication of the Weyerhaeuser Sales Company, 12 Jy. 1922, p. 3. For the quotation about staying with his decisions see Leslie Mallory interview, p. 44. Also see William Maxwell interview. Both in COL-OH. The Rowan quotation is in Frank and Lottie Rowan, interview 1. Also see Nell Wood Smith, interview 4; and, especially, the interview with Jones's niece, Mabelle Nickell Morris, interview 1, all in LCHS-OH. Additional information on T. P. and Marjorie Jones can be found in John B. Miller, *The Trees Grew Tall* (Moscow, Id.: John Miller, 1972). For background on the Shelby oil boom see Michael P. Malone and Richard B. Roeder, *Montana: A History of Two Centuries* (Seattle: University of Washington Press, 1976), p. 256. Jones had earlier been president of a mine in the Hoodoo area of Latah County. See Palouse *Republic*, 22 Jy. 1910.

[11]For details on this earliest construction see Deary to Jones, 7 Apr. 1905; and Deary to C. A. Weyerhaeuser, 8 Apr. 1905, both in Box 2, Letterbook #9; Deary to Turrish, 31 Jy. 1905, Box 4, Letterbook #26; Deary to Wilkinson, 1 Aug. 1905, Box 5; Wilkinson to Thatcher, 22 Sept. 1905, Box 5, all in PLC-UISC; and Deary to Thatcher, 29 Je. 1905, WI&M papers, Box 61, LN.

[12]Palouse *Republic*, 22 Sept. 1905.

[13]See Deary to Wilkinson, 3 Mar. 1905, Box 2, Letterbook #9; Deary to C. A. Weyerhaeuser, 8 Aug. 1905, Box 5, both in PLC-UISC; and *The Family Tree*, Mar. 1939, p. 4.

[14]For background on completion of the rail line to Potlatch see two articles by Arlie Decker, A. W. Laird's son-in-law, in the Moscow *Daily Idahonian*, 9 Jy. 1956 and 13 Jy. 1956; and H. L. Rofinot, "Logging in the Pacific Northwest," unpublished typescript, RG 7, Box 29, pp. 6-7, WEYER. Construction details can also be followed in considerable correspondence in Boxes 2 and 3, PLC-UISC. The "official" grand opening of the WI&M to Potlatch was not held until November, when 400 Inland Empire residents were invited by the company to travel by train to visit the construction site. See Palouse *Republic*, 17 Nov. 1905.

[15]For temporary housing details see Laird to G. A. Dehart, Ritzville, 10 Oct. 1905, Box 4, Letterbook #26; and Wilkinson to C. A. Weyerhaeuser, 13 Oct. 1905 and 1 Dec. 1905, Box 5, all in PLC-UISC.

[16]The quotation is from Wilkinson to Matt Culbertson, Troy, 16 Mar. 1906. For numbers of men at the construction site see Wilkinson to Thatcher, 9 Nov. 1905, and 22 Nov. 1905. Preference for hiring local men is outlined in Wilkinson to M. L. Seymour, 14 Aug. 1905. All of the above are in Box 5, PLC-UISC. For the company's frustration at being unable to hire enough men see Deary to Thatcher, 31 Oct. 1905, WI&M Papers, Box 62, LN; while a typical advertisement for employees, running under the heading "Potlatch Lumber Company Needs 500 Men," can be found in Palouse *Republic*, 31 Mar. 1905.

[17]For the "ducks feathers" quotation see Wilkinson to C. A. Weyerhaeuser, 6 Oct. 1905, Box 5. The inadequate water supply and attempts to relieve the situation are covered in Anonymous to A. W. Laird, 9 Nov. 1905, and Wilkinson to Thatcher, 22 Nov. 1905, both in Box 5. For Thanksgiving and Christmas at the camp see, respectively, Wilkinson to C. A. Weyerhaeuser, 1 Dec. 1905 and 29 Dec. 1905, both in Box 5. For Deary's admonition to get rid of the whiskey or leave town, see Deary to Robert Roberts, 14 Apr. 1906, Box 3, Letterbook #21. The quotation concerning a police officer is in Wilkinson to Deary, 8 Jan. 1906, Box 6. All in PLC-UISC.

[18]Wilkinson to Thatcher, 22 Nov. 1905, Box 5, PLC-UISC.

[19]Wilkinson to C. A. Weyerhaeuser, 29 Dec. 1905. Also see M. L. Seymour to Thatcher, 8 Nov. 1905; Wilkinson to Thatcher, 22 Nov. 1905; and Wilkinson to Ira Warren, Little Falls, Mn., 26 Oct. 1905. All in Box 5, PLC-UISC.

[20]A "Complete Bill of Timber for Saw Mill" placed with the Palouse mill was found in "Contracts" file, PLC. For a description of the millsite just prior to dismantling in the 1980s see Keith Petersen, "Farewell to the Potlatch Mill," *Latah Legacy*, vol. 12, no. 3, Fall 1983, pp. 16-26. A file of several hundred photographs documenting interiors and exteriors of millsite buildings, taken just prior to dismantling, is maintained at LCHS.

[21]Construction progress during this time can be traced in many letters in Letterbooks #21 and #22, Box 3; and in the Box 5 correspondence files, PLC-UISC.

²²The other incorporators were Potlatch Lumber Company employees H. P. Henry and F. C. McGowan, who by 1907 had moved to the new town of Deary at the request of the company to manage sales of town lots through the Deary Townsite Company.

²³For background on the Tertelings see Peter Terteling's handwritten reminiscences, SC/TER-2, LCHS; "The Tertelings . . . Builders," *America's Builders*, Oct. 1952, pp. 1-6; Marguerite Laughlin, "Bigger Buckets, Fill 'em Full, Swing 'em Fast: The Story of the Terteling Family," *Latah Legacy*, vol. 13, no. 4, Winter 1984, pp. 24-6; and "The Terteling Company, Inc.," in Merle Wells and Arthur A. Hart, *Idaho: Gem of the Mountains* (Northridge, Ca.: Windsor Publications, 1985), pp. 196-99. Joseph Terteling's obituary, which includes a concise biography, can be found in Boise *Idaho Daily Statesman*, 29 Je. 1940. Stories in the following issues of the Palouse *Republic* detail the growth of the Palouse and Potlatch brick manufacturing firms: 8 Jan. 1904; 22 Apr. 1904 (quotation); 28 Jy. 1905; 12 Oct. 1906; 29 Mar. 1907; 28 Je. 1907; 29 Je. 1923. Contracts and correspondence between the Potlatch Lumber Company and John Gamble and J. A. Pettifor of Spokane – including the lumber company's takeover of the brick manufacturing facilities at Potlatch – as well as contracts with Terteling, were in "Potlatch Brick Co." file, PLC. Finally, see Wilkinson to Laird, 2 Dec. 1905; Wilkinson to M. L. Seymour, 4 Oct. 1905; and Wilkinson to C. A. Weyerhaeuser, 29 Dec. 1905, all in Box 5, PLC-UISC, for further background on early brick manufacturing at Potlatch.

²⁴For the early days of mill testing see Palouse *Republic*, 7 Sept. 1906 and 14 Sept. 1906; *The Potlatch Story*, Sept. 1965, pp. 2-7; Laird to C. A. Weyerhaeuser, 23 Aug. 1906, Box 3, Letterbook #23, PLC-UISC; and Laird to George Long, 14 Sept. 1906, Box 36; C. A. Weyerhaeuser to Long, 3 Sept. 1906, 10 Sept. 1906, Box 37; in RG 1, WEYER.

²⁵Palouse *Republic*, 14 Sept. 1906.

²⁶LaVoy's comment is in *The Family Tree*, Oct. 1946, p. 5.

²⁷Deary to Seymour, 22 Sept. 1911, RG 7, Box 6, "Potlatch Lumber Co." file, WEYER.

²⁸For descriptions of the mill see Palouse *Republic*, 14 Sept. 1906 and 29 May 1914; *Potlatch Lumber Company: Manufacturers of Fine Lumber, Idaho White Pine, Western Pine and Larch* (Potlatch: Potlatch Lumber Co., 1907); Clifford Lewis Imus, "A Social Study of Potlatch, Idaho," unpublished bachelor of arts thesis, State College of Washington, 1910; Arthur W. Stevens, "A Study of the Lumbering Methods of the Potlatch Lumber Company, December 17-23, 1911," Cage 1583, WSU MASC, which was published in *Latah Legacy*, vol. 11, no. 4, Winter 1982, pp. 14-20; Special "Potlatch-Elk River Edition" of the *Salesmen's Log*, published by the Weyerhaeuser Sales Company, 12 Jy. 1922; "Interesting Facts About Potlatch Plant, Jan. 1, 1936," File 1, PLC-LCHS; address by S. E. Andrew, manager, Potlatch Unit, 18 Sept. 1958, "Addresses" file, PLC; Petersen, "Farewell to Potlatch Mill"; and the following issues of *The Family Tree*: Dec. 1944, pp. 4-5; Sept. 1945, pp. 1, 4-5; May 1946,

pp. 1, 4-5; Oct. 1946, pp. 1, 4-5; Nov. 1946, p. 8. The following oral history interviews provide excellent details on the plant and working conditions. From COL-OH: A. N. Frederickson; Maxwell Williamson; Laboring Men of Potlatch. From LCHS-OH: James Bacca; Gus Demus, nos. 2, 3; Lee Gale, nos. 1, 2; Glen Gilder, no. 2; Charles Jelleberg; Carl Lancaster; Ed Muhsal; Mike Stefanos; Arthur Sundberg, nos. 2, 3, 4, 5; Emmett Utt, nos. 2, 3. I am especially indebted to Lee Gale for his assistance on this section.

[29] For alterations in the 1920s see *The Family Tree*, Mar. 1946, p. 5; Laird to directors, 5 Dec. 1925, Box 5, PLC-LN; William Maxwell interview, pp. 66, 80; R. E. Irwin interview, pp. 4-10; and A. N. Frederickson interview, pp. 14-15, all in COL-OH. Also see Lee Gale, interview 2, LCHS-OH.

[30] See *The Family Tree*: May 1940, pp. 1, 3; Dec. 1944, pp. 4-5; Sept. 1945, pp. 1, 4-5; *Potlatch Story*, Sept. 1965, pp. 2-7; and "General Information Manual, Potlatch Unit," 31 Jy. 1961, Box 9, PLC-UISC.

[31] The Weyerhaeuser statement is quoted in Billings to PFI executive committee, 18 Oct. 1946; the Jewett quotation is in Jewett to Billings, 20 Sept. 1946, both in Box 43, JEWETT. Also see Laird Bell to George Little, Laird-Norton Co., 31 Dec. 1947, Box 8, PFI-LN. The Moscow *Daily Idahonian* issues of 22 Apr. 1948 and 6 May 1948 discuss the mill's new diversified capabilities.

[32] Lee Gale, "Corliss Engine Summary," 26 Mar. 1959, typescript, Box 13, File #321, PLC-UISC; Lee Gale, interview no. 2, LCHS-OH; *Potlatch Story*, Sept. 1965, p. 6.

[33] *Potlatch Story*, Sept. 1965, pp. 6-7; Lee Gale, interview no. 2, LCHS-OH.

[34] Lee Gale, interview 2, LCHS-OH. Numerous news stories and editorials concerning the "temporary" and permanent closures of the plant can be found in the region's daily and weekly newspapers for August 1981 and March 1983.

CHAPTER FIVE

[1] Spokane *Spokesman-Review*, 16 Oct. 1905; Moscow *Daily Idahonian*, 13 Jy. 1956.

[2] Very little work has been done on Onaway. For the town as a stage stop and the 1905 plat see Boone, *From A to Z in Latah County*, p. 74; and "Potlatch History: Towns," typescript, n.d., SC/POT-4, LCHS.

[3] The three quotations are from, respectively, Palouse *Republic*, 20 Apr. 1906; 25 Jan. 1907; and 8 Feb. 1907. For the anti-saloon petition see Laird to Sheriff J. J. Keane, Moscow, 10 Je. 1907, Box 3, Letterbook #24, PLC-UISC. For the private detectives see Palouse *Republic*, 18 Feb. 1910.

[4] Musser to Thatcher, 18 Nov. 1905, WI&M papers, Box 61, LN.

[5]Bell to Thatcher, 14 Sept. 1905, Box 1, PLC-LN.

[6]Deary to Bell, 25 Aug. 1905; Deary to Thatcher, 30 Aug. 1905, Box 4, Letterbook #26, PLC-UISC.

[7]Thatcher to C. R. Musser, 20 Nov. 1905, WI&M papers, Box 61, LN; Deary to Thatcher, 12 Mar. 1906; Laird to James Towey, Winona, 1 Mar. 1906, all in Box 3, Letterbook #21, PLC-UISC.

[8]See *Exhibit of the U.S. Bureau of Labor at the Louisiana Purchase Exposition*, U.S. House of Representatives, Doc. #343, part 5, 58th Cong., 20 Sess., especially pp. 1191-4. For some positive images of company towns and model industrial communities in the popular press see Lawrence Lewis, "Uplifting 17,000 Employees," *The World's Work*, Mar. 1905, pp. 5939-50; Graham Taylor, "Creating the Newest Steel City," *Survey*, Apr. 1909, pp. 20-36; and George D. McCarthy, "Morgan Park – A New Type of Industrial Community," *The American City*, Feb. 1916, pp. 150-3. Not all popular coverage of company towns has been positive. For examples of damning essays, albeit from a slightly later period, see "Life in a Company Town," *The New Republic*, 22 Sept. 1937, p. 171; Zachariah Chafee, Jr., "Company Towns in the Soft Coal Fields," *The Independent*, 15 Sept. 1923; pp. 102-4; "The Company Community in the American Coalfields," *The New Statesman*, 15 Oct. 1927, pp. 6-8; Frank Tannenbaum, *Darker Phases of the South* (New York: G. P. Putnam's Sons, 1924); and "Potlatch – A Slacker City," *The Public*, 18 Jan. 1919, pp. 62-3. For an excellent analysis of perceived positive effects accruing from company town architecture see Leland M. Roth, "Three Industrial Towns by McKim, Mead & White," *Journal of the Society of Architectural Historians*, vol. 38, no. 4, Dec. 1979, pp. 317-47. For Pullman, Illinois, see Stanley Buder, *Pullman: An Experiment in Industrial Order and Community Planning, 1880-1930* (New York: Oxford University Press, 1967); and for a general overview of western company towns, James B. Allen, *The Company Town in the American West* (Norman: University of Oklahoma Press, 1966).

[9]Laird to R. D. Musser, 20 Mar. 1906, Box 3, Letterbook #21, PLC-UISC.

[10]Ibid.

[11]For the effort to call the town "Thatcher" and Musser's disapproval of "Potlatch," see Musser to Thatcher, 23 Je. 1905, Box 1, PLC-LN; and notes from PLC Director's meeting, 10 Jy. 1905, RG 7, Box 19, "Potlatch" file, WEYER. There was already a "Potlatch Junction" in Latah County on the Northern Pacific Railroad line, and Potlatch officials had to convince railroad officials to change the name of the junction, which the railroad readily agreed to. The company finally received confirmation from the Post Office department in late October 1905 that their name of "Potlatch" was approved. See Thatcher to H. J. Elliot, President, Northern Pacific, 26 Je. 1905; 14 Jy. 1905; and Elliot to Thatcher, 5 Jy. 1905, WI&M papers, Box 61, LN; and Laird to Thatcher, 31 Oct. 1905, Box 4, Letterbook #28, PLC-UISC.

[12]For Hayward see Kohlmeyer, *Timber Roots*, pp. 259-73; and Hidy, *Timber and Men*, pp. 89-91. For Cloquet see *Timber and Men*, p. 189; and A. N. Fredericksen interview, pp. 11-12, COL-OH.

13Deary to Thatcher, 12 Mar. 1906; Laird to Crossett Lumber Co., Crossett, Ark., 23 Feb. 1906, both in Letterbook #21; Laird to C. A. Weyerhaeuser, 30 Je. 1906, Letterbook #22; Laird to J. A. Roebings Sons Co., Trenton, N.J., 15 Aug. 1906, Letterbook #23. All in Box 3. Laird to R. M. Weyerhaeuser, 18 Jan. 1906, Box 4, Letterbook #28. All in PLC-UISC.

14The quotation is from Laird to C. R. Musser, 29 Nov. 1905, Letterbook #28. For more on the town layout decision see Deary to Thatcher, 15 Je. 1905, Letterbook #26; all above in Box 4, PLC-UISC. Also see Bell to Thatcher, 14 Sept. 1905; and Laird to Bell, 9 Nov. 1905, Box 1, PLC-LN; C. R. Musser to Thatcher, 18 Nov. 1905; Thatcher to Musser, 20 Nov. 1905; and Laird to Bell, 25 Oct. 1905, WI&M papers, Box 61, LN.

15For biographical sketches of White see N. W. Durham, *Spokane and the Inland Empire* (Spokane and Chicago: S. J. Clarke Publishing Co., 1912), vol. 2, pp. 391-4; and Jonathan Edwards, *An Illustrated History of Spokane County, State of Washington* (W. H. Lever, 1900), p. 621. Additional information came from the files of the City of Spokane Historic Preservation Office. For Cutter see Michael Schmeltzer, "The Cutter Mystique," *Washington: The Evergreen State Magazine*, vol. 1, no. 5, March/April 1985, pp. 49-57. For a brief introduction to Spokane architecture, including descriptions of the *Review* building and many other structures built during the Spokane boom of 1890-1910, see Roland Colliander, et al., *Spokane Sketchbook* (Seattle: University of Washington Press, 1974).

16White's contract, dated 19 Jan. 1906, was in "Small House Construction" file, PLC. The contract did require White to furnish his services free for houses costing less than $1,000. Furthermore, the company constructed the town inexpensively with its own lumber, largely utilizing its own work crews, thus making construction expenses—and White's 5 percent—comparatively low. Even so, White recouped a tidy sum. For construction cost-cutting on the part of the company see notes from various correspondence of G. W. Morgan, Potlatch Townsite Division superintendent, 1907-1909, R.G. 7, Box 19, "Potlatch" file, WEYER.

17The quotation is in Davis to W. H. Laird, 23 Jan. 1906, Box 1, PLC-LN. For the number of houses built and families living in town prior to White's hiring see Wilkinson to C. A. Weyerhaeuser, 23 Jan. 1906, Box 6. For hiring another builder for smaller houses see Laird to E. W. Swails, Murray, Id., 12 Jan. 1906, Box 4, Letterbook #28. Both in PLC-UISC.

18The first quotation is from Laird to White, 12 Jan. 1906, Box 4, Letterbook #28, PLC-UISC; the second from the Palouse *Republic*, 20 Apr. 1906.

19Pullman *Herald*, 3 Feb. 1906; F. McGowan to P. M. Lachmund, 24 Jy. 1906, Box 3, Letterbook #22, PLC-UISC.

20For details on Potlatch's rapid growth see Laird to C. A. Weyerhaeuser, 23 Feb. 1906, Box 3, Letterbook #21; and McGowan to C. J. Bettis, 18 Aug. 1906, Box 3, Letterbook #23; both in PLC-UISC. Also see the Palouse *Republic*, 25 Jan. 1907.

21A few of White's blueprints and elevations have been preserved and are in PLC-UISC. For more information on Potlatch architecture see Keith

Petersen and Mary Reed's unpublished reports, "Reconnaissance Survey: City of Potlatch," 1984; and "Potlatch Historic Site Survey: National Register Nominations," 1985. Both are at the Idaho State Historic Preservation Office, Boise. Duplicate copies are also at LCHS. A document entitled "Potlatch Townsite Buildings, December 1950," in "Townsite Division" files, PLC, provided original construction dates, costs, and number of rooms for every Potlatch house. Also see Imus, "Social History of Potlatch," pp. 14-15.

[22]See Laird to White, 10 Mar. 1906 and 17 Mar. 1906, both in Letterbook #21; and 9 Je. 1906, Letterbook #22. All in Box 3, PLC-UISC.

[23]For biographical details on Seymour see Thatcher to Deary, 12 Jy. 1905 (quotation), WI&M papers, Box 62; Bell to C. A. Weyerhaeuser, 13 Mar. 1905, Box 4, F. S. Bell papers; and C. A. Weyerhaeuser to Laird-Norton Company, 29 May 1905, Box 1, PLC. All in LN. An obituary is in the Palouse *Republic,* 7 Aug. 1925. Blueprints of the Seymour and other Nob Hill houses are in UISC. For the radiator heating system see Arnold-Evans Company to White, 25 Oct. 1906; and Laird to White, 29 Oct. 1906; both in PLC.

[24]Blueprints of some boardinghouses are in UISC. Sanborn Fire Insurance Company maps of Potlatch, 1910 and 1928, UISC, provide additional construction and location information. Also see Imus, "Social History of Potlatch," pp. 33, 35.

[25]No contract specifications for the original Potlatch houses exist, but in 1916 the company contracted to build a one-story, five-room working-class cottage at 715 Elm Street, which cost $322 to construct. The contract specifications, which give an indication of the quality of workmanship expected, read in part, "All plates are to be doubled. All openings three feet or wider are to be trussed. Double up joists under all partitions. . . . Double up all trimmers and headers for all openings with the same sized material. . . . All work done for the proper erection and completion of the building must be of the best and subject to the approval of the Company. All lath shall be nailed to every bearing. . . . All plaster to be two coats with carpet float. Second coat is to be carefully worked out to a smooth, even and true surface. . . . When the work is completed all plaster must be absolutely free from cut faces or imperfections of any kind whatsoever." Contract made 1 Aug. 1916 between Potlatch Lumber Co. and H. E. Crose of Palouse and Matt Wilkinson of Spokane, PLC.

[26]For descriptions of town size and the number of houses completed at the time of mill opening see notes from correspondence, Laird to H.M. Foulk, Oshkosh, Wi., 2 Aug. 1906, RG 7, Box 19, "Potlatch" file, WEYER; and Palouse *Republic,* 14 Sept. 1906. For problems with the use of green lumber and inexperienced work crews see Maxwell interview, p. 7, COL-OH; and G. W. Morgan to T. J. Humbird, 22 Feb. 1907, and Morgan to J. B. Kehl, 23 Jan. 1908, both in Box 35, PLC-UISC. The report about some directors being concerned houses were too well built comes in Laird to Laird-Norton Co., 26 Sept. 1906, Box 1, PLC-LN. Laird's "rather crude" comment is in Laird to James Tawney, Winona, 5 Sept. 1906,

Box 3, Letterbook #23. The anti-shack quotation is in Deary to Seymour, 21 Jan. 1907, Box 6. For more on shack removal see Morgan to "Occupant of this Shack," 9 Nov. 1907, Box 35. All above in PLC-UISC.

[27]W. J. Gamble, interview 1, p. 15, LCHS-OH.

[28]For early details of church services in Potlatch see Laird to Rev. H. H. Hubbell, Lewiston, 14 May 1906; Laird to Rev. E. E. Hench, Palouse, 14 Jy. 1906; Laird to C. A. Weyerhaeuser, 17 Jy. 1906, all in Box 3, Letterbook #22; and Laird to Rev. W. J. A. Hendricks, Moscow, 4 Jan. 1906, Box 4, Letterbook #28. All in PLC-UISC. Also see notes from PLC Board of Directors' meeting, 12 May 1906, RG 7, Box 19, "Potlatch" file, WEYER; and the Palouse *Republic*, 15 Dec. 1906; 21 Dec. 1906; 19 Apr. 1907.

[29]For a summary of Catholicism in Potlatch see Rev. Kenneth J. Arnzen, "The Celebration of the Diamond Jubilee of St. Mary's Church," typescript, 1982, LCHS. For details on the church dedication see R. D. Musser to Bell, 16 Sept. 1907, Box 2, PLC-LN; and Palouse *Republic*, 20 Sept. 1907. Deary regularly contributed to the Catholic church's fund drives, and paid house rent for priests. See Deary to A. A. McDonald, 21 Nov. 1907, Box 4, Letterbook #30; and G. W. Morgan to Lee Oakes, 30 Dec. 1908, Box 36, both in PLC-UISC. Fred Kohlmeyer, "Northern Pine Lumbermen: A Study in Origins and Migrations," *Journal of Economic History*, vol. 16, no. 4, Dec. 1956, pp. 529-38, states that 95 percent of leading lumbermen in the Great Lakes States were Protestant, the remainder Catholic or agnostic.

[30]Palouse *Republic*, 11 Jan. 1907.

[31]See *The Lutheran-Presbyterian Parish* (Potlatch: Grace Lutheran Church and Community Presbyterian Church, 1981); and an early history of the church written by the Rev. C. R. Scafe in Moscow *Daily Star-Mirror*, 7 Dec. 1912. For dedication of the first Union Church, and its overcrowding by 1911, see Palouse *Republic*, 10 Jan. 1908; 17 Jan. 1908; and 26 May 1911. Further background on the church can be found in Moscow *Daily Idahonian*, 31 Jy. 1951; and *The Family Tree*, Sept. 1941, p. 2; Aug. 1952, p. 10. Construction details for the two buildings can be found in Sanborn Fire Insurance Maps of Potlatch, 1910 and 1928, UISC. The original, small Union Church later housed the Potlatch High School, and was razed for a parking lot in 1941. The larger church was destroyed by fire in July 1951.

[32]See *The Lutheran-Presbyterian Parish*; and Moscow *Daily Idahonian*, 10 Jy. 1956.

[33]Laird to Thatcher, 14 Je. 1906, Box 3, Letterbook #22, PLC-UISC.

[34]Deary to Thatcher, 29 May 1906, Box 3, Letterbook #22, PLC-UISC.

[35]For details on planning and construction of the school see numerous letters between Laird and company directors, Box 3; and "Potlatch School History," typescript, ca. 1953, Box 38. All above in PLC-UISC. Also see Palouse *Republic*, 31 Aug. 1906; 15 Dec. 1906; 9 Aug. 1907.

[36]For the first town hospital see Palouse *Republic*, 13 Dec. 1907; and Sanborn Fire Insurance Company map of Potlatch, 1910, UISC. For the jail see G. W. Morgan to Deary, 27 Oct. 1908, Box 35. For the ice house and ice harvesting see Wilkinson to C. A. Weyerhaeuser, 6 Oct. 1905, 4 Dec. 1905, Box 5. All in PLC-UISC.

[37]The quotation is from Laird to Laird-Norton Co., 26 Sept. 1906, Box 1, PLC-LN. For good background on the Merc's history see *The Family Tree*, Feb. 1937, pp. 7-8. Also see the Palouse *Republic*, 1 Feb. 1907; 14 Je. 1907. The Sanborn Fire Insurance Company map of Potlatch, 1910, UISC, details the building's division.

[38]Deary to J. B. Kehl, 16 Nov. 1907, Box 4, Letterbook #30, PLC-UISC. Hotel blueprints are in UISC. Also see Palouse *Republic*, 25 Jan. 1907; Sanborn Fire Insurance Company maps of Potlatch, 1910 and 1928, UISC.

[39]Deary to Thatcher, 22 May 1906; Laird to Palouse Light and Power Co., 7 Je. 1906. Both in Box 3, Letterbook #22, PLC-UISC.

[40]Laird to Laird-Norton Co., 8 Nov. 1905; Thatcher to Laird, 16 Nov. 1905, WI&M papers, Box 62, LN.

[41]For plank streets see Arthur Sundberg, interview 2, pp. 39-40, LCHS-OH; and G. W. Morgan to Deary, 6 Je. 1908, Box 35, PLC-UISC. For street lights see Palouse *Republic*, 15 Mar. 1907. Information on first street oiling can be found in Palouse *Republic*, 1 Jy. 1927; and Laird to A. E. Velguth, Spokane, 22 May 1926, "Contracts" file, PLC. Also see Imus, "Social History of Potlatch," pp. 7-9, for details on Potlatch streets and sidewalks.

[42]For trees and lawns see Palouse *Republic*, 19 Apr. 1907; 20 Apr. 1907; Laird to G. W. Morgan, 27 Sept. 1907, Box 4, Letterbook #25; and Morgan to A. Miller & Sons, 26 Sept. 1908, Box 35, PLC-UISC. The first city park was located approximately where the company's administration building was constructed in 1917. See Palouse *Republic*, 17 May 1907; and an early, undated town plat map in PLC.

[43]See M. L. Seymour to Will Hayes Laird, 8 May 1906, Box 1, PLC-LN; Laird to J. H. Cunningham, Portland, 8 Mar. 1906, Letterbook #21 and Laird to J. A. Roebings Sons Co., Trenton, N.J., 15 Aug. 1906, Letterbook #23, both in Box 3, PLC-UISC; Laird to Surgeon General, Washington, D.C., 2 Nov. 1926, File 3, PLC-LCHS; William Maxwell interview, pp. 37-9, COL-OH; and Sanborn Fire Insurance Company map of Potlatch, 1910, UISC.

CHAPTER SIX

[1]The ad, or similar ones, ran frequently in area newspapers in the spring of 1905. See, for example, Palouse *Republic*, 31 Mar. 1905. For the number of men employed by November see Deary to Thatcher, 17 Nov. 1905, Box 4, Letterbook #28, PLC-UISC. For the hundreds of job applications see notes from correspondence, Laird to T. J. Humbird, 28 Aug. 1906; and

Laird to Tom McNeill, 13 Oct. 1906, both in RG 7, Box 19, "Potlatch" file, WEYER.

[2]For the various statistics see Palouse *Republic*, 28 Apr. 1916; 12 Jan. 1917; 16 Feb. 1917.

[3]For architecturally designed buildings see C. E. Isenberger to H. G. Adams, Pullman, 27 Apr. 1903, Box 1, Letterbook #1, PLC-UISC; Palouse *Republic*, 9 Jy. 1915; and numerous advertisements in the *Republic*, 1915-1916. One farm building designed by Potlatch, the T. A. Leonard round barn three miles southeast of Pullman, was deemed sufficiently significant to be registered on the prestigious Historic American Buildings Survey in 1985, one of the few structures in eastern Washington so recognized. Potlatch sold all of the required lumber and designs for the barn for $645. For an advertisement concerning this structure see the Palouse *Republic*, 6 Oct. 1916. Information on the Leonard barn can be found at the Office of Archaeology and Historic Preservation in Olympia, Washington. For cordwood see *Republic*, 23 Dec. 1910; and for Potlatch's egg, butter, and poultry requirements the issue of 19 Nov. 1909.

[4]Details on the growth of Potlatch Yards can be found in various letters in Box 1, Letterbook #1, PLC-UISC; and Frank Kendall, "A Brief History of the First Forty-Five Years of Potlatch Yards," unpublished typescript, 12 May 1950, Box 28, Norton Clapp papers, LN. The "small pox" quotation is in a short-lived Potlatch newsletter entitled *Splinters*, 24 Apr. 1920 issue, Box 4, PLC-LN. For biographical details on John Kendall see Kendall to Bell, 13 May 1935, Box 2, F. S. Bell papers, LN; and Kohlmeyer, *Timber Roots*, pp. 209, 217-18, 308.

[5]Eugene V. Smalley, "Pullman, Palouse City, and Colfax," originally printed in *Northwest Magazine*, Sept.-Oct. 1892; reprint, *The Record*, 1970, pp. 54-85, quotation p. 68. Smalley was a Northern Pacific Railroad publicist. For comparisons on the time needed to clear prairie and timbered land see Michael Williams, "Pioneer Farm Life and Forest Use," in Davis, *Encyclopedia of American Forest and Conservation History*, vol. 2, pp. 529-34.

[6]The quotation is from Dick Benge, interview 1, p. 13, LCHS-OH. Also see biographical sketch of Walter A. Fiscus, 3 Oct. 1934 in James E. Lindsey papers, WSU MASC. There are many similar stories of meager, hard cutover lifestyles in LCHS-OH. See, for example, the following interviews: William Burkland; Elmer Flodin; Glen Gilder; Carl Olson; Kenneth Wilkins.

[7]Palouse *Republic*, 21 Jy. 1905.

[8]For Kehl see Kehl to Laird-Norton Co., 22 Jy. 1902, Box 1, PLC-LN. For 1905 sales see Deary to R. D. Musser, 1 Apr. 1905, Box 2, Letterbook #9; and for the quotation, Laird to Hammond & Sons, Plains, Montana, 29 Apr. 1907, Box 3, Letterbook #24. Both in PLC-UISC. In later years the lumber company worked extensively with the University of Idaho attempting to find easy ways to remove stumps. At one point the university established an experiment station on the company's cutover lands, and the company purchased one of the largest stump pullers ever made

for the university to use. They found no easy, affordable method of stump removal, however. Eventually, technological advances made it possible for farmers to use heavy equipment to undertake the task. See the University of Idaho *Argonaut*, 7 Feb. 1917 and 14 Mar. 1917; and an undated 1910 clipping in the E. L. Hulme scrapbooks, MG 42, UISC.

[9]The quotations are from *A Home and Prosperity* (Potlatch: Potlatch Lumber Co., 1916), VF 2132/254, WSU MASC; and *The Fertile Logged-Off Lands of Latah County, Idaho* (Potlatch: Potlatch Lumber Co., n.d.), File 2, PLC-LCHS.

[10]Purchase terms are outlined in *Home and Prosperity*; *Logged-Off Lands*; and Palouse *Republic*, 21 May 1909. For the success of cutover land sales see Laird to Bell, 31 Oct. 1910, Box 2, PLC-LN; and *The Timberman*, Dec. 1912, p. 62. For comparative purposes, a good discussion of the effort to move settlers onto cutover lands in western Washington, and the difficulties encountered by farmers there, can be found in Richard White, *Land Use, Environment, and Social Change: The Shaping of Island County, Washington* (Seattle: University of Washington Press, 1980), pp. 113-41.

[11]Glen Gilder, interview 3, p. 21, LCHS-OH.

[12]Palouse *Republic*, 5 Jy. 1905.

[13]Palouse *Republic*, 30 Je. 1916.

[14]Palouse *Republic*, 6 Apr. 1906; 28 Aug. 1908.

[15]Palouse *Republic*, 14 May 1909. For the Trumbull wayhouse see Miller, *Trees Grew Tall*, pp. 74-5; and Mary Reed, "The Outdoor Life in Latah County," *Latah Legacy*, vol. 14, no. 4, Winter 1985, pp. 1-19.

[16]For the town yell see Palouse *Republic*, 4 Feb. 1910. Other details of the boom can be followed in numerous *Republic* stories for that year. The brochure sent in 1910 followed a cooperative effort among many Inland Empire town boosters to distribute the Spokane and Inland Empire Railway's *The Truth About the Palouse Country* a year earlier. The Palouse Businessmen's Association diligently answered all inquiries to both mailings; and while most were enthusiastic, a few were penned by skeptics. Wrote one in 1909: "It strikes me that the description of the country is greatly overdrawn, or the bargains would have been taken up long ago. The descriptions read as tho [sic] they were made to get rid of bad bargains. If they are not, yours must be a wonderful country." The files of the Palouse Businessmen's Association for this period are in the Boomerang Museum, Palouse.

[17]The quotation is in Palouse *Republic*, 5 Oct. 1906.

[18]For the peak and decline of Palouse communities around 1910 see Meinig, "Environment and Settlement in the Palouse," p. 140.

[19]Palouse *Republic*, 18 Aug. 1911.

[20]Palouse *Republic*, 10 Nov. 1911.

[21]Palouse *Republic*, editorial, 19 May 1916. Efforts of the paper to spark the town are evident in virtually every issue of the *Republic* from 1912 through 1916.

[22]The quotations are from, respectively, Humiston to Bell, 21 Mar. 1916, Box 4; Laird to Bell, 4 Jan. 1911, Box 2; Laird to Bell, 18 Jy. 1913, Box 3; Thatcher to Laird, 8 Mar. 1916, Box 4; and C. A. Weyerhaeuser to Laird, 9 Mar. 1916, Box 4. All in PLC-LN. Also see Palouse *Republic*, 13 Aug. 1915; 12 Nov. 1915.

[23]For the 1920s bus line see Palouse *Republic*, 30 Jan. 1925.

[24]The quotation is from Deary to Wakefield & Witherspoon, Spokane, 17 Oct. 1907, Box 4, Letterbook #30. Also see Deary to M. L. Seymour, 21 Sept. 1907, Box 4, Letterbook #30; and G. W. Morgan to Deary, 20 Sept. 1907, Box 35. All in PLC-UISC.

[25]For Onaway's Italian influence see James and Amelia Bacca interview, LCHS-OH.

[26]Palouse *Republic*, 2 Feb. 1917.

[27]See Karen Broenneke, "Princeton-Harvard," historical supplement, Moscow *Daily Idahonian*, 20 Je. 1980; and the Ruby Canfield Wheeler and George Nichols interviews, LCHS-OH.

[28]See Richard Waldbauer, "Deary," pp. 7-10, in Waldbauer and Keith Petersen, *Troy, Deary and Genesee: A Photographic History* (Moscow, Id.: Latah County Historical Society, 1979); Miller, *Trees Grew Tall*, pp. 111-15; and the following interviews in LCHS-OH: Arthur Bjerke, Joel Burkland, William Burkland, Alben Halen, and Albert Pierce. For a typical Deary Townsite Company ad see Palouse *Republic*, 3 Apr. 1908. Most local histories state that Henry and McGowan were hired by Potlatch Lumber Company to oversee the sale of Deary town lots, but actually Potlatch was no longer involved once these two former employees broke away from the company and went into business for themselves. See Palouse *Republic*, 13 Sept. 1907; and, for the quotation, Laird to C. A. Weyerhaeuser, 4 Oct. 1907, Box 2, PLC-LN.

[29]See Miller, *Trees Grew Tall*; Reed, "The Outdoor Life in Latah County"; Gwendolyn Bovill Lawrence, "A Long Way From Piccadilly and a Top Hat," unpublished typescript, SC/LAW-1, LCHS; the following interviews in LCHS-OH: Marie Fisher, Joseph Holland, Elsie Moore, Naomi Parker, Byers Sanderson, John Sanderson, Nellie Smith; and Palouse *Republic*, 28 Je. 1907. The quotation is from the *Republic*, 16 Aug. 1907.

[30]Billings to Potlatch Forests, Inc., Board of Directors, 2 Feb. 1946, Box 43, JEWETT.

[31]Palouse *Republic*, 28 Apr. 1911.

[32]Bell to Laird, 8 May 1912, Box 4, F. S. Bell papers, LN.

[33]Miller, *Trees Grew Tall*, p. 60.

[34]For background on Elk River and the Elk River mill see Miller, *Trees Grew Tall*, especially pp. 74-5, 115-22; "Potlatch-Elk River Edition," *Salesmen's Log* (Weyerhaeuser Sales Company), 12 Jy. 1922; *The Timberman*, Nov. 1910, p. 28; May 1911, p. 34; May 1912, p. 43; May 1913, p. 43; Palouse *Republic*, 22 Jy. 1910; 7 Oct. 1910; C. L. Billings to PFI Board of Directors, 29 Oct. 1936, Box 7, PFI-LN; and the following interviews from LCHS-OH: Axel Anderson, Marie Clark, John Diamantis,

Mabell Morris, Pete Paolini, George Schmaltz, George Torgeson, and Rannie Vine. For Andrew Bloom see *The Family Tree*, Jan. 1937, pp. 5-7; and William Maxwell interview, pp. 91-4, COL-OH.

[35]See Deary to C. A. Weyerhaeuser, 19 Feb. 1906; and Deary to J. B. Kehl, 7 Mar. 1906, both in Box 3, Letterbook #21, PLC-UISC; and Hidy, "Lumbermen in Idaho."

[36]Deary to C. A. Weyerhaeuser, 26 Oct. 1907, Box 4, Letterbook #30, PLC-UISC.

[37]For the difficulties of Idaho terrain and climate see notes from correspondence, C. A. Weyerhaeuser to Bradford D. Viles, Minneapolis, 6 Jan. 1930, RG 7, Box 14, "Idaho" file; and notes from Frederick E. Weyerhaeuser's Record, pp. 576-7, RG 7, Box 6, "PLC" file; both in WEYER. Also see Kohlmeyer, *Timber Roots*, p. 307; Hidy, *Timber and Men*, pp. 254-60; and Laura Barber Richards, "George Frederick Jewett: Lumberman and Conservationist," unpublished masters thesis, University of Idaho, 1969, pp. 5-6. The directors' anti-clearcutting order had been encouraged by young John P. (Phil) Weyerhaeuser, the founder's grandson, and one of the conglomerate's first advocates of selective cutting. In his later managerial positions with the Clearwater Timber Company and Potlatch Forests, Inc., Weyerhaeuser finally implemented his selective cutting ideas. See William Maxwell interview, pp. 75-6, and Maxwell Williamson interview, pp. 27-8, both in COL-OH; and Charles E. Twining, *Phil Weyerhaeuser: Lumberman* (Seattle: University of Washington Press, 1985), especially pp. 61-2, 69-74.

[38]For forest fires and timber protection see Curtis, *White Pines and Fires*. For insect pests see Norton Clapp, "Potlatch Forests, Inc.," unpublished typescript, c. 1951, Box 28, Norton Clapp papers, LN; and Hidy, *Timber and Men*, p. 259.

[39]Deary to C. R. Musser, 1 Aug. 1905, Box 4, Letterbook #26, PLC-UISC.

[40]For early shipments to the Lake States see C. E. Isenberger to Deary, 11 Aug. 1904, Box 1, Letterbook #5, PLC-UISC. For the efforts of the sales department and strong expectations for the Midwestern market see Maxwell Williamson interview, pp. 26-31, COL-OH; and Palouse *Republic*, 20 Feb. 1914. For 1907 and 1923 Inland Empire marketing statistics see *National Lumber Handbook* (National Lumber Manufacturers' Association), Series 2, no. 2, Apr. 1925, pp. 2, 11.

[41]Humiston to C. A. Weyerhaeuser, 28 Feb. 1918, Box 4, PLC-LN.

[42]Frederick K. Weyerhaeuser, *Trees and Men* (New York: The Newcomen Society, 1951), p. 15; Richard B. Madden, *Tree Farmers and Wood Converters: The Story of Potlatch Corporation* (New York: The Newcomen Society, 1975), p. 14; Kohlmeyer, *Timber Roots*, p. 307; Frederick K. Weyerhaeuser and John M. Musser interview, p. 62, COL-OH.

[43]A synopsis of Mason's "The Lumber Industry in the Inland Empire," 15 Je. 1916, can be found in RG 7, Box 14, "Idaho" file, WEYER. For more on Mason's important contributions to the industry see Elmo Richardson, *David T. Mason, Forestry Advocate: His Role in the Application*

of Sustained Yield Management to Private and Public Forest Lands (Santa Barbara, Ca.: Forest History Society, 1983).

CHAPTER SEVEN

[1]The quotations are from Deary to Seymour, 9 Dec. 1907, Box 4, Letterbook #30; and G. W. Morgan to Archie Sanders, 8 Mar. 1909, Box 35. Both in PLC-UISC.

[2]See Henry Oberg, All Nations Employment Agency, to Seymour, 8 Apr. 1908, 20 Apr. 1908; Seymour to Oberg, 16 Apr. 1908, 29 May 1908; R. M. Elliot, Northwestern Employment Agency, to Seymour, 3 Aug. 1908; and Seymour to Elliot, 1 Aug. 1908, 5 Aug. 1908. All in Box 6, PLC-UISC. In the mill's early years, the company contracted with a Seattle employment agency if it was unable to find "white men" and chose to hire Japanese. See W. J. Gamble, interview 2, pp. 14-15, LCHS-OH.

[3]The quotation is from Morgan to J. B. Kehl, 23 Jan. 1908, Box 35, PLC-UISC.

[4]The quotation about using a proper form letter is in Laird to Morgan, 31 May 1907, Box 3, Letterbook #24. The eviction notice, one of many in the PLC-UISC papers, is from Morgan to tenant, 22 Jy. 1908, Box 35. Both in PLC-UISC.

[5]It is unclear exactly when the night classes began, but they had been instituted at the Union Church at least by 1917 and were still being offered in 1936. See Palouse *Republic*, 2 Nov. 1917, 21 Oct. 1921; and J. J. O'Connell to "The Foremen," 29 Oct. 1936, Box 35, PLC-UISC. Ruth Hall was a Potlatch first grade teacher from 1909 until 1937, gaining a reputation for her dedication and innovative teaching techniques. See Ray K. Harris, "Life in Potlatch Was Different," *The Pacific Northwesterner*, vol. 20, no. 1, Winter 1976, pp. 7-8; and Edgar and Elsie Renfrew interview, 7 Oct. 1985, tape recording in possession of the family, hereafter cited as Edgar and Elsie Renfrew reminiscences.

[6]Arthur Sundberg, interview 2, p. 68, LCHS-OH; G. W. Morgan to Deary, 27 Oct. 1908, Box 35, PLC-UISC; Imus, "Social History of Potlatch," p. 15.

[7]The first quotation is from Edgar and Elsie Renfrew reminiscences; the second from Mike Stefanos interview, p. 14, LCHS-OH.

[8]For further information on Potlatch's ethnic groups and their segregation see Emmett Utt, interview 4, and W. J. Gamble, interview 2, both in LCHS-OH; Harris, "Life in Potlatch Was Different"; and Palouse *Republic*, 17 Je. 1919.

[9]Laird to Thatcher, 14 Je. 1906, Box 3, Letterbook #22, PLC-UISC.

[10]Laird to Clara Davis, 18 Jy. 1906, Box 3, Letterbook #22, PLC-UISC; Palouse *Republic*, 31 Aug. 1906. Also see Elsie and Malcolm Renfrew interview, LCHS-OH.

[11]Palouse *Republic*, 31 Aug. 1906; Reese, monthly billings to Townsite Department, 1907, Box 35, PLC-UISC. For Clifton see Allen, *Company Town in West*, p. 11.

[12]For teacher pay and housing see "Potlatch School History," typescript, c. 1953, Box 38, PLC-UISC; Potlatch Forests, Inc., to Carl Osterhout, 26 May 1939, and "Inventory of Furniture, Teachers' Dormitory," 26 May 1939, both in File 3, PLC-LCHS; Sanborn Fire Insurance Company map of Potlatch, 1928, UISC; "Potlatch Townsite Buildings, 1950," PLC; and Harris, "Life in Potlatch was Different," p. 7.

[13]The quotation is from Edgar and Elsie Renfrew reminiscences. Also see Elsie and Malcolm Renfrew interview, LCHS-OH.

[14]Palouse *Republic*, 1 Oct. 1909; 8 May 1914; 3 Jy. 1914; 24 May 1918; 31 Mar. 1933; *The Family Tree*, Jan. 1939, p. 5; May 1941, p. 6; Oct. 1941, p. 6; Harris, "Life in Potlatch Was Different," p. 7.

[15]The quotation is in Dr. Elmer Hall to Wilkinson, 12 Aug. 1905, Box 5, PLC-UISC. On the dangers of woods work see Andrew M. Prouty, *More Deadly Than War: Pacific Coast Logging, 1827-1981* (New York: Garland publishing, 1985).

[16]Contracts between the lumber company, Western Hospitals Association, and various doctors for the years 1904-1945 were in "Hospital contracts" file, PLC. For summaries of the history of company insurance policies and hospital care see Otto H. Leuschel to Board of Directors, 12 Feb. 1941, Box 7, PFI-LN; and C. L. Billings to Board of Directors, 21 Aug. 1943, Box 40, JEWETT. For Potlatch's first hospital see Palouse *Republic*, 13 Dec. 1907; and Potlatch Sanborn Fire Insurance Company map of Potlatch, 1910, UISC. For modernization of the Potlatch hospital see the following issues of the Palouse *Republic*: 2 Feb. 1923; 20 Apr. 1923; 20 Jy. 1923; 10 Aug. 1923; 10 Je. 1927. For biographical sketches of Gibson see *The Family Tree*, Jy. 1939, p. 6; and, especially, the excellent reminiscences of Dr. Frank Gibson, Jr., "My Father Was My Hero," typescript, 1985, LN. In 1945 the company assumed all medical expenses for employees, dropping the one dollar monthly fee.

[17]The quotations about the loud siren and the fire drill story are in Maxwell Williamson interview, pp. 12-14, COL-OH. The Renfrew quotation is in Edgar and Elsie Renfrew reminiscences. For further details on the Potlatch fire protection system see Sanborn Fire Insurance Company maps of Potlatch, 1910 and 1928, UISC; Laird to C. A. Weyerhaeuser, 30 Je. 1906, Box 3, Letterbook #22, PLC-UISC; "Fire Protection Setup," 20 Sept. 1949, miscellaneous correspondence files, PLC; Imus, "Social History of Potlatch," pp. 11-12; Arthur Sundberg, interview 3, pp. 97-9, and Lee Gale, interview 2, both in LCHS-OH; *The Family Tree*, Je. 1937, p. 4; Jy. 1938, p. 8; Oct. 1940, p. 3; *Potlatch Story*, Dec. 1961, pp. 2-7; and Palouse *Republic*, 19 Oct. 1906, 2 Nov. 1906.

[18]The quotation is from Harris, "Life in Potlatch Was Different," p. 4. Also see Imus, "Social History of Potlatch," p. 10.

[19]Laird's quotation is in Laird to Directors, 28 Apr. 1924, Box 5, PLC-LN. The quotation as to Bottjer's character is in Moscow *Star Mirror*,

30 Apr. 1924. Also see Spokane *Spokesman-Review*, 25 Apr. 1924; and Laird, Annual Report to Stockholders, 22 Jan. 1926, Box 21, PLC-UISC. In addition to serving town residents, the bank also catered to the needs of those in the region surrounding Potlatch.

20For a summary of banks and bank failures in the Latah County vicinity during the 1930s see Glen Barrett, *The First Bank of Troy, 1905-1971* (Boise, Id.: Graphic Services, 1974), pp. 39-51. For the Potlatch bank specifically see Billings to Directors, 6 Mar. 1933; 25 Mar. 1933, Box 6, PFI-LN; and for profits in the 1930s see Auditor's Reports, Potlatch State Bank, Box 52, JEWETT.

21Billings to R. M. Weyerhaeuser, 9 Apr. 1940; 15 Apr. 1940; 23 Apr. 1940; Billings to Directors, 13 May 1940; all in Box 36, JEWETT; and *The Family Tree*, May 1940, p. 4.

22A good summary of Potlatch library history can be found in *The Family Tree*, Oct. 1939, p. 5. Also see the issue of Oct. 1941, p. 5; and the following issues of Palouse *Republic*: 14 Feb. 1908; 2 Nov. 1917; 16 May 1930; 6 Je. 1930. For the involvement of the Bells and Mrs. Weyerhaeuser see Bell to Mrs. W. D. Humiston, 20 Sept. 1917; Mabel Kelley to Bell, 19 Oct. 1932; 3 Nov. 1932; and Bell to Kelley, 26 Oct. 1921; all in Box 2, F. S. Bell papers, LN; Laird to Bell, 5 Apr. 1926; 7 Je. 1930; Box 5, PLC-LN; and "Churches, Library, Cemetery," typescript, c. 1951, Box 36, PLC-UISC. For Mollie Humiston's involvement see Julian Humiston reminiscences, 1986, LCHS.

23See Maxwell Williamson interview, pp. 15-21; and for the Starr quotation, Laboring Men of Potlatch interview, p. 31, both COL-OH. Also see Palouse *Republic*, 29 Mar. 1907; 8 Aug. 1913; 5 Sept. 1913; 2 Oct. 1914.

24The quotation is from Palouse *Republic*, 23 Jan. 1914. Also see the issue of 26 Dec. 1913; and for biographical detail on Williamson, Maxwell Williamson interview, COL-OH.

25Laird to Thatcher, 31 Jan. 1916, Box 4, PLC-LN.

26Palouse *Republic*, 8 Dec. 1916.

27Palouse *Republic*, 2 Nov. 1917; 15 Feb. 1918; 24 May 1918; 6 Apr. 1923; 30 Jan. 1925; 9 Oct. 1925.

28For summaries of the history of the Potlatch Amateur Athletic Club and its 1937 revival see *The Family Tree*, Mar. 1937, p. 4; Dec. 1937, pp. 4-6.

29Allen, *Company Town in West*, pp. 128-39, asserts that the bad reputation of company stores is generally undeserved, a belief shared by Ole S. Johnson, whose *The Industrial Store: Its History, Operations and Economic Significance* (Atlanta: University of Georgia, 1952), is the major work in the field.

30For background on Marshall see C. A. Weyerhaeuser to George S. Long, 23 Mar. 1907, RG 1, Box 43, "Weyerhaeuser 1907" file, WEYER.

31For descriptions of the Merc and the types of items sold at various times see Palouse *Republic*, 14 Je. 1907; 21 Jy. 1911; 17 Jan. 1913; 9 Jy. 1915; 19 Je. 1925; 14 Mar. 1930.

[32]Annual reports for and correspondence about the ranch can be found in Box 34, PLC-UISC. Also see Imus, "Social History of Potlatch," pp. 25-6; and Palouse *Republic*, 10 Apr. 1908; 11 Je. 1909.

[33]The quotation is in a Palouse *Republic* advertisement, 4 Apr. 1913. McDonald also sold wholesale goods to smaller merchants in the region, which assisted him in reaching his goal of a million dollars in sales annually. See Imus, "Social History of Potlatch," p. 24.

[34]Arthur Sundberg interview 1, p. 24, LCHS-OH. The Merc's multi-page ads can be found several times each year in the Palouse *Republic*. Also see *The Family Tree*, Feb. 1937, pp. 7-8; Je. 1946, pp. 1-5; *Potlatch Story*, Sept. 1960, p. 16; and Harris, "Life in Potlatch Was Different," pp. 5-6, for more on Sales Days and McDonald's merchandising techniques.

[35]The automobile quotation is from the Palouse *Republic*, 15 Oct. 1915; the quotation about McDonald's leadership from the issue of 26 Nov. 1920. After leaving Potlatch, McDonald operated a dairy ranch near Choteau, Montana, for awhile before selling out to the Cloverland Dairy and Packing Company of Spokane. As part of the consideration of that sale, he assumed control of a meat packing plant in Enterprise, Oregon. During World War II he lived in Portland and worked in shipyards there. See Palouse *Republic*, 7 Jan. 1921; 27 May 1921; and *The Family Tree*, June 1946, p. 5. For his instructions to employees see McDonald to clerks, 1 May 1907, Box 34, PLC-UISC.

[36]The "famous artist" quotation is in Palouse *Republic*, 5 Oct. 1923. Merc annual reports of profits and losses can be found in Box 34, PLC-UISC, which also has considerable correspondence detailing the tenures of various managers, and the 1950s efforts to sell the store. Also see Janice C. Johnson, "The Potlatch Story," unpublished University of Idaho history paper, 1969, p. 12, LCHS.

[37]O'Connell's no-credit statement is in O'Connell to Ferguson, 14 Apr. 1939. The harsh anti-Merc statement is in "A Friend of Justice" to Rudolph Weyerhaeuser, 1936. Both in Box 34, PLC-UISC. For the Marshall Fields quotation see Harris, "Life in Potlatch Was Different," p. 14, and for scrip, p. 11. For more on scrip and store credit see Laboring Men of Potlatch interview, pp. 77-8, COL-OH; and Elsie and Malcolm Renfrew interview, LCHS-OH.

[38]Leases for various Potlatch businesses were found in PLC.

[39]The film controversy quotations were in O'Connell to B. C. Johnson, 4 Oct. 1940; and Johnson to O'Connell, 18 Oct. 1940, PLC. Also see Palouse *Republic*, 4 May 1917, for building construction details.

[40]For 1908 townsite department activities see notes from townsite files, 1907-09, RG 7, Box 19, "Potlatch" file, WEYER; and Kohlmeyer, *Timber Roots*, pp. 305-6. For 1938 activities see "Summary of Work Performed by Townsite Department, 1938," file 3, PLC-LCHS. For a 1940s townsite superintendent's job description see "Job Description for George Hudson," Box 10, PLC-UISC.

41Edgar and Elsie Renfrew reminiscences; Harris, "Life in Potlatch Was Different," p. 4.

42Hudson to tenant, 8 Sept. 1953, Box 9. For cleanup days and contests for best yards, see various circulars to employees and residents, Box 10. All in PLC-UISC.

43Arthur Sundberg, interview 1, pp. 13-14, LCHS-OH. Also see Harris, "Life in Potlatch Was Different," pp. 3-4; and Laird to W. E. McCroskey, 31 Aug. 1907, Box 4, Letterbook #25, PLC-UISC.

44For the opera house see Morgan to E. D. Wilkins, 7 Oct. 1908. For street noise see O'Connell to "All Employees and Members of Their Families," c. 1937. Both in Box 35. For dog control see Deputy Sheriff to "Owners of Dogs in Potlatch," 15 Mar. 1944, Box 10. All in PLC-UISC.

45For ice deliveries see Harris, "Life in Potlatch Was Different," p. 3; and Laird to Seymour, 15 Apr. 1909, Box 7, PLC-UISC. For street grading see Palouse Republic, 24 May 1907; and Edgar and Elsie Renfrew reminiscences. For water and electric services see The Salesman's Log, published by Weyerhaeuser Sales Co., 12 Jy. 1922, p. 1. A list entitled "Buildings Heated by Plant," 10 Oct. 1950 in "Townsite Budget" file, PLC, provided a listing of Potlatch's steam-heated buildings.

46See Billings to Executive Committee, 18 Oct. 1946, Box 43, JEWETT. Extant profit/loss figures for the townsite for 1931-1950 are in Box 21, PLC-UISC.

47For 1947 rent increases see Jewett to PFI directors, 10 Jan. 1947, Box 44, JEWETT.

CHAPTER EIGHT

1The quotation is the title of Harris's article in the Pacific Northwesterner, vol. 20, no. 1, Winter 1976, pp. 1-16.

2Laird to Bell, 31 Oct. 1907, Box 2, PLC-LN; Laird to L. C. Barrett, Spokane, 19 Je. 1907; Laird to C. A. Weyerhaeuser, 6 Aug. 1907; both Box 4, Letterbook #25, PLC-UISC.

3For the Scotts and the desirability of uphill progression among Potlatch residents see Johnson, "The Potlatch Story," p. 11, LCHS. The Schnurrs moved into a small Pine Street house in 1927 and left Potlatch fifty years and six houses later, their last home being on Nob Hill. Robert Schnurr, personal correspondence with the author, Feb. 1986. Large gaps in extant company records prohibit any detailed or quantitative analysis of Potlatch transiency or social mobility within town.

4Forty additional company houses were constructed in 1910, five in 1916, and twenty-six in 1923. See "Potlatch Townsite Buildings," 1950, "Miscellaneous Townsite Materials" file, PLC. For the location of shacks at various times see Sanborn Fire Insurance Company maps of Potlatch, 1910 and 1928, UISC; and Johnson, "The Potlatch Story," p. 9, LCHS.

[5]The first quotation is from William Maxwell interview, p. 39; the last from Laboring Men of Potlatch interview, p. 12; both COL-OH. For the middle quotation see Morgan to Deary, 1 March 1909, Box 35, PLC-UISC.

[6]A. N. Frederickson interview, p. 18, COL-OH.

[7]Harris, "Life in Potlatch Was Different," p. 9; Elsie and Malcolm Renfrew interview; Arthur Sundberg, interview 2, p. 75, both in LCHS-OH; and Charles Talbott, Jr., correspondence with the author, 15 Feb. 1986.

[8]See, for example, the Emmett and Anna Utt interviews, and Glen Gilder, interview 4, LCHS-OH.

[9]The quotation is from Malcolm Renfrew reminiscences, LCHS. Also see Harris, "Life in Potlatch Was Different," p. 10.

[10]For a comparison of living costs between Potlatch and neighboring towns in 1910 see Imus, "Social Study of Potlatch," pp. 27-35.

[11]O'Connell to E. E. Renfrew, 24 Mar. 1937, Box 35, PLC-UISC.

[12]Edgar and Elsie Renfrew reminiscences. For town violence see Palouse Republic, 21 Apr. 1911; 12 Nov. 1934; and Gibson reminiscences, LN. For school scandals see Malcolm Renfrew reminiscences, LCHS.

[13]The quotation is from Edgar and Elsie Renfrew reminiscences. Also see Alta O'Connell, "Twenty Years in Potlatch, Idaho," p. 4; Mrs. Earl J. Woods, reminiscences, p. 2; and Gordon Gleave, "My Boyhood at Potlatch," pp. 23-5, 40-5. The last three, along with several other reminiscences of Potlatch residents, can be found at LCHS.

[14]The first quotation is from Malcolm Renfrew, Elsie and Malcolm Renfrew interview, LCHS-OH; the second from Malcolm Renfrew reminiscences, LCHS; the third from Imus, "Social Study of Potlatch," p. 29. For Laird's requirements for residency, see Palouse Republic, 28 Apr. 1916. For the prostitution, bootlegging, and drinking occasionally tolerated by the management see Gus Demus interview 3, p. 6; Edward Muhsal interview, p. 27; and Mike Stefanos interview, p. 15. All in LCHS-OH.

[15]The quotation is from Edgar and Elsie Renfrew reminiscences. Also see Elsie and Malcolm Renfrew interview, LCHS-OH. For Young see Laboring Men of Potlatch interview, pp. 74-5, COL-OH. Various cleanup drive notices and rat and earwig extermination campaign notices can be found in file 3, PLC-LCHS.

[16]Laird to Jap Campbell, 18 Apr. 1907, Box 3, Letterbook #24, PLC-UISC. Also see Palouse Republic, 25 Jan. 1907; 1 Feb. 1907; 29 Mar. 1907; 30 Jan. 1925; and Malcolm Renfrew reminiscences, LCHS.

[17]For the Legion Cabin see Palouse Republic, 10 Jan. 1930.

[18]For the company's donation of Grizzle Camp to the Boy Scouts, see Palouse Republic, 2 Je. 1938.

[19]The Mothers' Club quotation is from the Palouse Republic, 29 Jy. 1927. Information on town clubs, lodges, and organizations came from various issues of the Republic, as well as from conversations with long-time Potlatch residents.

20The first quotation is from the Palouse *Republic*, 31 Jy. 1914; the second from Elsie and Malcolm Renfrew interview, LCHS-OH.

21See Morgan to Ben LaMott, Forrest, Id., 27 Nov. 1908, Box 35, PLC-UISC; and for the Jubilee Singers and Governor Brady quotations, respectively, the Palouse *Republic*, 16 Sept. 1927; 14 Oct. 1910.

22For the anniversary banquet see Palouse *Republic*, 13 Sept. 1907; for the 1925 basketball team, Malcolm Renfrew reminiscences, LCHS.

23Palouse *Republic*, 22 Jy. 1927; 18 Jy. 1930; *The Family Tree*, Sept. 1945, p. 7; Aug. 1946, pp. 4-5. The invitation to the marshmallow roast is in a scrapbook kept by Charlotte Laird, now in the possession of Allison Laird Decker of Spokane.

24Gleave, "My Boyhood at Potlatch," p. 8, LCHS.

25R. D. Musser to C. A. Weyerhaeuser, 19 Sept. 1907, Box 2, PLC-LN.

26The quotations are from, respectively, Laird to G. E. Hanson, St. Paul, 18 Jy. 1907, RG 7, "PLC" file, WEYER; and Laird to C. A. Weyerhaeuser, 23 Feb. 1906, Box 3, Letterbook #21, PLC-UISC.

27The quotation is from Morgan to Laird, 4 Mar. 1908. Also see Morgan to A. A. McMillan, 15 Jy. 1908; Morgan to William Anschultz, 20 Nov. 1908; and Morgan to James Bingham, 17 Mar. 1909. All in Box 35, PLC-UISC.

28See R. M. Balch to Lee Oakes, 28 Oct. 1908, Box 36, PLC-UISC; Palouse *Republic*, 24 Aug. 1906; and Arthur Sundberg, interview 2, pp. 67-8, LCHS-OH.

29For highway progress see the following issues of the Palouse *Republic*: 21 Feb. 1919; 31 Oct. 1919; 29 May 1925; 10 Jy. 1925; 20 May 1932; 11 Nov. 1932. Also see Edgar and Elsie Renfrew reminiscences.

30Elsie and Malcolm Renfrew interview, LCHS-OH.

31Ibid.

CHAPTER NINE

1Palouse *Republic*, 13 Apr. 1917.

2Details on the Potlatch war effort can be found in the Potlatch news column that ran regularly in the Palouse *Republic* during these years.

3Palouse *Republic*, 13 Sept. 1918.

4Palouse *Republic*, 2 Nov. 1917; 25 Jan. 1918; 16 May 1919.

5The quotations are from the Palouse *Republic*, 7 Je. 1918. For young boys in the mill during the war see Emmett Utt, interview 4, p. 18, LCHS-OH.

6Palouse *Republic*, 20 Apr. 1917; 17 May 1918. During the latter months of the war, Potlatch did face economic difficulties. It was unable to successfully compete on a sustained basis with west coast lumber companies in supplying lumber for shipbuilding, and government restrictions on construction projects, combined with higher wartime wages, diminished profits. But by the time these impacts were felt in the fall of 1918, the war was nearly over. See Laird to Albert Newald, Milwaukee, 31 Oct. 1918, Box 4, PLC-LN.

[7]The complimentary quotation is in R. E. Brown, Fisher Body Corporation, Detroit, to PLC, 26 Nov. 1918. For further details on the company's wartime production efforts see Laird to Thatcher, 21 Aug. 1918; Laird to Everett Griggs, Bureau of Aircraft Production, 24 Oct. 1918; and Laird to C. A. Weyerhaeuser, 5 Nov. 1918; 4 Dec. 1918. All above correspondence in Box 4, PLC-LN. The Laird quotation and a good summation of the company's airplane stock production can be found in the Palouse *Republic*, 25 Jy. 1919. For a technical look at the use of wood in airplane manufacturing during the war see Richard P. Hallion, "Wooden Aircraft and the Great War," *Journal of Forest History*, vol. 22, no. 4, Oct. 1978, pp. 200-202.

[8]The quotation is from the Palouse *Republic*, 20 Apr. 1917.

[9]Hershiel Tribble, interview 2, pp. 23-4. For more on Potlatch's logging camps see Axel Anderson, interview 1; and Lena Justice, interviews 1 and 2. All in LCHS-OH. •

[10]Byers Sanderson, interview 2, pp. 17-18, LCHS-OH. For the Bedbug Creek place name see Boone, *From A to Z in Latah County*, p. 6. For a general overview of conditions in Pacific Northwest logging camps at the time see Robert L. Tyler's *Rebels of the Woods: The I.W.W. in the Pacific Northwest* (Eugene: University of Oregon, 1967), pp. 89-91.

[11]The way of the IWW in the Pacific Northwest had been paved by the Knights of Labor, which enjoyed considerable success organizing in the region in the 1890s and early 1900s. For a discussion of the connections between the Knights and the IWW see Cox, *This Well-Wooded Land*, pp. 170-4.

[12]For the beginning of the strike and Wobbly demands see Tyler, *Rebels of the Woods*, pp. 91-3; and Joyce L. Kornbluh, *Rebel Voices: An I.W.W. Anthology* (Ann Arbor: The University of Michigan Press, 1965), pp. 252-3.

[13]The posted warning is quoted in the Palouse *Republic*, 15 Dec. 1916. Also see the issue of 22 Dec. 1916; Hugh T. Lovin, "The Red Scare in Idaho, 1916-18," *Idaho Yesterdays*, vol. 17, no. 3, Fall 1973, pp. 2-13; Robert Anthony Perrin, Jr., "Two Decades of Turbulence: A Study of the Great Lumber Strikes in Northern Idaho (1916-1936)," unpublished master's thesis, University of Idaho, 1961, pp. 42-3; and Laird to Directors, 25 Jy. 1917, Box 4, PLC-LN. For firsthand accounts of the strike in Latah County see Axel Anderson, interview no. 2; Dick Genge, interview 1; and Albert Justice interview, all in LCHS-OH. The Palouse *Republic* also ran frequent stories about the strike action in Potlatch's camps. With the exception of Lovin and Perrin, historians have missed the significant connection between the Bovill strike of December 1916 and the well-documented region-wide strikes of 1917. The best source for the Everett confrontation is Norman H. Clark, *Mill Town: A Social History of Everett*,

Washington, from Its Earliest Beginnings . . . to the Tragic and Infamous Event Known as the Everett Massacre (Seattle: University of Washington Press, 1970). No one knows exactly how many people died at Everett. The fatalities could have been as high as nineteen or twenty.

[14]Lovin, "Red Scare in Idaho," p. 4; Perrin, "Two Decades of Turbulence," pp. 57-9.

[15]Perrin, "Two Decades of Turbulence," pp. 43-4.

[16]Ibid., pp. 44-50; Lovin, "Red Scare in Idaho," p. 6.

[17]Tyler, *Rebels of the Woods*, p. 92.

[18]Perrin, "Two Decades of Turbulence," pp. 74-5; Laird to Directors, 25 Jy. 1917, Box 4, PLC-LN. For a brief biographical sketch of Flynn and her IWW activities see Patrick Renshaw, *The Wobblies: The Story of Syndicalism in the United States* (Garden City, New York: Doubleday & Co., 1967), pp. 100-4; 121-2; 237.

[19]Laird to Directors, 25 Jy. 1917, Box 4, PLC-LN; Perrin, "Two Decades of Turbulence," p. 75.

[20]Tyler, *Rebels of the Woods*, p. 93.

[21]Ibid., pp. 93-5.

[22]Laird to F. E. Weyerhaeuser, 4 Aug. 1917, Box 4, PLC-LN. For a sample of anti-Wobbly literature in the Inland Empire see Zane Grey, *The Desert of Wheat* (New York: Grosset & Dunlap, 1919). Though this anti-IWW novel focused on Wobblies in the agricultural areas, the same vitriolic attacks were issued against IWW woods workers.

[23]The quotation is from Laird to F. E. Weyerhaeuser, 4 Aug. 1917, Box 4, PLC-LN. For Laird's role on the Defense Council see Lovin, "Moses Alexander and the Idaho Lumber Strike of 1917: The Wartime Ordeal of a Progressive," *Pacific Northwest Quarterly*, vol. 66, no. 3, July 1975, pp. 115-22.

[24]Records of the Latah County Protective Association are in MG 40, UISC. The quotations are from the association's Board of Directors minutes, 14 Jy. 1917, which also contain an account of the governor's Moscow rally. For more on the governor's actions in northern Idaho see Perrin, "Two Decades of Turbulence," pp. 67-80, 99; Lovin, "Moses Alexander and the Idaho Lumber Strike"; Lovin, "Red Scare in Idaho"; and Laird to Directors, 25 Jy. 1917, Box 4, PLC-LN. For brief descriptions of the Bovill and Moscow bullpens see Frank C. Gibson, "My Father Was My Hero," typescript, pp. 21-2, LN; and Dick Benge, interview 1, p. 23, and Harry Sampson, interview 2, p. 20, LCHS-OH.

[25]For details on the Potlatch Home Guard see the following issues of the Palouse *Republic*: 20 Apr. 1917; 17 Aug. 1917; 7 Sept. 1917; 28 Sept. 1917; 12 Oct. 1917; 11 Apr. 1919. Also see papers of the Latah County Protective Association, UISC.

[26]Laird to Directors, 25 Jy. 1917, Box 4, PLC-LN.

[27]Palouse *Republic*, 24 Aug. 1917; Lovin, "Moses Alexander and the Lumber Strike of 1917," p. 119-20; Robert C. Sims, "Idaho's Criminal Syndicalism

Act: One State's Response to Radical Labor," *Labor History,* vol. 15, no. 4, Fall 1974, pp. 511-27.

[28]For Disque, the Spruce Division, and the Four L's, see Tyler, *Rebels of the Woods,* pp. 101-15; Robert L. Tyler, "The United States Government as Union Organizers: The Loyal Legion of Loggers and Lumbermen," *Mississippi Valley Historical Review,* vol. 47, no. 3, Dec. 1960, pp. 434-51; Vernon H. Jensen, *Lumber and Labor* (New York: Farrar & Rinehart, 1945), pp. 129-37; and especially, Harold M. Hyman, *Soldiers and Spruce: Origins of the Loyal Legion of Loggers and Lumbermen* (Los Angeles: University of California, 1963).

[29]Bloom to Taylor, 28 Feb. 1918; Taylor to Bloom, 15 Mar. 1918, Box 10, JEWETT; Palouse *Republic,* 19 Apr. 1918.

[30]University of Idaho *Argonaut,* 3 Apr. 1918; Palouse *Republic,* 10 May 1918. There are many interviews in LCHS-OH describing IWW activities in the Latah County woods as well as the strike of 1916-17. For an excellent synopsis of that collection's interviews dealing with the event see Schrager, " 'The Early Days': Narrative and Symbolism of Logging Life in the Inland Northwest," pp. 39-65, 268-305.

[31]For the flu epidemic at Potlatch see the following issues of the Palouse *Republic:* 6 Dec. 1918; 3 Jan. 1919; 10 Jan. 1919; 17 Jan. 1919; 24 Jan. 1919; 31 Jan. 1919.

[32]For various post-war activities in Potlatch see the following issues of the Palouse *Republic:* 24 Jan. 1919; 27 Je. 1919; 14 Nov. 1919; 26 Mar. 1920.

[33]Arthur Sundberg, interview 4, p. 185, LCHS-OH. Even Zane Grey, after 360 pages of castigating the IWW, had a mild change of heart. "I've switched a little in my ideas about the I.W.W.," he has one of his characters assert at the end of his book. "I'm bound to say that now thousands of I.W.W. laborers are loyal to the United States, an' that made me switch." *Desert of Wheat,* pp. 362-4.

[34]Laird to Directors, 30 Oct. 1929, Box 5, PLC-LN.

[35]The quotation is from John Philip Weyerhaeuser, Jr. interview, p. 17, COL-OH. For Pacific Northwest lumber production statistics during this period see Michael Edwin Thompson, "The Challenge of Unionization: Pacific Northwest Lumber Workers During the Depression," unpublished master's thesis, Washington State University, 1968, p. 28. Also see Cox, *This Well-Wooded Land,* p. 217.

[36]See Laird to Mrs. W. M. Bowe, Chippewa Falls, 18 Dec. 1929; and Laird to Directors, 29 Jy. 1930, Box 5, PLC-LN. By 1930, Phil Weyerhaeuser and C. L. Billings had been experimenting with selective logging for three years at the Clearwater Timber Company, and the other Idaho Weyerhaeuser affiliates finally began to take heed. See H. A. Simons, "Harvesting Idaho's White Pine Forests for the Future," *Lewiston Morning Tribune,* 20 April 1930, which was originally published in *4 Square News,* 15 Mar. 1930; and Twining, *Phil Weyerhaeuser,* p. 69.

[37]See Laird to All Employees, 29 Dec. 1930, Box 5, PLC-LN; and notes from PLC Directors minutes, 23 Jan. 1931; 1 April 1931, RG 7, Box 19, "Potlatch" file, WEYER.

³⁸J. P. Weyerhaeuser to Directors, 15 Oct. 1932, Box 6, PFI-LN; Palouse *Republic*, 18 Mar. 1932; Twining, *Phil Weyerhaeuser*, p. 90.

³⁹For the first quotation see Maxwell Williamson interview, p. 17, COL-OH. Notice of the "permanent" mill closure can be found in the Palouse *Republic*, 28 Oct. 1932; and, for the quotation, in the Moscow *Star-Mirror*, 22 Oct. 1932. Irwin's reply is in the *Star-Mirror* of 27 Oct. 1932. Also see Richards, "George F. Jewett," pp. 11-12. The company always followed a policy of providing little or no warning prior to shutdowns, despite the hardship this caused employees. Lee Gale recalled the frequent stops and starts of the Potlatch plant during the Depression: "They just shut down without warning. You were told that the plant's going down today at noon and that would be it until further notice." Lee Gale, interview 2, LCHS-OH.

⁴⁰The quotation, typical of many in this period, is in George Little to E. A. Duff, Nebraska City, 7 Dec. 1933. For the 1932 losses see C. L. Billings to Directors, 17 Feb. 1933. For the 1935 wage reductions see Billings to Directors, 25 Mar. 1935. All above in Box 6, PFI-LN. For the company's inability to pay taxes and bills in 1933, see notes from correspondence, Billings to F. E. Weyerhaeuser, 28 Feb. 1933; J. P. Weyerhaeuser to R. M. Weyerhaeuser, 20 Apr. 1933; and J. P. Weyerhaeuser to Charles Donnelly, Northern Pacific, 18 Apr. 1933, all in RG 7, Box 19, "Potlatch" file, WEYER. For accumulated losses in the 1930s see Billings to Stockholders, July 1946, Box 43, JEWETT.

⁴¹Twining, *Phil Weyerhaeuser*, pp. 61 (quote), 69, 88.

⁴²Bell to F. E. Weyerhaeuser, 12 Je. 1928, Box 5, PLC-LN.

⁴³Julian G. Humiston reminiscences, 1986, LCHS; The *Journal of Commerce*, 22 Mar. 1930; undated (1916) clipping concerning Humiston from *American Lumberman*, GEN/BIO H-109, LCHS.

⁴⁴Later the lab moved to the upstairs of the main office building.

⁴⁵The *Journal of Commerce*, 22 Mar. 1930.

⁴⁶The quotation is in F. E. Weyerhaeuser to Laird, 14 Je. 1930. Also see Laird to F. E. Weyerhaeuser, 20 Je. 1930. Both in Box 5, PFI-LN. For Pres-to-Logs see Hidy, *Timber and Men*, especially pp. 361, 520; and *Potlatch Story*, vol. 1, no. 1 (1959), p. 7; Dec. 1962, p. 16.

⁴⁷Some Weyerhaeuser concerns did quite actively pursue research efforts through and beyond the 1930s. In fact, the Weyerhaeuser Company eventually had the largest non-governmental research organization in the industry, a much more significant undertaking than the research supported by PFI after 1931, despite the impressive early start made at the Potlatch and Clearwater companies. Bowling's work throughout the 1930s and 1940s, however—largely the effort of one man working on a limited budget—truly was a significant contribution. See Hidy, *Timber and Men*, pp. 323, 361, 527, 556. Virtually no work has been done on the significant early Potlatch Lumber Company and PFI research activities, but a recent (1986) donation by Potlatch Corporation of its Research Division papers to UISC will facilitate future historical efforts along this line.

Some of the material for this section came from correspondence, 1929-1931, in these files, which at the time were still unprocessed. For a good summary of early research efforts see Humiston, "Report to the Directors on the Research Activities of the Potlatch Lumber Company," 31 May 1930, Box 6, PFI-LN. Also helpful is the Frederick K. Weyerhaeuser and John M. Musser interview, pp. 73-5, COL-OH. For a summary of more recent Potlatch research efforts see *Potlatch Story*, no. 5 (1977?), pp. 7-12. For Humiston's basement lab see the Malcolm Renfrew reminiscences, and Julian Humiston reminiscences, both in LCHS. Renfrew, who became a nationally acclaimed Dupont chemist and was one of the inventors of Teflon, worked in Humiston's lab during the summer between his junior and senior years in college. The entire field of forest products research has largely been ignored by scholars, particularly the role of industry in research. For a brief overview see Herbert O. Fleischer, "Forest Products Research," in Davis, *Encyclopedia of American Forest and Conservation History*, vol. 1, pp. 231-4. For the Madison lab see Charles A. Nelson, *A History of the U.S. Forest Products Laboratory* (Madison: USFS Forest Products Laboratory, 1971).

[48]The sporadic operations of the mill during the 1930s can be traced in the following issues of the Palouse *Republic*: 25 Sept. 1931; 20 Apr. 1934; 6 Apr. 1935; 13 Mar. 1936; 31 Mar. 1939. The planing mill ran a bit more regularly, and the company also employed a small maintenance crew throughout the Depression, providing employment for a few men.

[49]The Palouse *Republic* details the various effects of the Depression. For the WI&M see the issue of 21 Oct. 1932; for the schools, 8 Apr. 1932; for the library, 23 Oct. 1931, 16 Sept. 1932, 28 Dec. 1934; and for the athletic club, 1 Apr. 1932, 23 Sept. 1932, 5 May 1939.

[50]For McGibbon and Irwin see R. E. Irwin interview; J. P. Weyerhaeuser, Jr. interview, p. 22; William Maxwell interview, pp. 77-8; and Laboring Men of Potlatch interview, pp. 56, 59, all in COL-OH. Also see Hidy, *Trees and Men*, pp. 364, 521-2. For O'Connell see *The Family Tree*, Jan. 1937, p. 6; and Alta O'Connell, "Twenty Years in Potlatch," typescript, LCHS. For the differences some town residents perceived between the "old guard" and the "new," see Elsie and Malcolm Renfrew interview, LCHS-OH.

[51]Similarly, as the company gradually came out of the Depression, hired more people, and increased wages in the late 1930s, it increased rents again. See Laird to All Employees, 29 Dec. 1930, Box 5, PLC-LN; and numerous letters from O'Connell to Potlatch tenants in the fall of 1937 concerning wage increases, Box 35, PLC-UISC.

[52]The quotation is from O'Connell to Department Heads, 27 Jan. 1937, Box 35. Also see Daisy Bardgett to O'Connell, 1935; and O'Connell to Bardgett, 22 Mar. 1935, Box 8. All in PLC-UISC.

[53]Laboring Men of Potlatch interview, pp. 24-5, COL-OH; Malcolm Renfrew reminiscences, LCHS.

[54]See Elsie and Malcolm Renfrew interview; Lee Gale, interview 2; and Glen Gilder, interview 3, pp. 25-6, all in LCHS-OH. For further

information on the Depression in Potlatch see Laboring Men of Potlatch interview, pp. 24-5, COL-OH; Ray Cameron, "A Memorable Christmas," typescript, 1985, LCHS; Palouse *Republic*, 16 Sept. 1932; and "A Friend of Justice" to Rudolph Weyerhaeuser, 1936, Box 34, PLC-UISC.

[55]The quotation is from Laird Bell to F. S. Bell, 14 Oct. 1936, F. S. Bell papers, Box 1, LN. For profits and losses during this period see C. L. Billings, Reports to Stockholders, 31 Dec. 1936, 4 Feb. 1938, 31 Dec. 1938, all in Box 7, PFI-LN; PFI Annual Financial Statements, Box 21, PLC-UISC; and Palouse *Republic*, 7 Jan. 1938.

[56]See O'Connell to E. E. Renfrew, 24 Mar. 1937, Box 35, PLC-UISC; O'Connell to N. T. MacKenzie, Weyerhaeuser Sales Company, St. Paul, 8 Nov. 1937, "Small House Construction" file, PLC; and Malcolm Renfrew reminiscences, LCHS.

[57]Records from the theater during the 1930s were found in "Potlatch Theatre" file, PLC. The Palouse *Republic* for this period noted various other Potlatch social and civic activities.

[58]Charles G. Talbott, Jr., reminiscences, LCHS.

[59]For an excellent description of the Palouse hobo jungle see the Palouse *Republic*, 9 Aug. 1935. For background on that town's relief fund see the issues of 15 Jan. 1932 and 22 Jan. 1932.

[60]Lee Gale, interview 2, LCHS-OH.

[61]For Chambers, Trotter, and Owens, see the following issues of *The Family Tree*: Je. 1942, p. 8; Je. 1943, p. 6; Sept. 1943, p. 7; Aug. 1945, p. 6 (quotation); Oct. 1945, pp. 1, 4. For Hicks see *The Family Tree*, Dec. 1943, p. 8. Unfortunately, Potlatch had no local correspondence column in the Palouse *Republic* during the war years. However, Mabel Kelley's dutiful monthly reporting of town and plant activities in *The Family Tree* during this period helps to fill that void.

[62]For the Larsons see *The Family Tree*, Mar. 1939, p. 1, and Feb. 1945, p. 7; for the Berrys and Goodnoughs the issue of Jy. 1944, pp. 4-5, 8.

[63]Stories of these and other Potlatch individuals can be found in the war-time issues of *The Family Tree*. Information on Honda and Matsura came from Lee Gale, interview 2, LCHS-OH, and from a personal interview with the author; and Dwight Strong personal interview with the author, April 1986. Also see Alta O'Connell, "Twenty Years at Potlatch," LCHS.

[64]Palouse *Republic*, 24 Jan. 1941; *The Family Tree*, Feb. 1942, p. 8.

[65]*The Family Tree*, Sept. 1942, p. 5; May 1943, p. 2; Feb. 1944, p. 6.

[66]For these various wartime activities see O'Connell to "Residents of Potlatch," 14 May 1942, Box 35, PLC-UISC; Palouse *Republic*, 29 Sept. 1944; 23 Nov. 1945; and *The Family Tree*, Feb. 1942, p. 6; Nov. 1942, p. 6; Apr. 1943, p. 8; Apr. 1944, p. 8.

[67]See numerous wartime circulars from O'Connell to "All Employees," Box 10, PLC-UISC; and *The Family Tree*, Aug. 1942, p. 8; Oct. 1943, p. 7; Nov. 1943, p. 5.

[68]The quotation is in an O'Connell circular of 3 Nov. 1941. Also see his circulars of Jan. 1942 and 6 Apr. 1942 in Box 13, PLC-UISC; and the following issues of *The Family Tree*: Apr. 1942, p. 7; Jy. 1942, p. 7; Feb. 1943, p. 2; Apr. 1943, p. 6; Feb. 1944, p. 6; Mar. 1944, p. 7.

[69]*The Family Tree*: Feb. 1942, p. 1; Apr. 1942, p. 1; Jy. 1942, p. 1; Mar. 1943, pp. 1-2; Jy. 1943, p. 7; Mar. 1944, pp. 1, 4-8.

[70]For the first quotation see Billings to Directors, 22 Jy. 1942, Box 38. For more on PFI's labor shortages see O. H. Leuschel to Directors, 25 Aug. 1942, Box 38; and Billings to Directors, 21 Aug. 1943, Box 40. All in JEWETT. For the second quotation see O'Connell, "Get Thar Fustest with the Mostest," typescript, Nov. 1942, Box 8, PLC-UISC. For University student employees see *The Family Tree*, Dec. 1942, p. 4.

[71]For the investigation of Weyerhaeuser mills see Billings to J. P. Weyerhaeuser, 16 Je. 1942, Box 38, JEWETT. The Moscow *Daily Idahonian*, 17 Dec. 1942, contains an excellent section on women's work at the Potlatch Unit. Also see *The Family Tree*, Sept. 1942, p. 5; Oct. 1943, p. 7; and Ed Muhsal, interview 1, pp. 9-10; Ella Benje, interview 4, p. 60; and Lee Gale, interview 2, all in LCHS-OH.

[72]See O'Connell, "Get Thar Fustest with the Mostest," typescript, Nov. 1942, Box 8, PLC-UISC; and Lee Gale, interview 2, LCHS-OH. For log artwork see *The Family Tree*, Dec. 1942, p. 6.

[73]*The Family Tree*, May 1943, pp. 1, 3; Aug. 1943, p. 5.

[74]Mabel Kelley's columns in *The Family Tree* detail many of the community's wartime activities. By 1944 the Palouse *Republic* also began to more regularly publish Potlatch town news.

[75]See various circulars concerning victory celebrations in Box 10, PLC-UISC; C. L. Billings to All Employees, 7 Jy. 1945, Billings papers, Idaho State Historical Society; Palouse *Republic*, 29 Sept. 1944; and *The Family Tree*, Aug. 1945, p. 3; Jan. 1946, p. 1; Apr. 1946, p. 3.

CHAPTER TEN

[1]For Weyerhaeuser's characterization of "Potlatch" as an appropriate name see notes from F. E. Weyerhaeuser's Record, vol. 4, pp. 576-77, RG 7, Box 6, "Potlatch Lumber Co." file, WEYER. PLC profit and loss figures for the years 1909-1931 can be found in the company's annual reports, Box 20, PLC-UISC. Annual PFI reports for later years are in Box 21. For an overall summary of company finances for 1908-1930, see Hidy, "Lumbermen in Idaho," p. 10. It is difficult to obtain a true picture of profits and losses simply by looking at annual reports because of peculiar bookkeeping techniques characteristic of the lumber industry, particularly before federal income tax legislation of 1913. "Since many of the figures used were arbitrary and determined by a vote of the stockholders, it would be difficult to gain a realistic view of their financial or profit position in any given year without completely adjusting their chosen methods of accounting. The profits or losses were in effect planned by the

stockholders," wrote Fred Kohlmeyer, *Timber Roots*, p. 281. While book-keeping is more accurate after 1913, it is still difficult to know if figures in the annual reports truly reflect a year's business operations. In 1936, for example, PFI general manager C. L. Billings debated with Laird Bell about whether to offset profits that year by declaring a loss on abandoning the Elk River plant, even though that mill had actually been abandoned several years earlier. Wrote Laird Bell to his father, 14 Oct. 1936, Box 1, F. S. Bell Papers, LN: "Billings thinks that after normal charges he may have two hundred or two hundred and fifty thousand dollars of profit. He proposes to eliminate this by charging off the Elk River plant as a loss on abandonment. Elk River stood on the books at $229,000 at the end of last year. . . . I pointed out that abandonment was a question of fact and that the [Internal Revenue] Bureau would undoubtedly do its best to show that the plant had in fact been abandoned in previous years when there was no profit and that if it succeeded Potlatch would have undistributed profits subject to . . . tax. While they will actually tear down the plant this year . . . it is some stretch of the imagination to say that the plant could have run up until this year." While actual profit and loss figures are therefore difficult to judge, the company's overall financial health at various times can be gauged by correspondence between company managers and stockholders, and these letters serve as the primary source for the information in this section concerning company finances.

[2]The quotation is from Laird to C. A. Weyerhaeuser, 3 Mar. 1906, Box 3, Letterbook #21, PLC-UISC. For Deary's unhappiness see Laird to F. S. Bell, 31 Oct. 1907, and for a typical critical letter, C. A. Weyerhaeuser to Deary, 8 Nov. 1907, both in Box 2, PLC-LN. For various problems provoking financial difficulties in these early years and steps taken to rectify the situation see Deary to Kehl, 7 Mar. 1906, Box 3, Letterbook #21; Deary to Frederick Weyerhaeuser, 24 Mar. 1906, Box 3, Letterbook #21; Laird to C. A. Weyerhaeuser, Je. 1907, Box 3, Letterbook #24; Deary to F. E. Weyerhaeuser, 30 Sept. 1907, Box 4, Letterbook #30, all above in PLC-UISC; notes from correspondence, Laird to C. A. Weyerhaeuser, 21 Aug. 1906, RG 7, Box 19, "Potlatch" file, WEYER; and the Palouse *Republic* for 15 Dec. 1906; 29 Mar. 1907.

[3]See the Palouse *Republic,* 7 Aug. 1908; 19 Feb. 1909; 18 Je. 1909.

[4]The quotation is in Laird to C. A. Weyerhaeuser, 25 Nov. 1911, Box 2, PLC-LN. In the same box see, for 1910 fire details, Deary to C. A. Weyerhaeuser, 3 Aug. 1910; Deary to Bell, 23 Aug. 1910; 24 Aug. 1910; C. A. Weyerhaeuser to Bell, 2 Sept. 1910. Also see William Maxwell interview, pp. 46-7, COL-OH. For an account of the 1910 fires in the Latah County vicinity see Keith Petersen and Mary Reed, "Latah Vignettes: The 1910 Fire," *Latah Legacy*, vol. 13, no. 2, Summer 1984, pp. 10-12. For more general overviews see Stan Cohen and Don Miller, *The Big Burn: The Northwest's Forest Fire of 1910* (Missoula, Mt.: Pictorial Histories Publishing Co., 1978); *When the Mountains Roared: Stories of the 1910 Fire* (Coeur d'Alene, Id.: U.S. Forest Service, Idaho Panhandle National Forests, 1982); Julian S. Marshall, "The Idaho Fire of 1910,"

The Pacific Northwesterner, vol. 7, no. 3, Summer 1963, pp. 33-42; and Stewart H. Holbrook, *Burning an Empire: The Story of American Forest Fires* (New York: The Macmillan Co., 1952), pp. 121-133.

[5]For the effects of the depression of 1913 on Potlatch's profits see Bell to Laird, 1 Aug. 1913, Box 3, PLC-LN; notes from correspondence, Laird to F. E. Weyerhaeuser, 4 Aug. 1913, RG 7, Box 19, "Potlatch" file, WEYER; *The Timberman,* Aug. 1913, p. 57; and William Maxwell interview, p. 45, COL-OH.

[6]The quotation about the special train and details of Deary's death can be found in Laird to Thatcher and Bell, 11 May 1913, Box 3, PLC-LN. Several letters in this box from Laird to directors give accounts of Deary's lingering illness and treatment. For Weyerhaeuser's impression of Deary see notes from correspondence, C. A. Weyerhaeuser to C. R. Musser, 22 May 1913, RG 7, Box 5, "Northland Pine Co." file, WEYER. Funeral details can be found in Directors' Minutes, 2 Je. 1913, RG 7, Box 19, "Potlatch" file, WEYER; Elk River *Sentinel,* 16 May 1913; and Palouse *Republic,* 9 May 1913; 16 May 1913.

[7]The first quotation is from Laird to Laird-Norton Co., 11 May 1913; the second from Bell to Laird, 14 May 1913. Both in Box 3, PLC-LN.

[8]Bell's quotation is in Bell to Laird, 1 Aug. 1913. Weyerhaeuser's displeasure about the mill closure is outlined in Bell to Laird, 21 Jy. 1913. Thatcher's opposition to having a Weyerhaeuser assistant is detailed in Laird to Laird-Norton Co., 11 May 1913. All in Box 3, PLC-LN.

[9]Hidy, *Timber and Men,* p. 248.

[10]The quotation is in notes from F. E. Weyerhaeuser's Record, vol. 4, RG 7, Box 6, "Potlatch Lumber Co." file, WEYER. For summaries of the difficulties of lumbering in northern Idaho generally, and Potlatch problems in particular, see Hidy, "Lumbermen in Idaho"; Hidy, *Timber and Men,* pp. 258-60; Kohlmeyer, *Timber Roots,* pp. 286-310; Twining, *Phil Weyerhaeuser,* p. 10; Richards, "George F. Jewett," pp. 5-6; and Madden, *Tree Farmers and Wood Converters,* p. 13.

[11]Laird to Directors, 1919 annual report, 31 Jan. 1920, Box 4, PLC-LN.

[12]The quotation is from Laird to Bell, 27 Aug. 1921. For further details on the impact of the 1921 depression upon Potlatch see Laird to C. A. Weyerhaeuser, 3 May 1931; 30 Jy. 1921, all above in Box 4, PLC-LN; and Palouse *Republic,* 7 Jan. 1921; 1 Apr. 1921; 12 Aug. 1921. Phil Weyerhaeuser's desire to sell the town is outlined in notes from correspondence, Phil Weyerhaeuser to C. A. Weyerhaeuser, 31 Jan. 1921, RG 7, Box 19, "Potlatch" file, WEYER.

[13]For the first quotation see William Maxwell interview, p. 73, COL-OH; the second is in Louise Heighes, correspondence with the author, 22 Feb. 1986; and the third is from Laird to Directors, 19 Mar. 1924, Box 5, PLC-LN.

[14]The quotation is from a Humiston speech, "What Ails the Lumber Industry of the Intermountain Region?" ca. 1928, Box 9, PLC-UISC.

¹⁵Most historians, including Twining, *Phil Weyerhaeuser*, and Hidy, *Timber and Men*, deal with the merger as a matter of concern arising in the 1920s, but actually consolidation talk long predated that decade. The quotation is from C. A. Weyerhaeuser to James Norton, 3 Nov. 1902, Box 41, Northland Pine Co. papers, LN. For an example of his early advocacy of a merger of northern and southern interests see C. A. Weyerhaeuser to P. M. Musser, 9 Apr. 1906, Box 1, PLC-LN. Periodically, merger rumors even became public. See, for example, the story about an anticipated Potlatch-Clearwater merger in the Palouse *Republic*, 11 Aug. 1911. For the history of Boise Cascade see Hidy, *Timber and Men*, pp. 260-7, 534-50.

¹⁶The quotations are from C. A. Weyerhaeuser to Laird, 5 Sept. 1919. Also see Laird to F. S. Bell, 18 Sept. 1919. Both in Box 4, PLC-LN.

¹⁷For background on the development of the Clearwater Timber Company see Twining, *Phil Weyerhaeuser*, pp. 56-76, with the quotation on p. 62; and Hidy, *Timber and Men*, pp. 515-20. For the enmity between Laird and the Weyerhaeusers see Twining, *Phil Weyerhaeuser*, pp. 71, 87; and J. Philip Weyerhaeuser, Jr. interview, p. 22, COL-OH. See notes from correspondence, F. E. Weyerhaeuser to F. S. Bell, 27 Jy. 1926, RG 7, Box 14, "Idaho" file, WEYER, for the optimism among some associates that a merger might finally be possible once Clearwater began production.

¹⁸See F. E. Weyerhaeuser to C. R. Musser, 6 Jan. 1930, which also contains a copy of Jewett's consolidation proposal, Box 5, PLC-LN.

¹⁹Laird to F. S. Bell, 9 Oct. 1930, Box 5, PLC-LN. For background on Laird Bell and the formation of the merger committee see Twining, *Phil Weyerhaeuser*, pp. 79-82; Hidy, *Timber and Men*, pp. 522-3; and especially the excellent Charles J. McGough interview, pp. 33-40, COL-OH. McGough was a part of the merger team and provides excellent "insider" information. Those interested in Laird Bell should also see the fine biography of his father-in-law, a prominent Chicago businessman and philanthropist, written by Laird Bell's daughter, Helen de Freitas, *Nathaniel Kellogg Fairbank, 1829-1903* (self-published, n.d.). A copy is available at LN.

²⁰Twining, *Phil Weyerhaeuser*, pp. 86-7; Hidy, *Timber and Men*, pp. 522-3.

²¹Like Deary, Laird was not buried in Potlatch. His body was cremated, with the ashes deposited in Los Angeles. For details on the Potlatch memorial services see Palouse *Republic*, 8 May 1931; and Elk River *News*, 8 May 1931.

²²A. N. Frederickson interview, pp. 18-19, COL-OH; Edgar and Elsie Renfrew reminiscences; Moscow *Star-Mirror*, 22 Oct. 1932; 27 Oct. 1932.

²³F. K. Weyerhaeuser to Billings, 12 Jy. 1939; Billings to F. K. Weyerhaeuser, 15 Jy. 1939, Box 35, JEWETT.

²⁴Weyerhaeuser's letter is quoted in Billings to Executive Committee, 18 Oct. 1946, Box 43, JEWETT. Potlatch had the highest production costs of the three plants. In 1945 it took 20.20 man hours per thousand board feet to produce logs and saw them into lumber at Clearwater, 21.88 man

hours at Coeur d'Alene, and 23.07 man hours at Potlatch. See Billings to Office of Price Administration District Office, Portland, 7 Feb. 1946, Box 8, PFI-LN.

[25]Details of the study and its acceptance can be found in Jewett to Billings, 20 Sept. 1946; Billings to Executive Committee, 18 Oct. 1946, Box 43; Board of Directors minutes, 24 May 1946, Box 44; Executive Committee minutes, 6 Nov. 1946, Box 44. All in JEWETT. Laird Bell's characterization is in Bell to George Little, Winona, 11 Aug. 1947, Box 8, PFI-LN.

[26]For biographical sketches of Billings see *4 Square News*, 15 March 1930; *Lewiston Morning Tribune*, 21 Je. 1948; *The Family Tree*, Je. 1948, p. 3; and Twining, *Phil Weyerhaeuser*, pp. 50-1, 69. There is a small collection of Billings's papers at the Idaho State Historical Society, Boise. There is also a substantial clippings file on him at LCHS.

[27]For a summary of company profits and expansion in the early 1950s see Norton Clapp, "Potlatch Forests, Inc.," typescript, 24 Jan. 1952; "Fernstrom Paper Mills, Inc.," typescript, 30 Apr. 1952; W. P. Davis to PFI Directors, 22 Feb. 1953; and Thomas Taylor, "Potlatch Forests, Inc.," typescript, 26 Jan. 1954, all in Box 28, Norton Clapp papers, LN. For the 1950 study into the possible closure of the Potlatch mill and the beginning of discussions concerning selling the town see Executive Committee minutes, 19 Sept. 1950; and Board of Directors minutes, 10 Nov. 1950, Box 49, JEWETT.

[28]The quotations are in, respectively, F. K. Weyerhaeuser to Davis, 29 Nov. 1951; Clapp to Davis, 19 Nov. 1951; and Davis to Clapp, 23 Nov. 1951, all in Box 28, Norton Clapp papers, LN. For background on F. K. Weyerhaeuser's training at Potlatch see Twining, *Phil Weyerhaeuser*, pp. 27, 44-6.

[29]For negotiations concerning sales of the water and power systems see Executive Committee minutes, 17 Nov. 1947, Box 44, JEWETT; Board of Directors minutes, 20 May 1948, Box 46, JEWETT; and O'Connell circular to tenants, 18 Oct. 1948, Box 10, PLC-UISC. For the school transition see *The Family Tree*, Je. 1948, p. 7.

[30]Details on planning for the town sale, as well as sale terms, were found in "Townsite Budget," "Village of Potlatch," and "Relative to Selling Townsite" files, PLC. For the number of buildings owned by the company see "Disposal Townsite Property," typescript, Box 36, PLC-UISC.

[31]The quotation was in M. E. Jones to H. L. Torsen, 22 Sept. 1953, "Relative to Selling Townsite" file, PLC. For the numbers of houses sold by fall 1953 see T. G. Youmans to M. E. Jones, 8 Sept. 1953, Box 36, PLC-UISC.

[32]The quotations were in, respectively, "Proposed Rental Increases," 1 Feb. 1953; Sven Alsager to C. J. Hopkins, 7 Je. 1954; Charles Talbott, Sr., to PFI, 15 Je. 1954; H. H. Hanson to M. E. Jones, 18 Feb. 1955; and Hopkins to Talbott, 21 Je. 1954, all in "Village of Potlatch" file, PLC. Similar correspondence can also be found in Box 36, PLC-UISC.

[33]J. J. O'Connell to W. P. Davis, 2 Aug. 1954, "Relative to Selling Townsite" file, PLC; T. G. Youmans, Jr., to M. E. Jones, 22 Sept. 1954, Box 36, PLC-UISC.

[34]Details on company donations and improvements prior to turning over the town's government can be found in various places. See George Hudson to Myrtle Garrelto, 23 Jan. 1953, "Small House Construction" file, PLC; PFI correspondence with landscape architect J. Haslett Bell, and H. L. Torsen to W. P. Davis, 16 Oct. 1953, "Relative to Selling Townsite" file, PLC; F. K. Weyerhaeuser to W. P. Davis, 29 Nov. 1951, Box 28, Norton Clapp papers, LN; "Churches, Library, Cemetery," typescript, ca. 1951, Box 36, PLC-UISC; and *The Lutheran-Presbyterian Parish.*

[35]Elder, Elder & Smith, attorneys to W. P. Davis, n.d., Box 36; Village of Potlatch Board of Trustees circular to residents, 3 Apr. 1953, Box 10. Both in PLC-UISC. Also see Moscow *Daily Idahonian,* 9 Apr. 1953; 29 Apr. 1953.

[36]M. E. Jones to J. J. O'Connell, 5 Jan. 1954; S. E. Andrew to L. K. Floan, 25 Sept. 1958. Both in "Relative to Selling Townsite" file, PLC. Also see George Hudson to Charles Francis, 24 Nov. 1954; and M. E. Jones to Village of Potlatch Board of Commissioners, 8 Je. 1955. Both in Box 9, PLC-UISC.

[37]For formation of the Chamber see an announcement of Aug. 1953, Box 10. There are numerous details of the booster group's activities in Box 38. Both in PLC-UISC. For a good description of an early Community Day celebration see Moscow *Daily Idahonian,* 30 Jy. 1956.

[38]The first quotation is from *Idaho: A Guide in Word and Pictures* (New York: Oxford University Press, 1950), p. 225; the second from *Lewiston Morning Tribune,* 18 Jan. 1959. Since Potlatch was not incorporated until 1953, the 1960 census is the first one to give a separate population figure for the community, making census comparisons with earlier times impossible. In 1960 the town had a population of 880 and in 1970 numbered 871. In both counts it was Latah County's second largest community.

[39]For the landscape architect's proposed community improvements see J. Haslett Bell, "Proposed Plan for the Improvement of the Town of Potlatch, Idaho, and Its Immediate Vicinity," File 11, PLC-LCHS.

EPILOGUE

[1]The quotations are from the *Lewiston Morning Tribune,* 17 Mar. 1983.

[2]*Lewiston Morning Tribune,* 13 Aug. 1981.

[3]For a summary of PFI diversification and expansion see Benton Cancell, PFI president, address before the Seattle Society of Investment Men, 13 Apr. 1965, Box 29, Norton Clapp papers, LN. Issues of *Potlatch Story,* which began publication in 1959, also provide details on company growth and changes.

[4]Richard B. Madden, Potlatch Corporation Chief Executive Officer, provided a summary of Potlatch's operations during the 1979-1985 period in his address given as part of the University of Idaho College of Forestry, Wildlife and Range Sciences distinguished lecturer series, 2 Apr. 1986. A summary of his statements can be found in the *Lewiston Morning Tribune*, 3 Apr. 1986.

[5]See Keith Petersen and Mary E. Reed, "Reconnaissance Survey Report, City of Potlatch," Sept. 1984; and Petersen and Reed, "Potlatch Historic Site Survey, National Register Nominations," Dec. 1985. Both are available at the Idaho State Historic Preservation Office, Boise, and at LCHS.

[6]For news of the plant closure see the *Lewiston Morning Tribune* issues of 24, 25, and 26 Jy. 1985. For the union/management settlement see the issue of 27 Nov. 1985. For the new sawmill see the issues of 3 and 4 May 1986.

[7]"Greenmail" is a legal, often lucrative, move made by hostile stock bidders who threaten to buy a company, acquire a considerable number of its shares, then agree to back away if the company will buy back the stock. Belzberg made nearly nine million dollars when Potlatch bought his stock, plus another million when the company agreed to reimburse him for expenses involved in the takeover attempt. In return, Belzberg agreed to refrain from purchasing Potlatch stock for five years. See the *Lewiston Morning Tribune* issues of 5 Nov. through 13 Nov. 1985 for details on the takeover attempt.

[8]For the quotation and a feature article on Rev. Onstot's dual ministry see the Pullman *Daily News*, 20 Dec. 1985.

Bibliographical Essay

This book began as a project in local public history. In 1979, as Director of the Latah County Historical Society, I developed a museum exhibit on the town of Potlatch and became intrigued by its past. Over the years, as I continued researching the town and company, I discovered that many key components in the Potlatch story, while not completely ignored, had largely been overlooked by scholars. This led me to look more deeply not only into Potlatch's particular history, but also into that of forestry and company towns generally.

Until recently, the history of the lumber industry had been generally slighted. Paul Gates, "Weyerhaeuser and the Chippewa Logging Industry," in O. Fritiof Ander, ed., *The John H. Hauberg Historical Essays* (Rock Island, Il.: Augustana Library Publications, 1954), pointed out how little we knew at that time about even major industry leaders. Twenty years later historians still decried the lack of progress in the field. "The subject of lumbering has been paid scant and very tardy attention by American historians," noted Charles E. Twining in *Downriver: Orrin H. Ingram and the Empire Lumber Company* (Madison: The State Historical Society of Wisconsin, 1975), p. v. Philip L. White, *Beekmantown, New York: Forest Frontier to Farm Community* (Austin: University of Texas Press, 1979), pp. 357-60, seconded that sentiment, asserting that historians of the frontier have ignored timber resources as a primary economic cause of westward migration.

In the past two decades, though, thanks largely to the efforts of the Forest History Society, whose *Journal of Forest History* is essential reading for anyone interested in the field, writings on lumbering have burgeoned. It is not my intention here to replicate this book's endnotes, but among the major works I found most useful for my study were the following: Ralph W. Hidy, Frank Ernest Hill, and Allan Nevins, *Timber and Men: The Weyerhaeuser Story* (New York: The Macmillan Co., 1963); Fred W. Kohlmeyer, *Timber Roots: The Laird, Norton Story, 1885-1905* (Winona, Mn.: Winona County

Historical Society, 1972); Charles E. Twining, *Phil Weyerhaeuser: Lumberman* (Seattle: University of Washington Press, 1985); Thomas R. Cox, *Mills and Markets: A History of the Pacific Coast Lumber Industry to 1900* (Seattle: University of Washington Press, 1974); and Robert E. Ficken, "Weyerhaeuser and the Pacific Northwest Timber Industry, 1899-1903," *Pacific Northwest Quarterly*, vol. 7, no. 4, Oct. 1979, pp. 146-54.

For background on the connection between the Great Lakes region and the westward movement of the lumber industry, in addition to Twining's biograpy of Orrin Ingram cited above, I found the following the most helpful: Agnes M. Larson, *History of the White Pine Industry in Minnesota* (Minneapolis: University of Minnesota Press, 1940); Theodore C. Blegen, "With Ax and Saw: A History of Lumbering in Minnesota," *Forest History*, vol. 7, no. 3, Fall 1963, pp. 2-13; and Robert F. Fries, *Empire in Pine: The Story of Lumbering in Wisconsin, 1830-1900* (Madison: The State Historical Society of Wisconsin, 1951).

By far the most outstanding book for a general overview of American forest history is the work by Thomas R. Cox, Robert S. Maxwell, Phillip D. Thomas, and Joseph J. Malone, *This Well-Wooded Land: Americans and Their Forests From Colonial Times to the Present* (Lincoln: University of Nebraska Press, 1985). Also useful are Richard C. Davis, ed., *Encyclopedia of American Forest and Conservation History*, 2 vols. (New York: Macmillan Publishing Co., 1983), and, for assistance in finding further sources, Ronald J. Fahl's *North American Forest and Conservation History: A Bibliography* (Santa Barbara, Ca.: A.B.C.-Clio Press, 1977).

Despite the significant impact lumbering had on the development of Idaho and the Inland Empire, historians have virtually ignored this field. For the few good works to date see S. Blair Hutchison, "A Century of Lumbering in Northern Idaho," *The Timberman*, 3 parts, vol. 39, nos. 10, 11, 12, Aug.-Oct. 1938; Samuel Alan Schrager, " 'The Early Days': Narrative and Symbolism of Logging Life in the Inland Northwest," Ph.D. dissertation, University of Pennsylvania, 1983, an account by the region's leading folklorist; John Fahey, "Big Lumber in the Inland Empire: The Early Years, 1900-1930," *Pacific Northwest Quarterly*, vol. 76, no. 3, July 1985, pp. 95-103; Fahey, *The Inland Empire: Unfolding Years, 1879-1929* (Seattle: University of Washington Press, 1986), especially pp. 188-213; Robert W. Swanson, "A History of Logging and Lumbering on the Palouse River, 1870-1905," master's thesis, Washington State College, 1958; Laura

Barber Richards, "George Frederick Jewett: Lumberman and Conservationist," master's thesis, University of Idaho, 1969; Ralph Hidy, "Lumbermen in Idaho: A Study in Adaptation to Change in Environment," *Idaho Yesterdays*, vol. 6, no. 4, Winter 1962, pp. 2-17; W. Hudson Kensel, "The Early Spokane Lumber Industry," *Idaho Yesterdays*, vol. 12, no. 1, Spring 1968, pp. 25-31; Robert A. Perrin, Jr., "Two Decades of Turbulence: A Study of the Great Lumber Strikes in Northern Idaho, 1916-1936," master's thesis, University of Idaho, 1961; and Hugh T. Lovin, "Moses Alexander and the Idaho Lumber Strike of 1917: The Wartime Ordeal of a Progressive," *Pacific Northwest Quarterly*, vol. 66, no. 3, Jy. 1975, pp. 115-22.

While historians of recent years have begun making inroads into the vast field of forest history generally, one area still remains understudied. "The literature of American history is punctuated with accounts of many kinds of communities: the New England village, the Socialistic Utopian community, the frontier outfitting post, the rough-and-tumble mining camp, the cow town of the Great Plains, the Mormon village . . . and . . . the big city and its sprawling suburbs," noted James B. Allen twenty years ago. "Almost neglected, however, has been the company-owned town." The statement is as true today as it was two decades ago. This lack of literature helps explain why scholars have successfully rebutted many false notions about the lumbering West yet still perpetuate others concerning company towns. Thus, while William G. Robbins's article "Labor in the Pacific Slope Timber Industry: A Twentieth Century Perspective," *Journal of the West*, vol. 25, no. 2, Apr. 1986, pp. 8-13, leads to a better understanding of real working conditions, his broad, inclusive summary of company towns is wide of the mark, at least if Potlatch was typical: "Whether they were attached to a large or a small camp, loggers worked in isolated areas away from the comforts of hearth and home – and the cultural distraction of urban life. Even the sizeable company towns fit within this framework." Errors such as this are bound to be perpetuated until more work is undertaken to understand these communities. Company towns, particularly in the lumbering and mining districts, played a vital role in western settlement, and their history has been too long ignored.

James B. Allen's *The Company Town in the American West* (Norman: University of Oklahoma Press, 1966) remains the only overview in the field. For the few attempts to study lumber company towns, some done more skillfully than others, see Thomas F. Gedosch, "Seabeck, 1857-1886, The History of a Company Town," master's thesis, University of Washington, 1967; Jack Held, "Scotia, the Town of Concern," *The Pacific Historian*, vol. 16, no. 2, Summer 1972, pp. 76-92; John Driscoll, "Gilchrist, Oregon, A Company Town," *Oregon Historical Quarterly*, vol. 85, no. 2, Summer 1984, pp. 135-53; Hugh Wilkerson and John van der Zee, *Life in the Peace Zone: An American Company Town* (New York: The Macmillan Company, 1971); Jon Humboldt Gates, *Falk's Claim: The Life and Death of a Redwood Lumber Town* (Eureka, Ca.: Pioneer Graphics, 1983); Curtis W. Wienker, "McNary: A Predominantly Black Company Town in Arizona," *Negro History Bulletin*, Aug./Sept. 1974, pp. 282-5; and Ruth B. Allen, *East Texas Lumber Workers: An Economic and Social Picture, 1870-1950* (Austin: University of Texas Press, 1961), which devotes an excellent chapter to company towns. I am also indebted to the work of two earlier writers on Potlatch, Clifford Lewis Imus, "A Social Study of Potlatch Idaho," bachelor's thesis, Washington State College, 1910; and Ray K. Harris, "Life in Potlatch was Different," *The Pacific Northwesterner*, vol. 20, no. 1, Winter 1976, pp. 1-16.

Works on non-lumbering company towns were also examined for comparative purposes. By far the best book to date on a single company town is Stanley Buder, *Pullman: An Experiment in Industrial Order and Community Planning, 1880-1930* (New York: Oxford University Press, 1967). Other valuable studies include Margaret F. Byington, *Homestead: The Households of a Mill Town* (Pittsburgh: University of Pittsburgh, 1974; reprint), first published in 1910 and still the classic study of mill town households; Leland M. Roth, "Three Industrial Towns by McKim, Mead & White," *Journal of the Society of Architectural Historians*, vol. 38, no. 4, Dec. 1979, pp. 317-47, the best look at company town architecture; and Tamara K. Hareven and Randolph Langenbach, *Amoskeag: Life and Work in an American Factory-City* (New York: Pantheon Books, 1978), which, though it deals with a single-industry community and not a true company town, should be examined for its skillful use of oral history and photography in studying such communities, two methodologies historians too often overlook. Similarly, researchers should note two outstanding studies of different types of mill towns, even though neither deals with company-owned communities. Both provide brilliant glimpses of outstanding scholarship applied to town studies: Norman H. Clark, *Mill Town: A Social History of Everett, Washington, From Its Earliest Beginnings on the Shores of Puget Sound to the Tragic and Infamous Event Known as the Everett Massacre* (Seattle: University of Washington Press, 1970); and Anthony F. C. Wallace, *Rockdale: The Growth of an American Village in the Early Industrial Revolution* (New York: W. W. Norton & Co., 1972). Two good earlier studies are Lois MacDonald, *Southern Mill Hills: A Study of Social and Economic Forces in Certain Textile Mill Villages* (New York: Alex L. Hilman, 1928); and Vera Shlakman, *Economic History of a Factory Town: A Study of Chicopee, Massachusetts* (Northampton, Ma.: Smith College, 1934). Two bibliographies, though somewhat outdated, provide access to both the popular and scholarly literature on company towns. See Rolf Knight, *Work Camps and Company Towns in Canada and the United States: An Annotated Bibliography* (Vancouver, BC: New Star Books, 1975); and J. Douglas Proteous, *The Single Enterprise Community in North America* (Monticello, Il.: Council of Planning Librarians, 1971).

I did most of the research for this project in archival and manuscript depositories. By far the most valuable group utilized was the large historical collection relating to the Potlatch Lumber Company. When I first began research, these papers were still in Potlatch, and the Potlatch Corporation allowed me access to them. During the course of my research the Corporation donated this valuable collection to the University of Idaho Library's Special Collections Department in Moscow, where it has since been processed as manuscript group (MG) 135. Other collections at the University of Idaho which were extremely useful included the papers of the Washington, Idaho and Montana Railway Company (MG 139); the George F. Jewett, Sr., papers (MG 43); the Charles O. Brown papers (MG 88); the papers of the Latah County Protective Association (MG 40); and the recently donated and still unprocessed papers of the research department of the Potlatch Lumber Company and Potlatch Forests, Inc.

Two well-organized company archives were indispensable to this study. One is the Laird-Norton Company Archives in Seattle and the other the Weyerhaeuser Company Archives in Tacoma. The latter contains the valuable Columbia University oral history project transcripts done in conjunction with the writing of *Timber and Men: The Weyerhaeuser Story*. Both are fine examples of the value of retaining and processing corporate records. I hope other companies will follow these examples.

Many collections in the Latah County Historical Society library in Moscow were used. During the course of this project, past and present Potlatch residents donated numerous reminiscences and photographs to the Society. These have now been processed and cataloged. The Society's oral history collection, one of the largest in the Pacific Northwest, includes several interviews with Potlatch residents and employees. Most of the interviews have been transcribed and all are indexed. The Society also has a small collection of Potlatch Lumber Company papers and numerous general reminiscences which were utilized in providing regional background. Researchers can gain access to these collections through various finding aids available at the Society.

Washington State University Library's Manuscripts, Archives and Special Collections in Pullman has a rich assortment of papers which also helped provide background on Palouse area history generally. Many of these are cited in the endnotes, and again, finding aids are available at the site. The small collection of C. L. Billings papers at the Idaho State Historical Society in Boise also contained some useful material.

I utilized several newspapers in compiling research, but for only one – the Palouse *Republic* – did I systematically go through each issue. The *Republic* is available on microfilm at the Washington State University Library, while bound volumes are accessible at the Boomerang Museum in Palouse. In the early years of the Potlatch Lumber Company's operations, the *Republic*'s coverage of the company and town is quite extensive. In later years, coverage is at times almost nonexistent. During some periods the *Republic* retained a local Potlatch reporter and ran a weekly column of news and gossip. Many times, however, there was no such column. By far the greatest frustration in undertaking this project was not having access to a truly local newspaper. For only a few issues in the 1950s did Potlatch have its own paper, a mimeographed sheet entitled the Potlatch *Pine Cone*. Extant copies of this paper are available at the Latah County Historical Society.

Three Potlatch corporate periodicals were helpful in providing information on company development. *The Family Tree* was begun in 1936 and continued until 1952. After a seven-year hiatus, it was replaced by *The Potlatch Story*, begun in 1959 and still being published. While *The Potlatch Story* covers corporate activities throughout Potlatch's broad operating range, *The Potlatch Times*, published in Lewiston, concentrates on operations in Idaho. Researchers can gain access to all three publications at either the Latah County Historical Society or the University of Idaho Library. Also valuable in understanding the corporation's history are the following short monographs: Richard B. Madden, *Tree Farmers and Wood Converters: The Story of Potlatch Corporation* (New York: The Newcomen Society, 1975); and Frederick K. Weyerhaeuser, *Trees and Men* (New York: The Newcomen Society, 1951).

Anyone attempting to research the history of the Palouse region should begin by reading Donald W. Meinig's outstanding *The Great Columbia Plain: A Historical Geography, 1805-1910* (Seattle: University of Washington Press, 1968). The other local and regional monographs cited in the endnotes can be found in one of three places: The Washington State University, University of Idaho, or Latah County Historical Society libraries. Researchers of Palouse history are fortunate to have access to two fine local history journals. Both the *Bunchgrass Historian*, the quarterly of the Whitman County Historical Society, and *Latah Legacy*, the quarterly of the Latah County Historical Society, were used extensively in this study.

Finally, I am convinced that one of the best ways to study a local community is simply to observe it. During the course of this project I photographed every building and house in town; walked every street many times; attended town functions and city council meetings; stood on street corners watching and listening; and talked with people on sidewalks and in businesses, restaurants, and taverns. Too often historians approach community studies as if they were viewing a museum artifact, examining towns as though they were dead. They arbitrarily limit research to a predetermined time period, ending their studies at a certain date a selected number of years in the past and giving little thought to present conditions. There is much to be learned about a town by studying historical records in a library. But a place like Potlatch is not dead, and though the community in 1986 differs considerably from its predecessor, there are many similarities. One of the values of history is in learning how we got to where we are. Potlatch obviously developed in certain ways because of its unusual history. One cannot determine what that historical legacy has meant without knowing the community today. In our efforts to uncover every shred of historical documentation about a place, we often forget that we are blessed with other outstanding forms of historical investigation: our senses of sight, hearing, taste, touch, and smell. Digging through musty archives, reading books, browsing newspapers, and viewing historical photographs gave me an appreciation for Potlatch, but it was the type of appreciation we get from studying a work of art under glass. We can admire the artwork and might even know the story behind its creation, but we are distant from the piece, and it is hard to truly identify with it. Only after repeated visits to Potlatch did I finally begin to feel that I really understood the community.

In this index   PFI = Potlatch Forests, Incorporated
                PLC = Potlatch Lumber Company
                WI&M = Washington, Idaho and Montana Railway.